Shojo Beat

Yurara

Volume 5

Story & Art by
Chika Shiomi

Contents

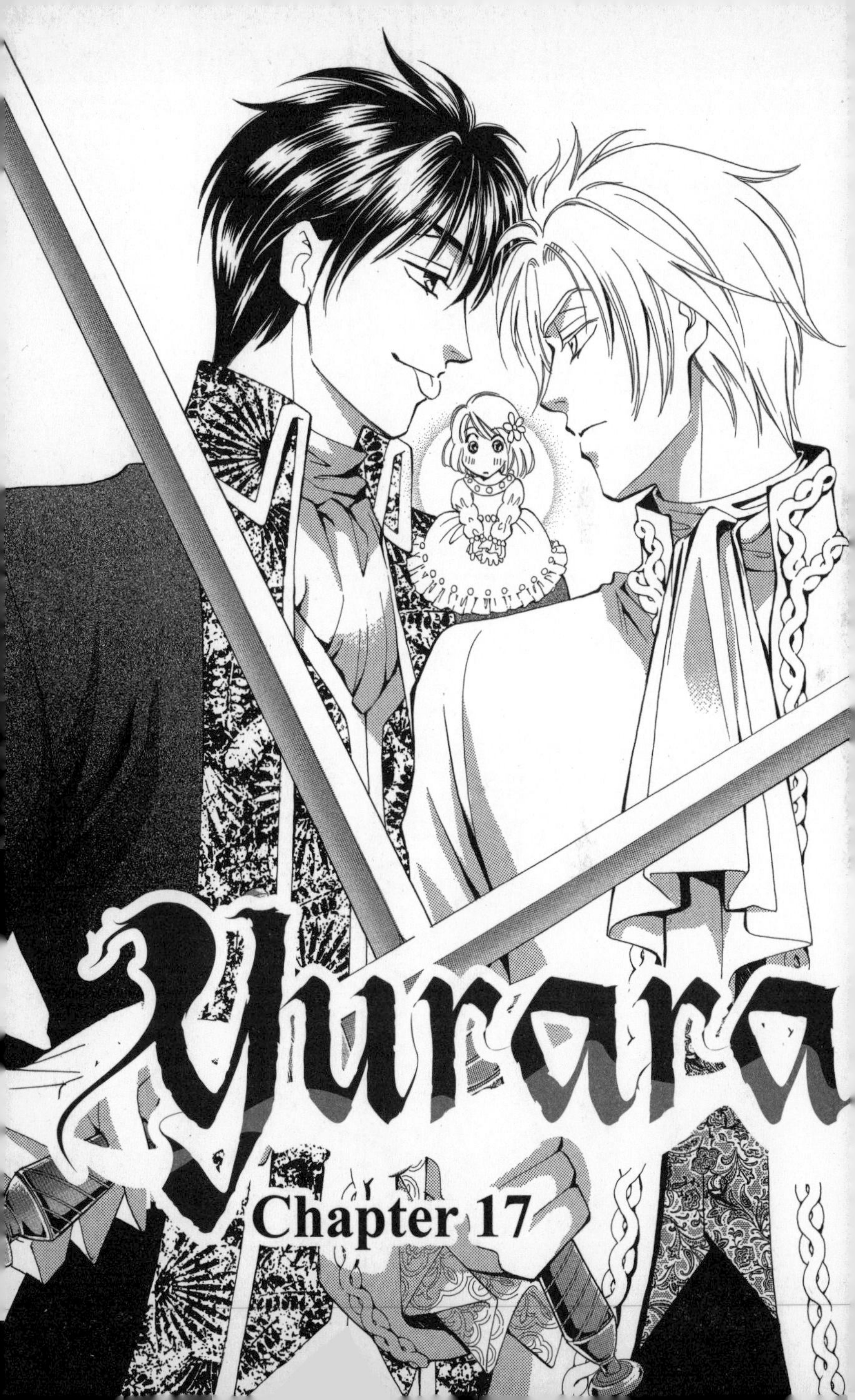
Yurara
Chapter 17

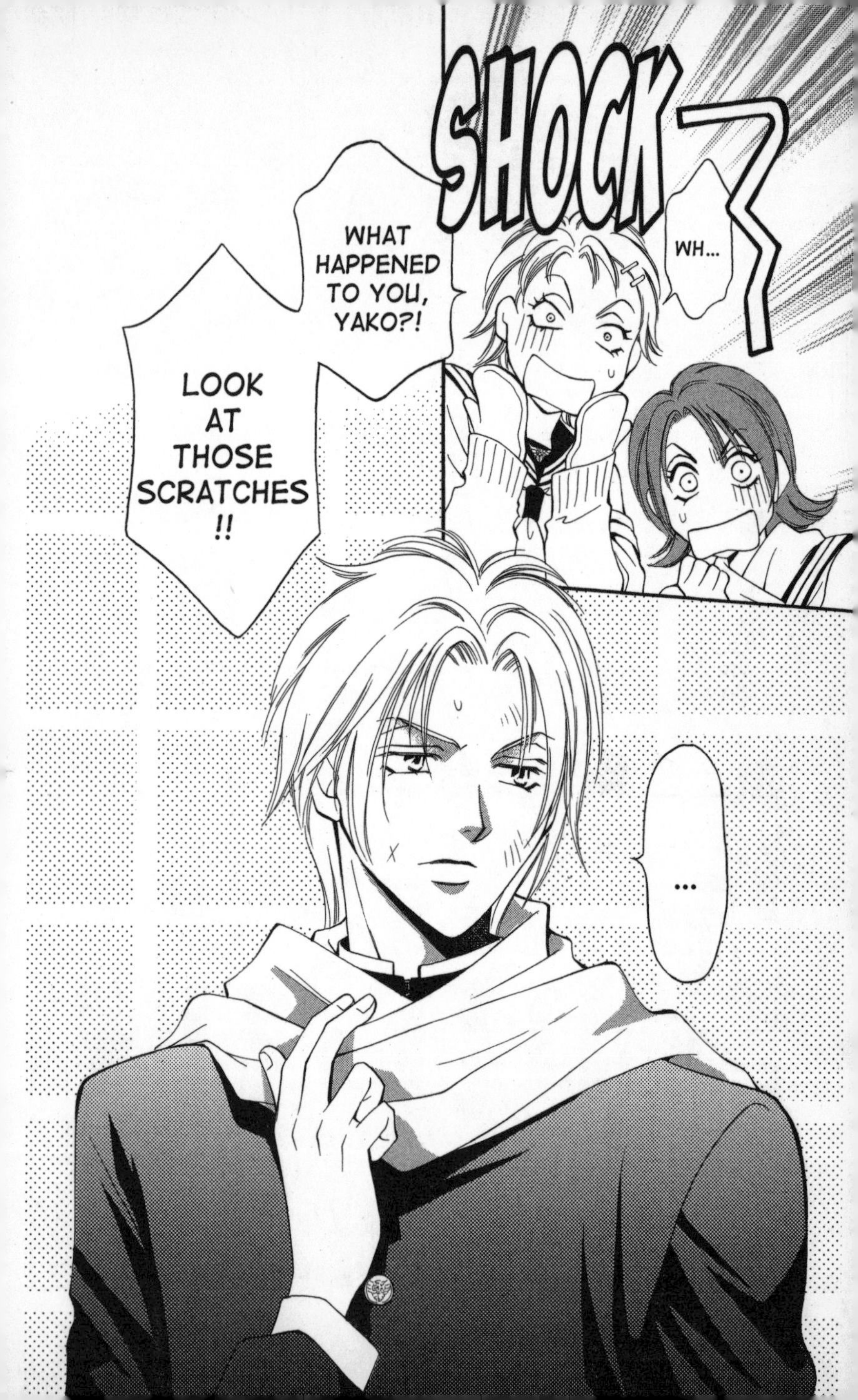
SHOCK
WH...
WHAT HAPPENED TO YOU, YAKO?!
LOOK AT THOSE SCRATCHES!!
...

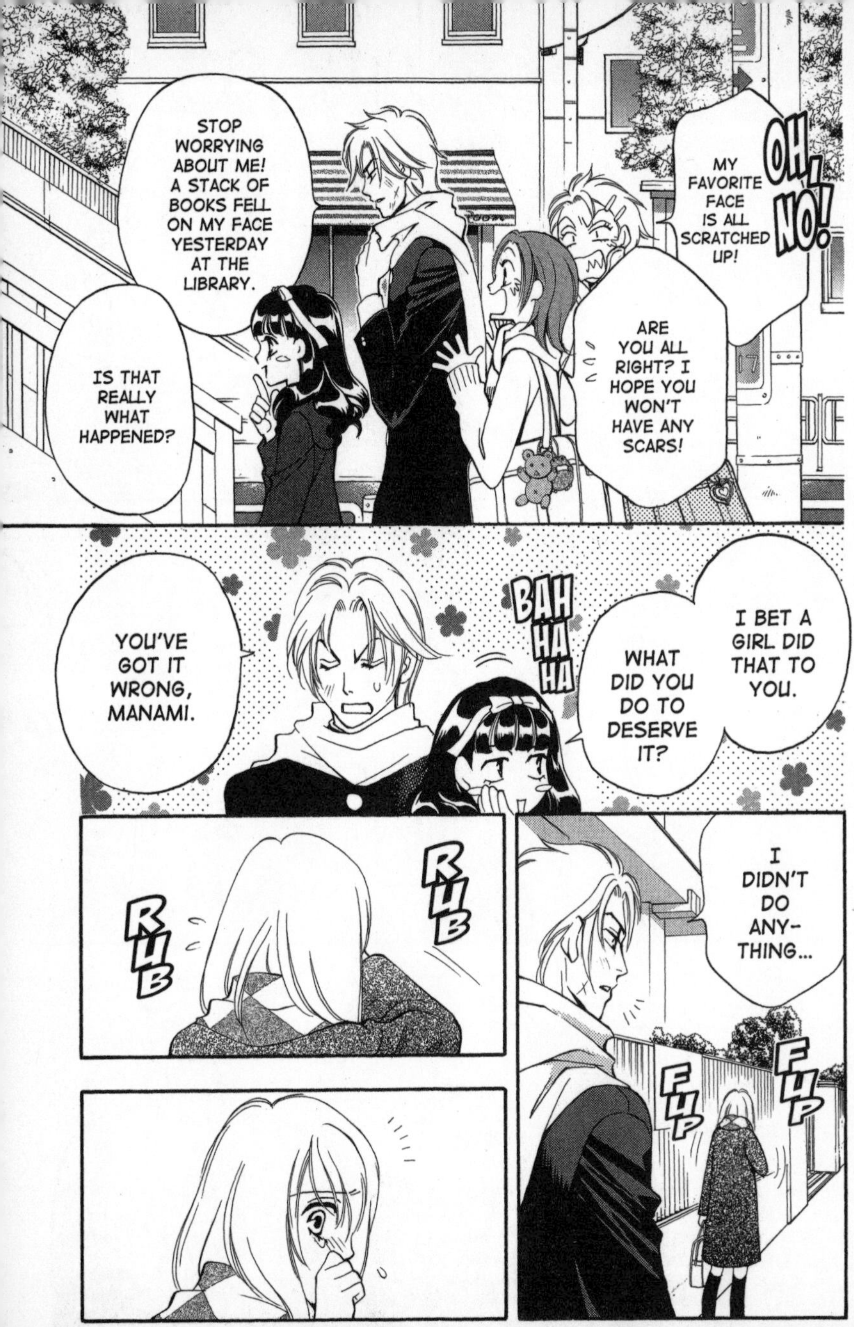
OH, NO!
MY FAVORITE FACE IS ALL SCRATCHED UP!
ARE YOU ALL RIGHT? I HOPE YOU WON'T HAVE ANY SCARS!
STOP WORRYING ABOUT ME! A STACK OF BOOKS FELL ON MY FACE YESTERDAY AT THE LIBRARY.
IS THAT REALLY WHAT HAPPENED?
I BET A GIRL DID THAT TO YOU.
WHAT DID YOU DO TO DESERVE IT?
BAH HA HA
YOU'VE GOT IT WRONG, MANAMI.
I DIDN'T DO ANY-THING...
FUP
FUP
RUB
RUB

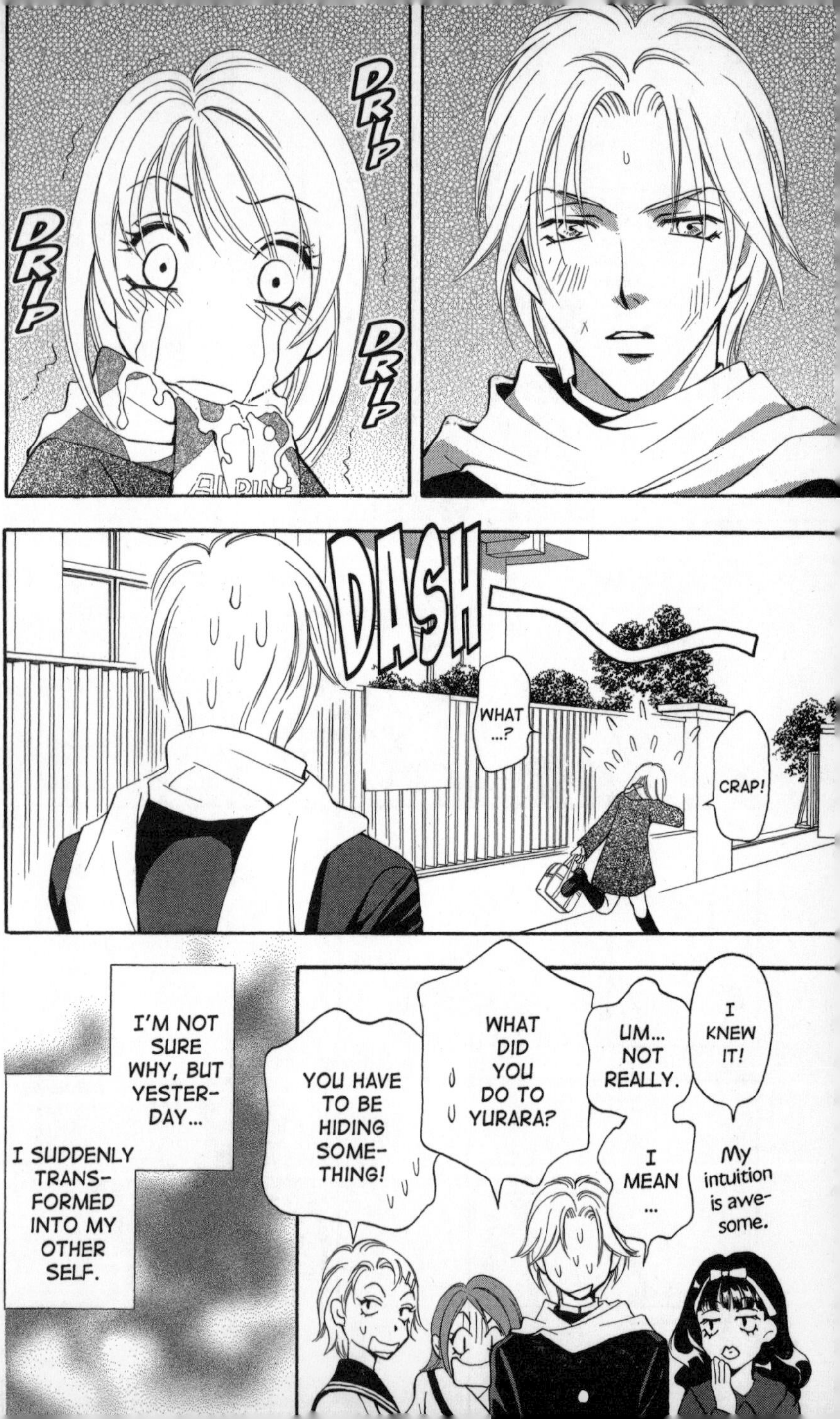
DRIP
DRIP
DRIP
DASH
CRAP!
WHAT ...?
I KNEW IT!
My intuition is awesome.
UM... NOT REALLY.
I MEAN ...
WHAT DID YOU DO TO YURARA?
YOU HAVE TO BE HIDING SOMETHING!
I'M NOT SURE WHY, BUT YESTERDAY...
I SUDDENLY TRANSFORMED INTO MY OTHER SELF.

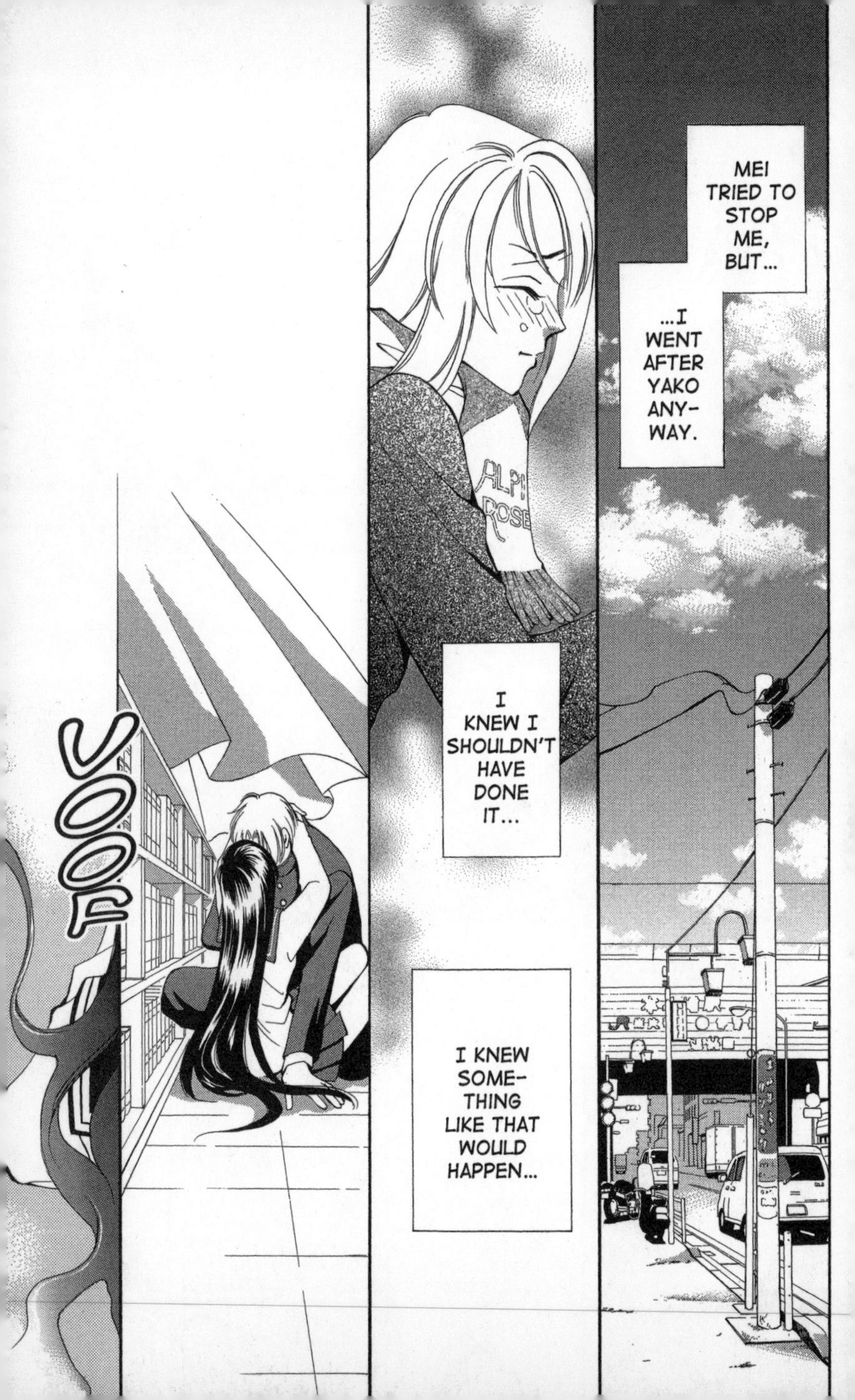
MEI TRIED TO STOP ME, BUT...
...I WENT AFTER YAKO ANYWAY.
I KNEW I SHOULDN'T HAVE DONE IT...
I KNEW SOMETHING LIKE THAT WOULD HAPPEN...
VOOF

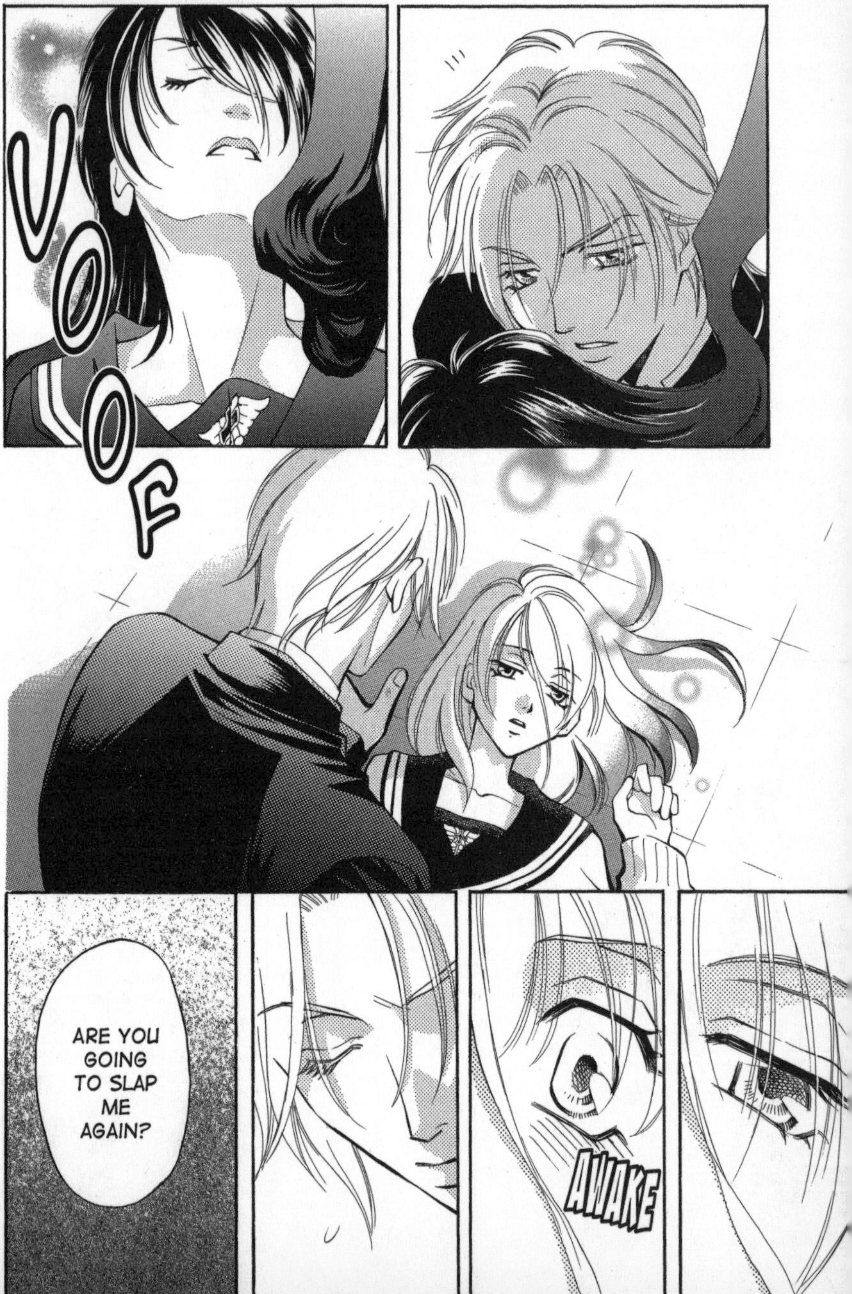
VOOF
AWAKE
ARE YOU GOING TO SLAP ME AGAIN?

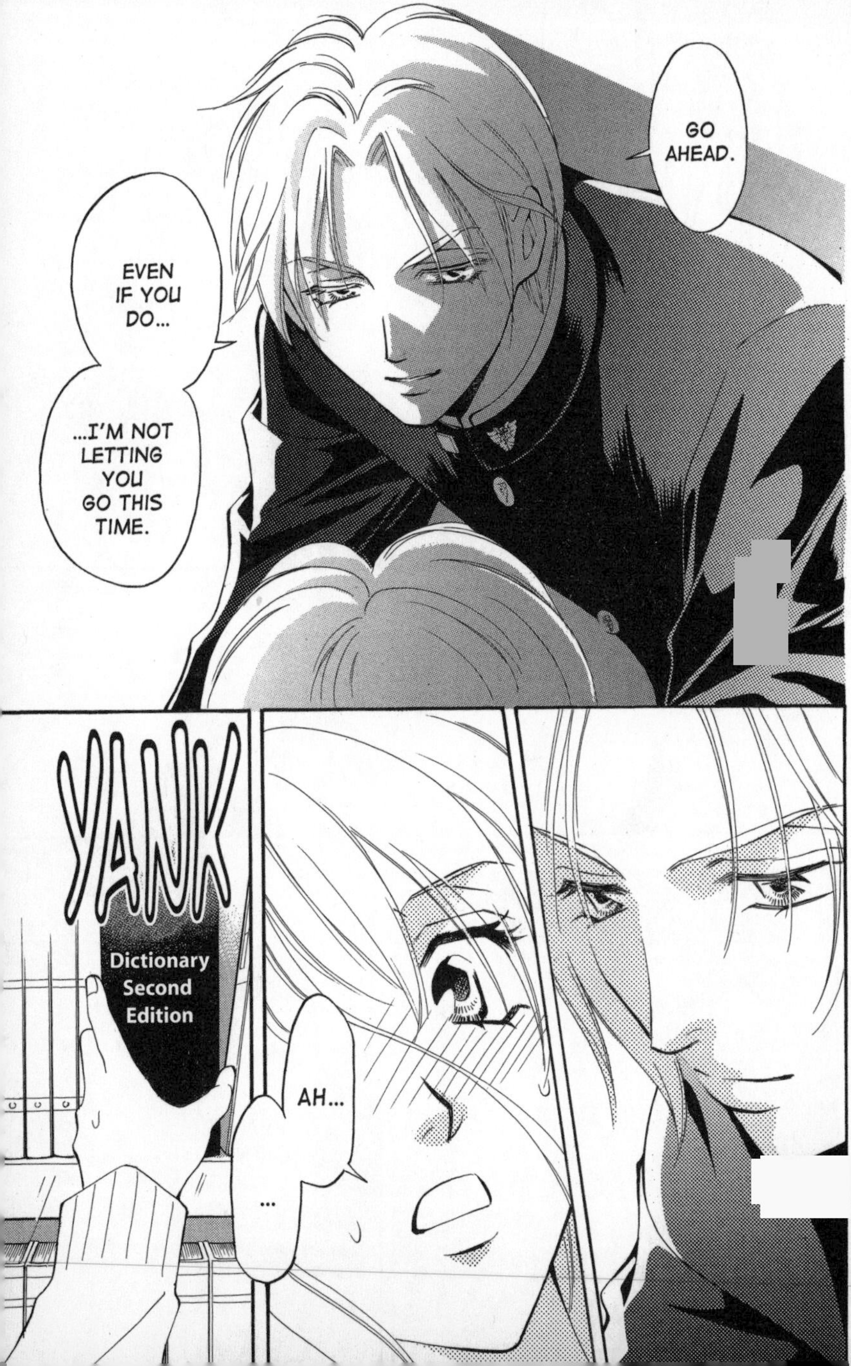
GO AHEAD.
EVEN IF YOU DO...
...I'M NOT LETTING YOU GO THIS TIME.
AH...
...
YANK
Dictionary Second Edition

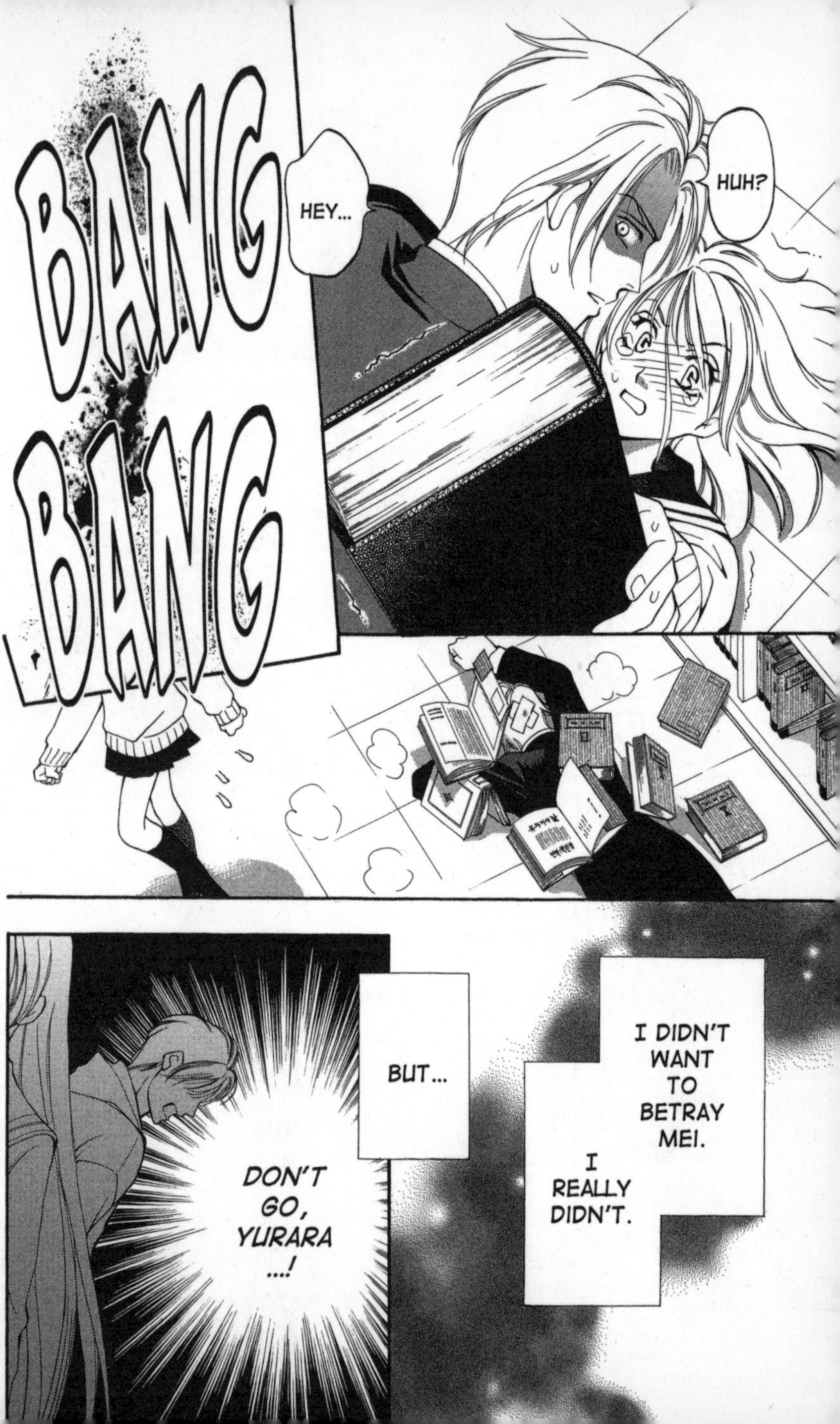
HUH?
HEY...
BANG
BANG
I DIDN'T WANT TO BETRAY MEI.
I REALLY DIDN'T.
BUT...
DON'T GO, YURARA ...!

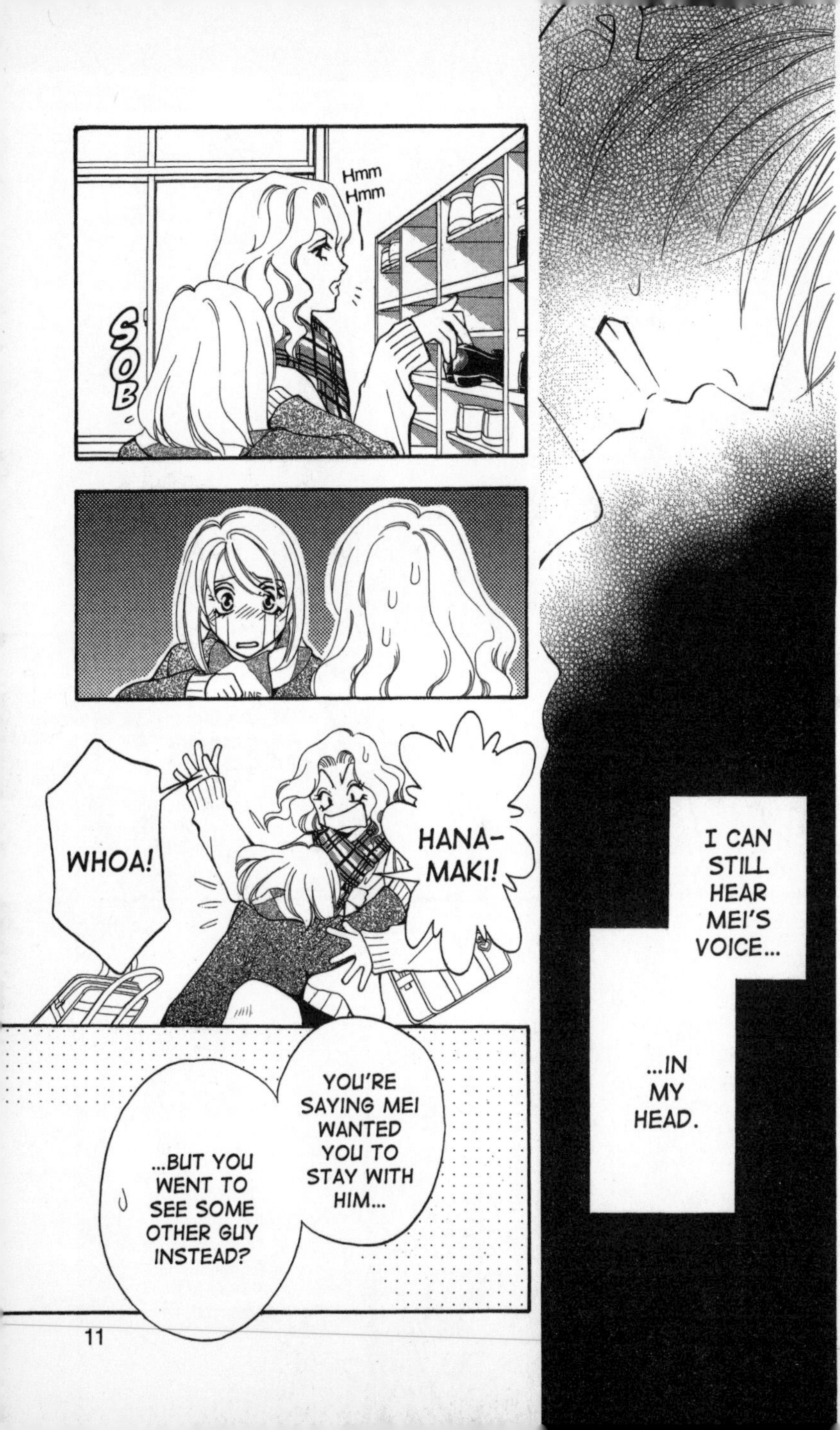
I CAN STILL HEAR MEI'S VOICE...
...IN MY HEAD.
Hmm Hmm
SOB
HANA-MAKI!
WHOA!
YOU'RE SAYING MEI WANTED YOU TO STAY WITH HIM...
...BUT YOU WENT TO SEE SOME OTHER GUY INSTEAD?

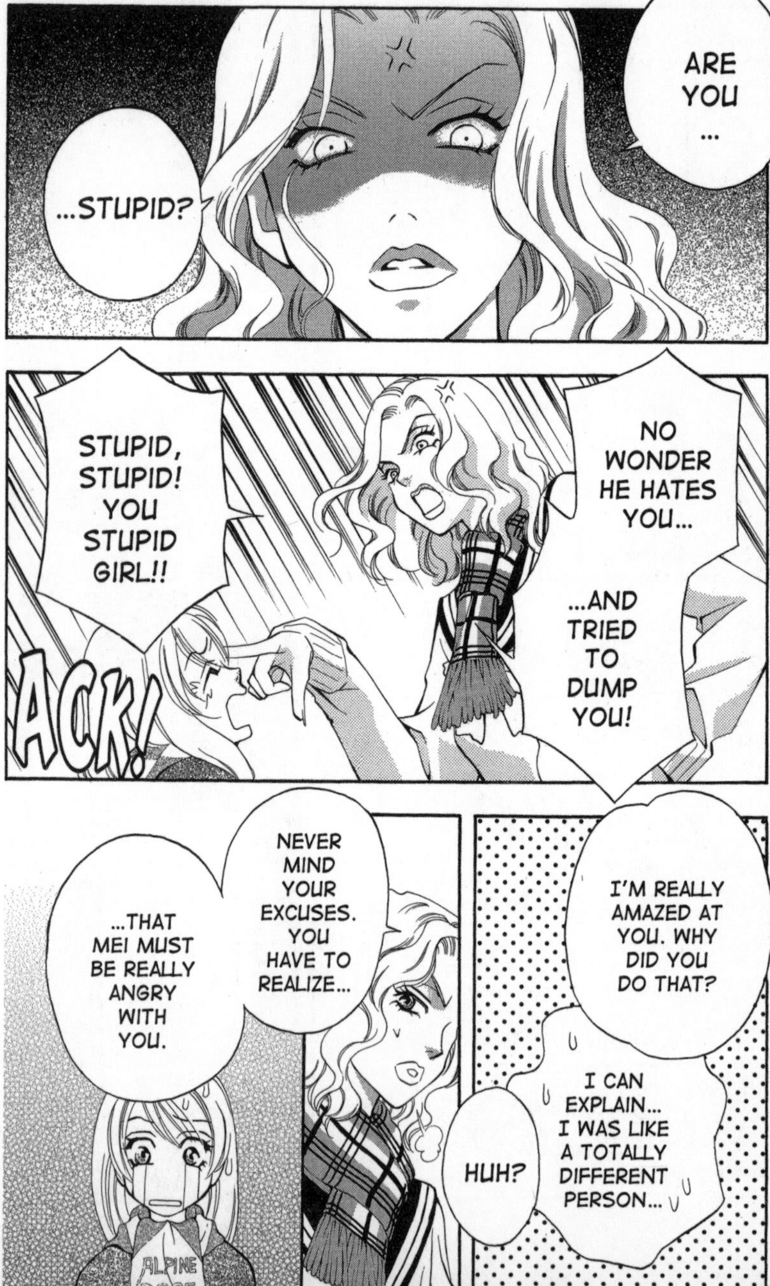
ARE YOU ...
...STUPID?
NO WONDER HE HATES YOU...
...AND TRIED TO DUMP YOU!
STUPID, STUPID! YOU STUPID GIRL!!
ACK!
I'M REALLY AMAZED AT YOU. WHY DID YOU DO THAT?
I CAN EXPLAIN... I WAS LIKE A TOTALLY DIFFERENT PERSON...
HUH?
NEVER MIND YOUR EXCUSES. YOU HAVE TO REALIZE...
...THAT MEI MUST BE REALLY ANGRY WITH YOU.
ALPINE ROSE

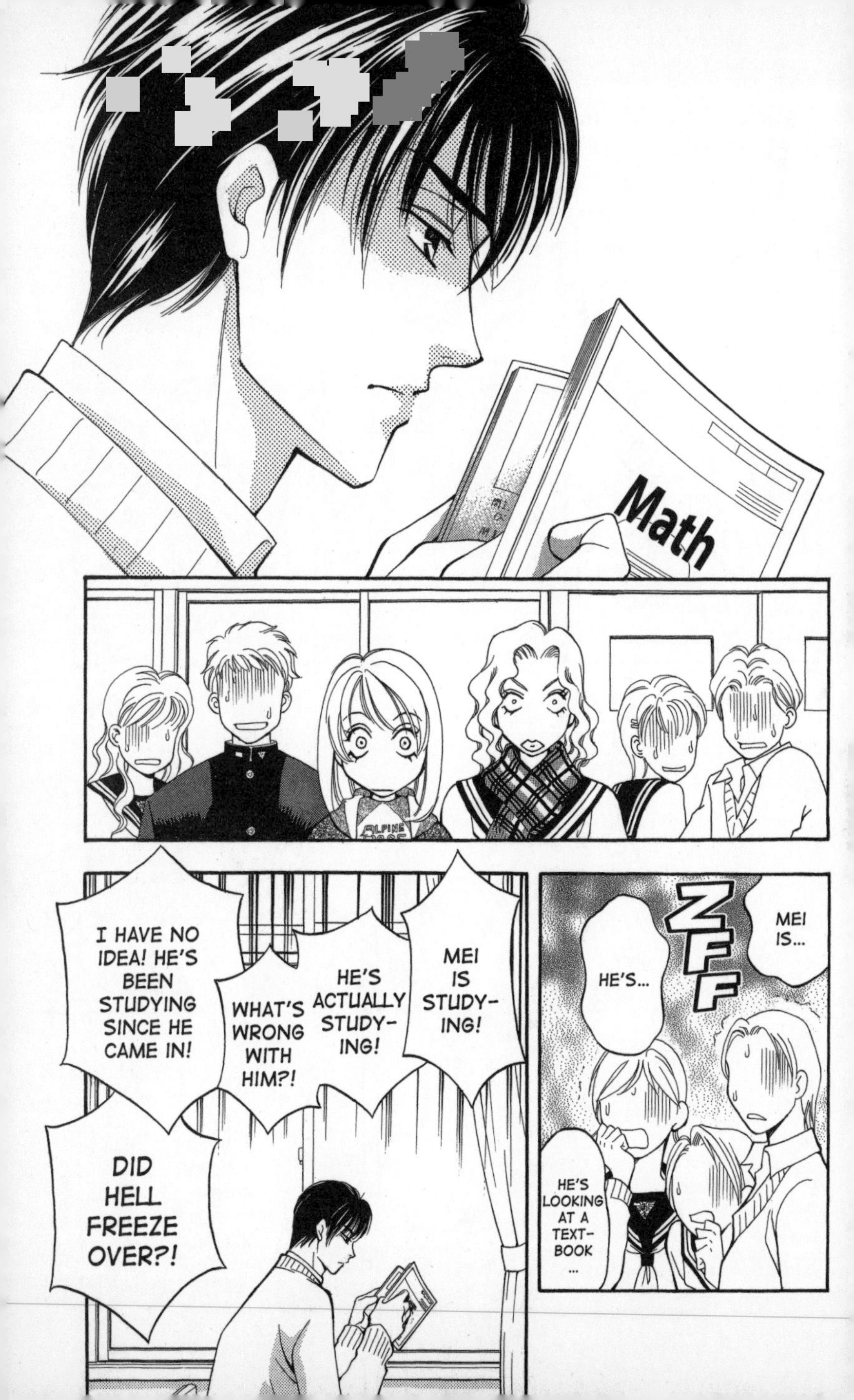
Math
MEI IS...
HE'S...
ZFF
HE'S LOOKING AT A TEXT-BOOK...
MEI IS STUDY-ING!
HE'S ACTUALLY STUDY-ING!
WHAT'S WRONG WITH HIM?!
I HAVE NO IDEA! HE'S BEEN STUDYING SINCE HE CAME IN!
DID HELL FREEZE OVER?!

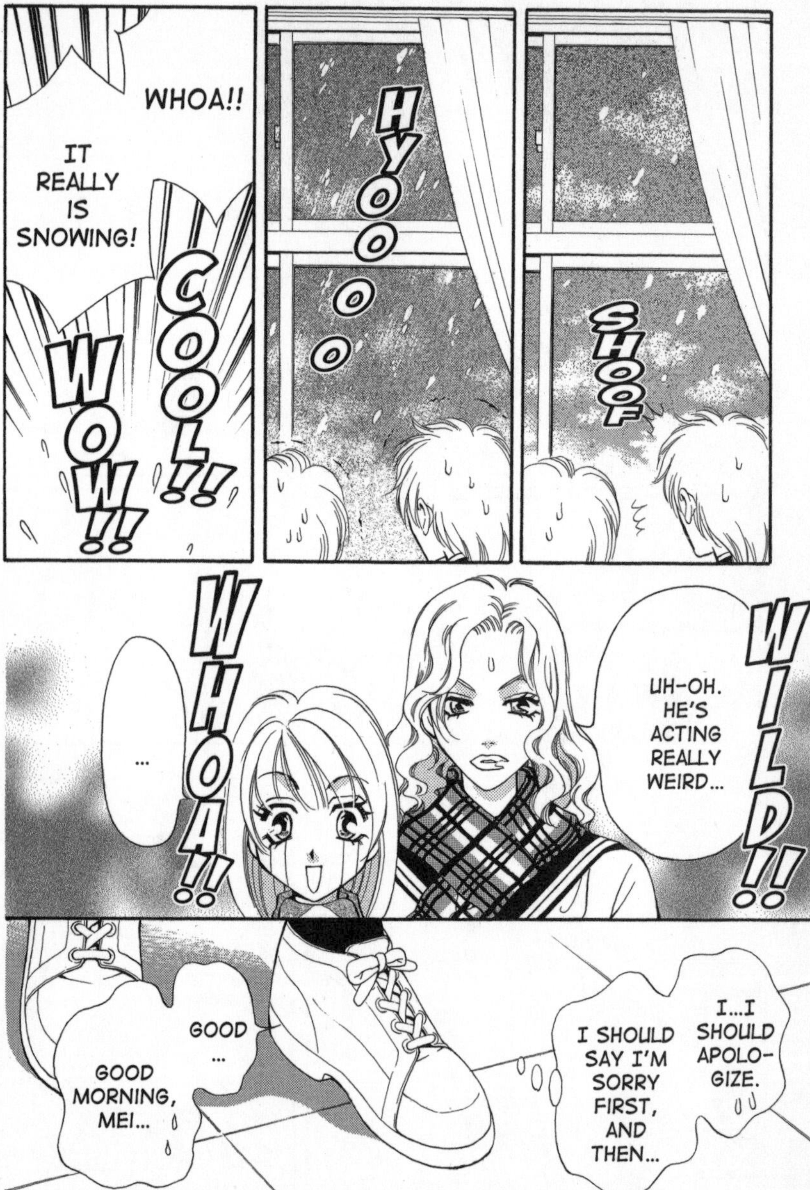
SHOOF
HYOOOOO
WHOA!!
IT REALLY IS SNOWING!
COOL!!
WOW!!
WILD!!
UH-OH. HE'S ACTING REALLY WEIRD...
WHOA!!
...
I...I SHOULD APOLOGIZE.
I SHOULD SAY I'M SORRY FIRST, AND THEN...
GOOD...
GOOD MORNING, MEI...

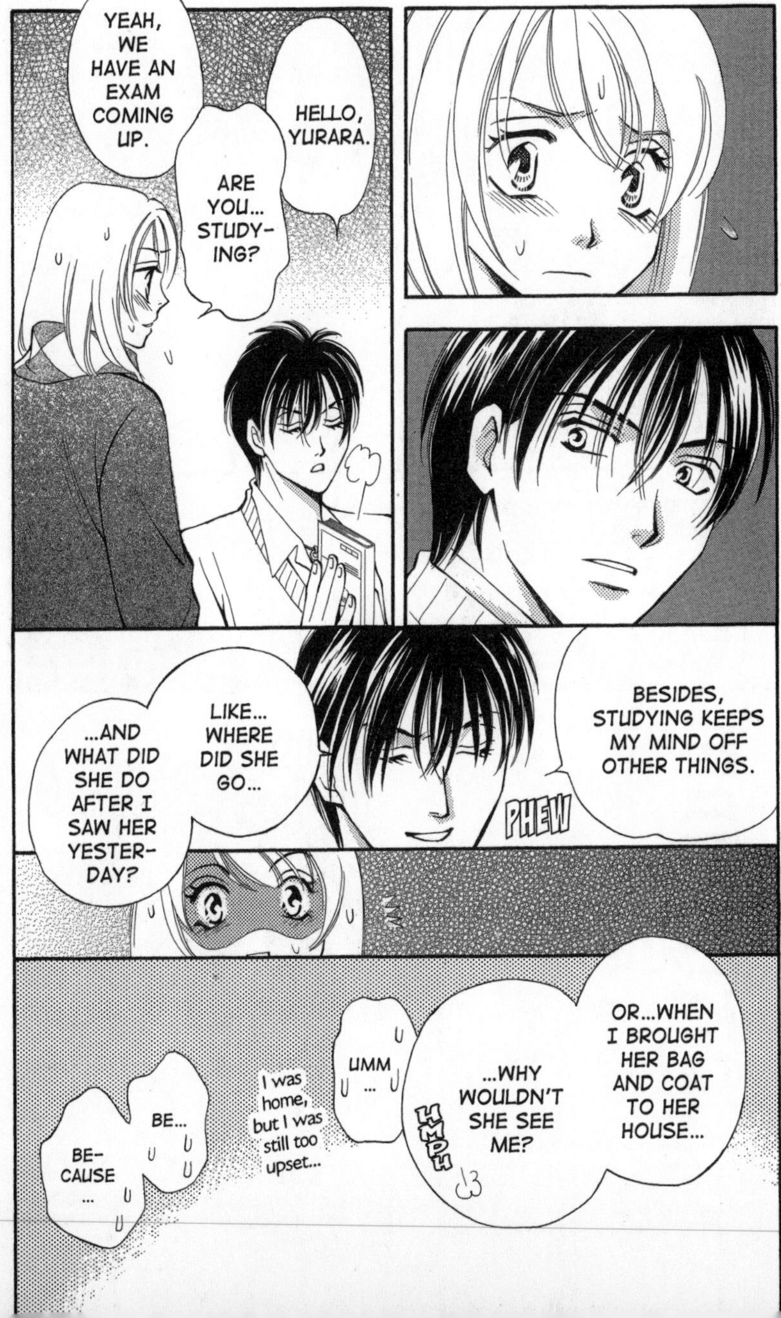
HELLO, YURARA.
ARE YOU... STUDYING?
YEAH, WE HAVE AN EXAM COMING UP.
BESIDES, STUDYING KEEPS MY MIND OFF OTHER THINGS.
PHEW
LIKE... WHERE DID SHE GO...
...AND WHAT DID SHE DO AFTER I SAW HER YESTERDAY?
OR...WHEN I BROUGHT HER BAG AND COAT TO HER HOUSE...
...WHY WOULDN'T SHE SEE ME?
HMPH
UMM...
I was home, but I was still too upset...
BE...
BE-CAUSE...

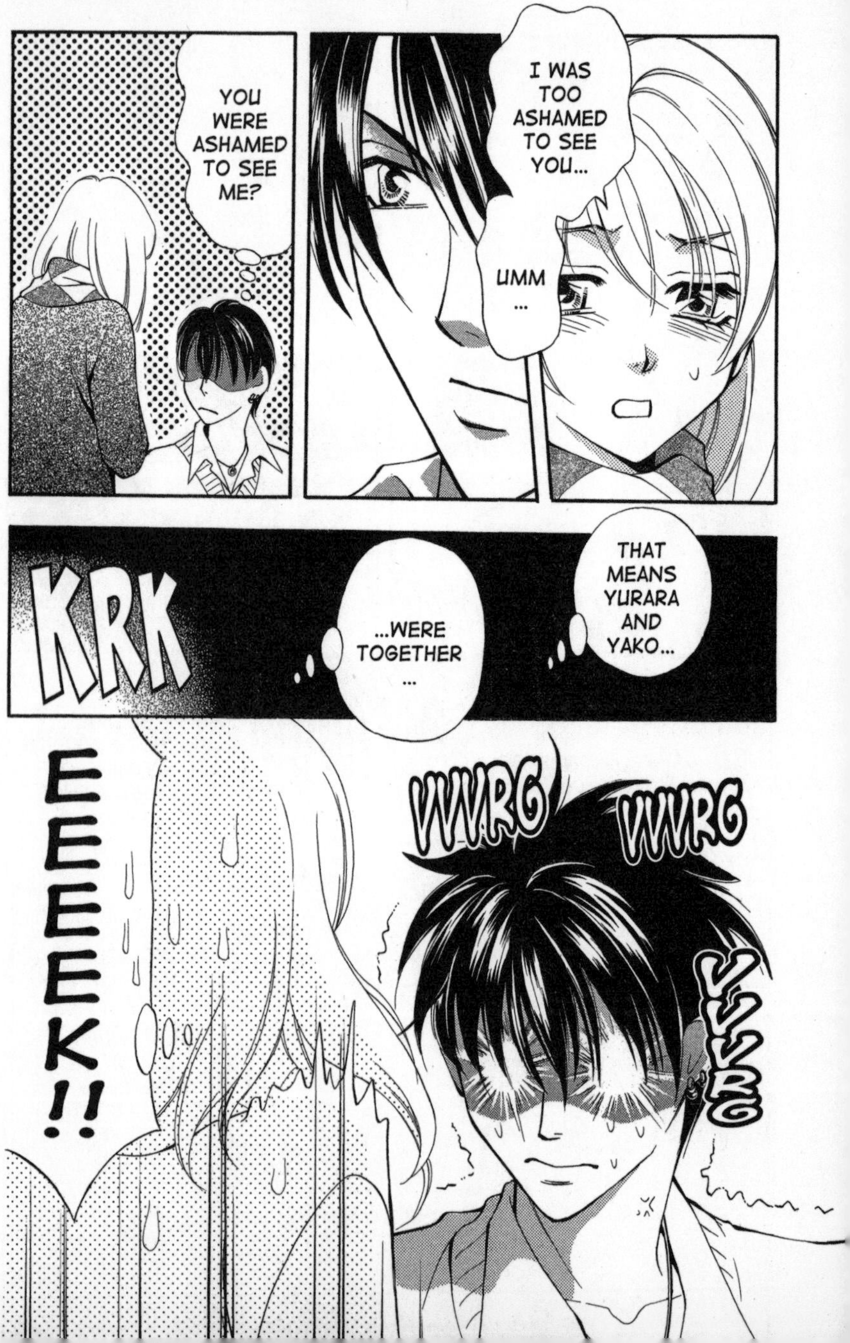
I WAS TOO ASHAMED TO SEE YOU...
UMM ...
YOU WERE ASHAMED TO SEE ME?
THAT MEANS YURARA AND YAKO...
...WERE TOGETHER ...
KRK
VVVRG
VVVRG
VVVRG
EEEEEK!!

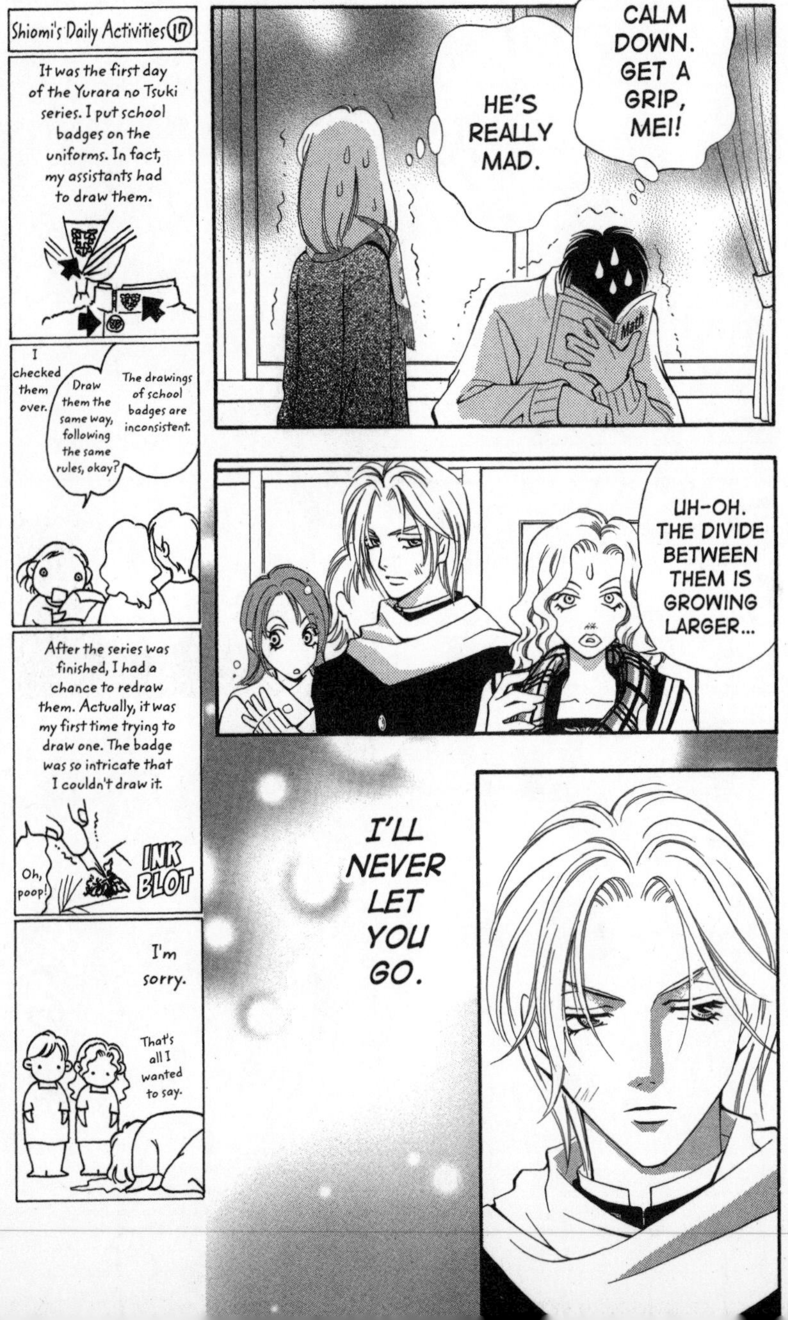
CALM DOWN. GET A GRIP, MEI!
HE'S REALLY MAD.
UH-OH. THE DIVIDE BETWEEN THEM IS GROWING LARGER...
I'LL NEVER LET YOU GO.
Shiomi's Daily Activities 17
It was the first day of the Yurara no Tsuki series. I put school badges on the uniforms. In fact, my assistants had to draw them.
The drawings of school badges are inconsistent.
Draw them the same way, following the same rules, okay?
I checked them over.
After the series was finished, I had a chance to redraw them. Actually, it was my first time trying to draw one. The badge was so intricate that I couldn't draw it.
INK BLOT
Oh, poop!
I'm sorry.
That's all I wanted to say.

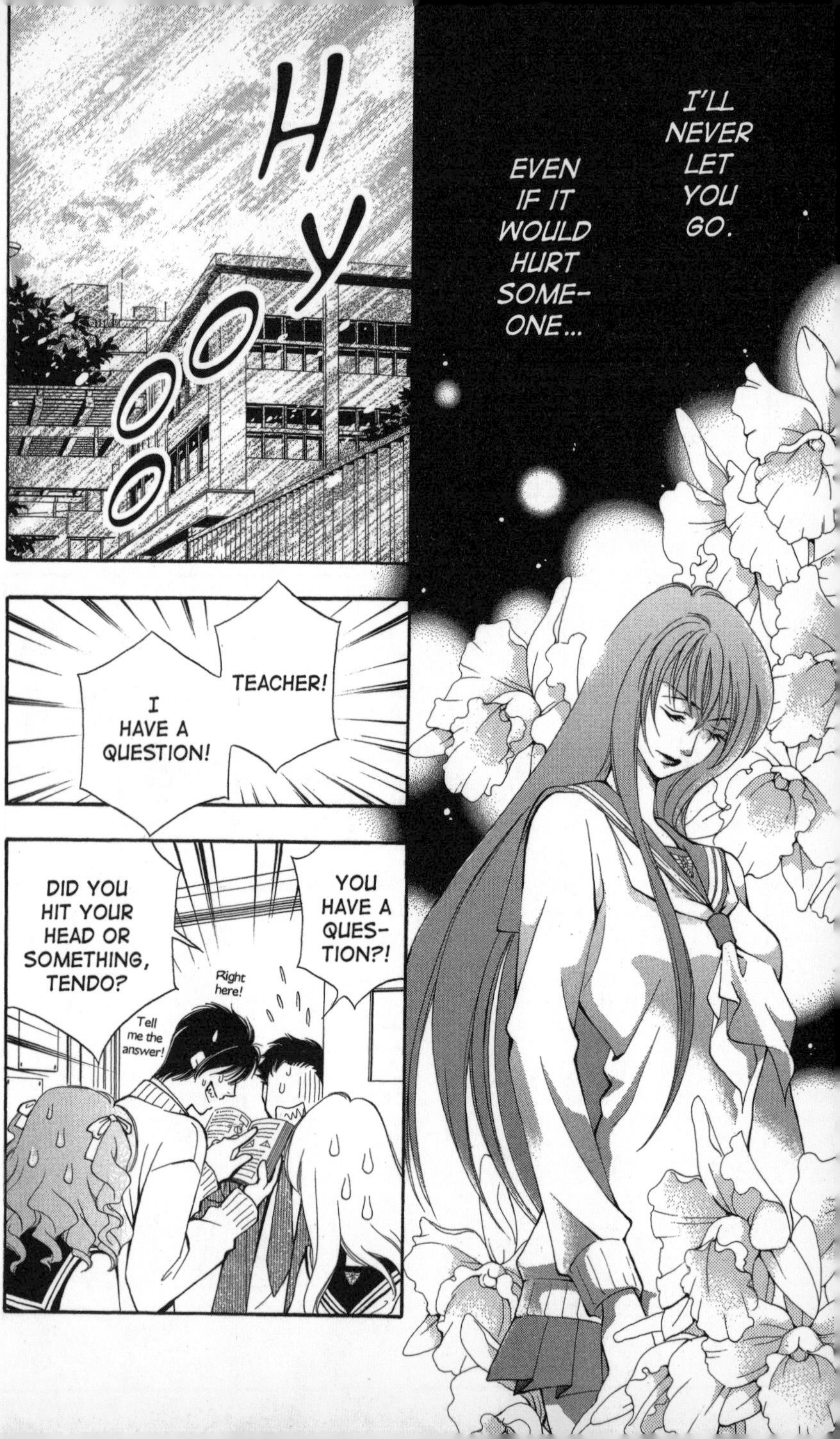
I'LL NEVER LET YOU GO.
EVEN IF IT WOULD HURT SOME-ONE...
HYOOOO
TEACHER!
I HAVE A QUESTION!
YOU HAVE A QUES-TION?!
DID YOU HIT YOUR HEAD OR SOMETHING, TENDO?
Right here!
Tell me the answer!

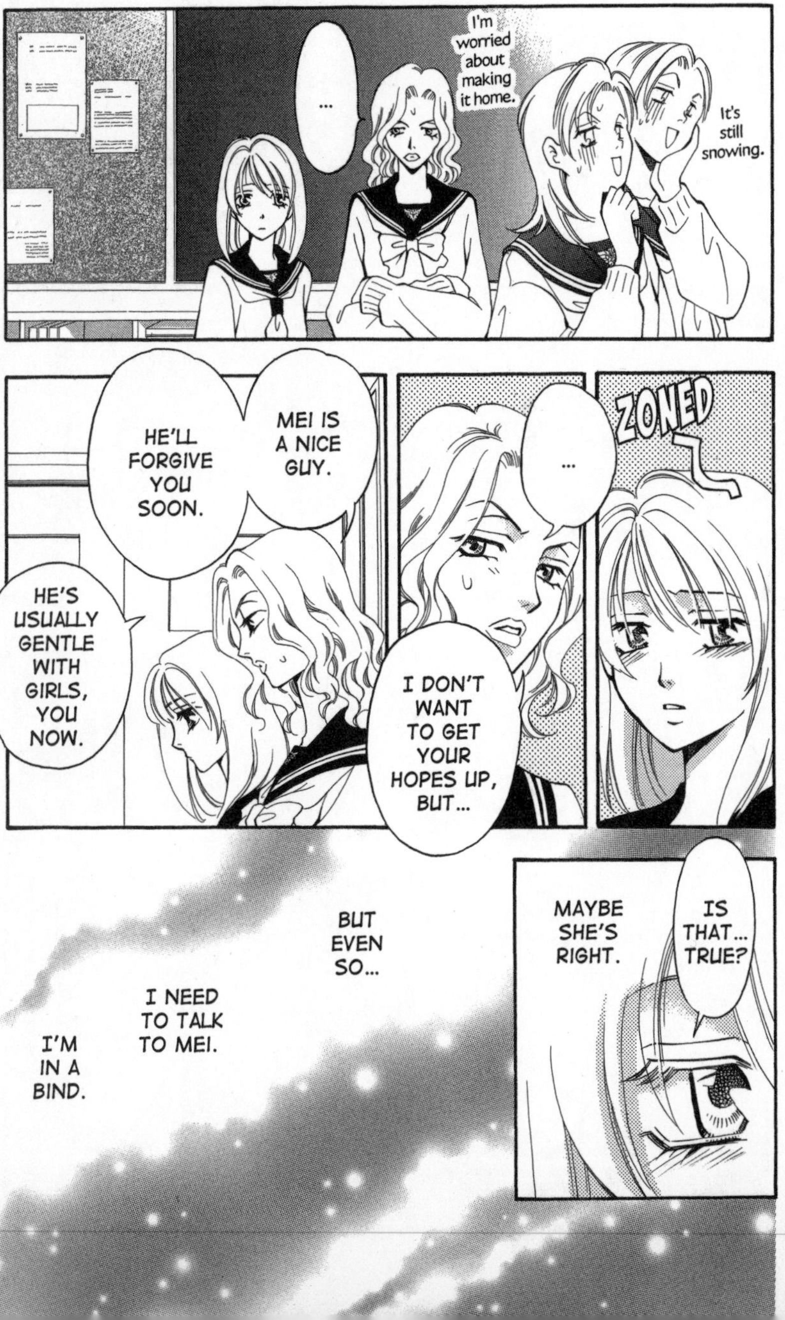
It's still snowing.
I'm worried about making it home.
...
ZONED
...
I DON'T WANT TO GET YOUR HOPES UP, BUT...
MEI IS A NICE GUY.
HE'LL FORGIVE YOU SOON.
HE'S USUALLY GENTLE WITH GIRLS, YOU NOW.
IS THAT... TRUE?
MAYBE SHE'S RIGHT.
BUT EVEN SO...
I NEED TO TALK TO MEI.
I'M IN A BIND.

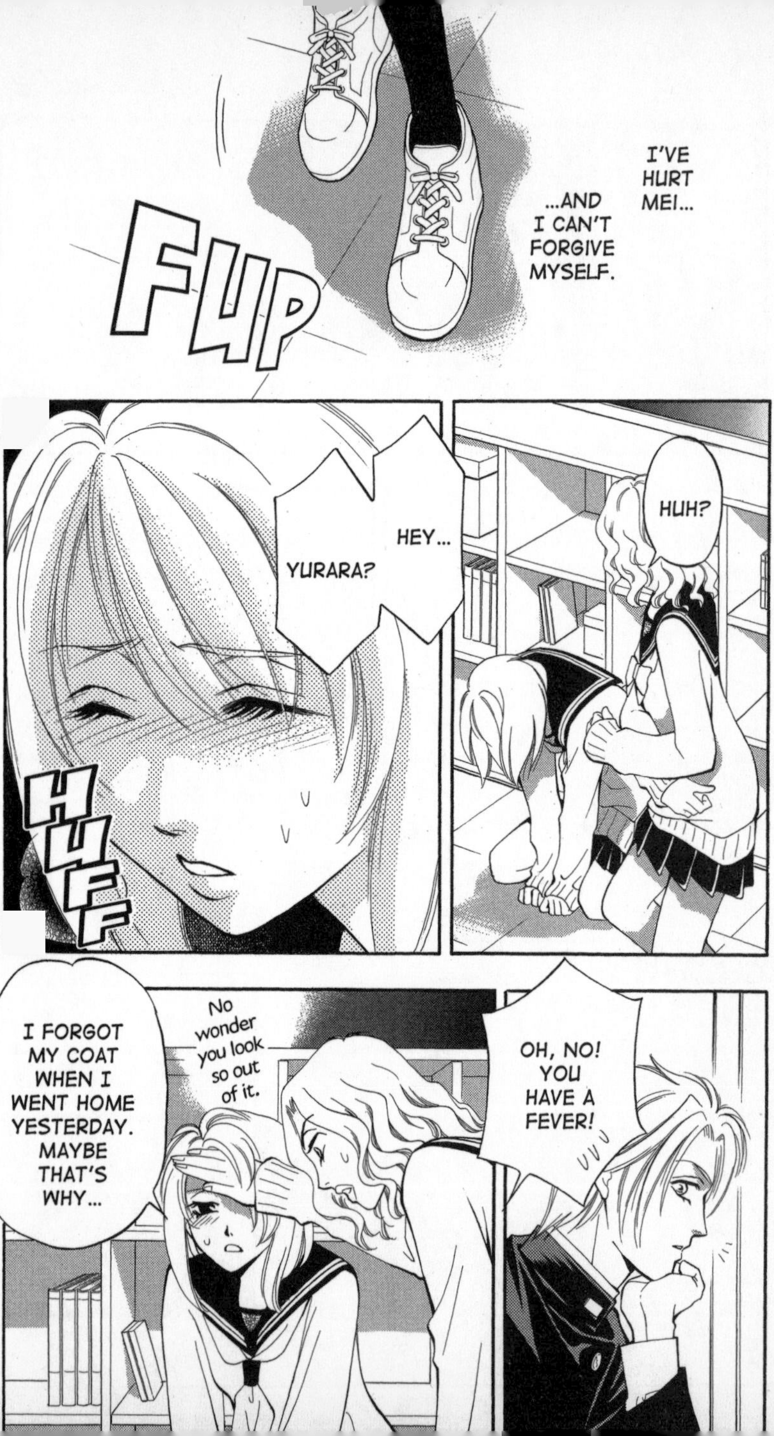
I'VE HURT MEI...
...AND I CAN'T FORGIVE MYSELF.
FUP
HUH?
HEY... YURARA?
HUFF
OH, NO! YOU HAVE A FEVER!
No wonder you look so out of it.
I FORGOT MY COAT WHEN I WENT HOME YESTERDAY. MAYBE THAT'S WHY...

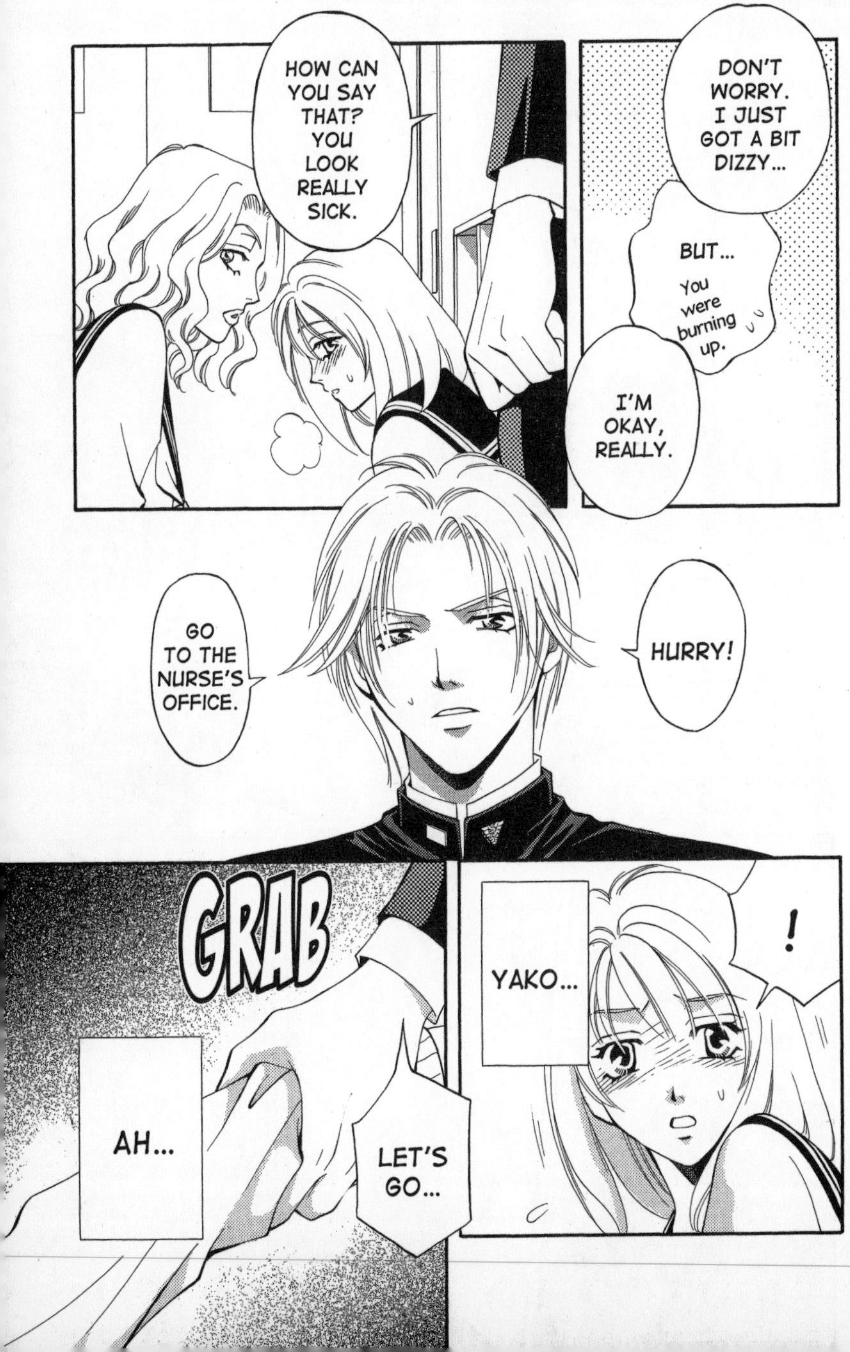
DON'T WORRY. I JUST GOT A BIT DIZZY...
BUT... You were burning up.
I'M OKAY, REALLY.
HOW CAN YOU SAY THAT? YOU LOOK REALLY SICK.
HURRY!
GO TO THE NURSE'S OFFICE.
!
YAKO...
GRAB
LET'S GO...
AH...

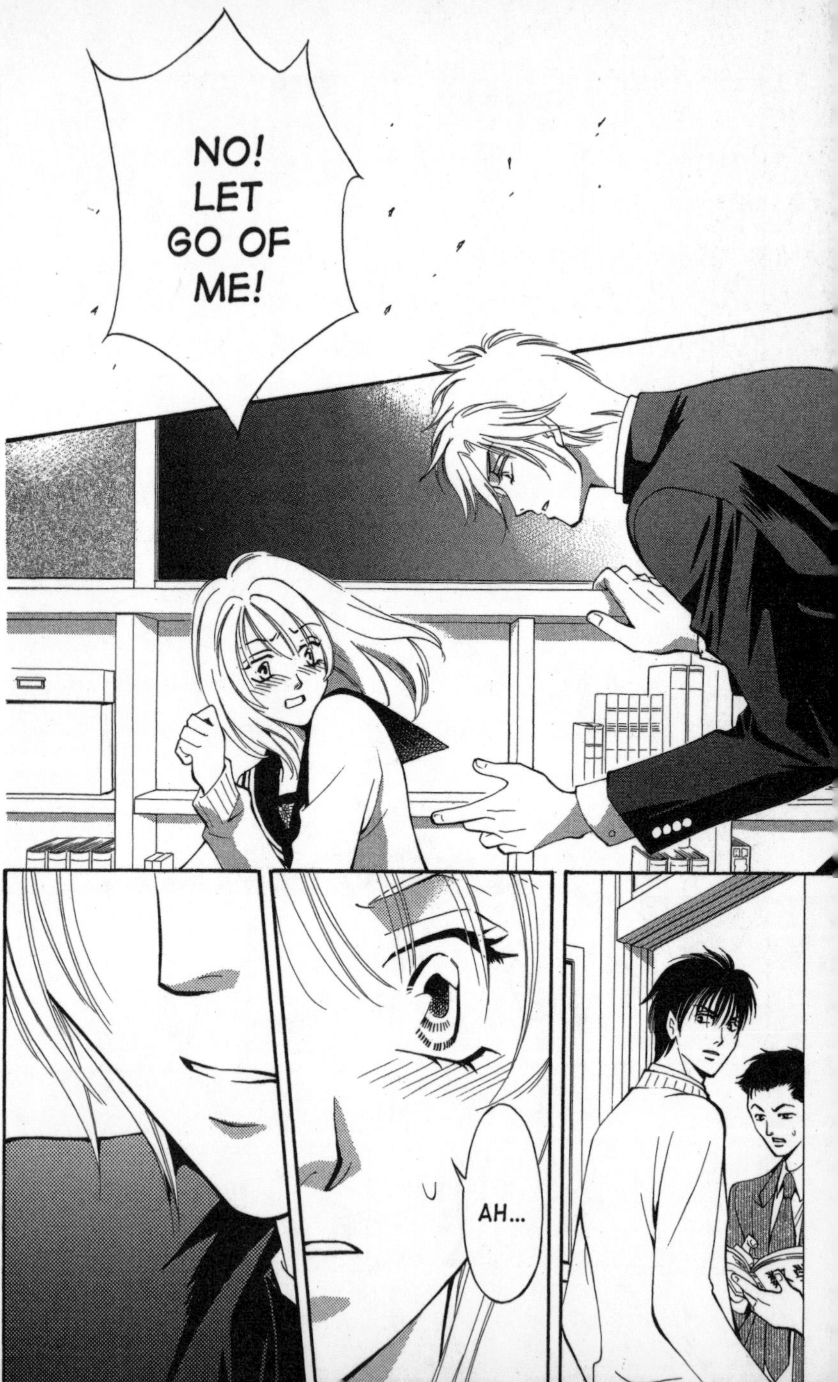
NO! LET GO OF ME!
AH...

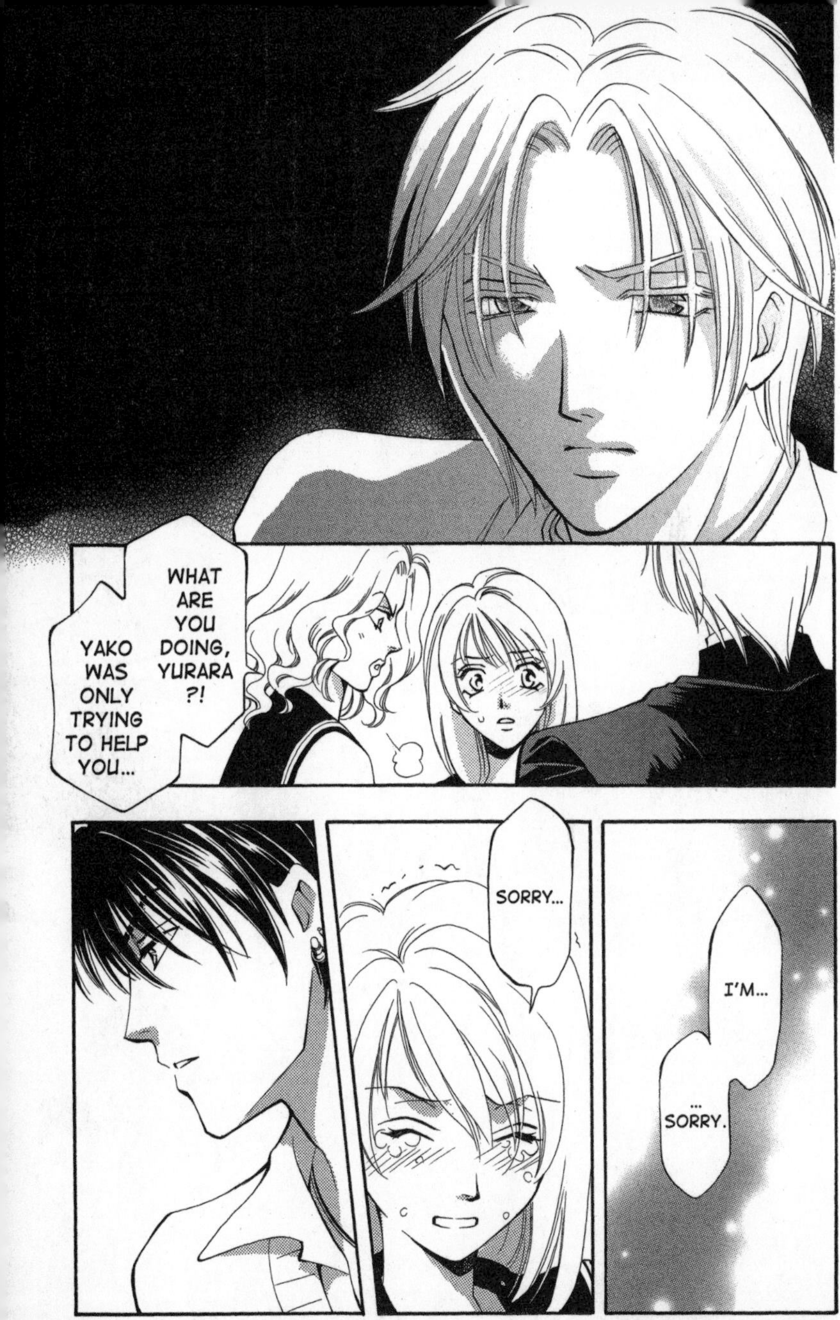
WHAT ARE YOU DOING, YURARA?!
YAKO WAS ONLY TRYING TO HELP YOU...
I'M... ...SORRY.
SORRY...

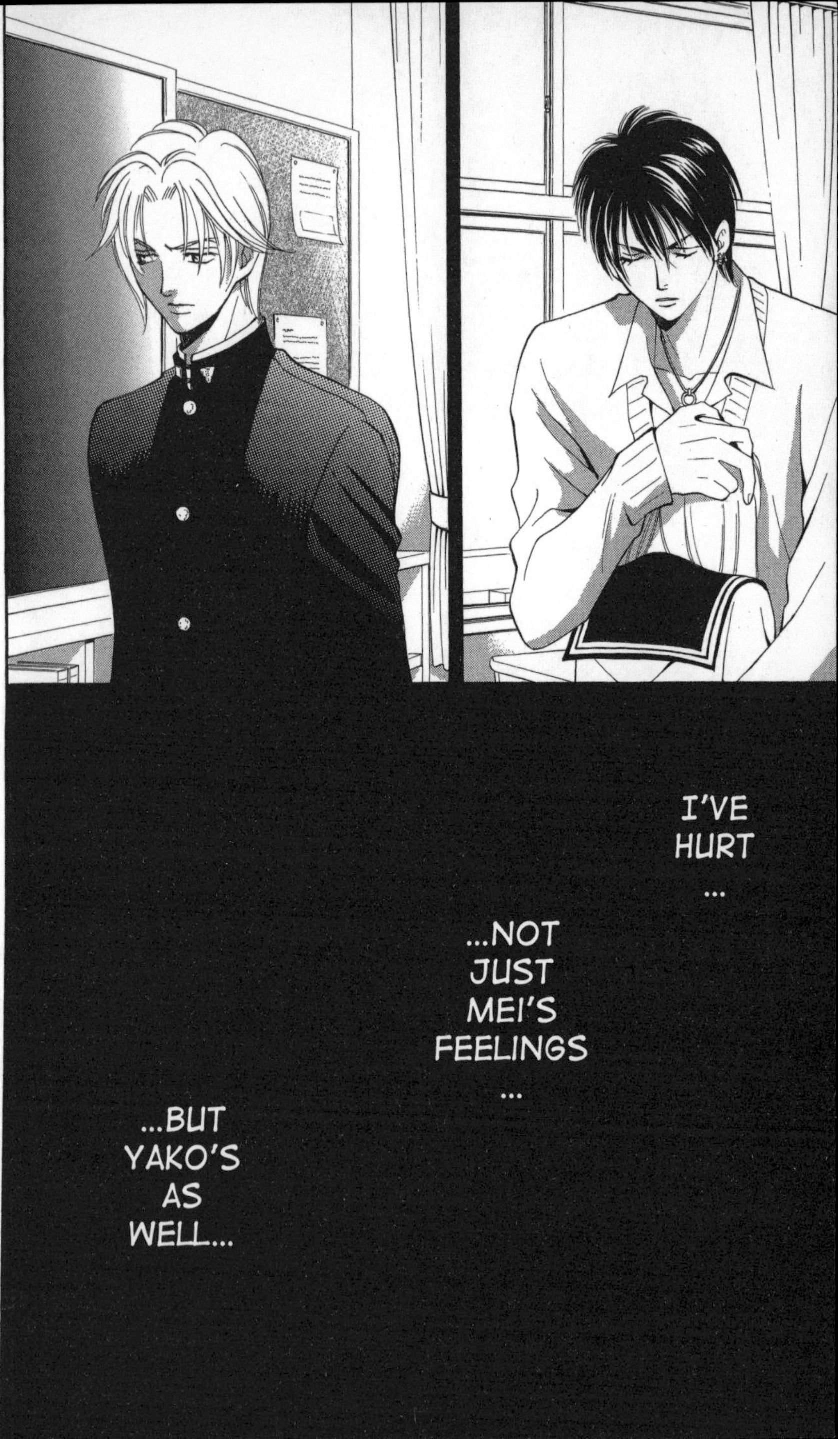
I'VE HURT ...
...NOT JUST MEI'S FEELINGS ...
...BUT YAKO'S AS WELL...

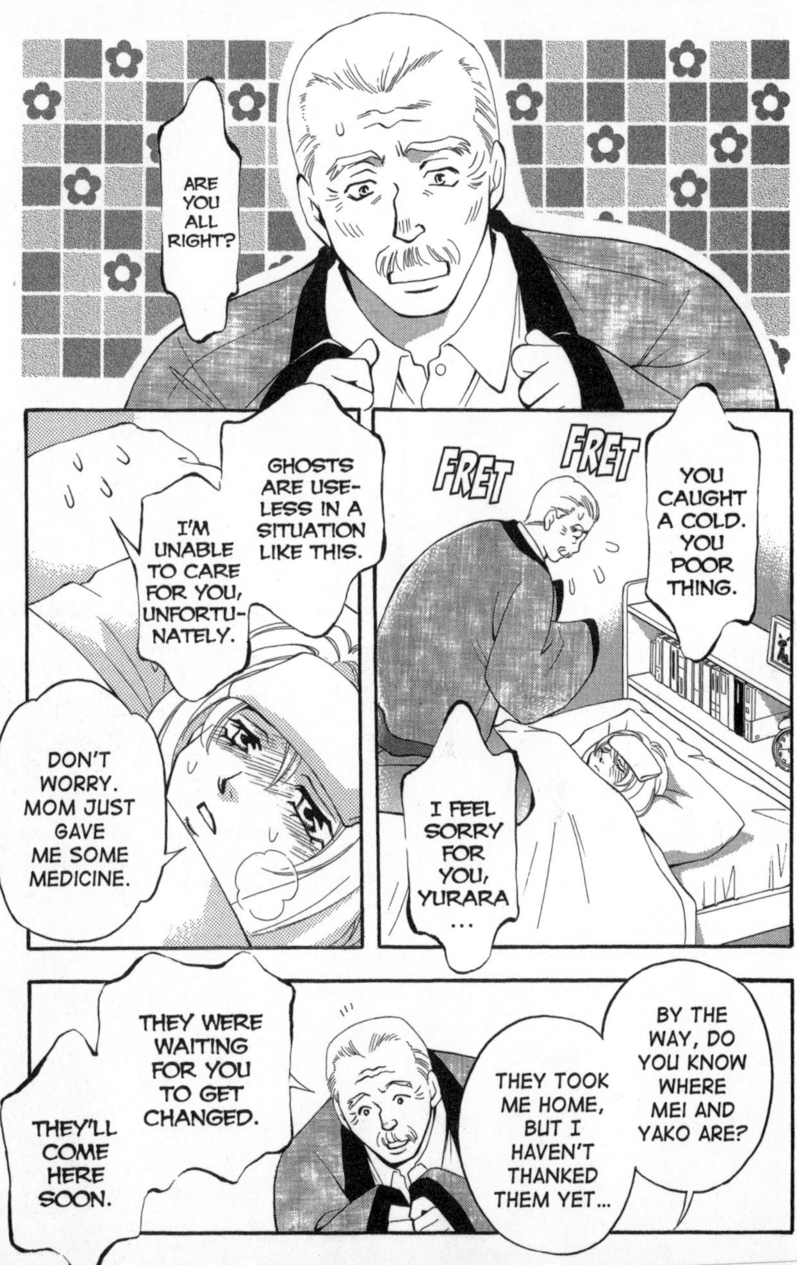
ARE YOU ALL RIGHT?
FRET FRET
YOU CAUGHT A COLD. YOU POOR THING.
I FEEL SORRY FOR YOU, YURARA ...
GHOSTS ARE USE-LESS IN A SITUATION LIKE THIS.
I'M UNABLE TO CARE FOR YOU, UNFORTU-NATELY.
DON'T WORRY. MOM JUST GAVE ME SOME MEDICINE.
BY THE WAY, DO YOU KNOW WHERE MEI AND YAKO ARE?
THEY TOOK ME HOME, BUT I HAVEN'T THANKED THEM YET...
THEY WERE WAITING FOR YOU TO GET CHANGED.
THEY'LL COME HERE SOON.

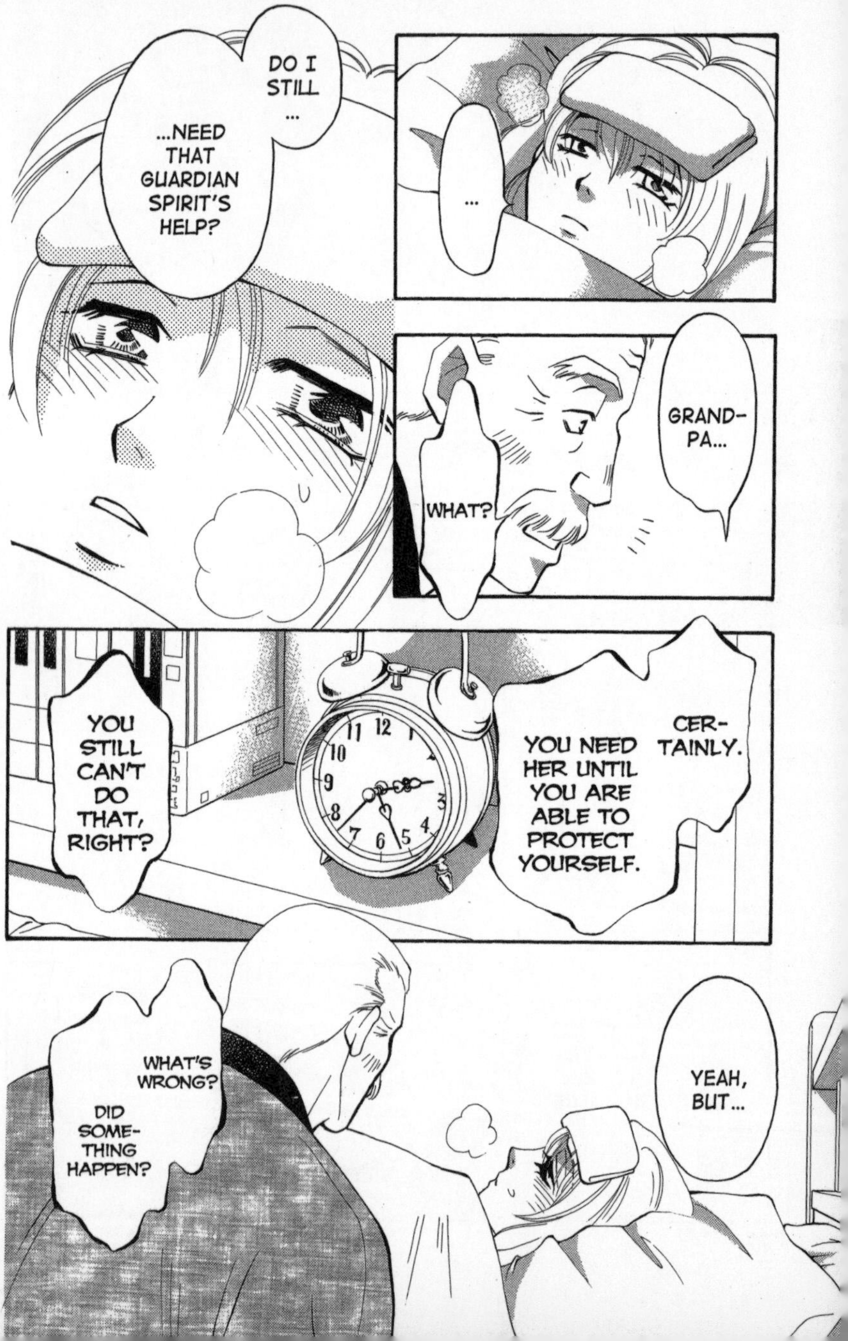
...
GRAND-PA...
WHAT?
DO I STILL ...
...NEED THAT GUARDIAN SPIRIT'S HELP?
CER-TAINLY.
YOU NEED HER UNTIL YOU ARE ABLE TO PROTECT YOURSELF.
YOU STILL CAN'T DO THAT, RIGHT?
YEAH, BUT...
WHAT'S WRONG?
DID SOME-THING HAPPEN?

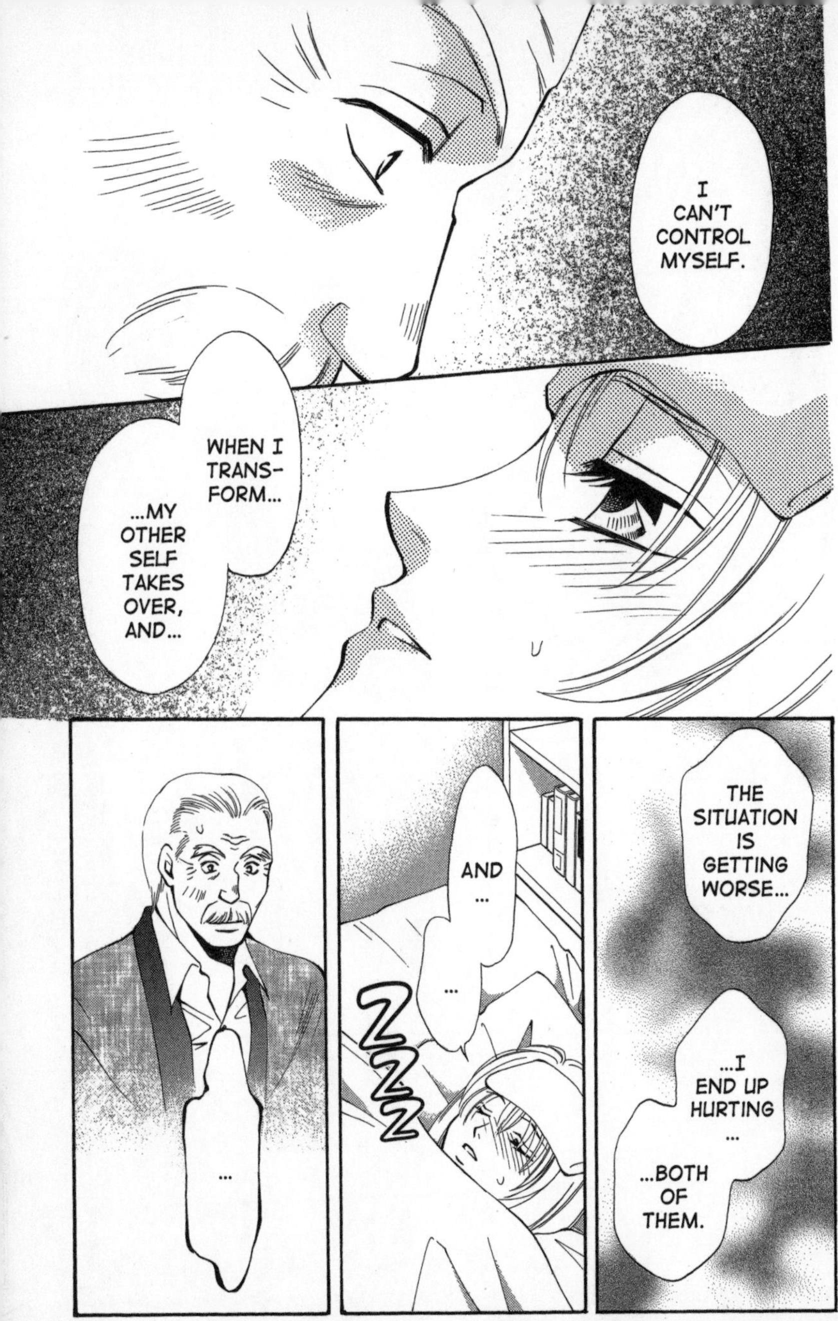
I CAN'T CONTROL MYSELF.
WHEN I TRANSFORM...
...MY OTHER SELF TAKES OVER, AND...
THE SITUATION IS GETTING WORSE...
...I END UP HURTING... ...BOTH OF THEM.
AND...
...
...

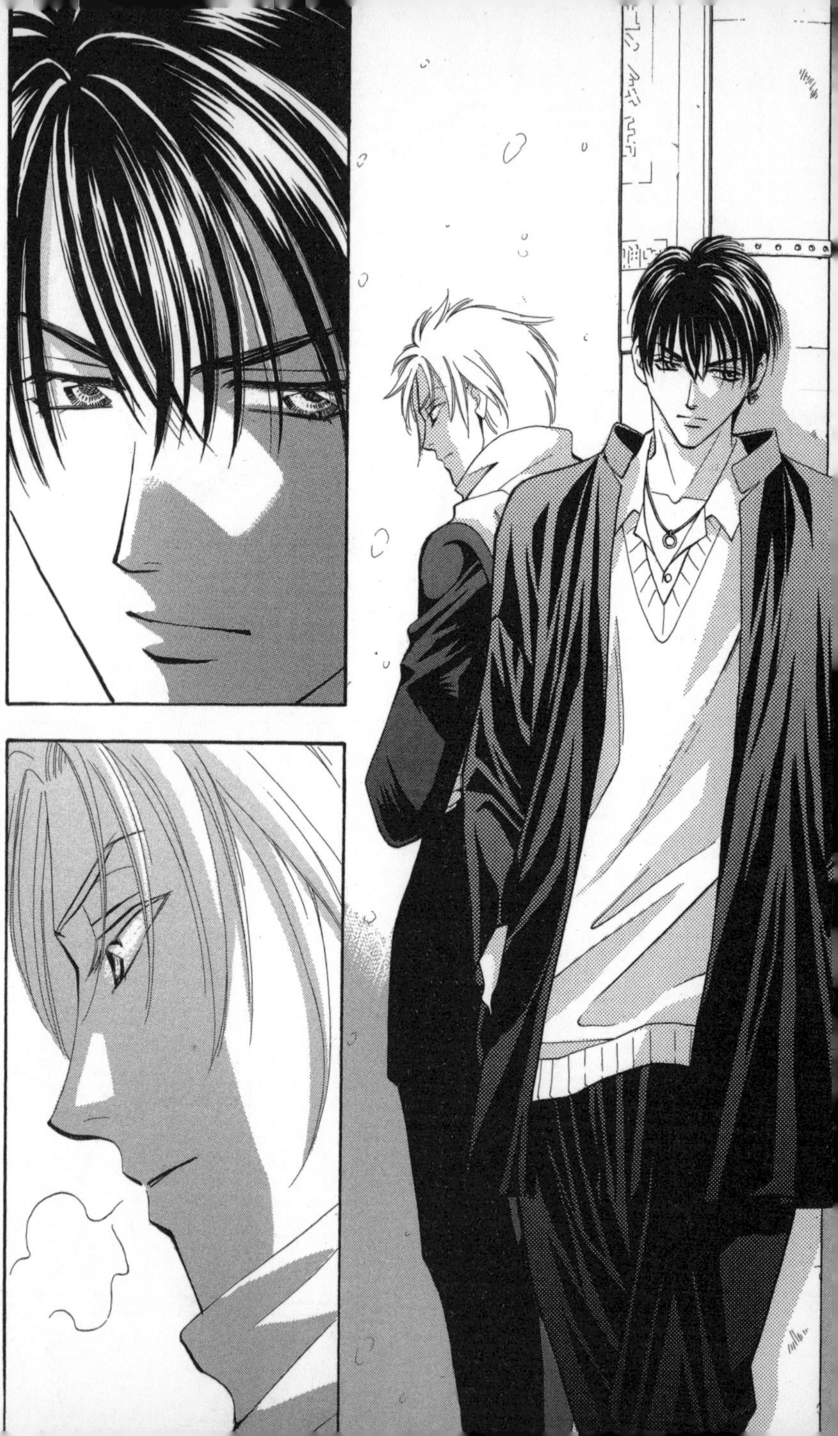

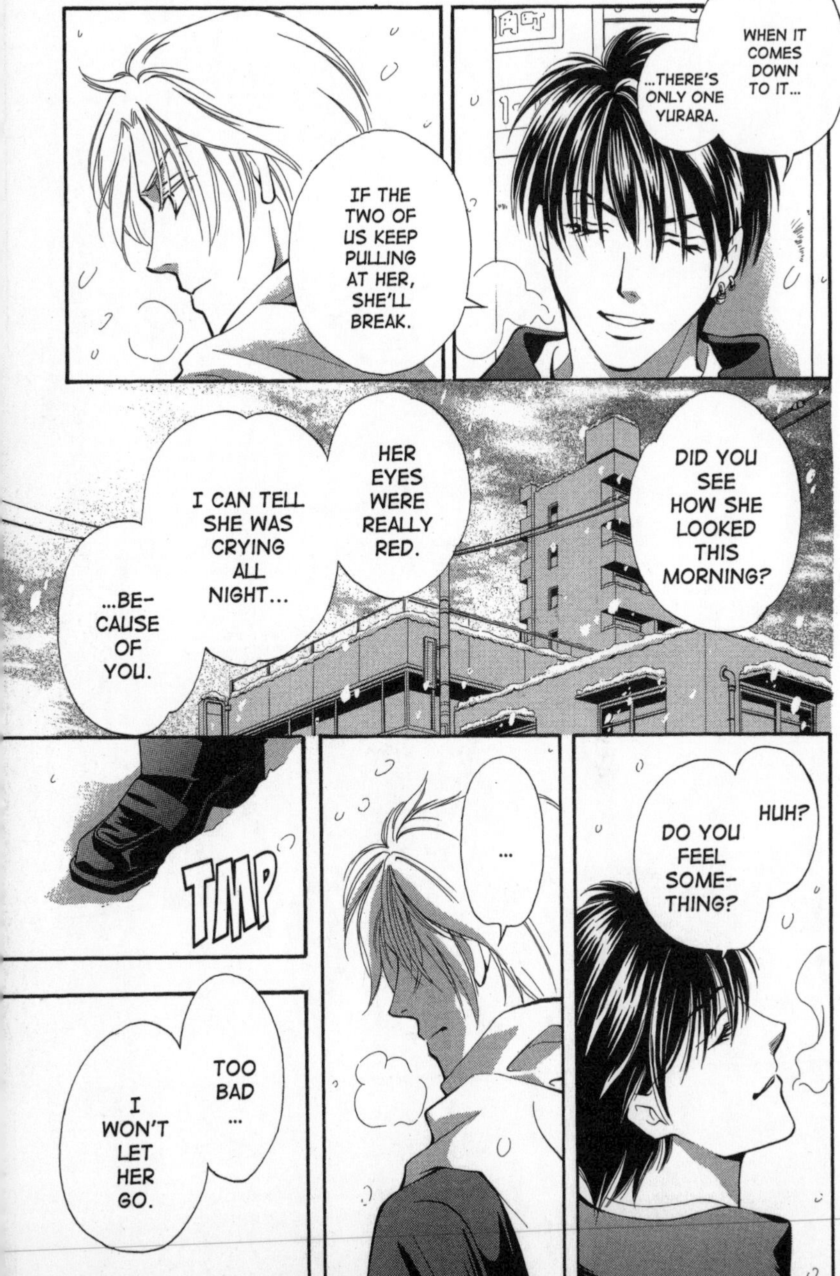
WHEN IT COMES DOWN TO IT...
...THERE'S ONLY ONE YURARA.
IF THE TWO OF US KEEP PULLING AT HER, SHE'LL BREAK.
DID YOU SEE HOW SHE LOOKED THIS MORNING?
HER EYES WERE REALLY RED.
I CAN TELL SHE WAS CRYING ALL NIGHT...
...BE-CAUSE OF YOU.
HUH?
DO YOU FEEL SOME-THING?
...
TMP
TOO BAD...
I WON'T LET HER GO.

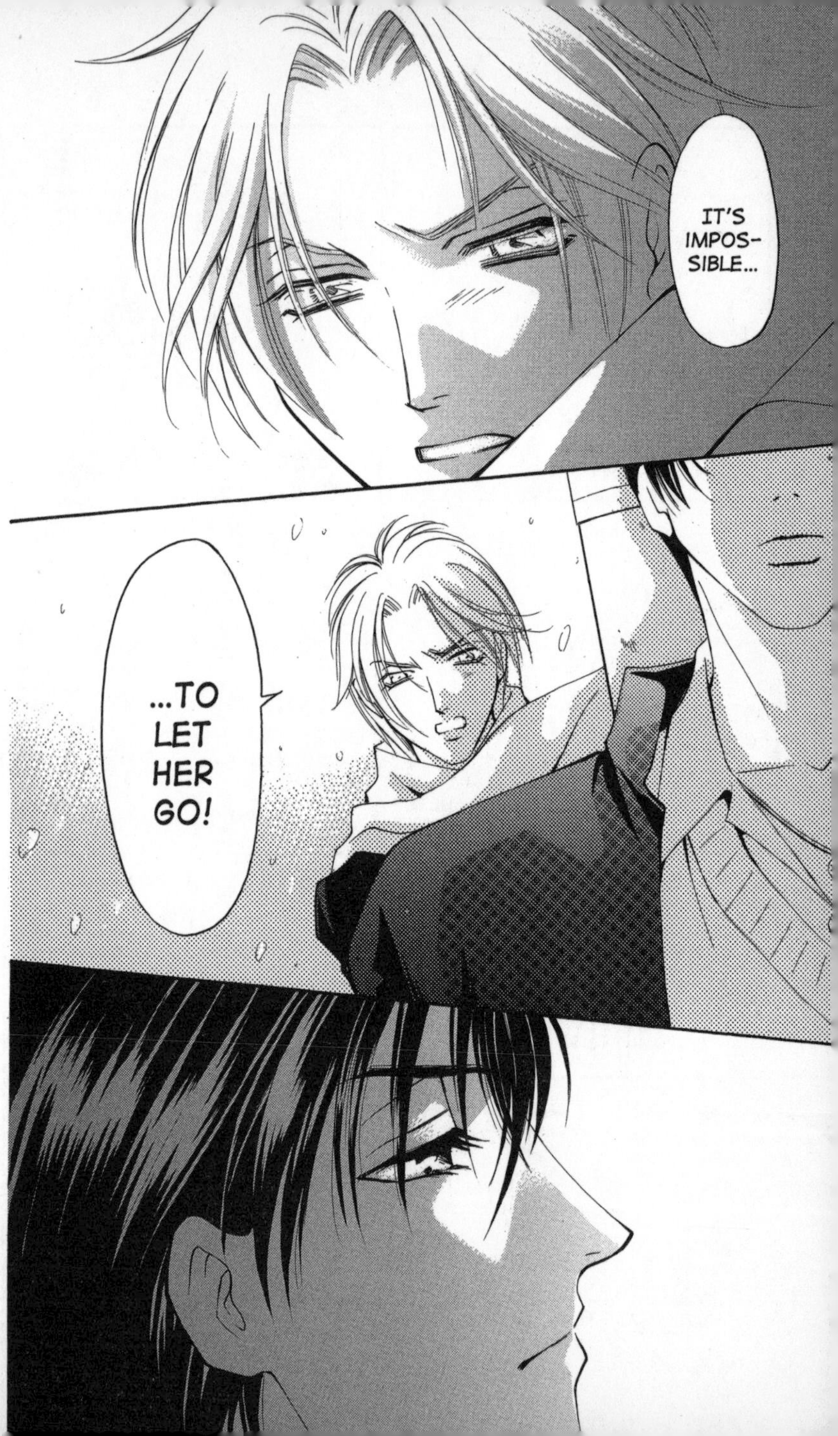
IT'S IMPOSSIBLE...
...TO LET HER GO!

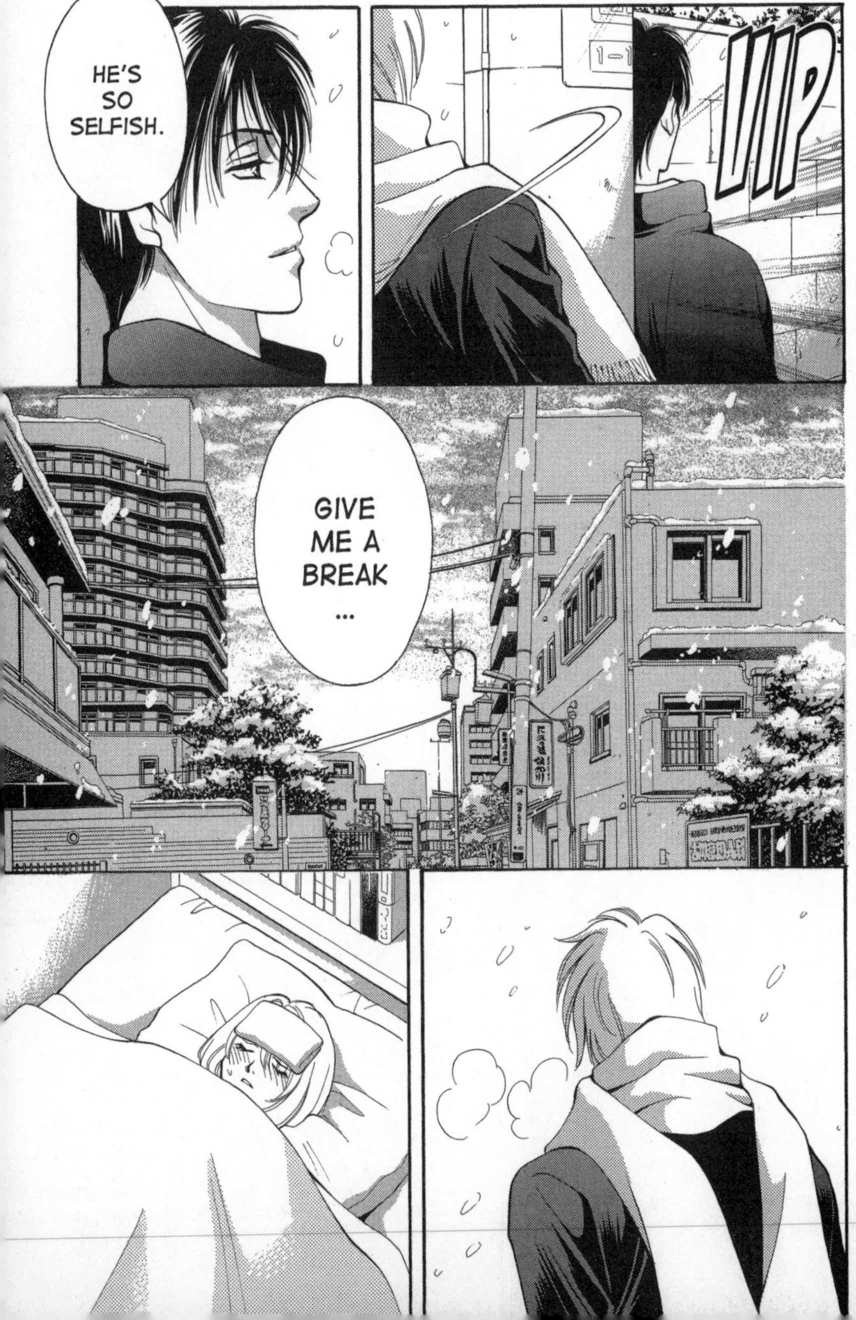
VIP
HE'S SO SELFISH.
GIVE ME A BREAK ...

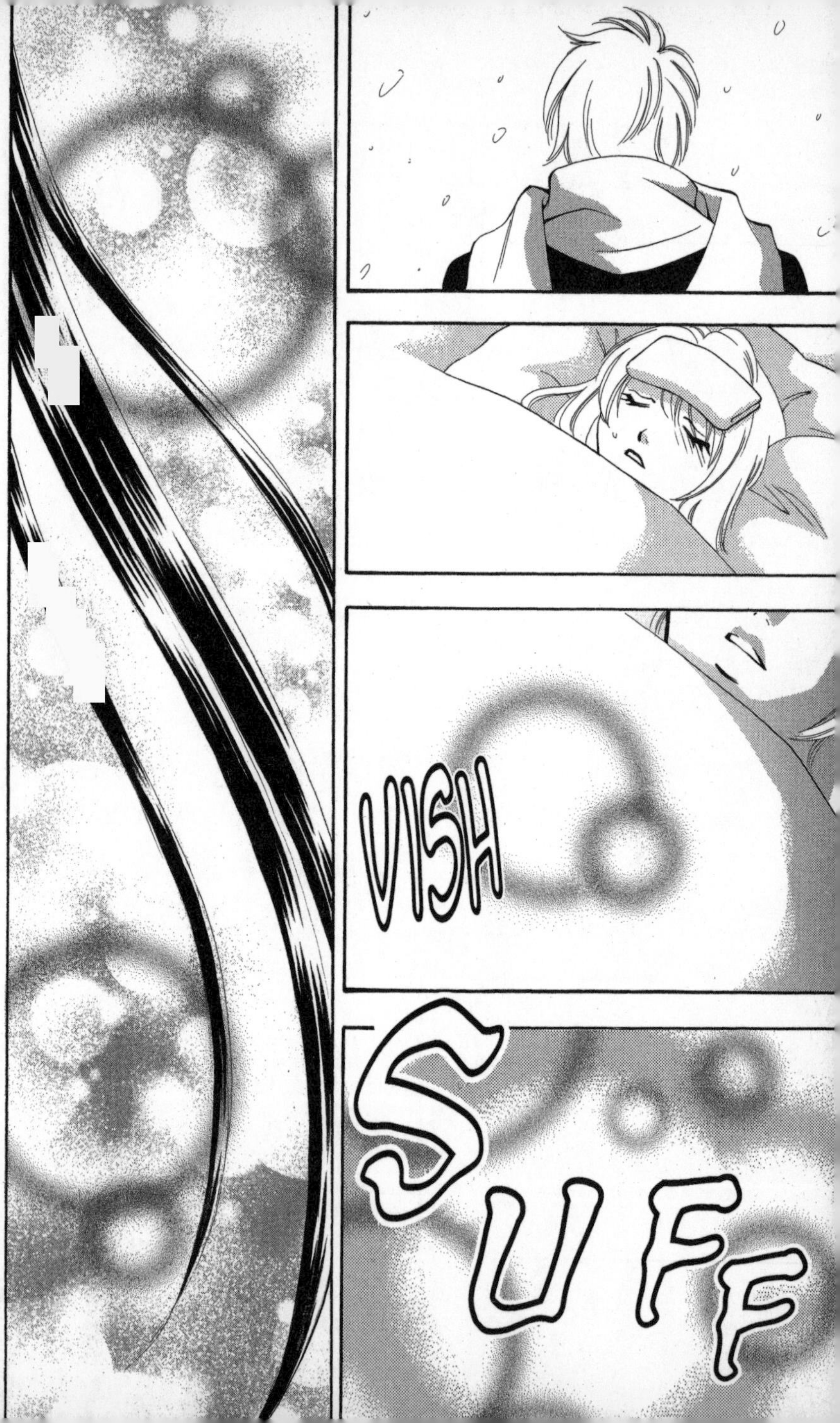
VISH
SUFF

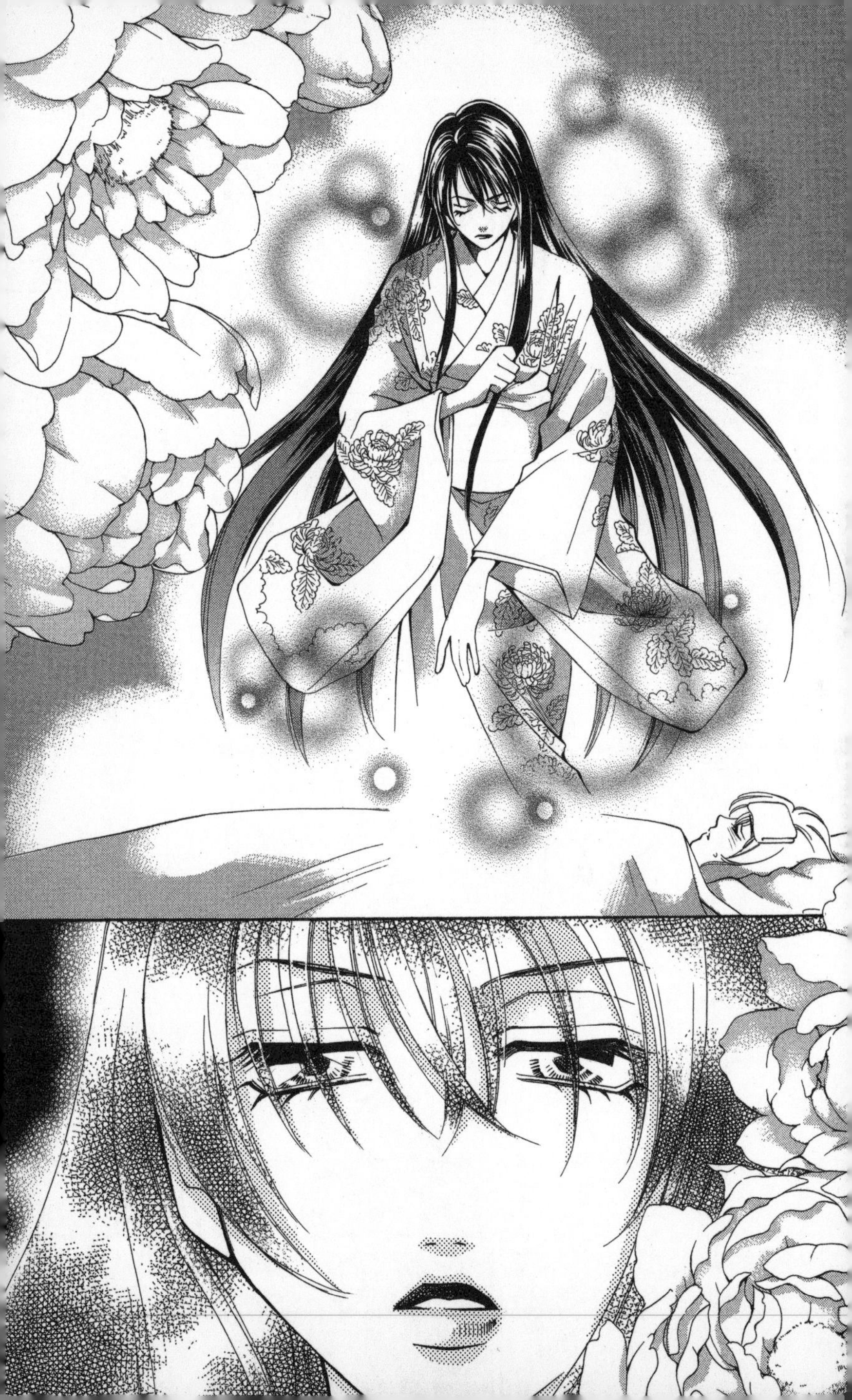

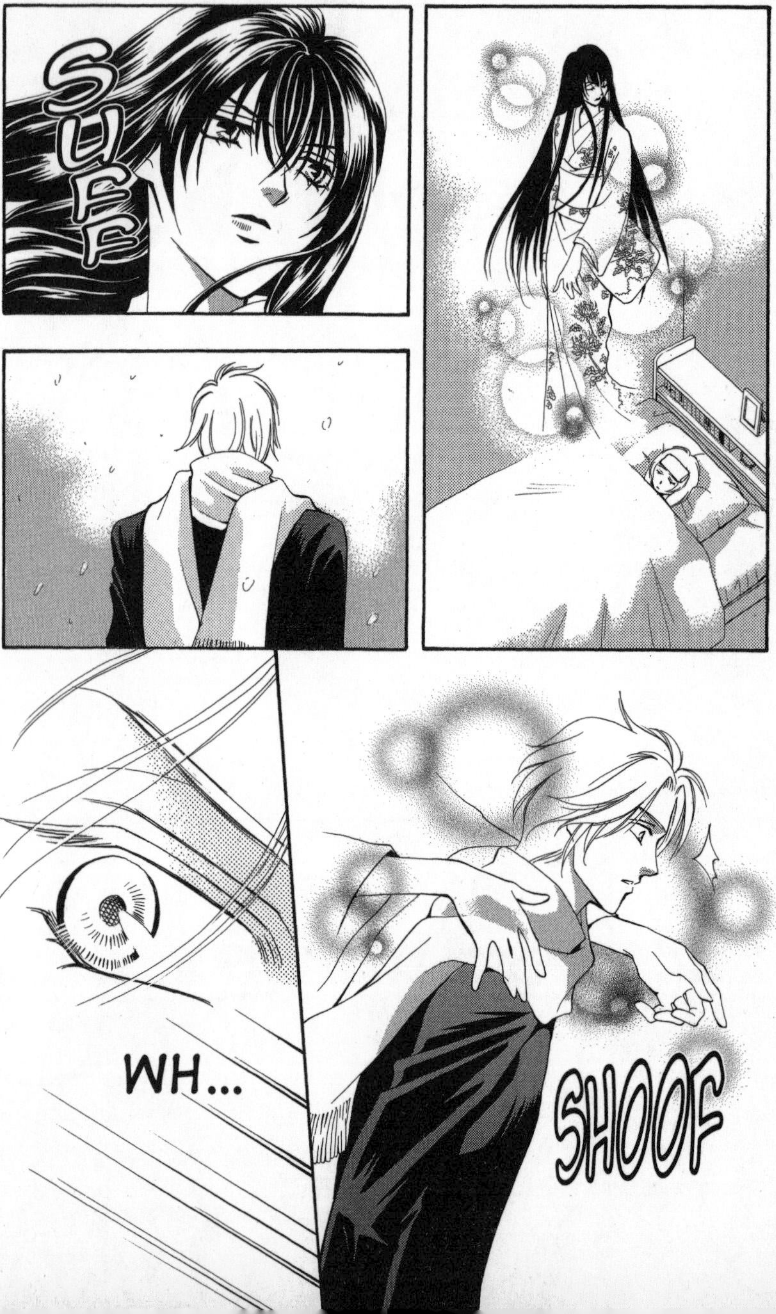
SUFF
SHOOF
WH...

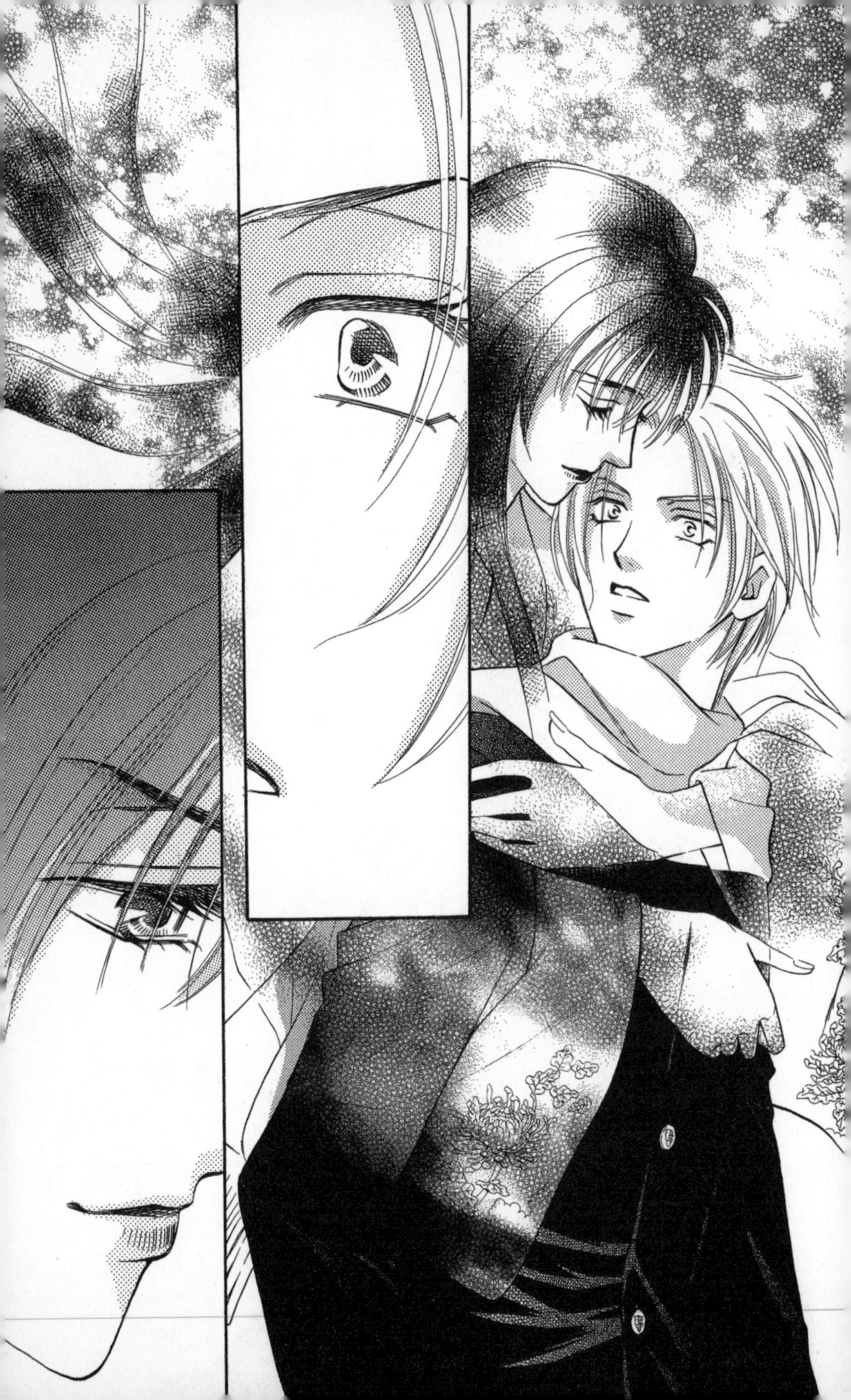

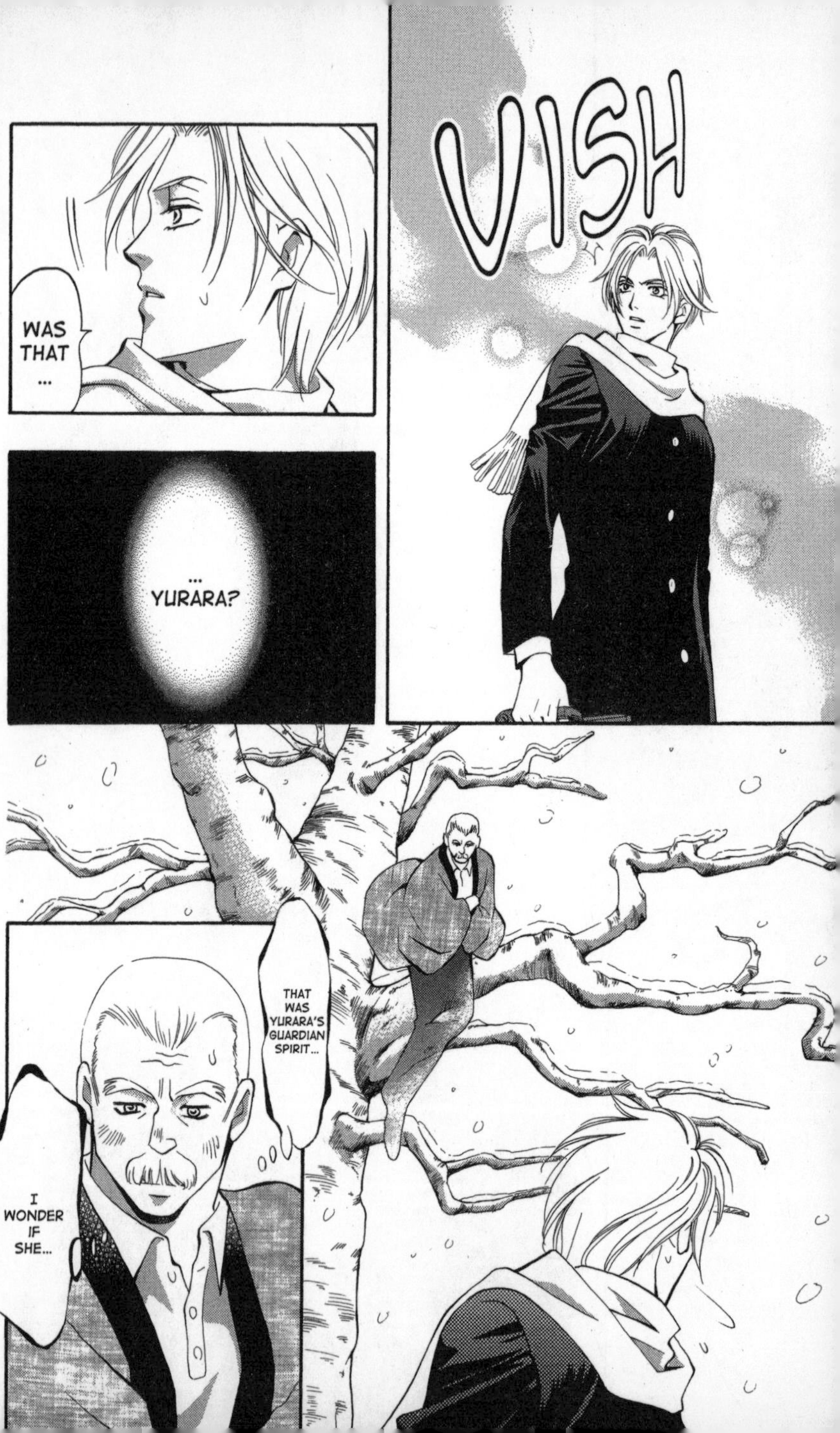
VISH
WAS THAT ...
... YURARA?
THAT WAS YURARA'S GUARDIAN SPIRIT...
I WONDER IF SHE...

SUFF

VISH

37

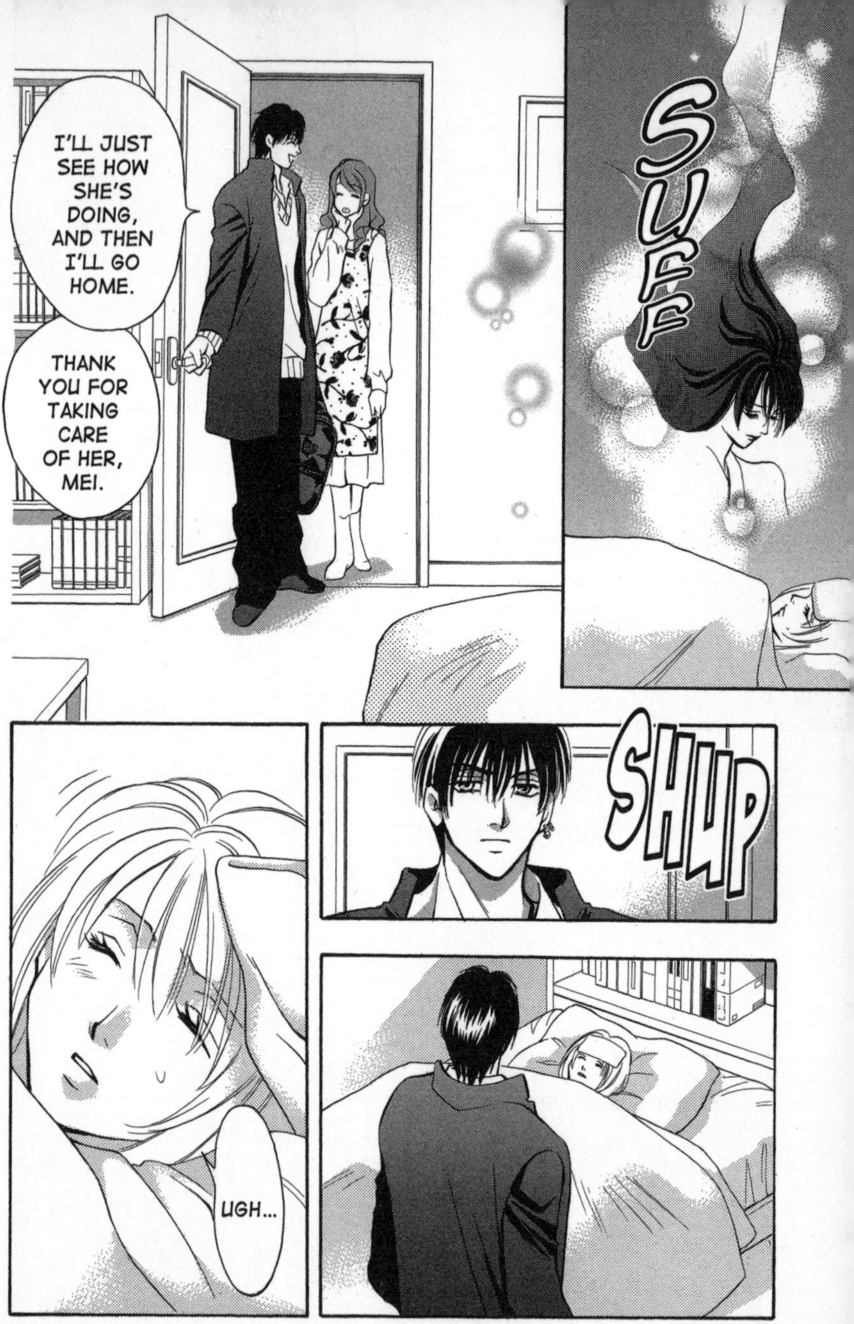
SUFF
I'LL JUST SEE HOW SHE'S DOING, AND THEN I'LL GO HOME.
THANK YOU FOR TAKING CARE OF HER, MEI.
SHUP
UGH...

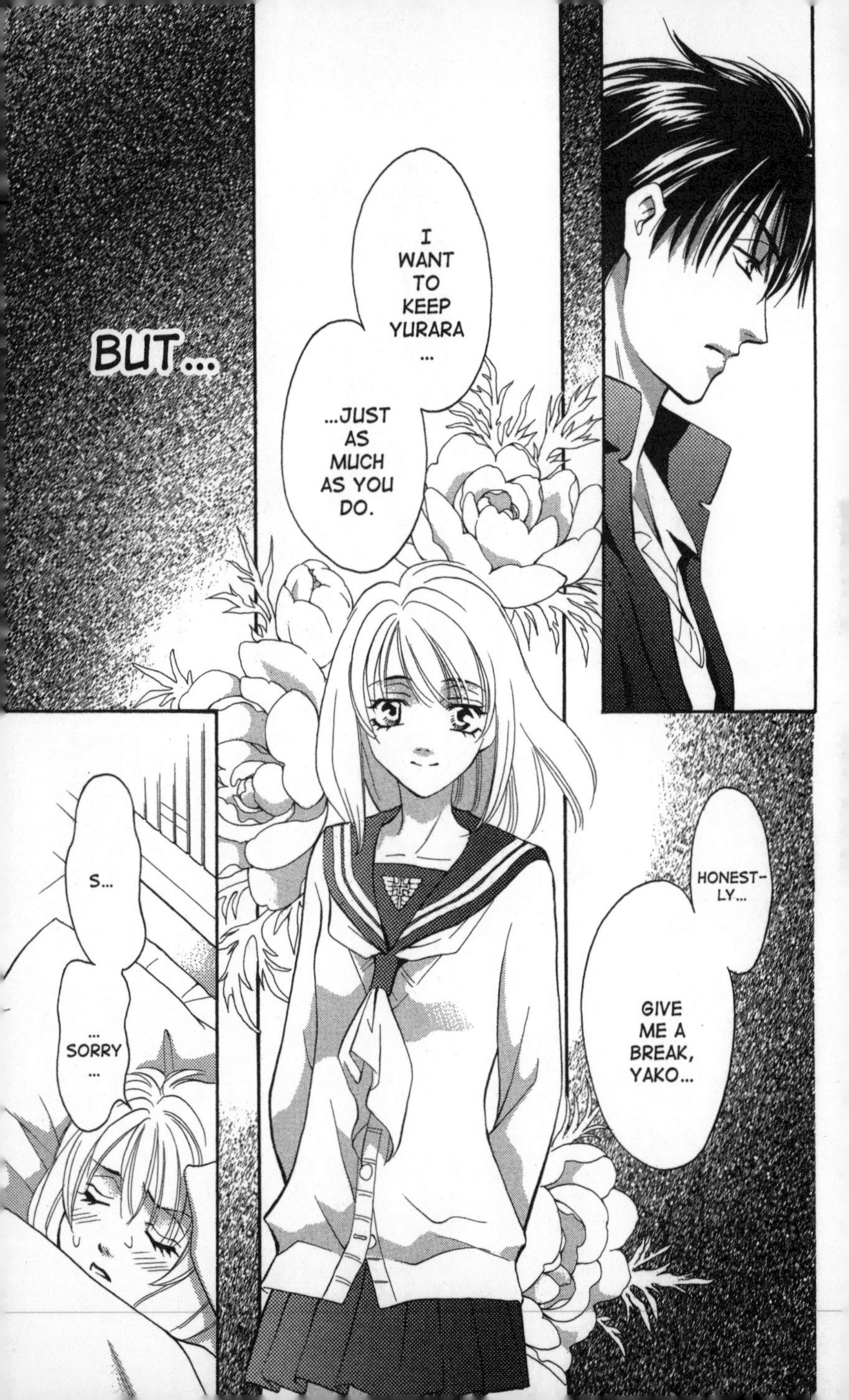
HONEST-LY...
GIVE ME A BREAK, YAKO...
I WANT TO KEEP YURARA ...
...JUST AS MUCH AS YOU DO.
BUT...
S...
... SORRY ...

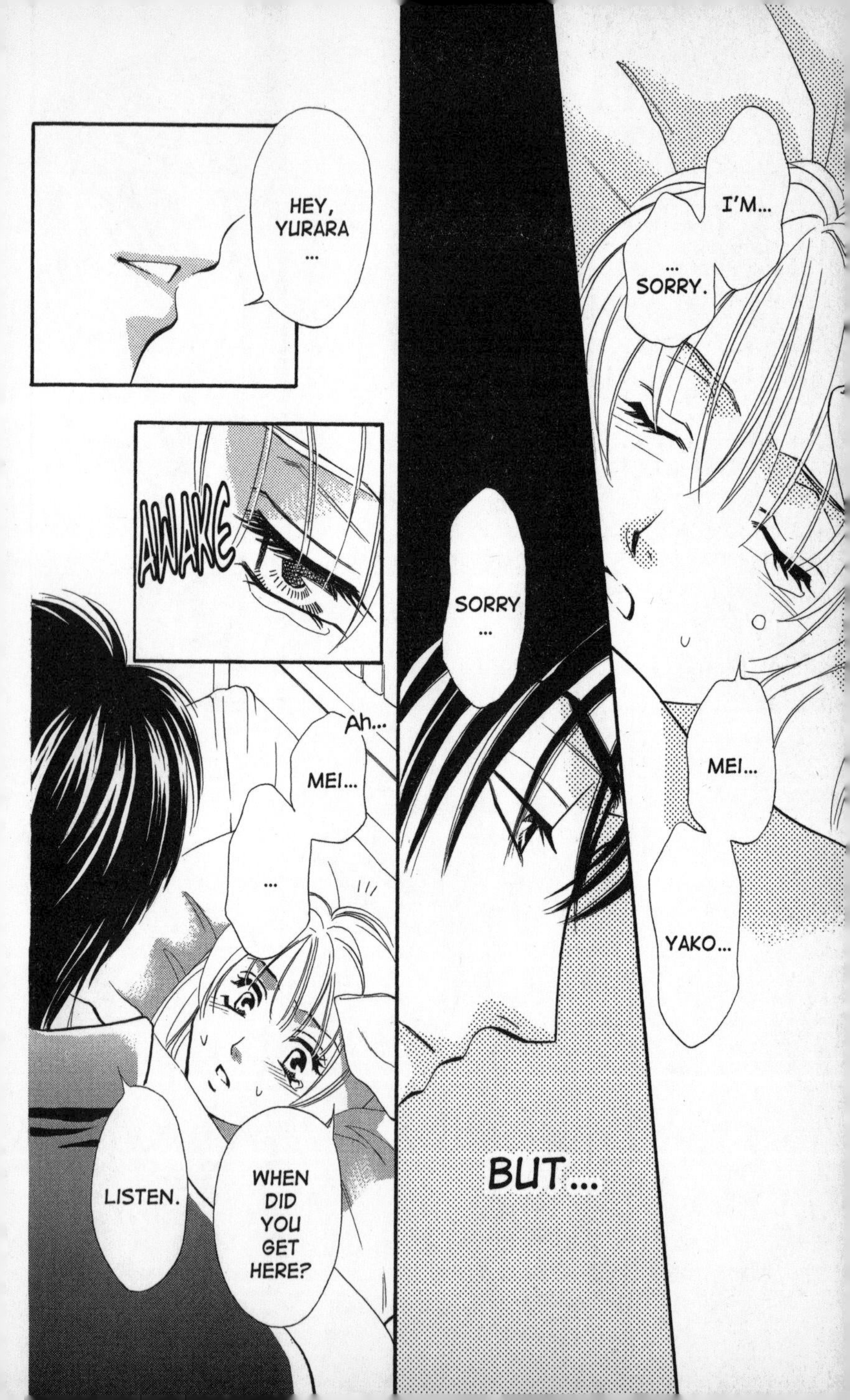
I'M...
...SORRY.
MEI...
YAKO...
SORRY...
BUT...
HEY, YURARA...
AWAKE
Ah...
MEI...
...
WHEN DID YOU GET HERE?
LISTEN.

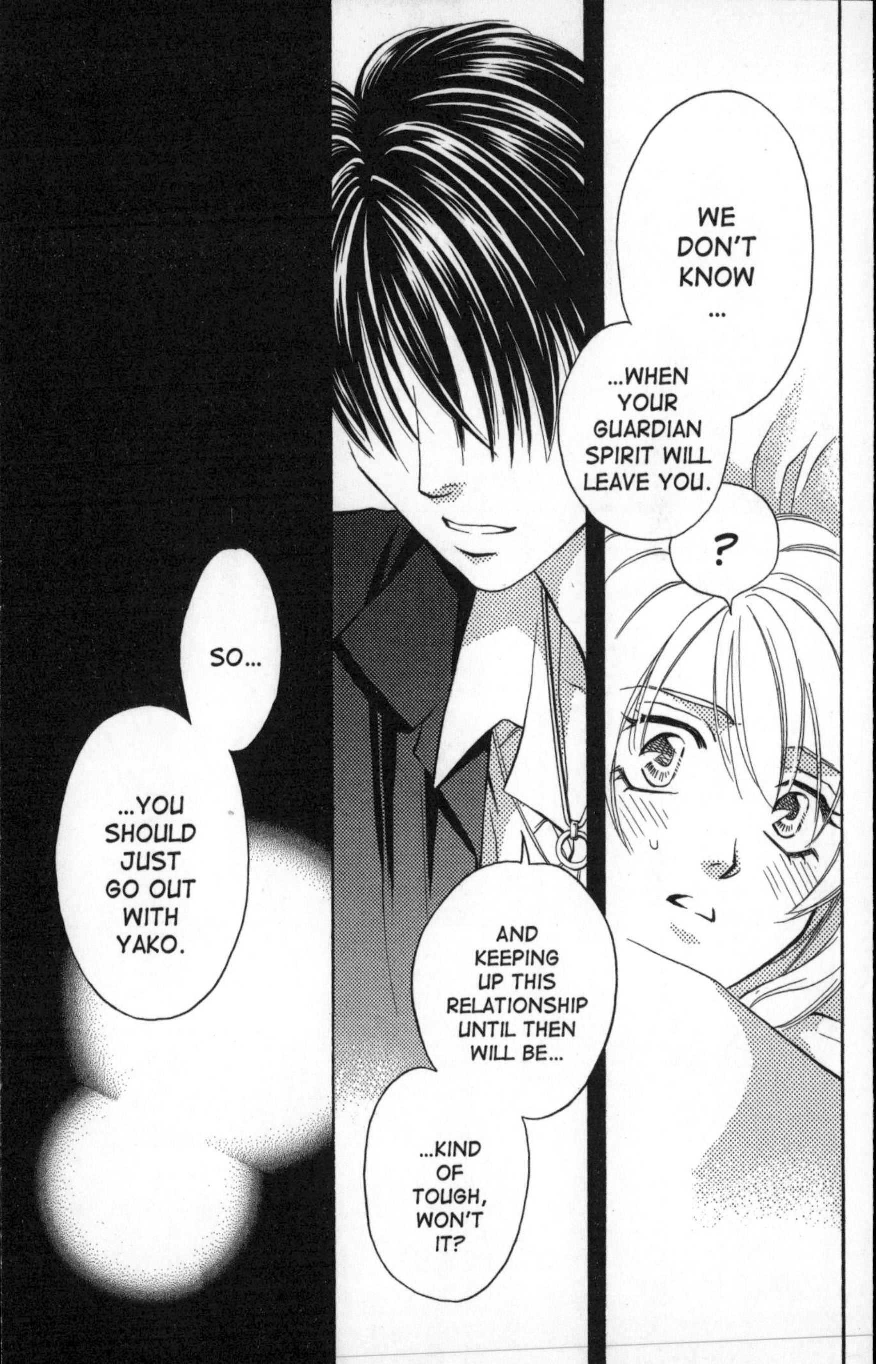
WE DON'T KNOW ...
...WHEN YOUR GUARDIAN SPIRIT WILL LEAVE YOU.
?
AND KEEPING UP THIS RELATIONSHIP UNTIL THEN WILL BE...
...KIND OF TOUGH, WON'T IT?
SO...
...YOU SHOULD JUST GO OUT WITH YAKO.

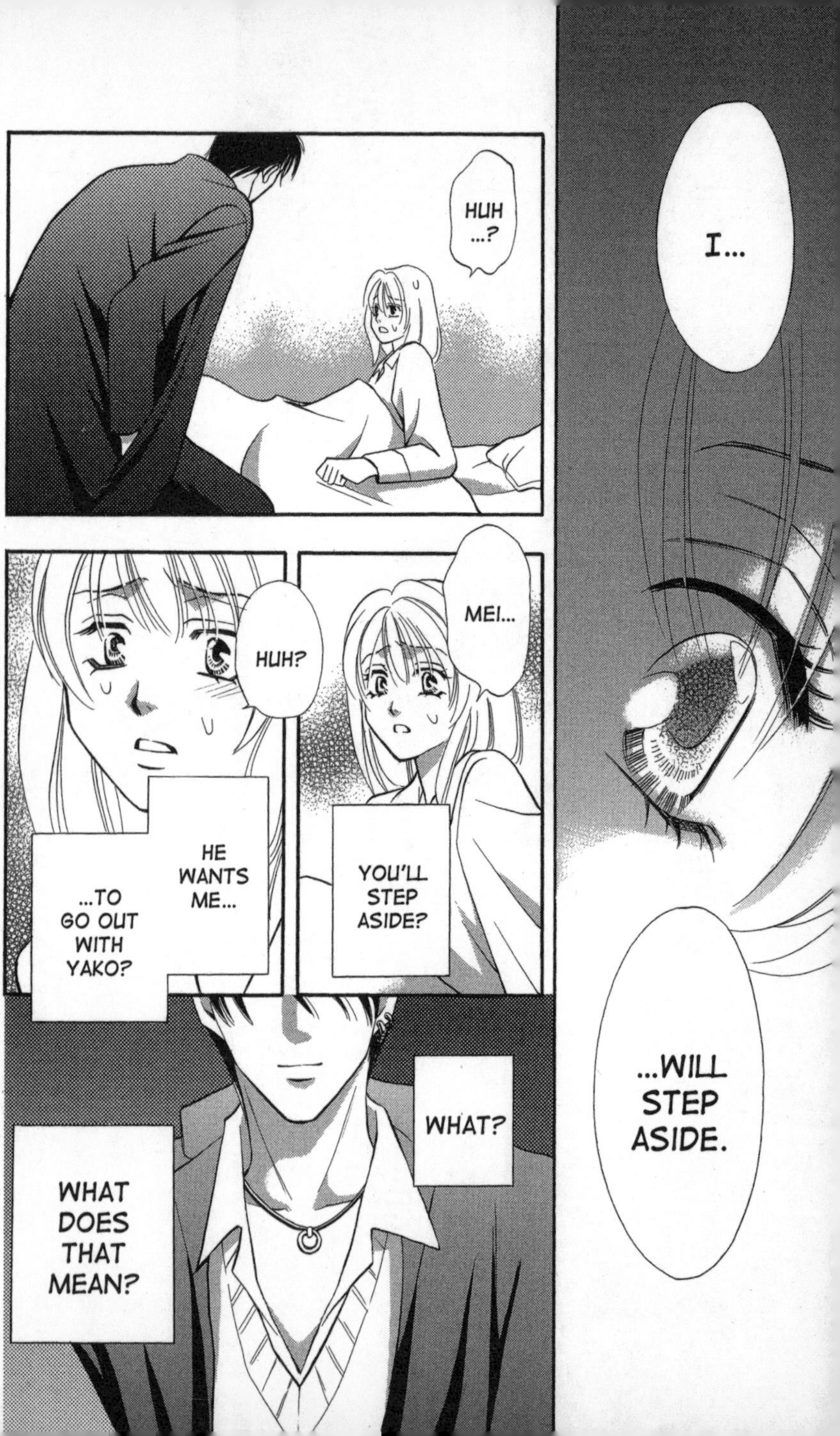
I...
...WILL STEP ASIDE.
HUH ...?
MEI...
YOU'LL STEP ASIDE?
HUH?
HE WANTS ME...
...TO GO OUT WITH YAKO?
WHAT?
WHAT DOES THAT MEAN?

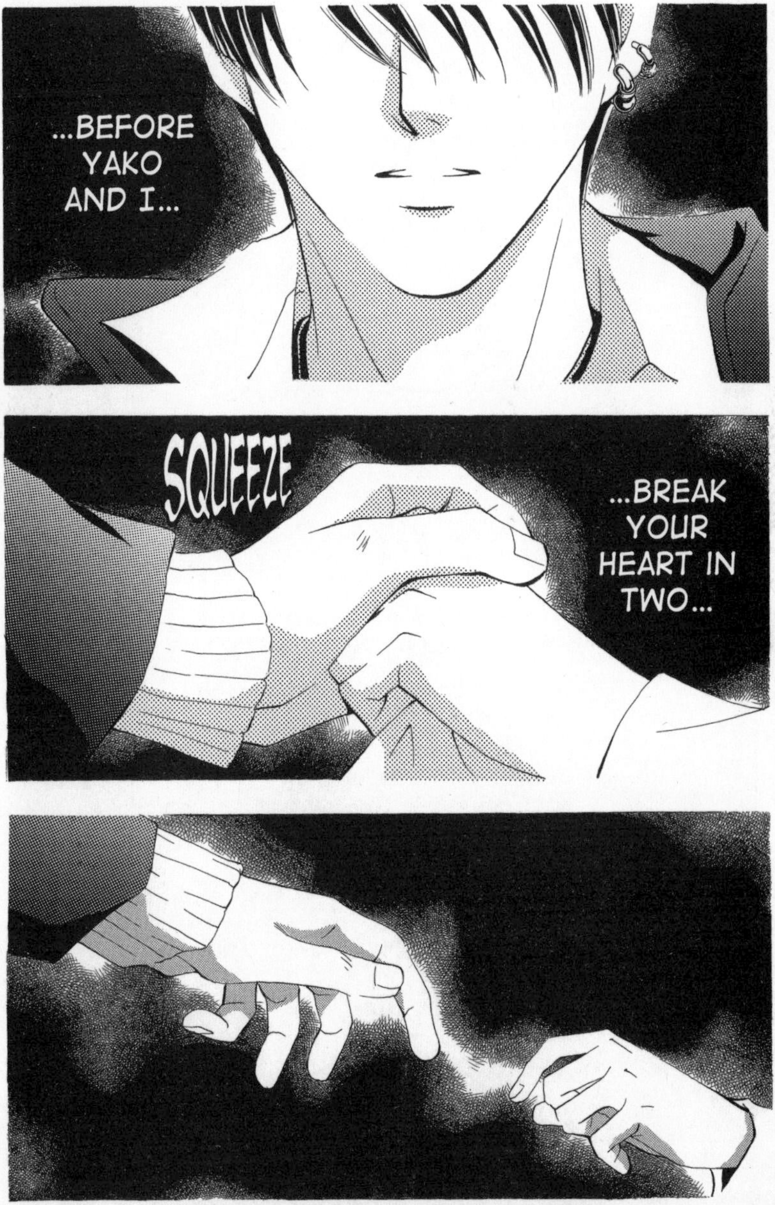
...BEFORE YAKO AND I...
...BREAK YOUR HEART IN TWO...
SQUEEZE

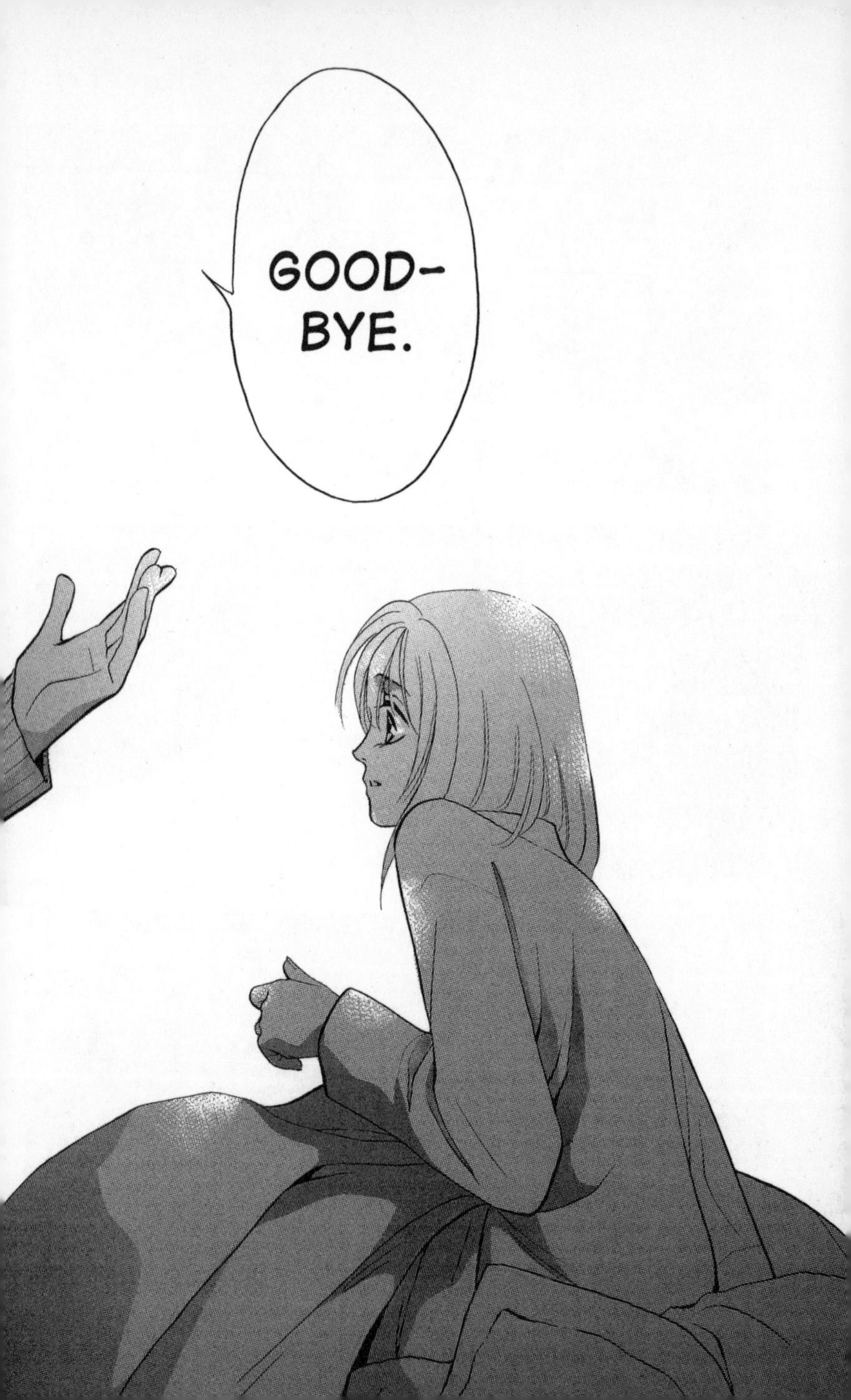
GOOD-BYE.

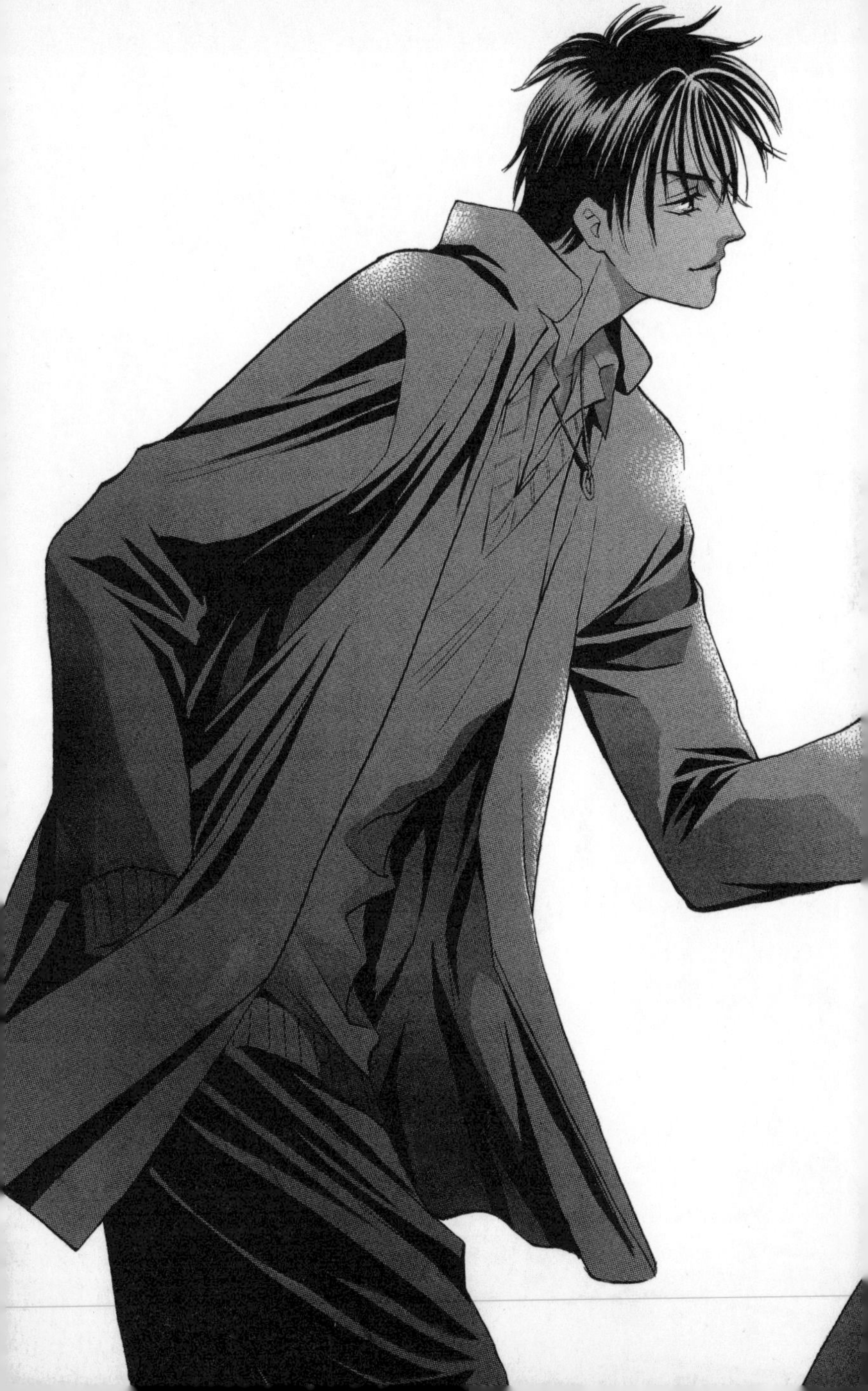

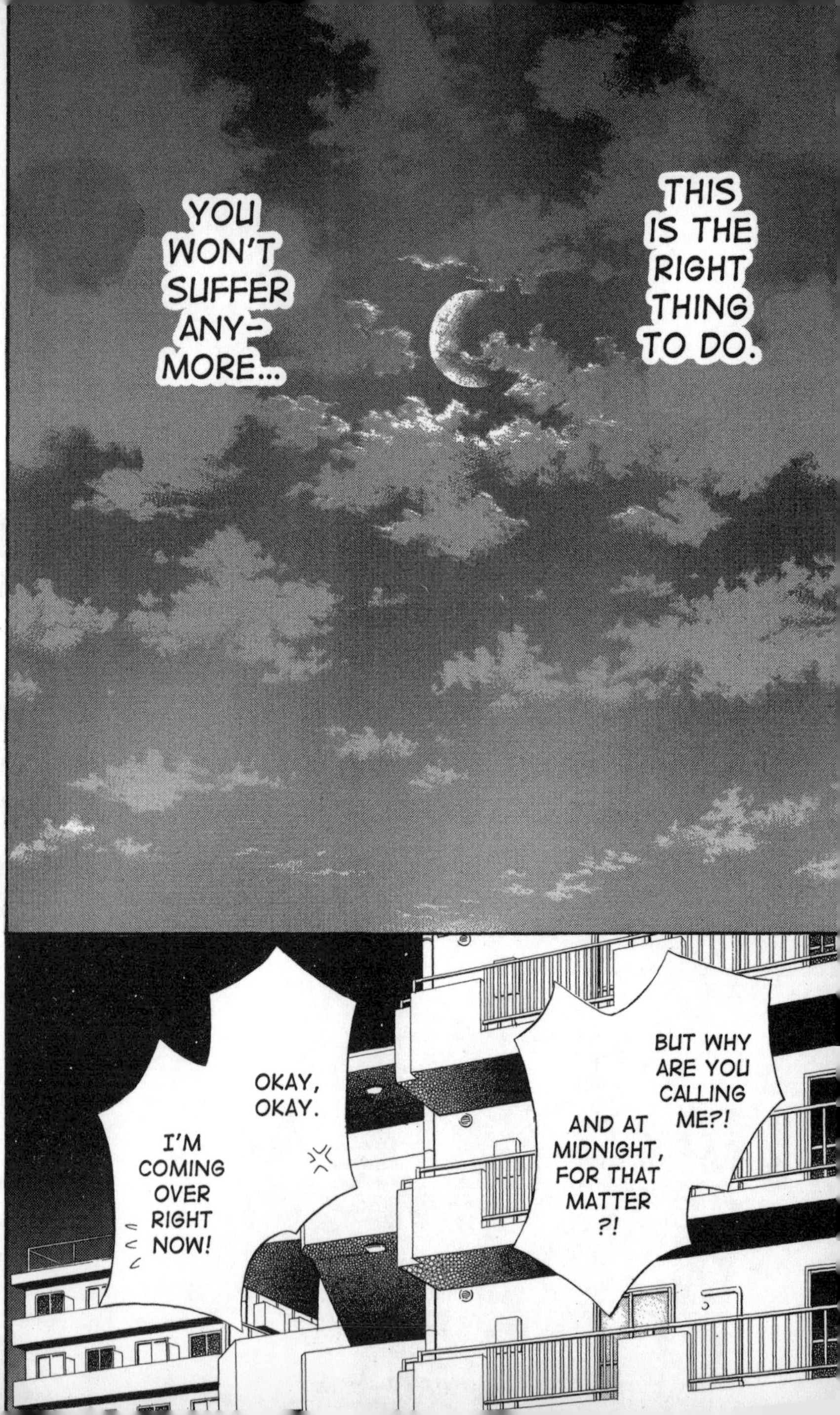
THIS IS THE RIGHT THING TO DO.
YOU WON'T SUFFER ANY-MORE...
BUT WHY ARE YOU CALLING ME?!
AND AT MIDNIGHT, FOR THAT MATTER?!
OKAY, OKAY.
I'M COMING OVER RIGHT NOW!

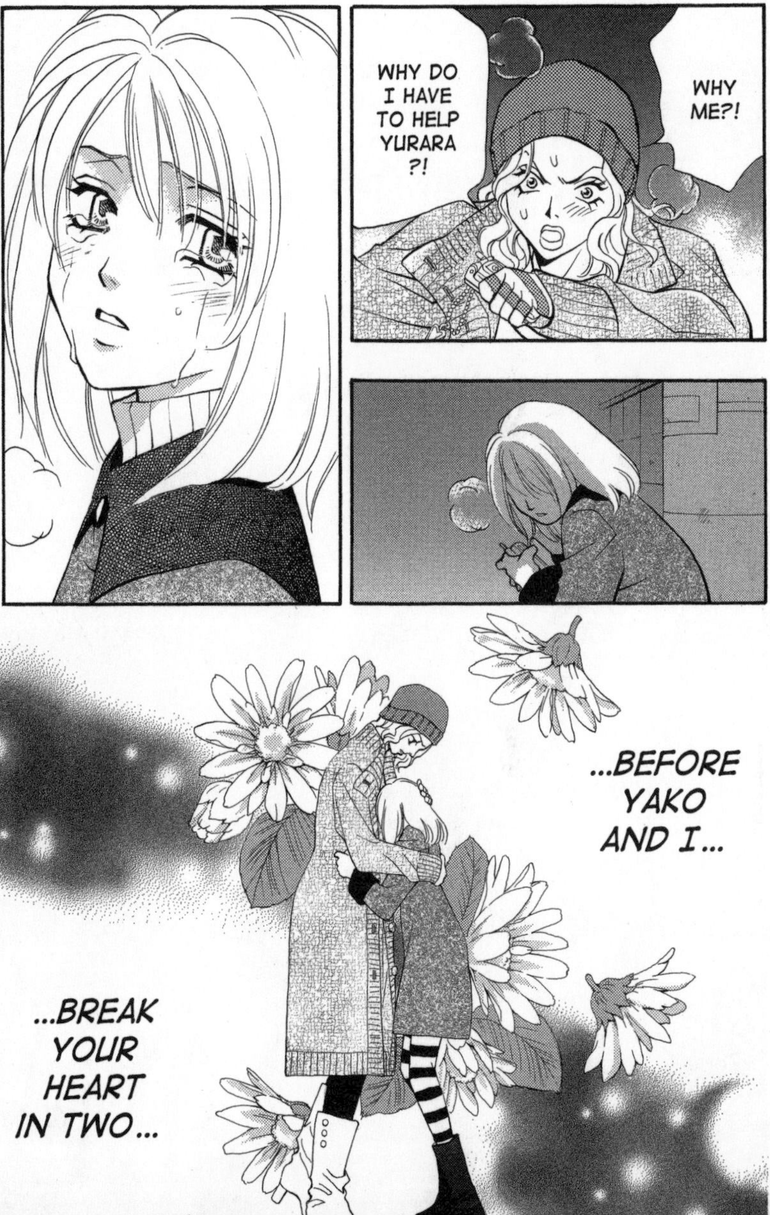
WHY ME?!
WHY DO I HAVE TO HELP YURARA ?!
...BEFORE YAKO AND I...
...BREAK YOUR HEART IN TWO...

Chapter 17 / End

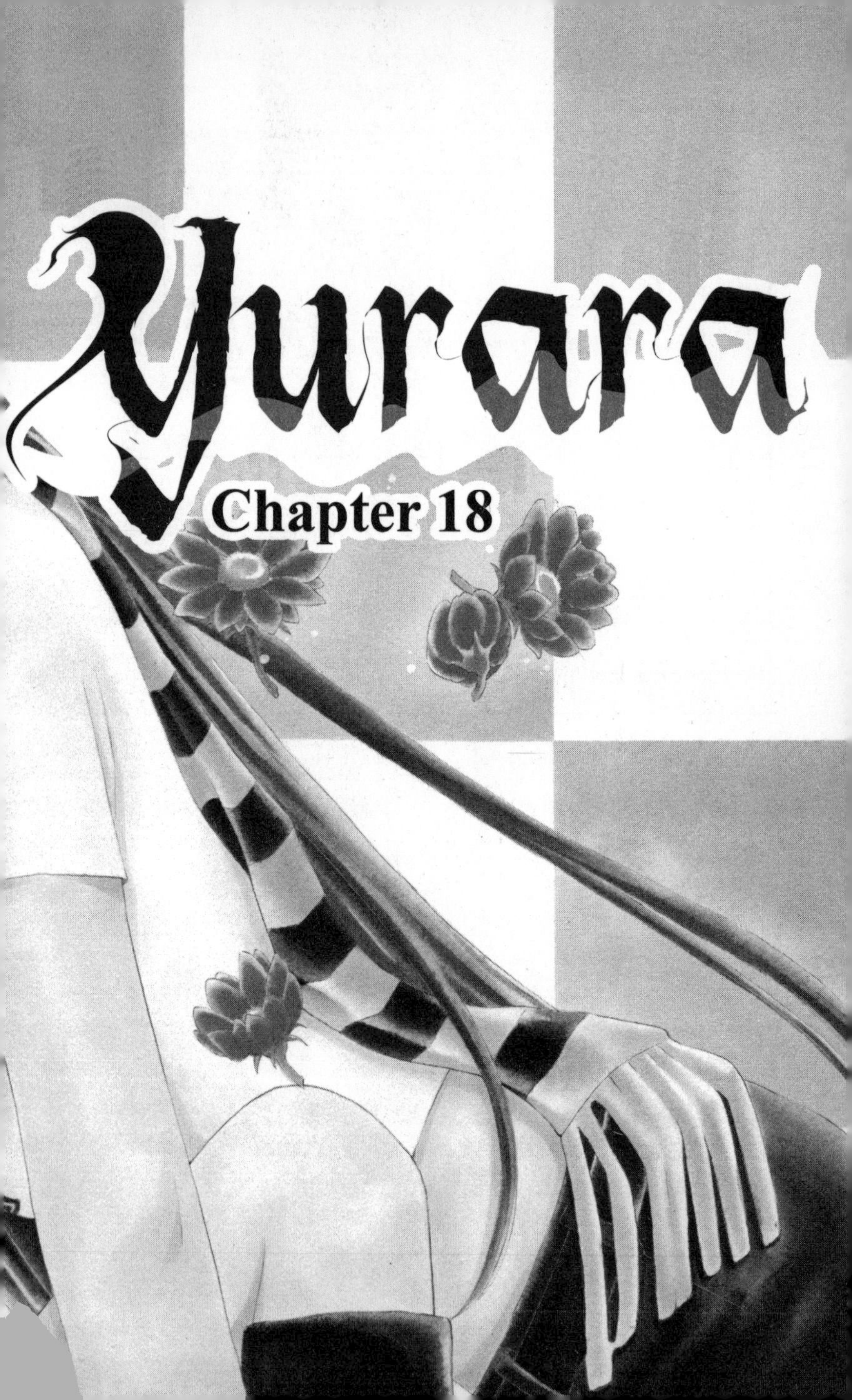
Yurara
Chapter 18

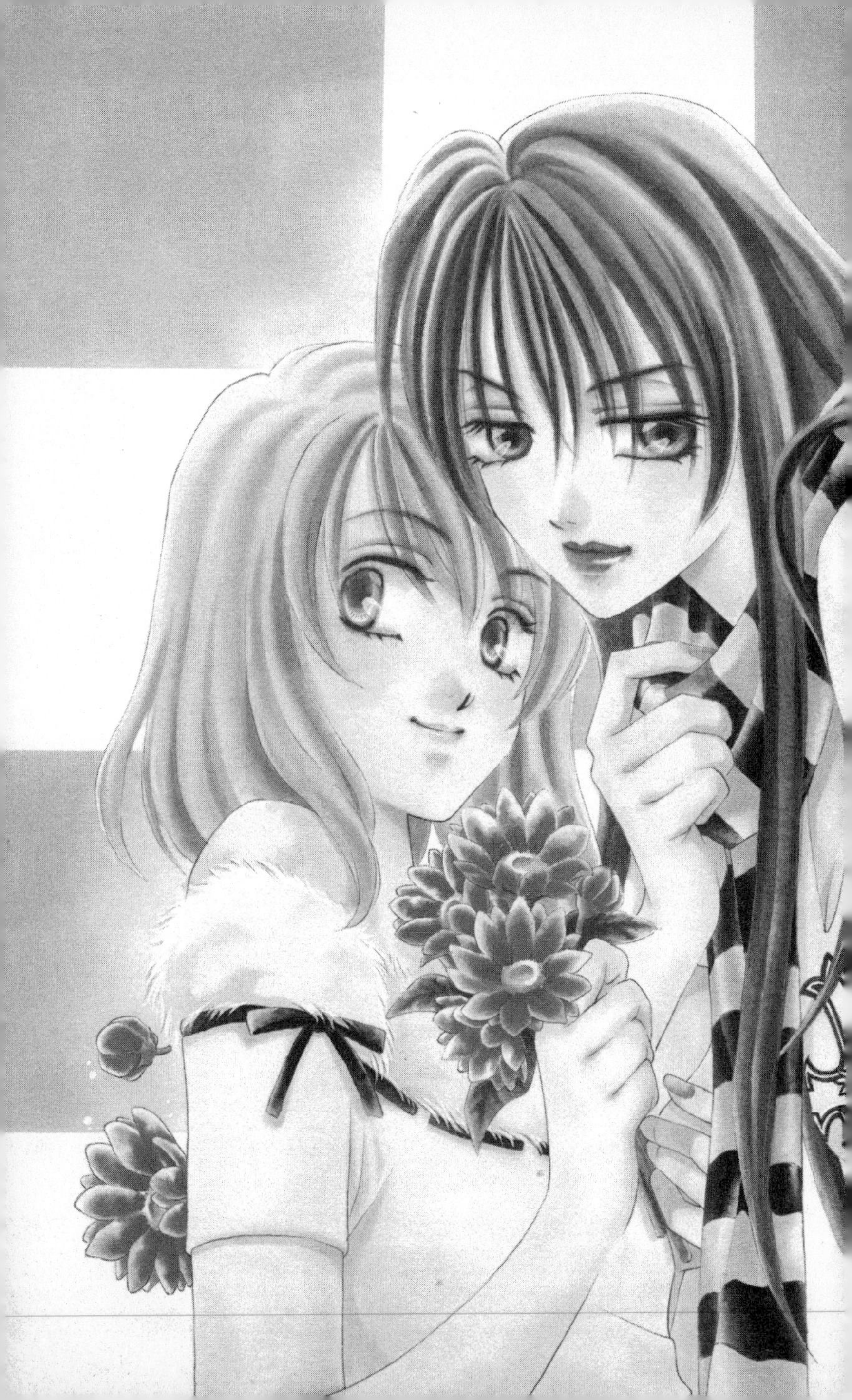

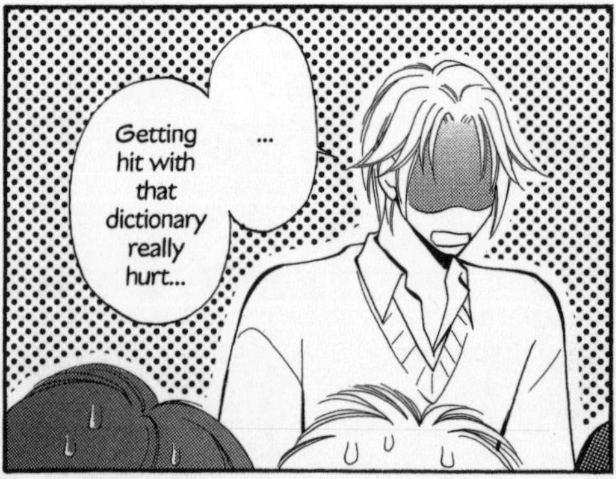
...
Getting hit with that dictionary really hurt...

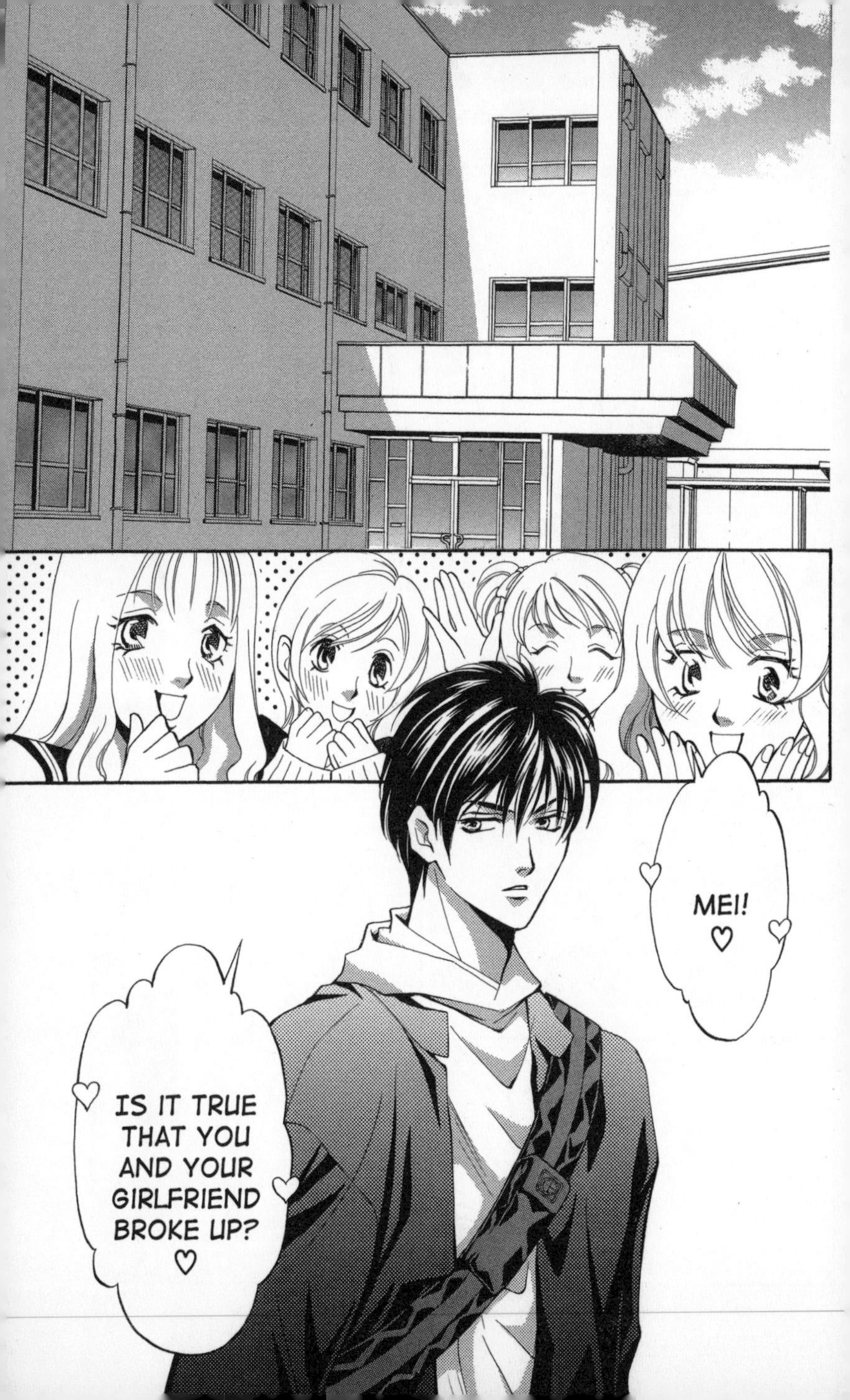
MEI! ♡
IS IT TRUE THAT YOU AND YOUR GIRLFRIEND BROKE UP? ♡

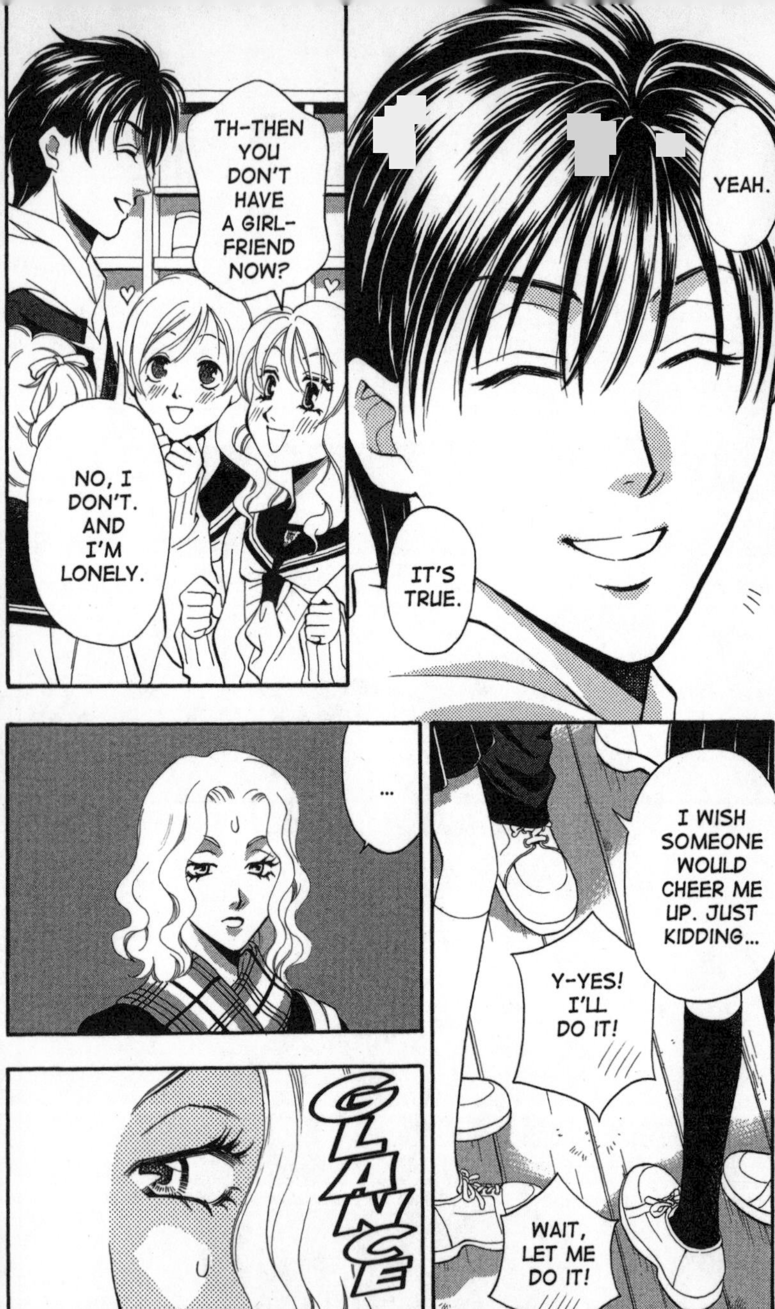
YEAH.
IT'S TRUE.
TH-THEN YOU DON'T HAVE A GIRL-FRIEND NOW?
NO, I DON'T. AND I'M LONELY.
I WISH SOMEONE WOULD CHEER ME UP. JUST KIDDING...
Y-YES! I'LL DO IT!
WAIT, LET ME DO IT!
...
GLANCE

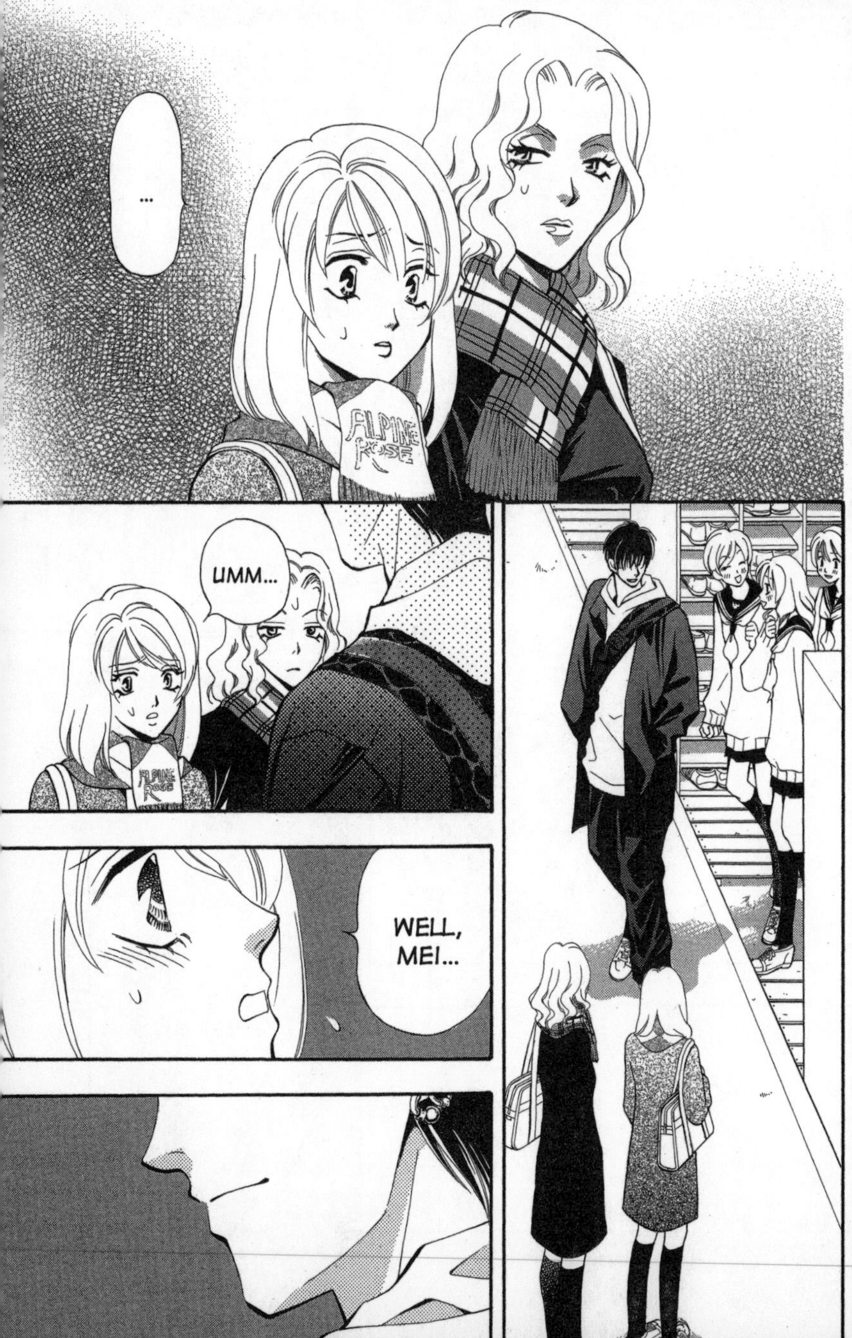
...
UMM...
WELL, MEI...

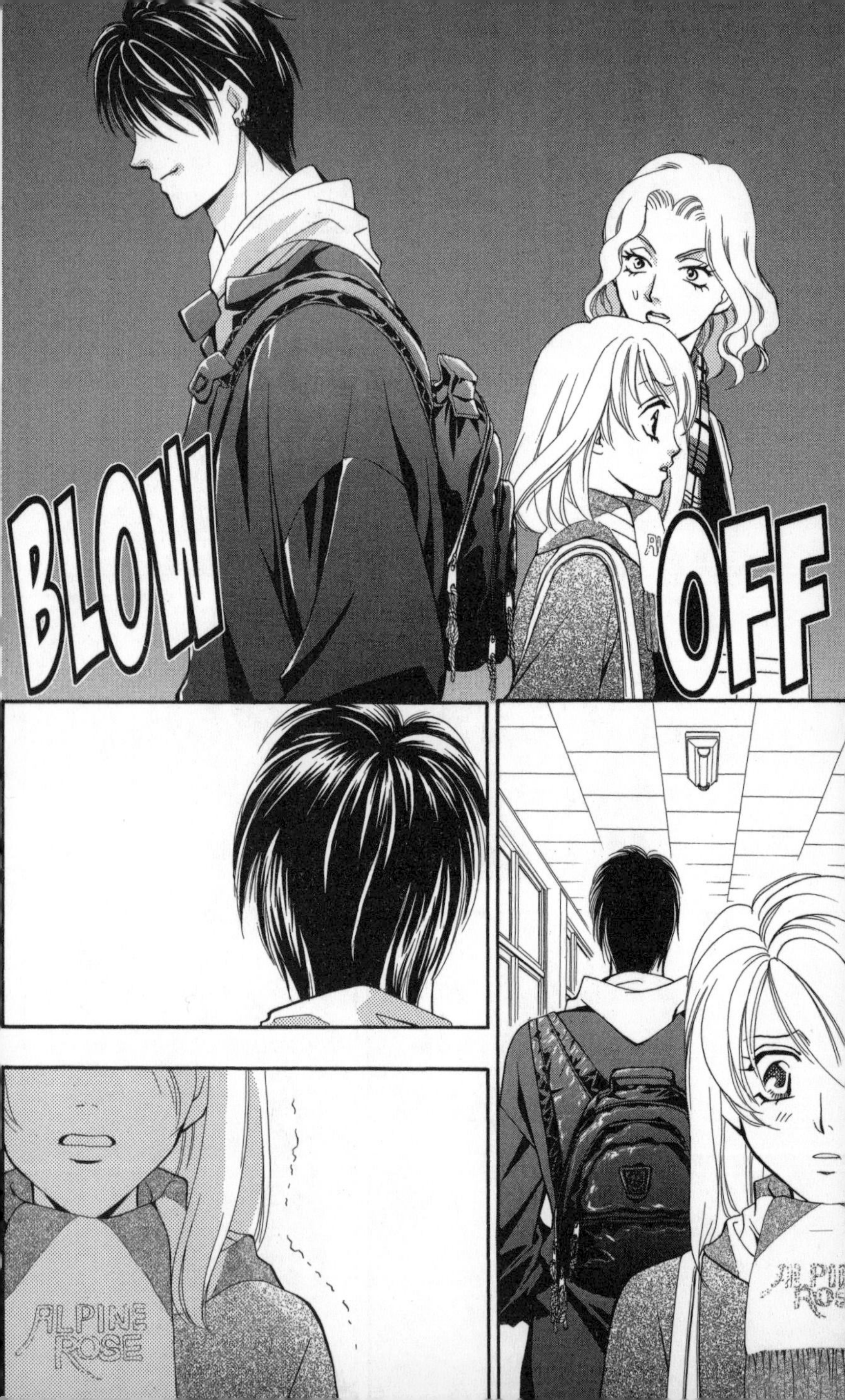
BLOW
OFF
ALPINE ROSE

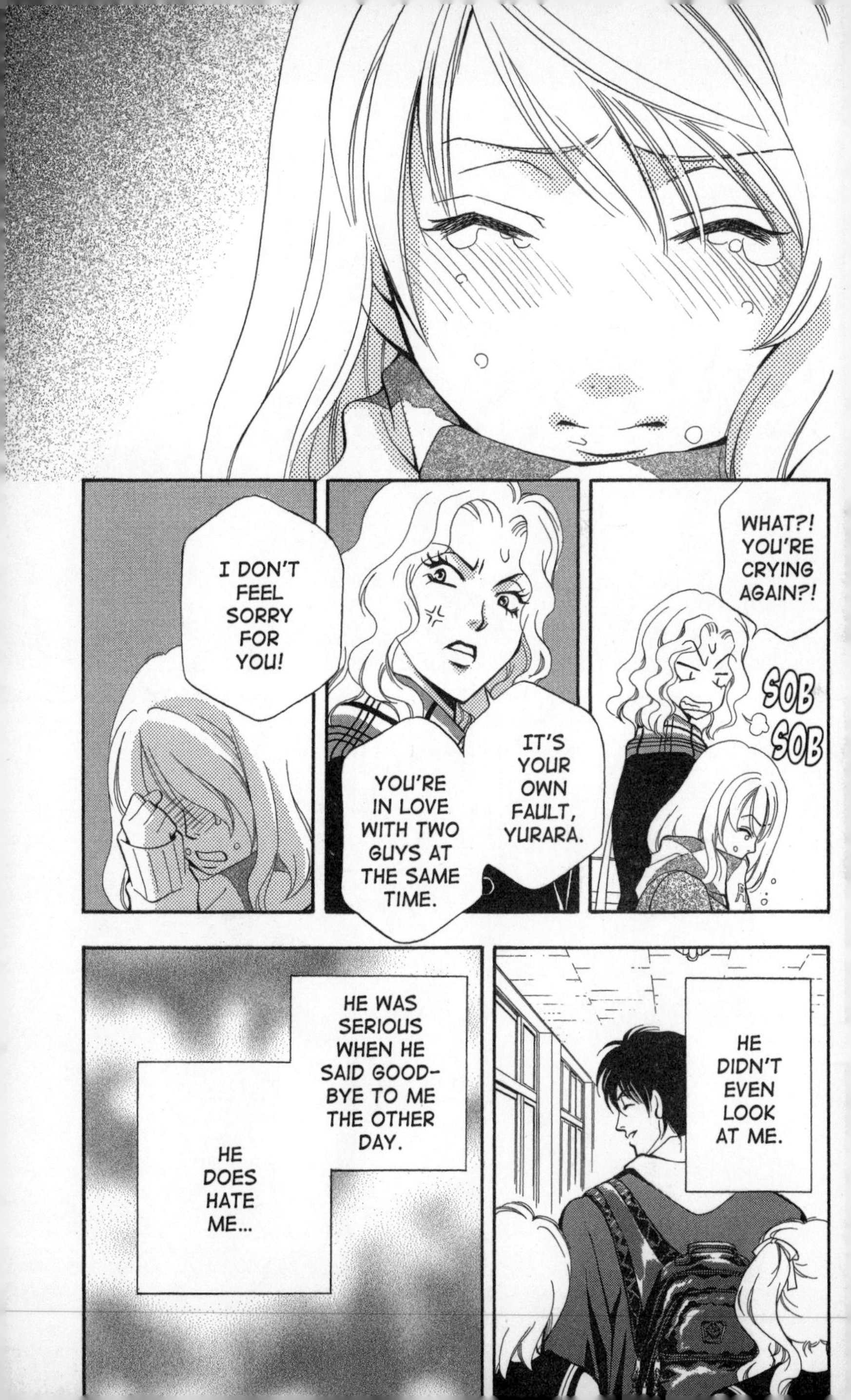
WHAT?! YOU'RE CRYING AGAIN?!
SOB SOB
IT'S YOUR OWN FAULT, YURARA.
YOU'RE IN LOVE WITH TWO GUYS AT THE SAME TIME.
I DON'T FEEL SORRY FOR YOU!
HE DIDN'T EVEN LOOK AT ME.
HE WAS SERIOUS WHEN HE SAID GOOD-BYE TO ME THE OTHER DAY.
HE DOES HATE ME...

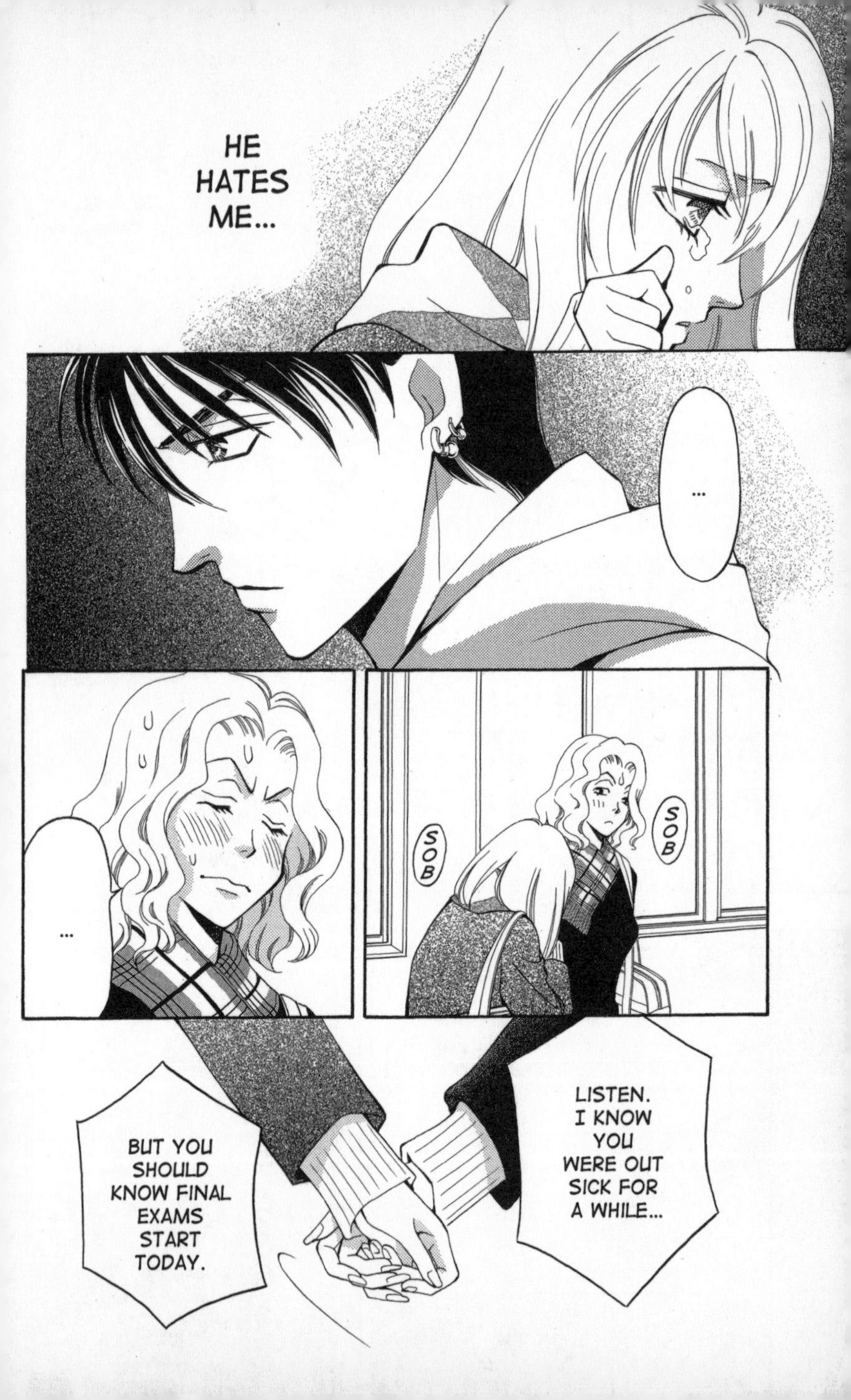
HE HATES ME...
...
SOB
SOB
...
LISTEN. I KNOW YOU WERE OUT SICK FOR A WHILE...
BUT YOU SHOULD KNOW FINAL EXAMS START TODAY.

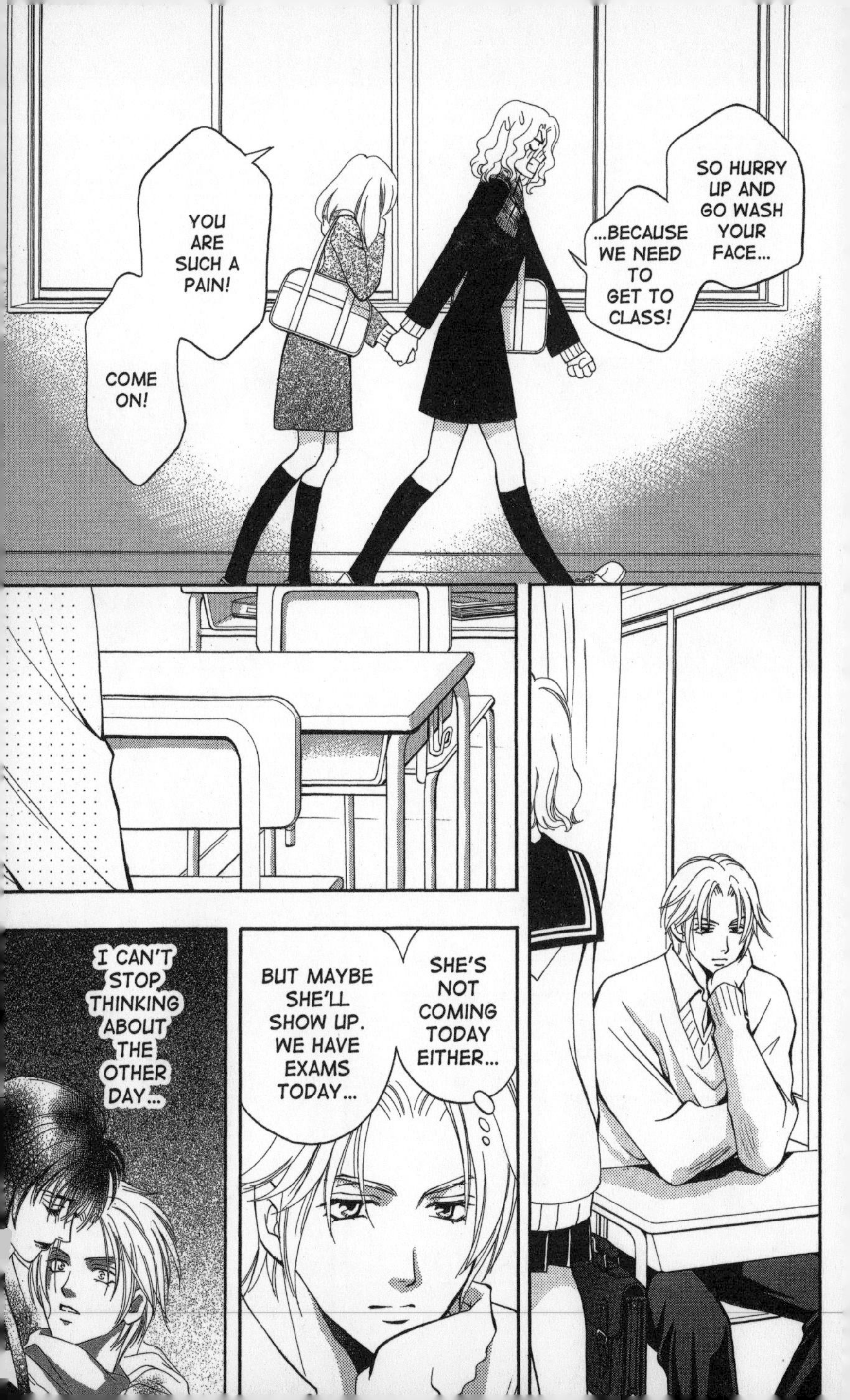
SO HURRY UP AND GO WASH YOUR FACE...
...BECAUSE WE NEED TO GET TO CLASS!
YOU ARE SUCH A PAIN!
COME ON!
SHE'S NOT COMING TODAY EITHER...
BUT MAYBE SHE'LL SHOW UP. WE HAVE EXAMS TODAY...
I CAN'T STOP THINKING ABOUT THE OTHER DAY...

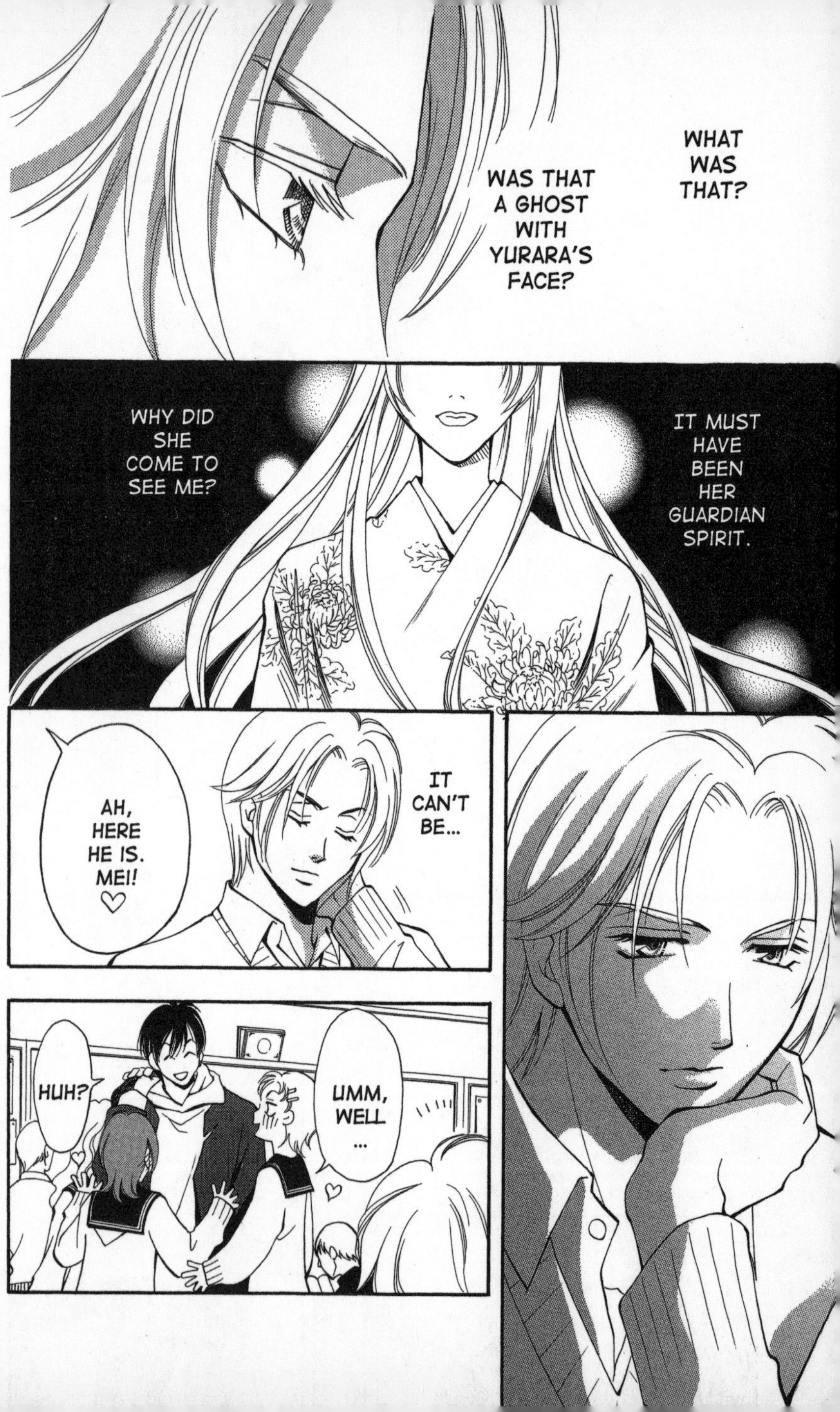
WHAT WAS THAT?
WAS THAT A GHOST WITH YURARA'S FACE?
IT MUST HAVE BEEN HER GUARDIAN SPIRIT.
WHY DID SHE COME TO SEE ME?
IT CAN'T BE...
AH, HERE HE IS. MEI! ♡
UMM, WELL ...
HUH?

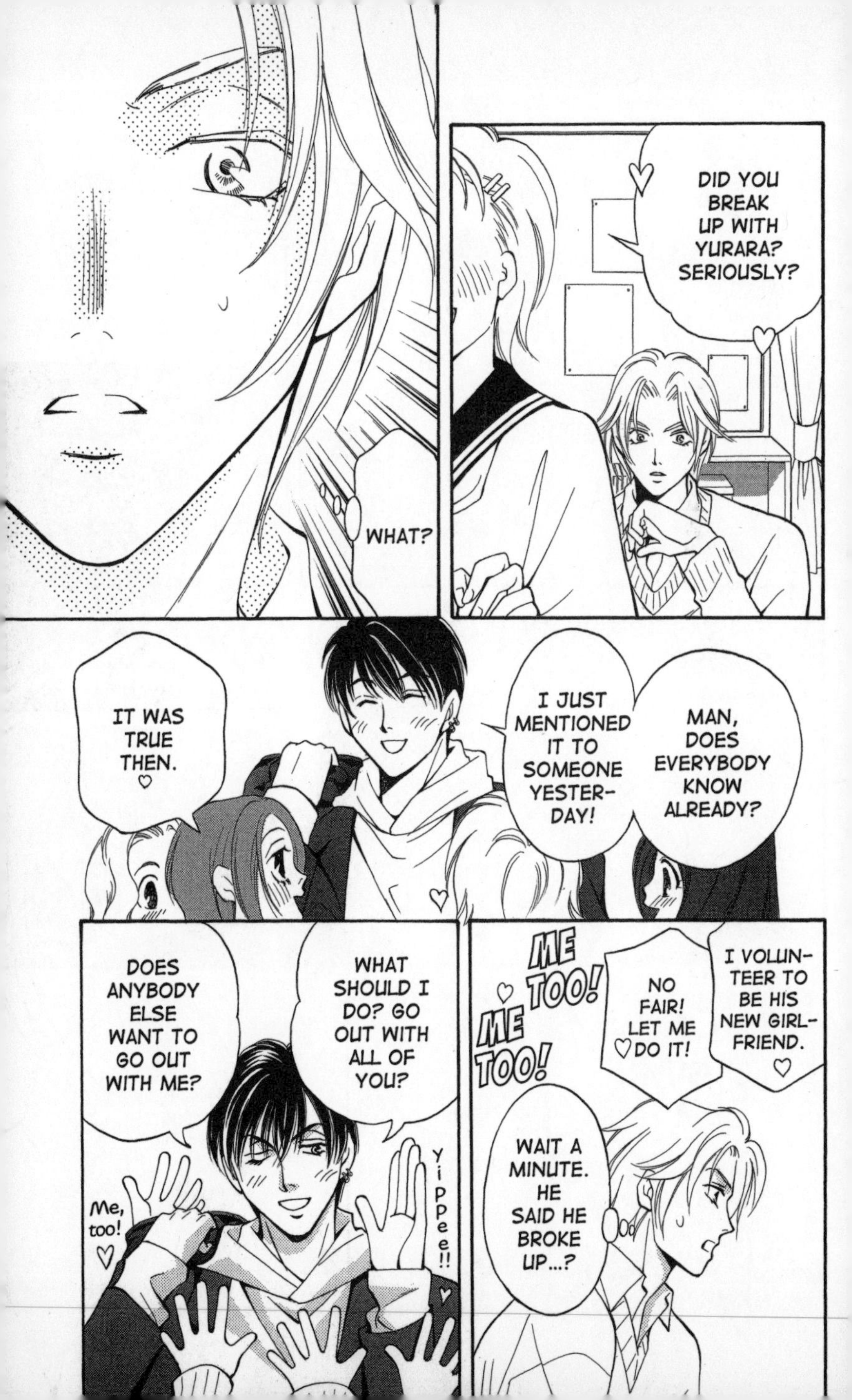
DID YOU BREAK UP WITH YURARA? SERIOUSLY?
WHAT?
MAN, DOES EVERYBODY KNOW ALREADY?
I JUST MENTIONED IT TO SOMEONE YESTERDAY!
IT WAS TRUE THEN. ♡
I VOLUNTEER TO BE HIS NEW GIRLFRIEND. ♡
NO FAIR! LET ME DO IT! ♡
ME TOO!
ME TOO!
WAIT A MINUTE. HE SAID HE BROKE UP...?
WHAT SHOULD I DO? GO OUT WITH ALL OF YOU?
Yippee!!
DOES ANYBODY ELSE WANT TO GO OUT WITH ME?
Me, too! ♡

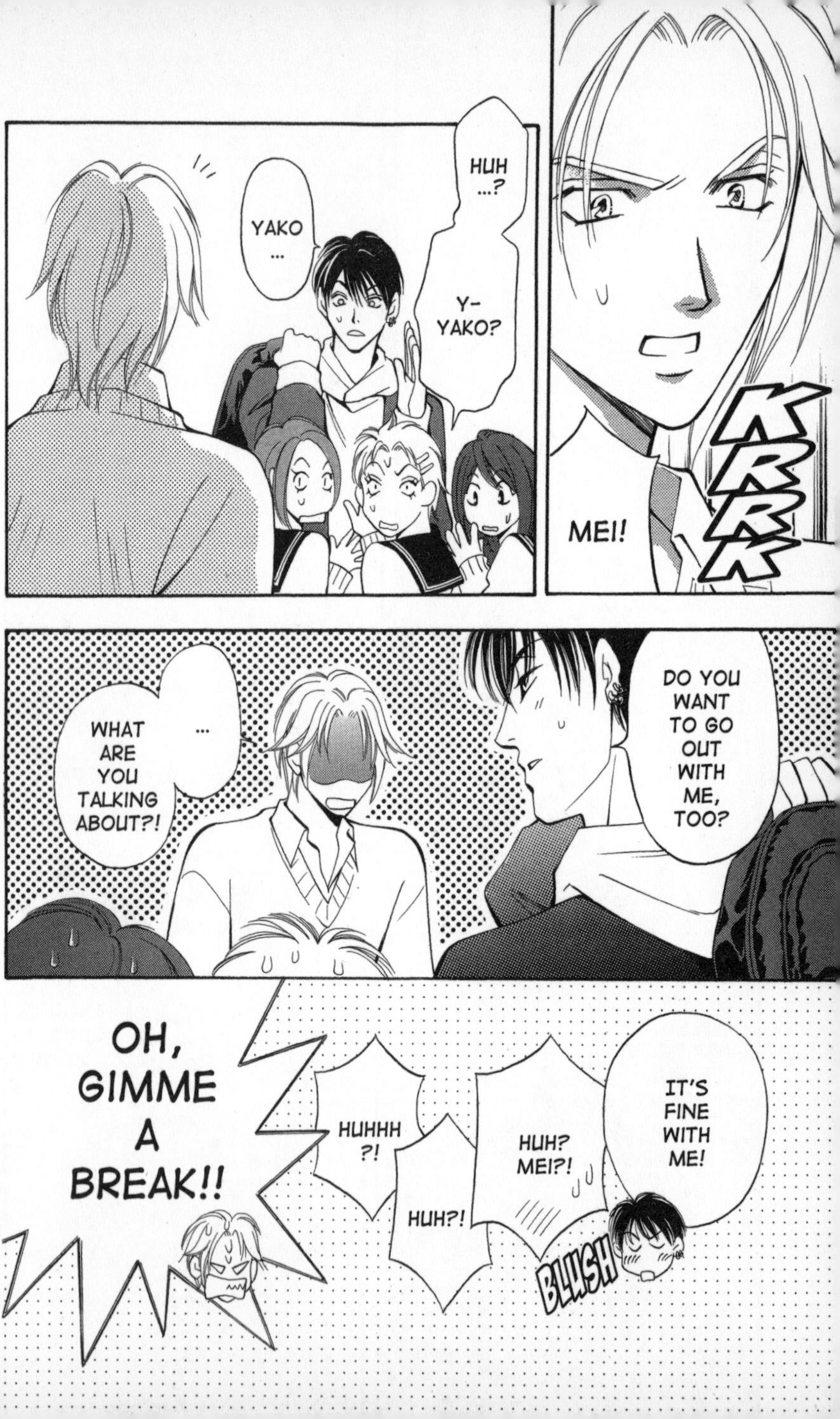
MEI!
KRRK
HUH ...?
Y-YAKO?
YAKO ...
DO YOU WANT TO GO OUT WITH ME, TOO?
...
WHAT ARE YOU TALKING ABOUT?!
IT'S FINE WITH ME!
BLUSH
HUH? MEI?!
HUH?!
HUHHH ?!
OH, GIMME A BREAK!!

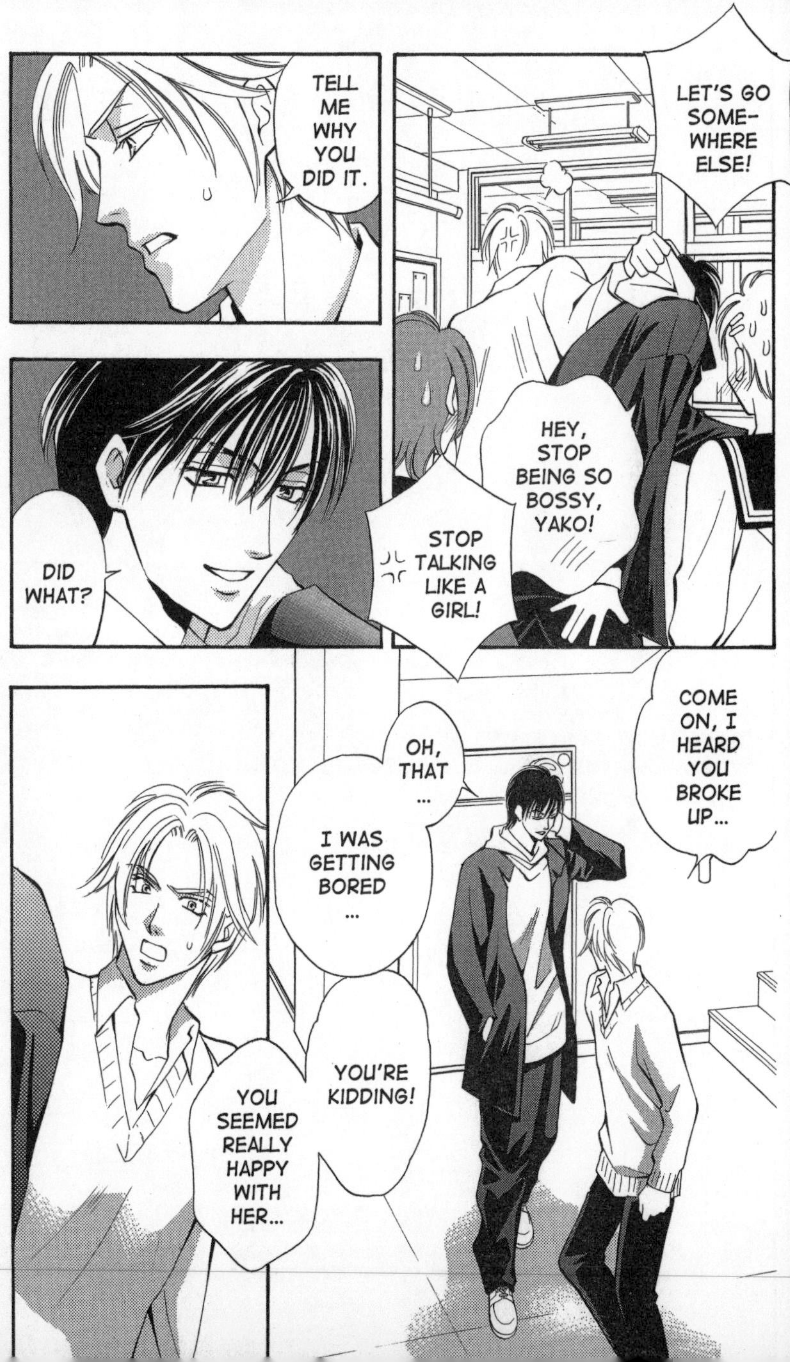
LET'S GO SOME-WHERE ELSE!
HEY, STOP BEING SO BOSSY, YAKO!
STOP TALKING LIKE A GIRL!
TELL ME WHY YOU DID IT.
DID WHAT?
COME ON, I HEARD YOU BROKE UP...
OH, THAT ...
I WAS GETTING BORED ...
YOU'RE KIDDING!
YOU SEEMED REALLY HAPPY WITH HER...

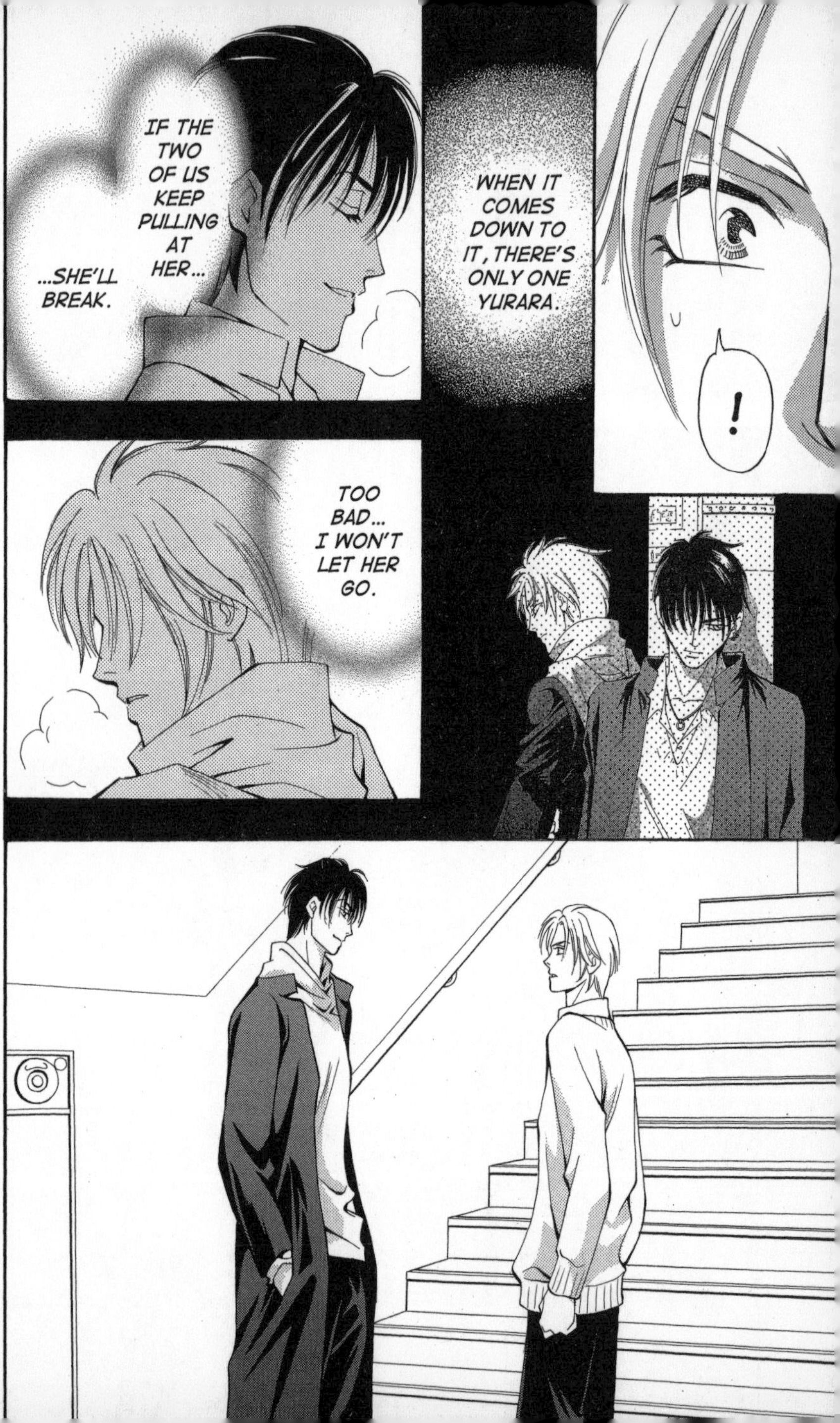
!
WHEN IT COMES DOWN TO IT, THERE'S ONLY ONE YURARA.
IF THE TWO OF US KEEP PULLING AT HER...
...SHE'LL BREAK.
TOO BAD... I WON'T LET HER GO.

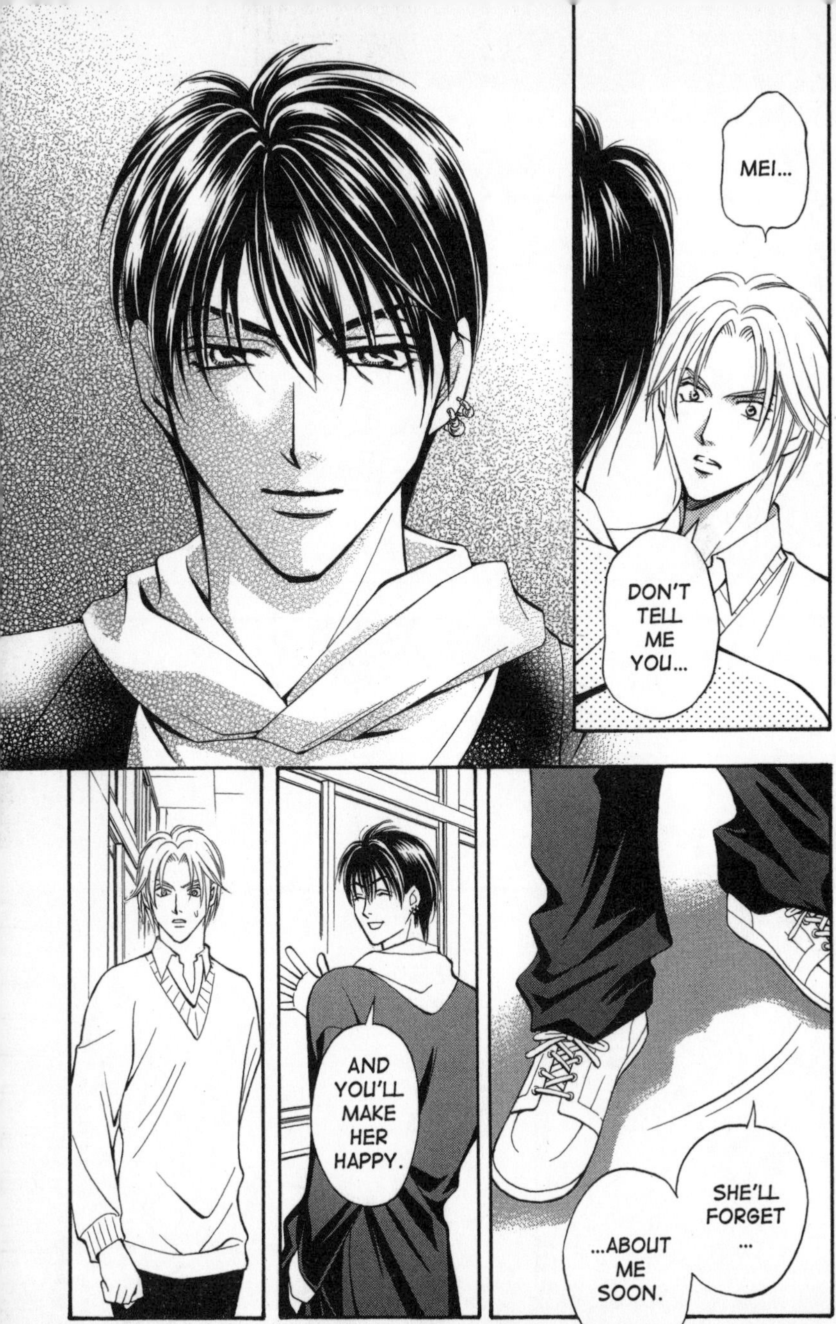
MEI...
DON'T TELL ME YOU...
SHE'LL FORGET ...
...ABOUT ME SOON.
AND YOU'LL MAKE HER HAPPY.

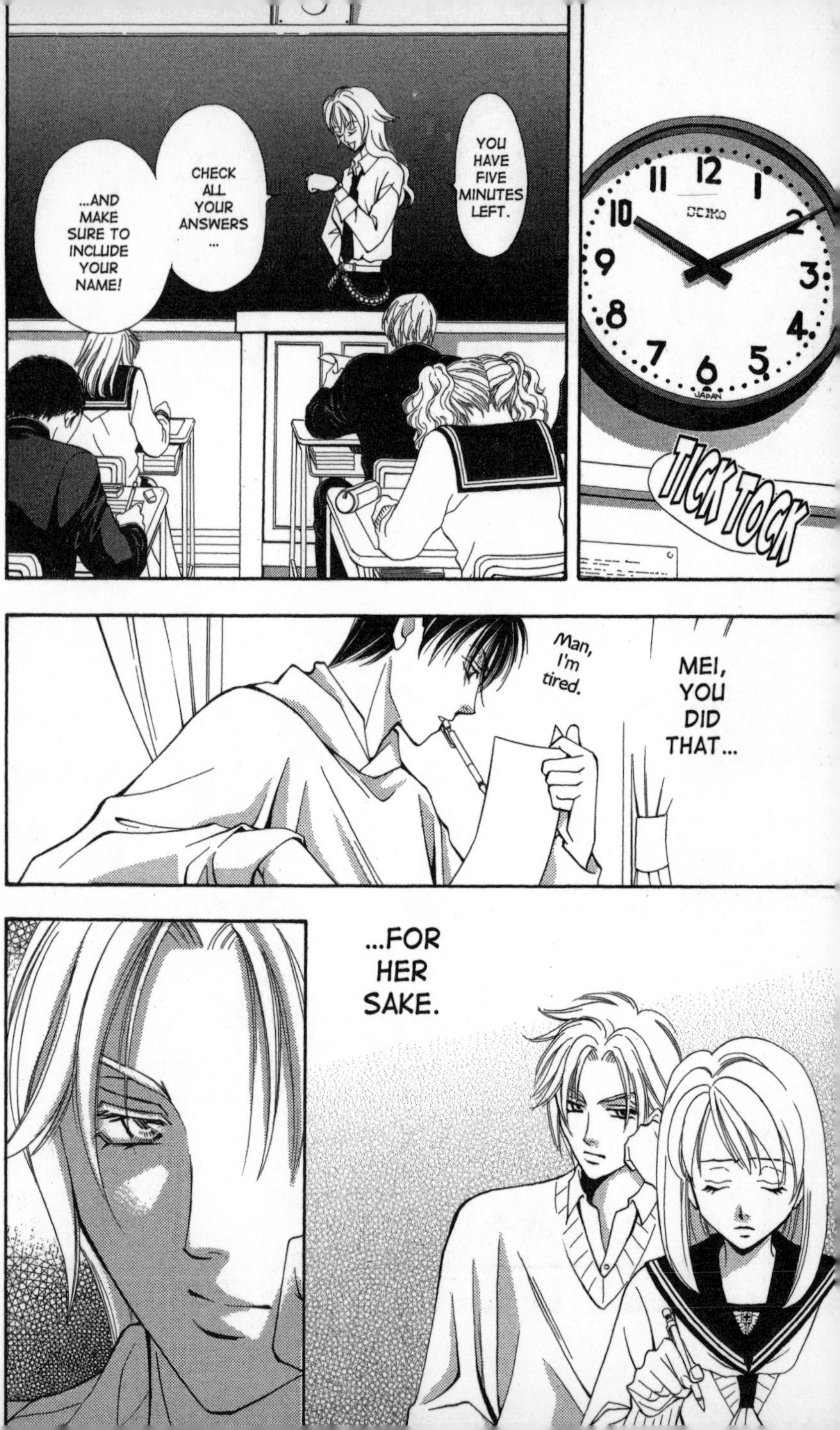
SEIKO
JAPAN
TICK TOCK
YOU HAVE FIVE MINUTES LEFT.
CHECK ALL YOUR ANSWERS ...
...AND MAKE SURE TO INCLUDE YOUR NAME!
MEI, YOU DID THAT...
Man, I'm tired.
...FOR HER SAKE.

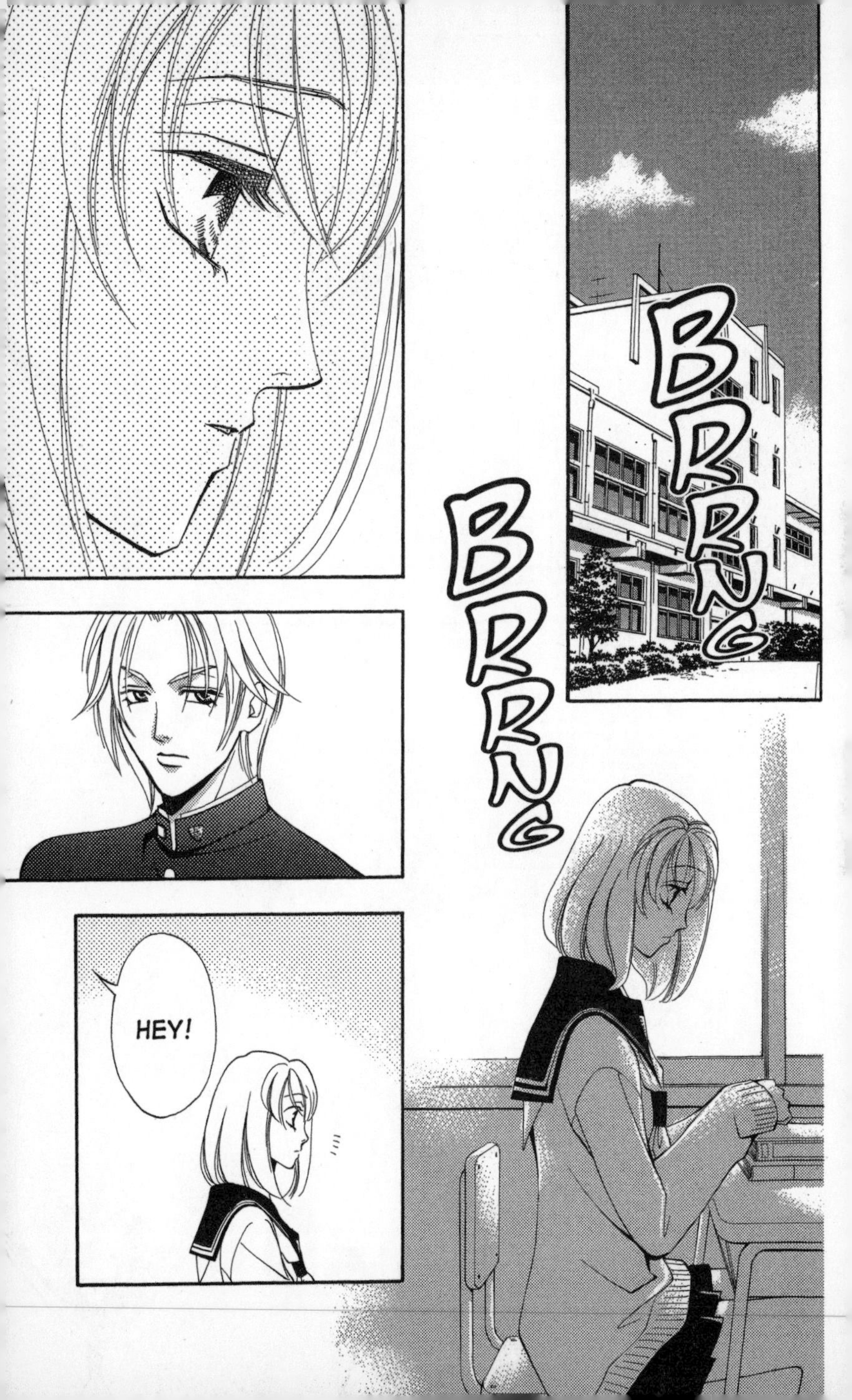
BRRRNG
BRRRNG
HEY!

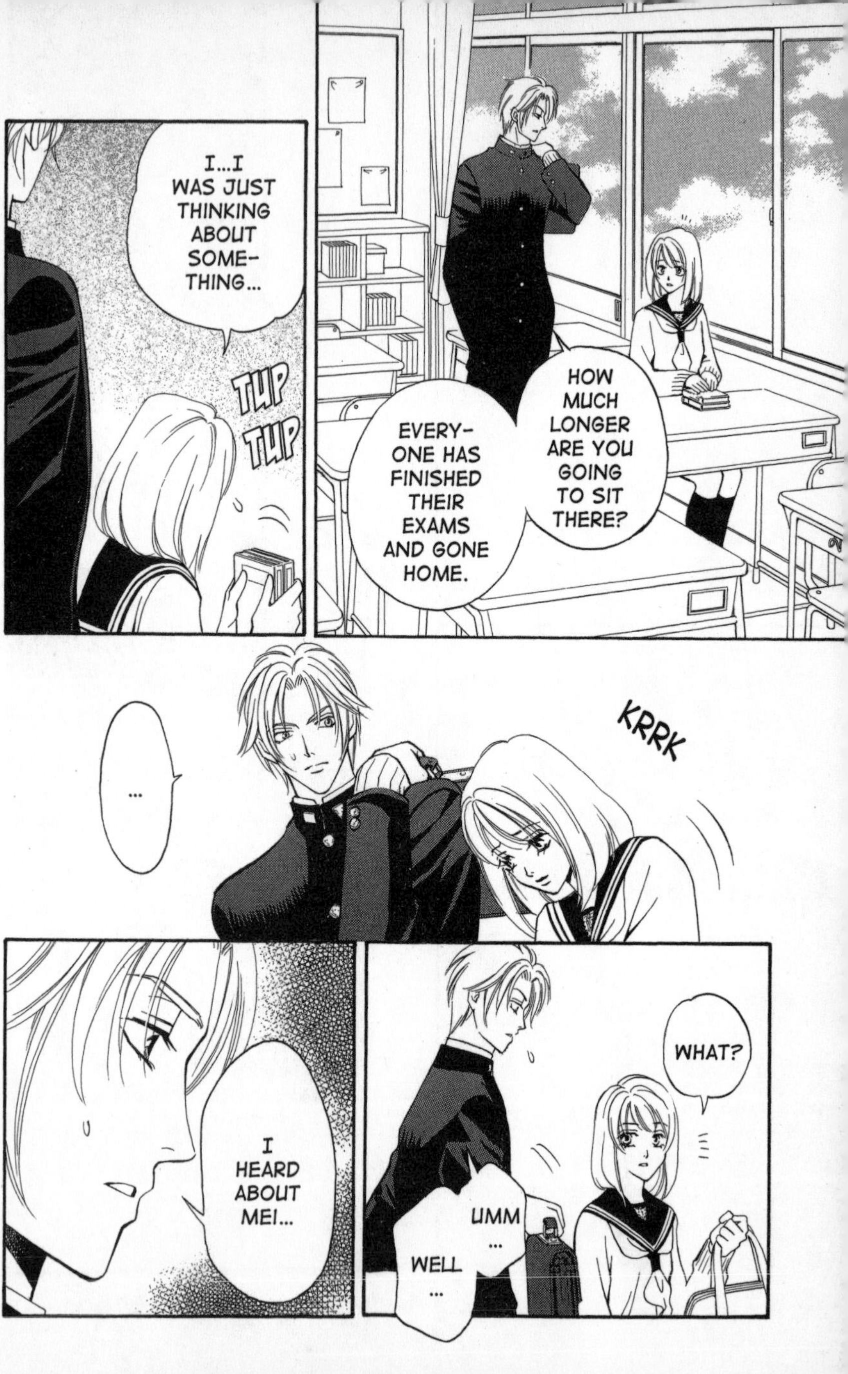
HOW MUCH LONGER ARE YOU GOING TO SIT THERE?
EVERYONE HAS FINISHED THEIR EXAMS AND GONE HOME.
I...I WAS JUST THINKING ABOUT SOME-THING...
TUP TUP
KRRK
...
WHAT?
UMM...
WELL...
I HEARD ABOUT MEI...

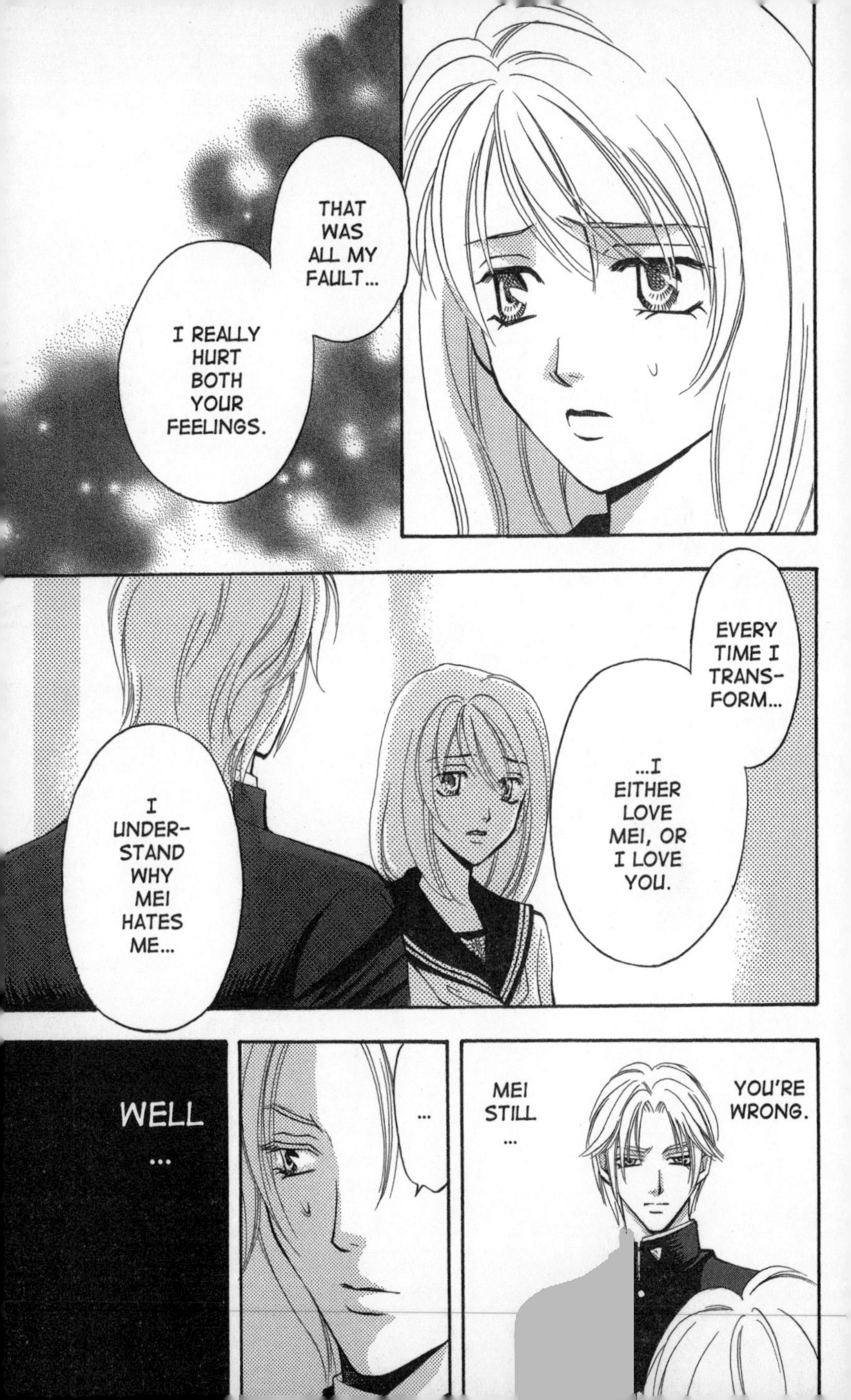
THAT WAS ALL MY FAULT...
I REALLY HURT BOTH YOUR FEELINGS.
EVERY TIME I TRANS-FORM...
...I EITHER LOVE MEI, OR I LOVE YOU.
I UNDER-STAND WHY MEI HATES ME...
YOU'RE WRONG.
MEI STILL ...
...
WELL ...

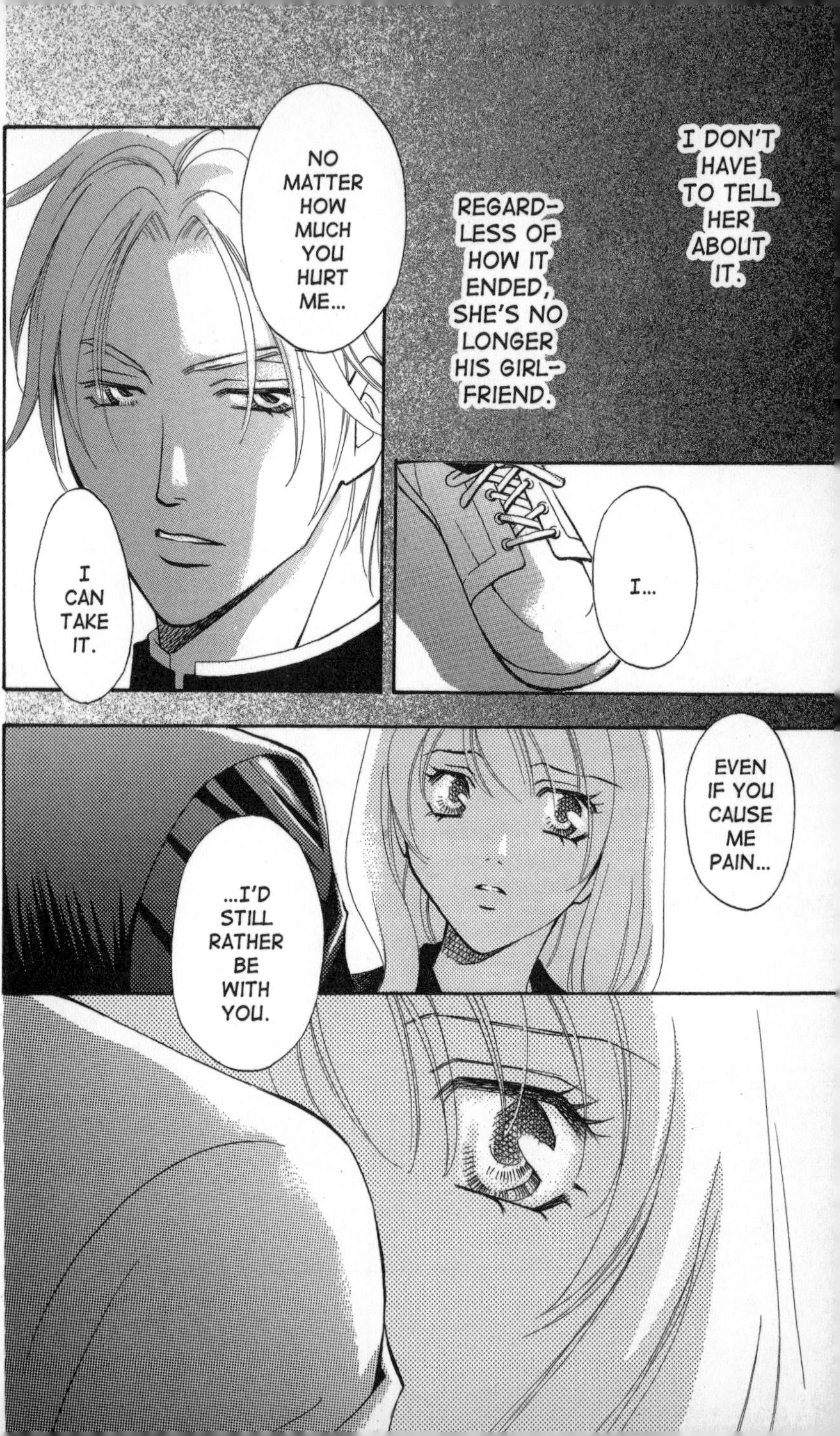
I DON'T HAVE TO TELL HER ABOUT IT.
REGARDLESS OF HOW IT ENDED, SHE'S NO LONGER HIS GIRLFRIEND.
I...
NO MATTER HOW MUCH YOU HURT ME...
I CAN TAKE IT.
EVEN IF YOU CAUSE ME PAIN...
...I'D STILL RATHER BE WITH YOU.

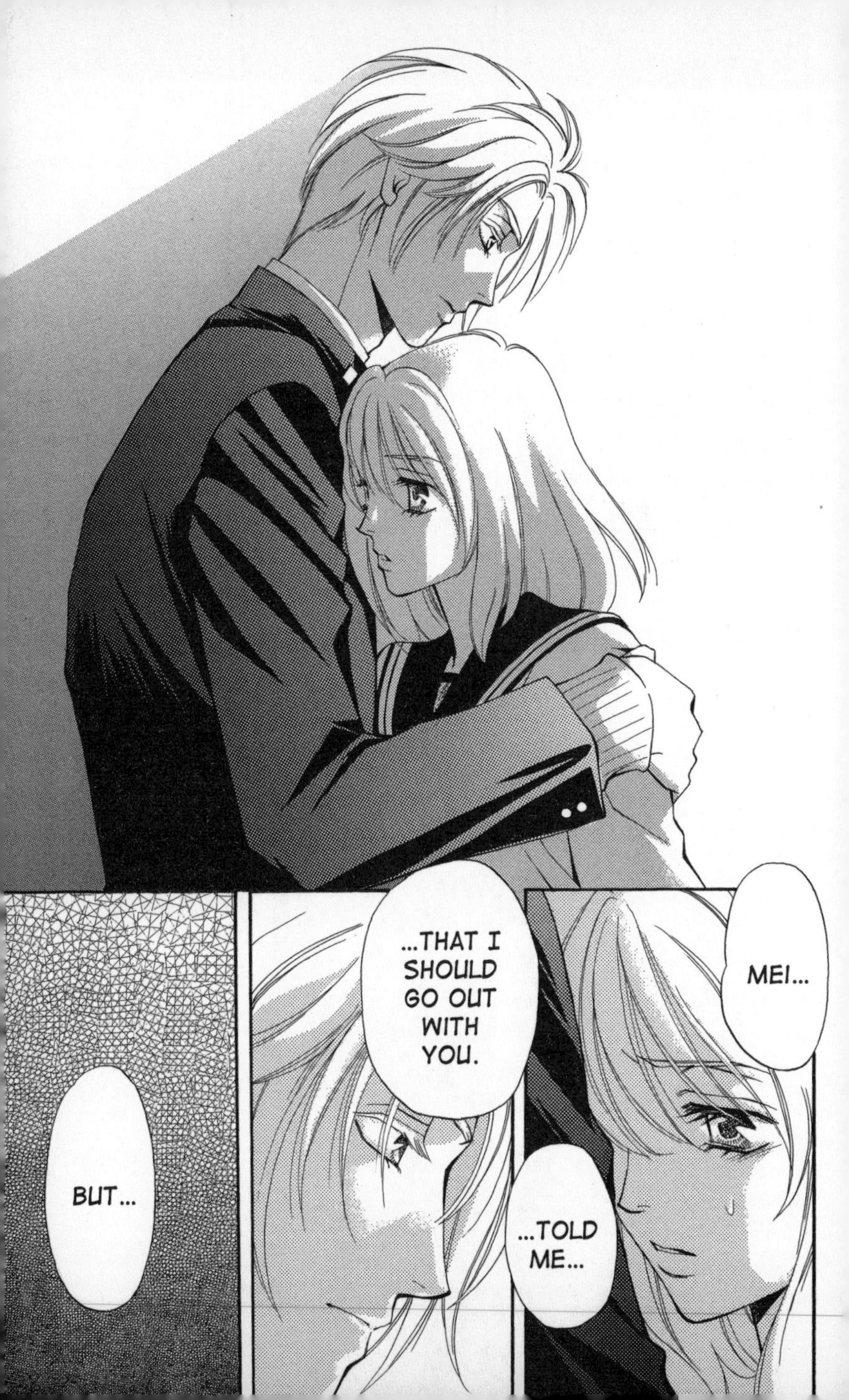
MEI...
...TOLD ME...
...THAT I SHOULD GO OUT WITH YOU.
BUT...

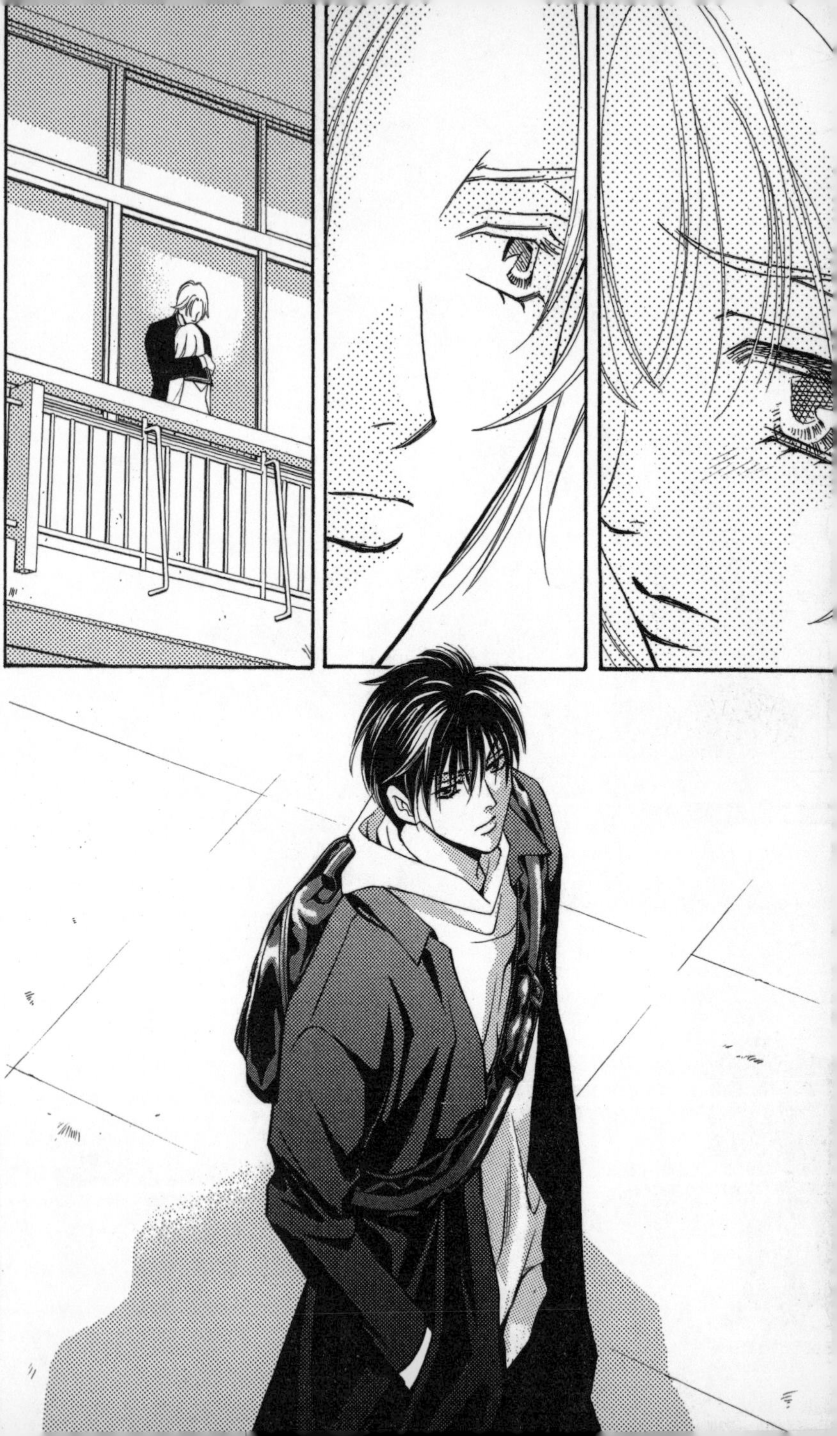

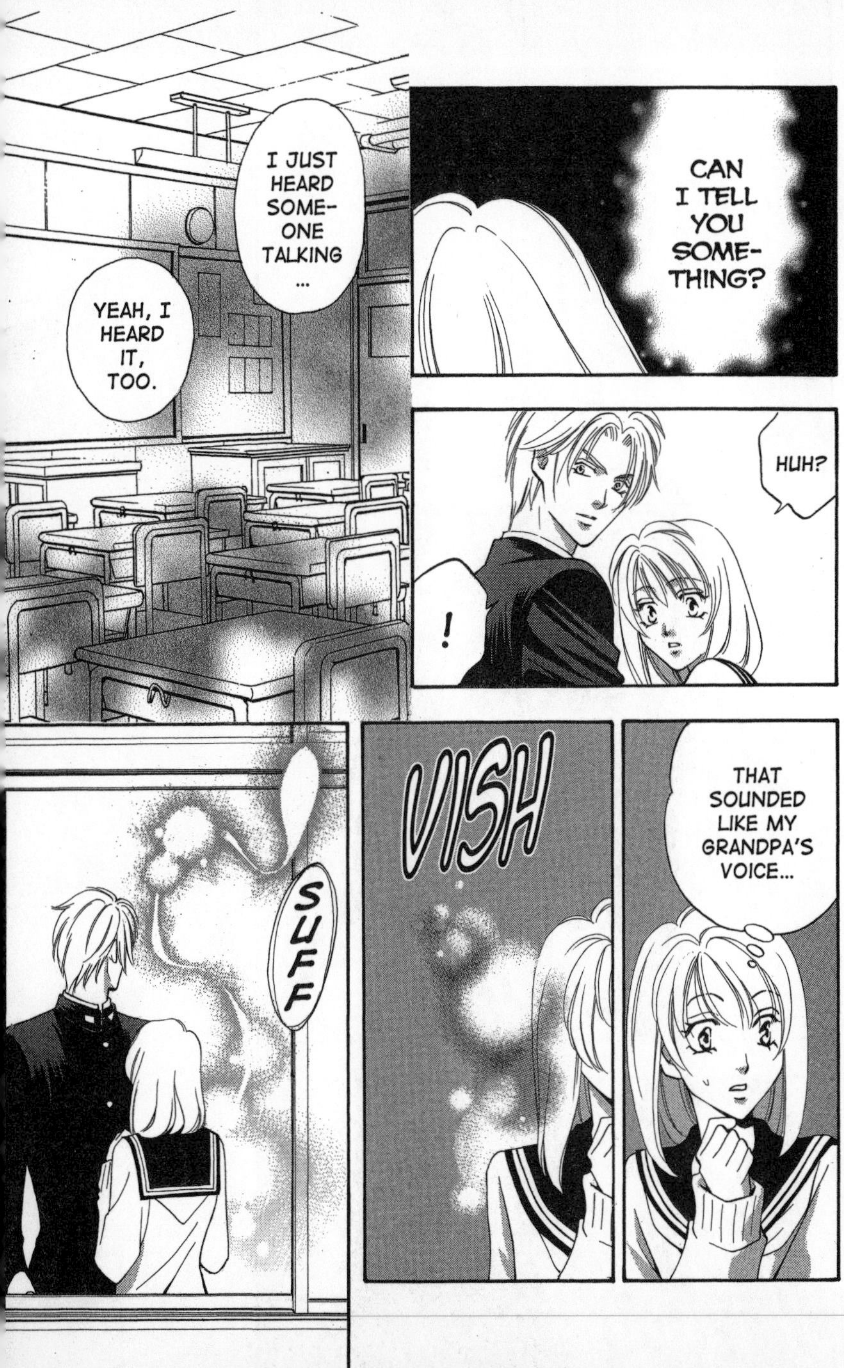
CAN I TELL YOU SOME-THING?
HUH?
!
I JUST HEARD SOME-ONE TALKING ...
YEAH, I HEARD IT, TOO.
THAT SOUNDED LIKE MY GRANDPA'S VOICE...
VISH
SUFF

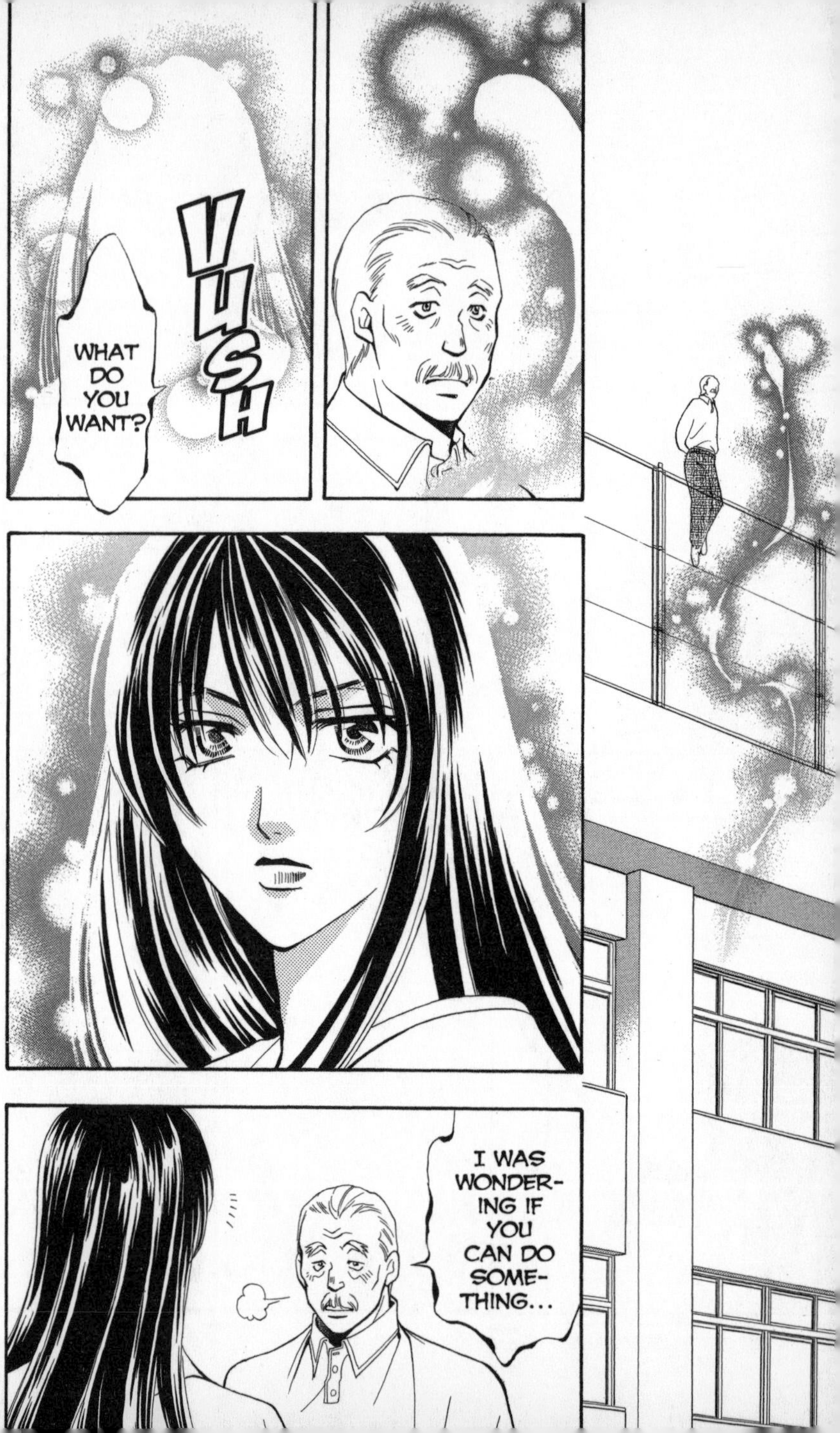
VUSH
WHAT DO YOU WANT?
I WAS WONDERING IF YOU CAN DO SOMETHING...

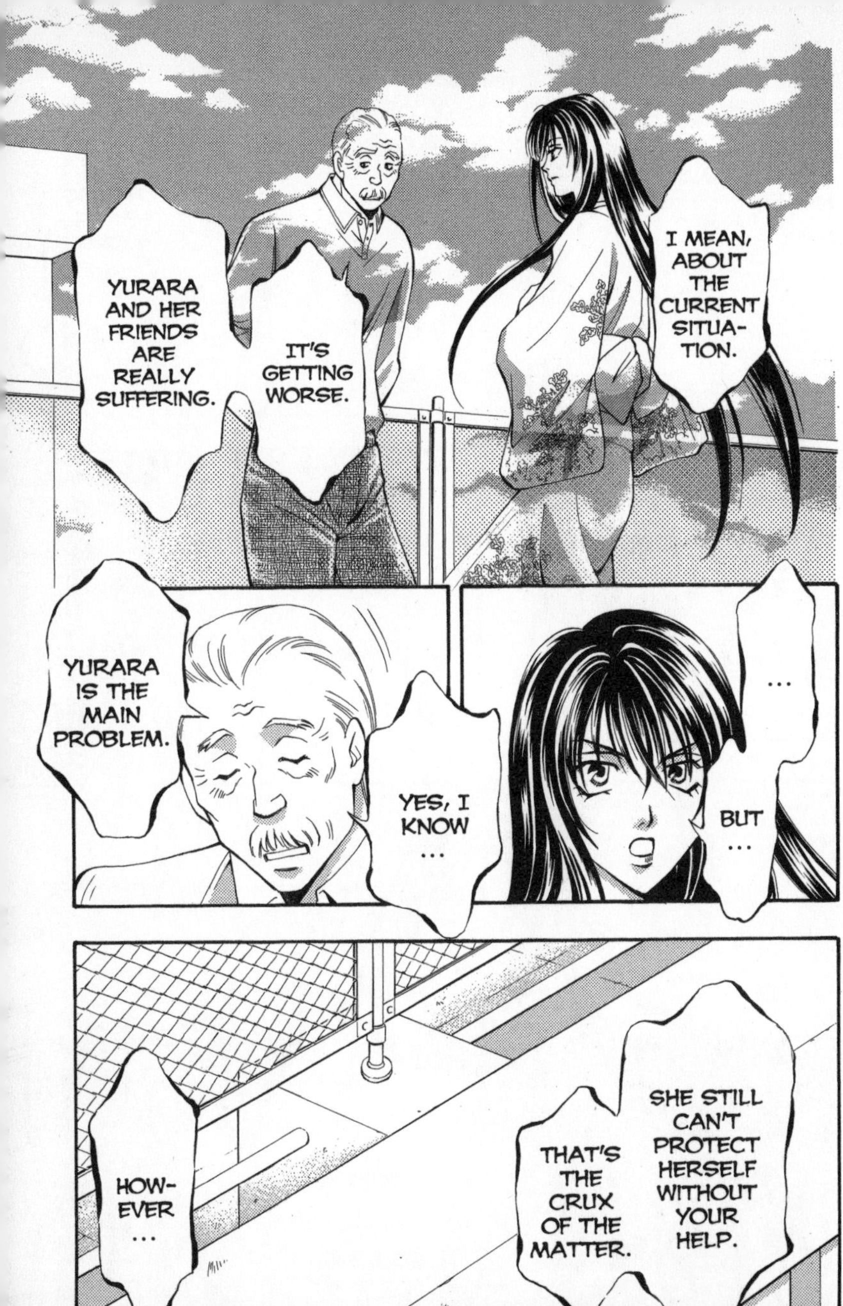
I MEAN, ABOUT THE CURRENT SITUA-TION.
IT'S GETTING WORSE.
YURARA AND HER FRIENDS ARE REALLY SUFFERING.
...
BUT ...
YES, I KNOW ...
YURARA IS THE MAIN PROBLEM.
SHE STILL CAN'T PROTECT HERSELF WITHOUT YOUR HELP.
THAT'S THE CRUX OF THE MATTER.
HOW-EVER ...

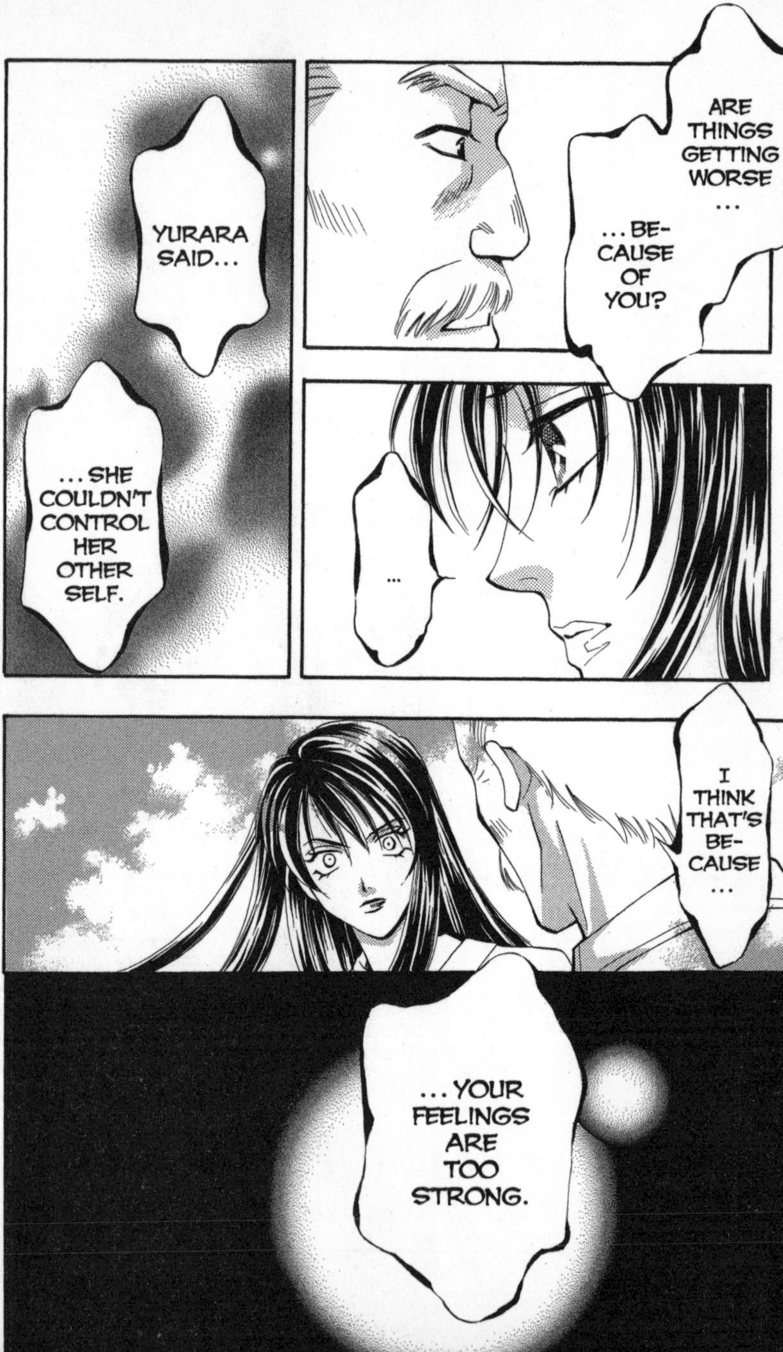
ARE THINGS GETTING WORSE...
...BECAUSE OF YOU?
...
YURARA SAID...
...SHE COULDN'T CONTROL HER OTHER SELF.
I THINK THAT'S BECAUSE...
...YOUR FEELINGS ARE TOO STRONG.

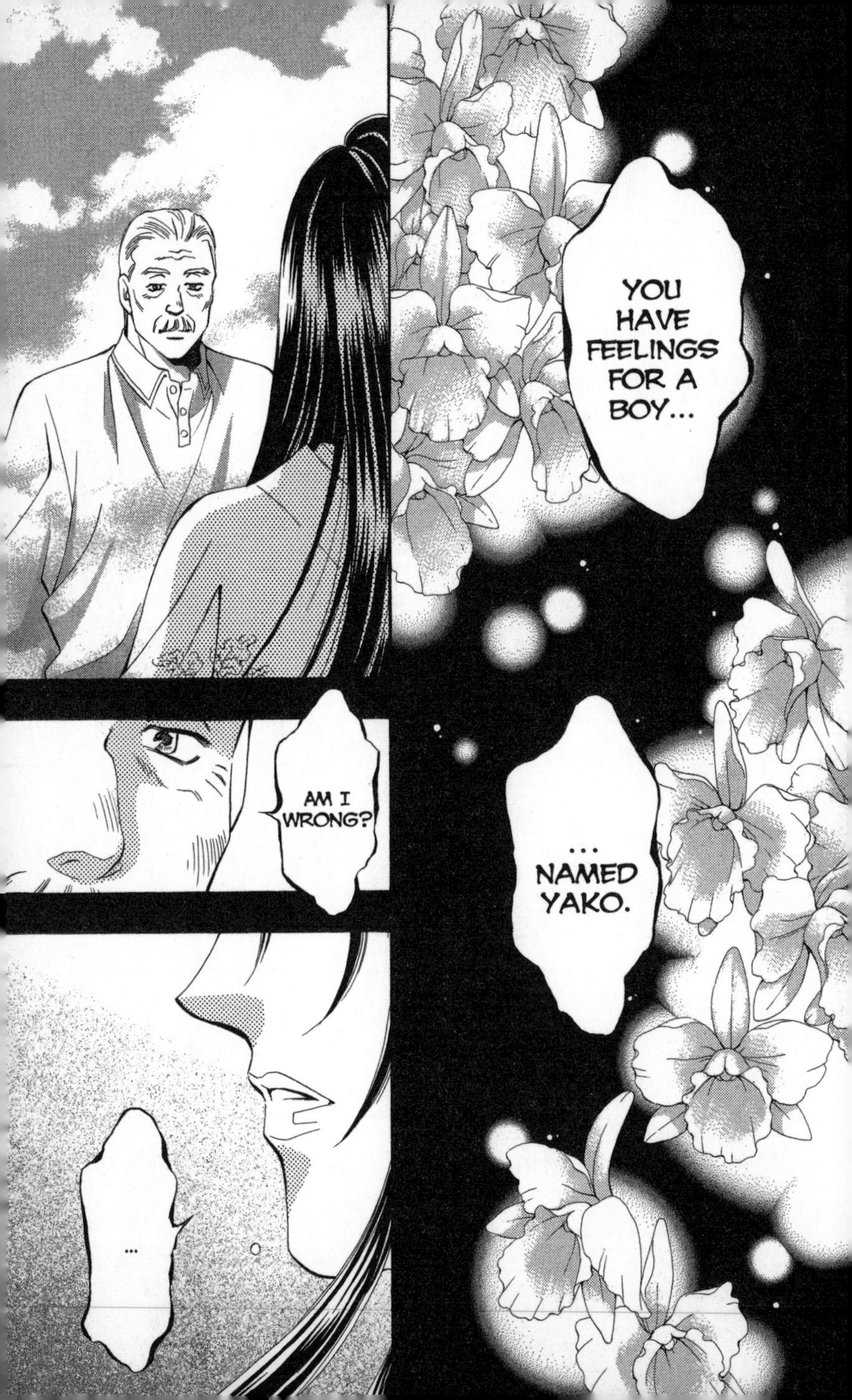
YOU HAVE FEELINGS FOR A BOY...
...NAMED YAKO.
AM I WRONG?
...

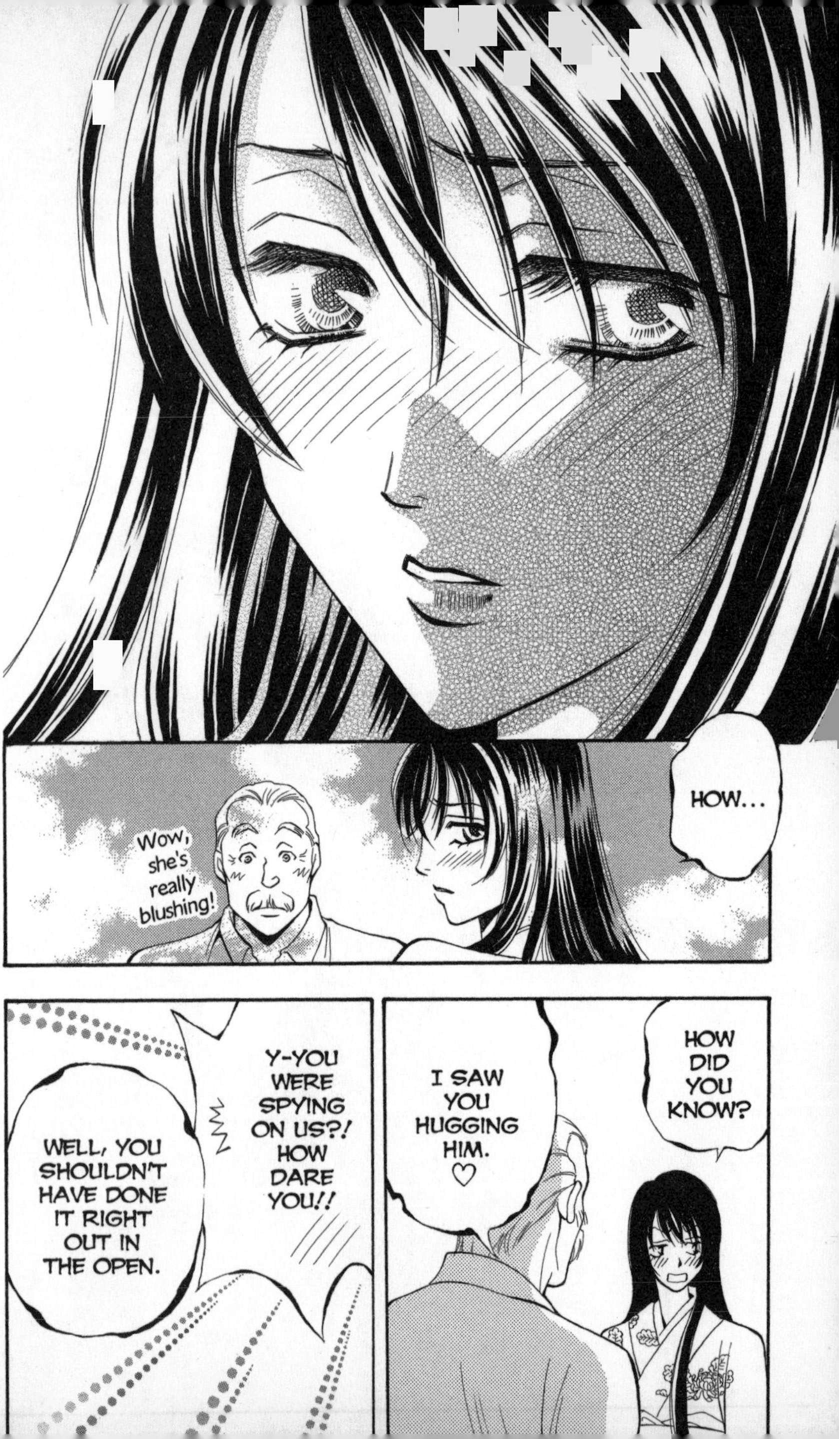
HOW...
Wow, she's really blushing!
HOW DID YOU KNOW?
I SAW YOU HUGGING HIM. ♡
Y-YOU WERE SPYING ON US?! HOW DARE YOU!!
WELL, YOU SHOULDN'T HAVE DONE IT RIGHT OUT IN THE OPEN.

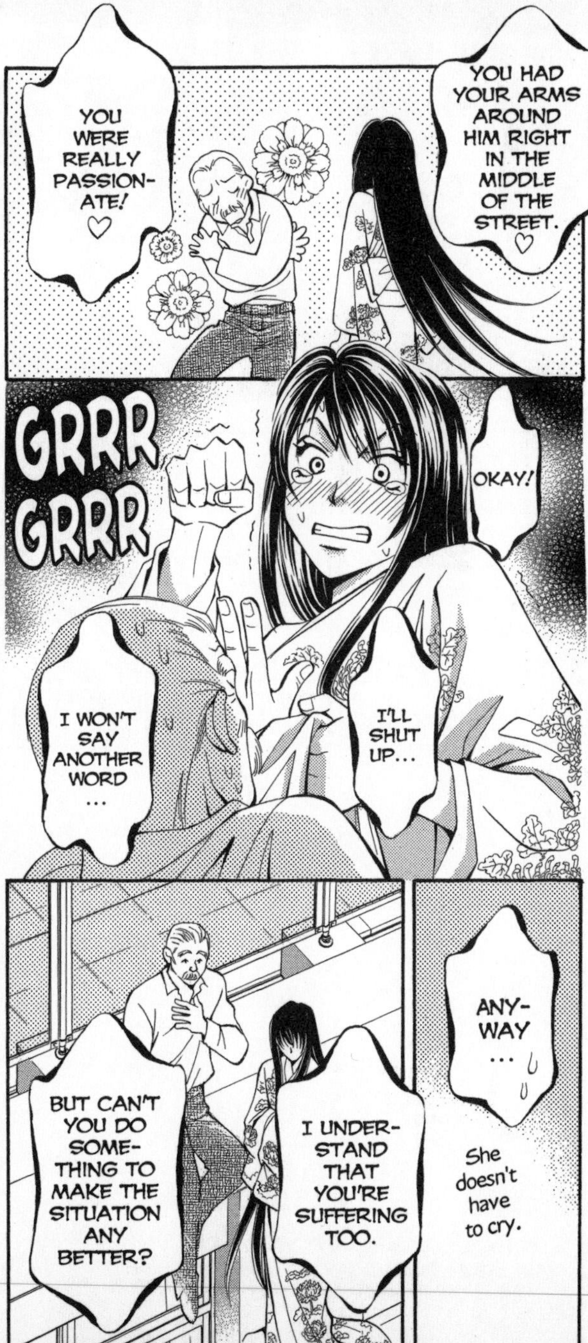
YOU HAD YOUR ARMS AROUND HIM RIGHT IN THE MIDDLE OF THE STREET. ♡
YOU WERE REALLY PASSION-ATE! ♡
OKAY!
GRRR GRRR
I'LL SHUT UP...
I WON'T SAY ANOTHER WORD ...
ANY-WAY ...
She doesn't have to cry.
I UNDER-STAND THAT YOU'RE SUFFERING TOO.
BUT CAN'T YOU DO SOME-THING TO MAKE THE SITUATION ANY BETTER?

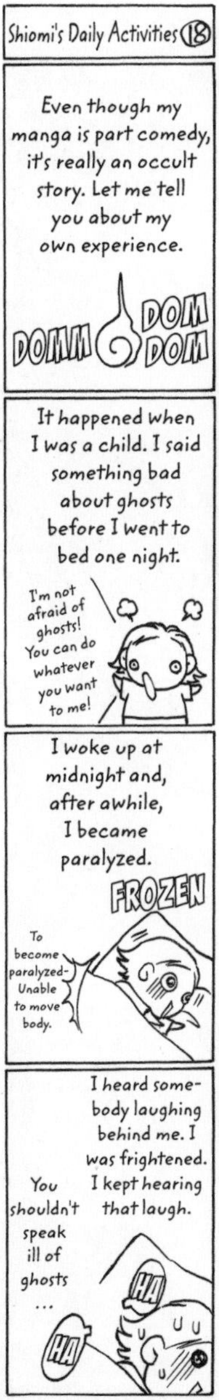
Shiomi's Daily Activities 18
Even though my manga is part comedy, it's really an occult story. Let me tell you about my own experience.
DOMM DOM DOM
It happened when I was a child. I said something bad about ghosts before I went to bed one night.
I'm not afraid of ghosts! You can do whatever you want to me!
I woke up at midnight and, after awhile, I became paralyzed.
FROZEN
To become paralyzed- Unable to move body.
I heard some-body laughing behind me. I was frightened. I kept hearing that laugh.
You shouldn't speak ill of ghosts ...
HA
HA

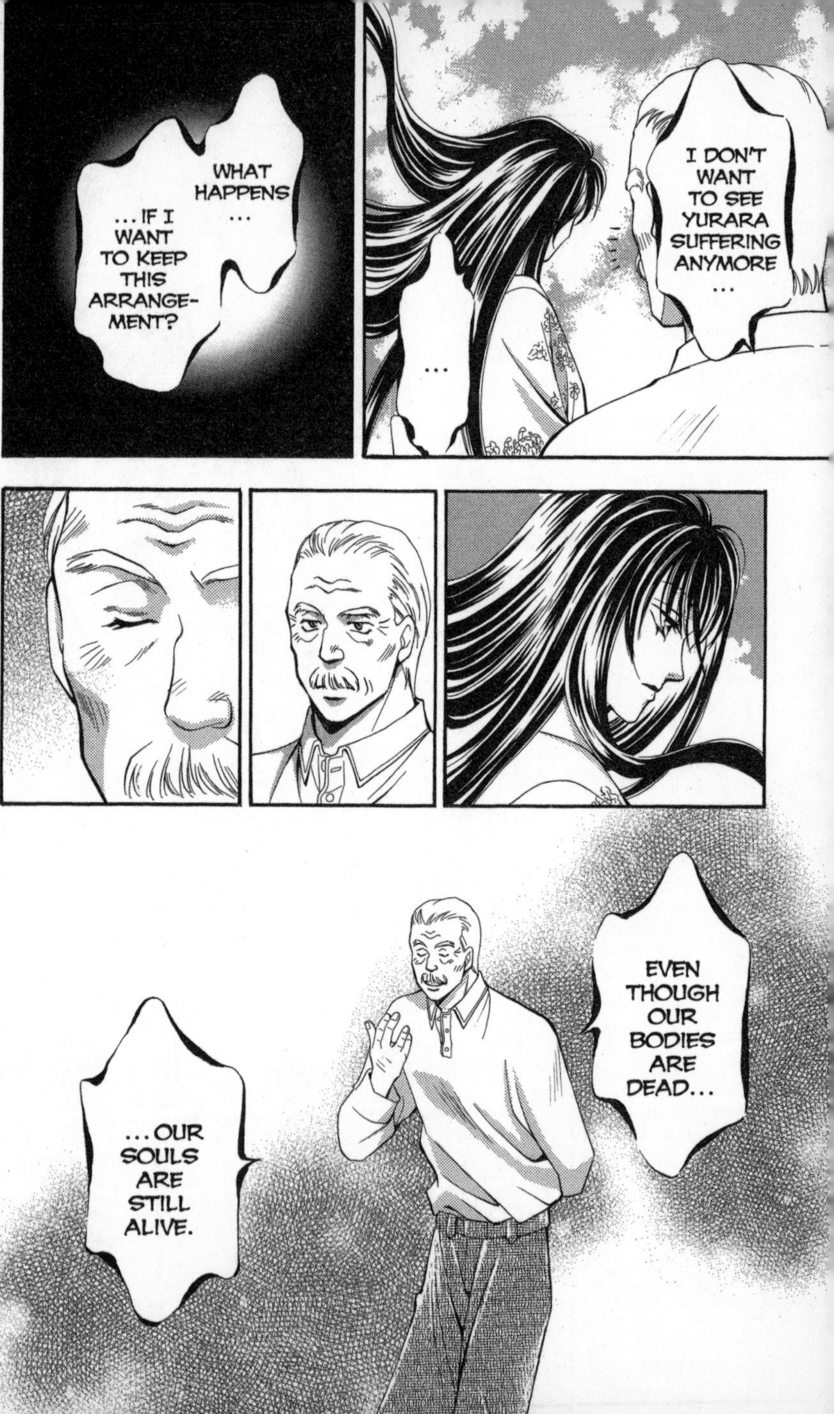
I DON'T WANT TO SEE YURARA SUFFERING ANYMORE...
...
WHAT HAPPENS...
...IF I WANT TO KEEP THIS ARRANGEMENT?
EVEN THOUGH OUR BODIES ARE DEAD...
...OUR SOULS ARE STILL ALIVE.

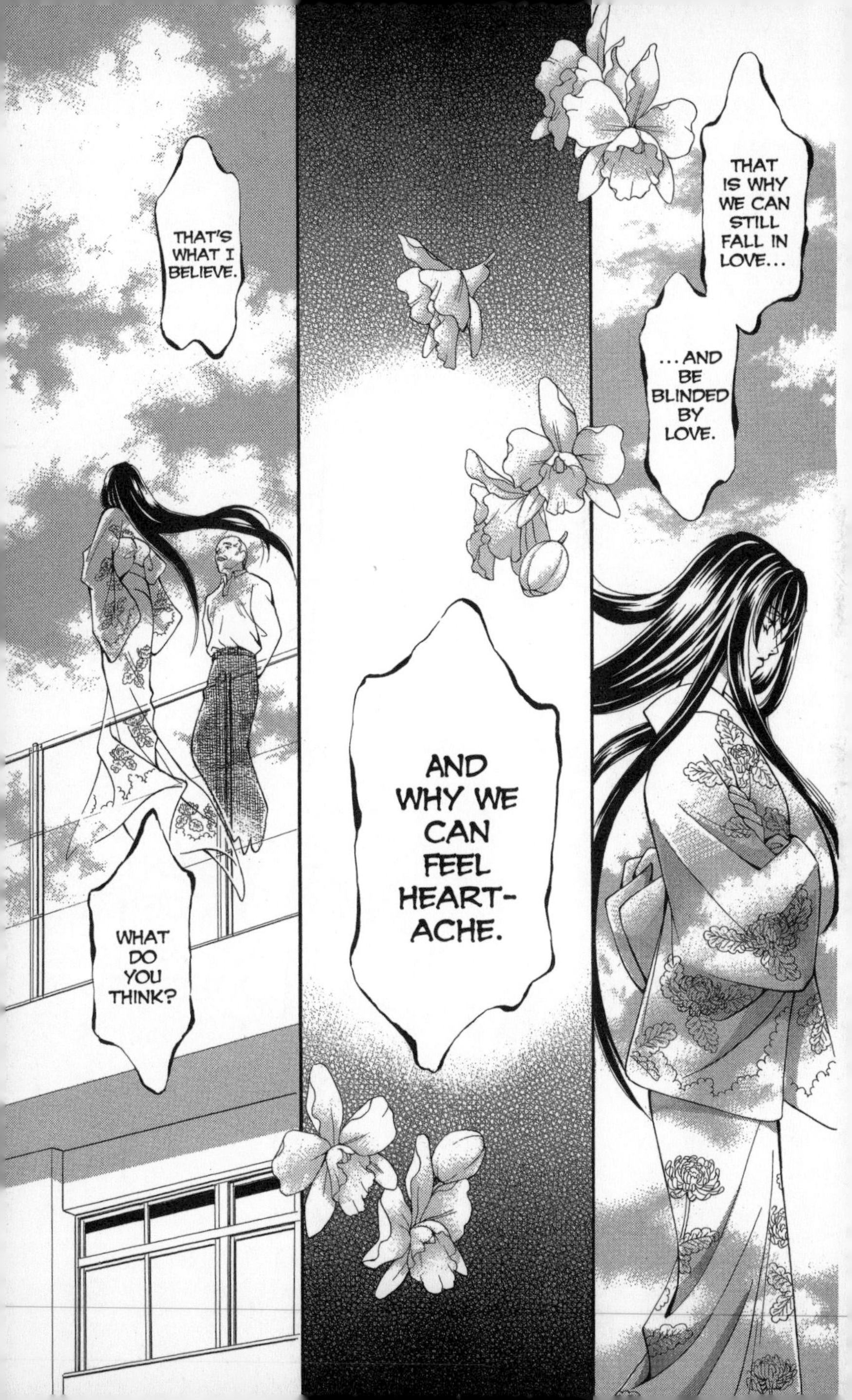
THAT IS WHY WE CAN STILL FALL IN LOVE...
...AND BE BLINDED BY LOVE.
AND WHY WE CAN FEEL HEART-ACHE.
THAT'S WHAT I BELIEVE.
WHAT DO YOU THINK?

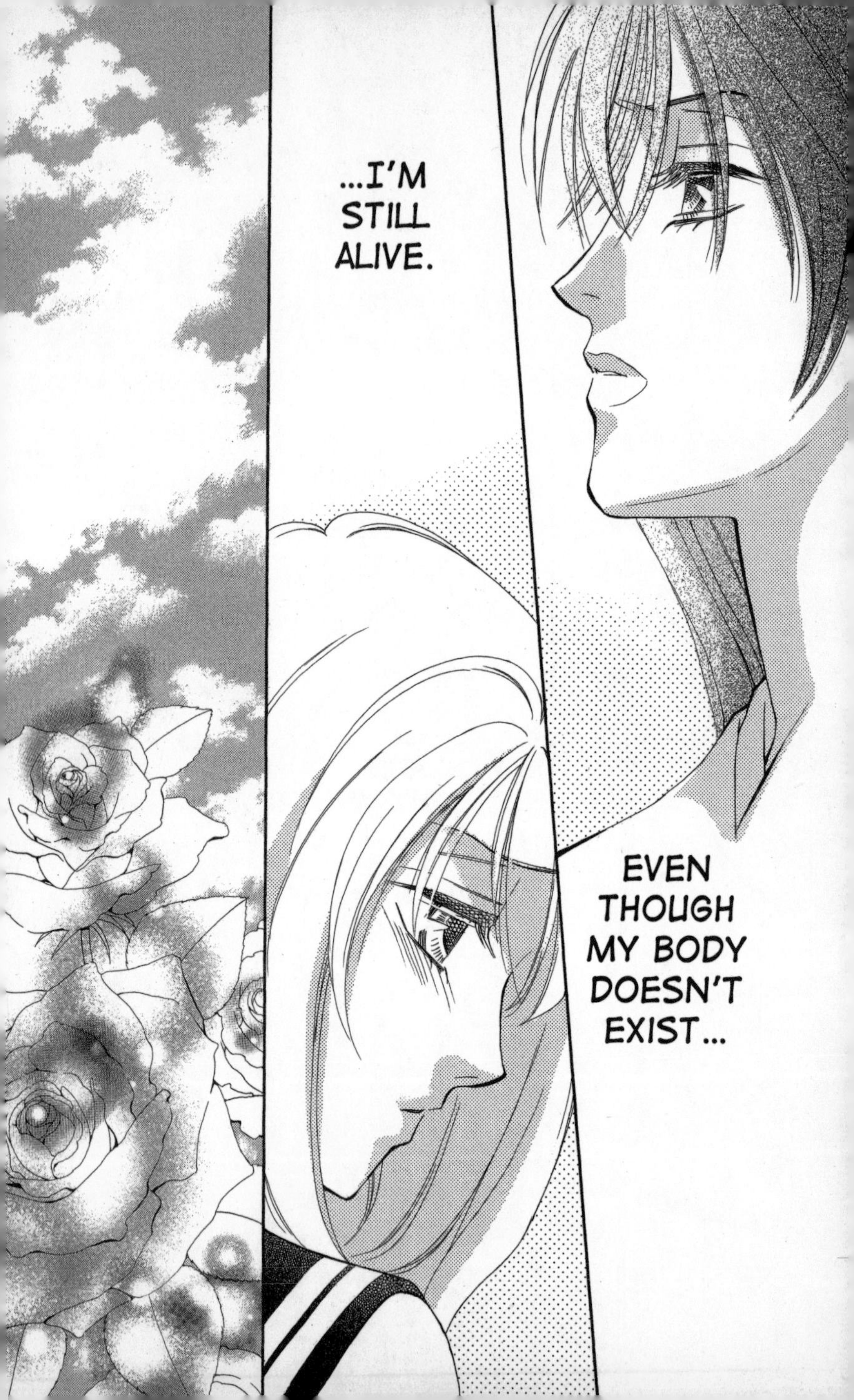
EVEN THOUGH MY BODY DOESN'T EXIST...
...I'M STILL ALIVE.

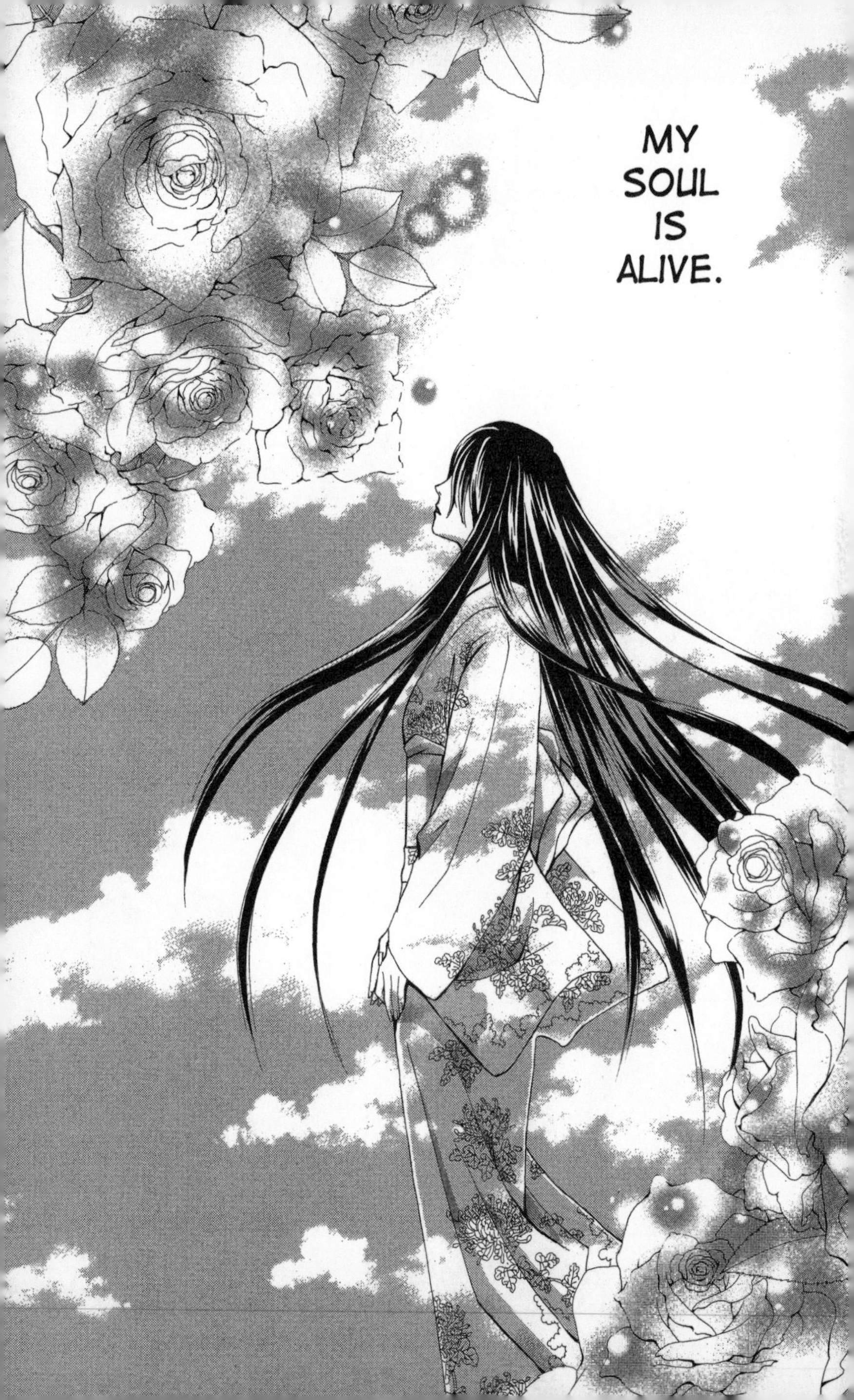
MY SOUL IS ALIVE.

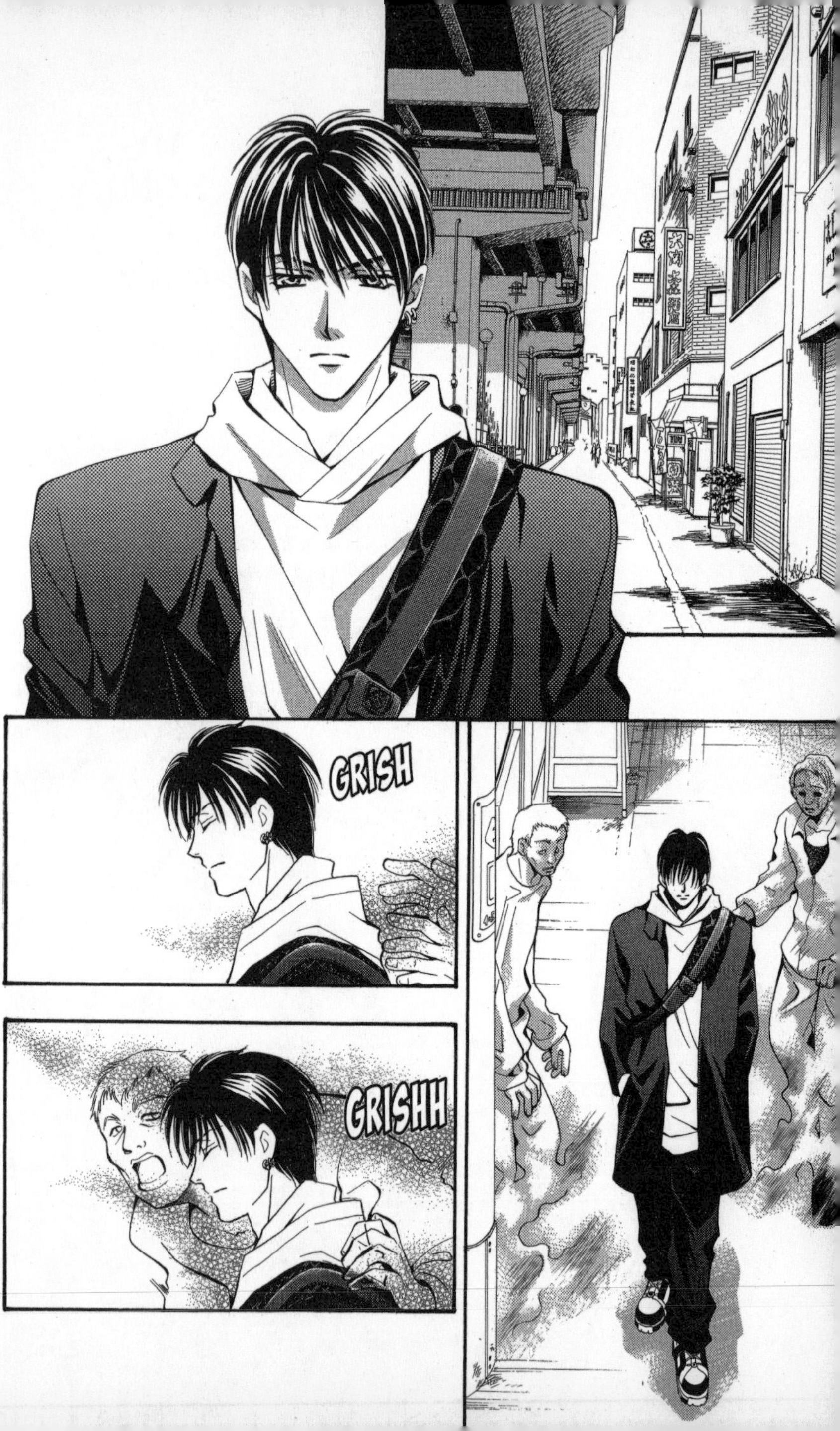
GRISH
GRISHH

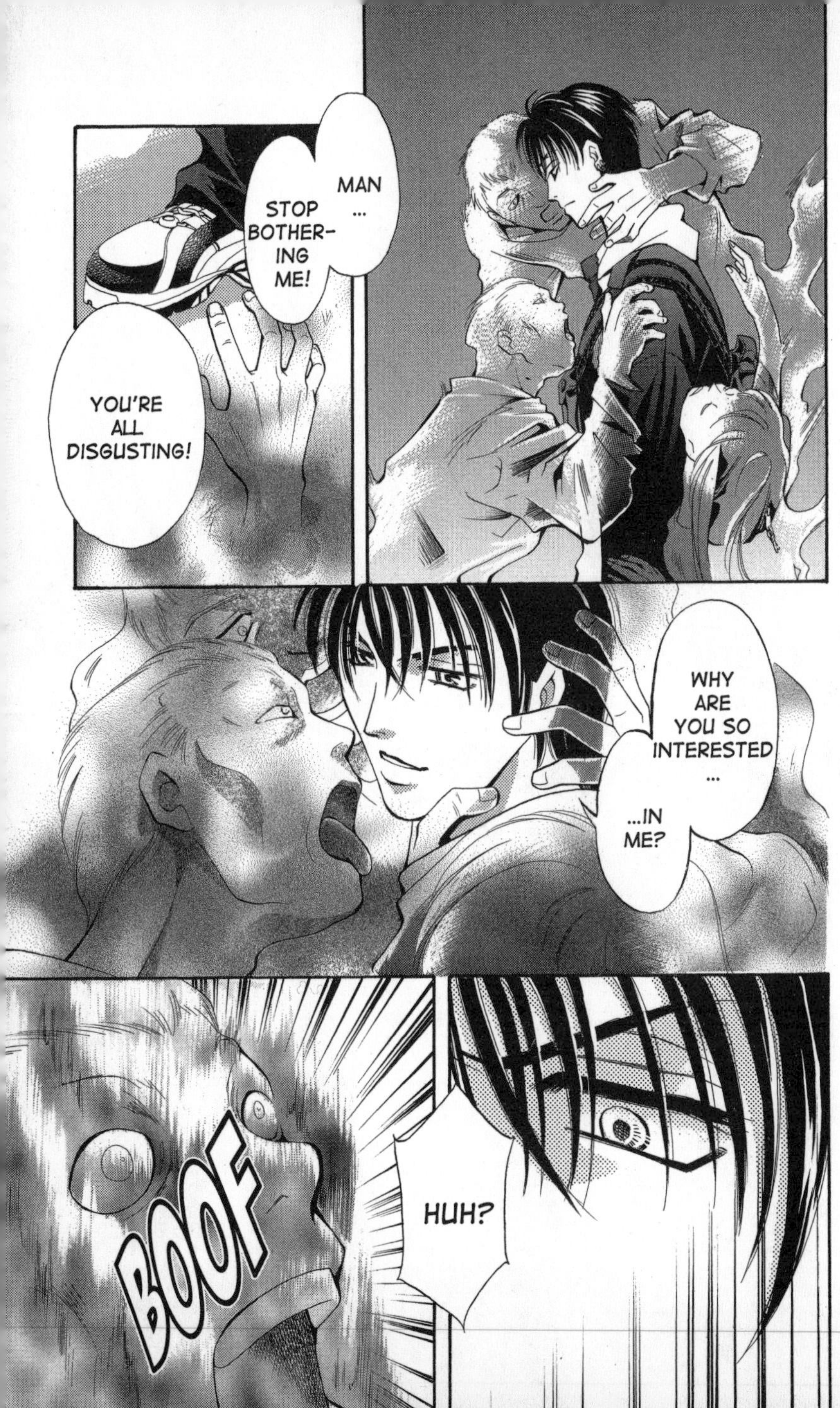
MAN ... STOP BOTHER-ING ME!
YOU'RE ALL DISGUSTING!
WHY ARE YOU SO INTERESTED ...
...IN ME?
HUH?
BOOF

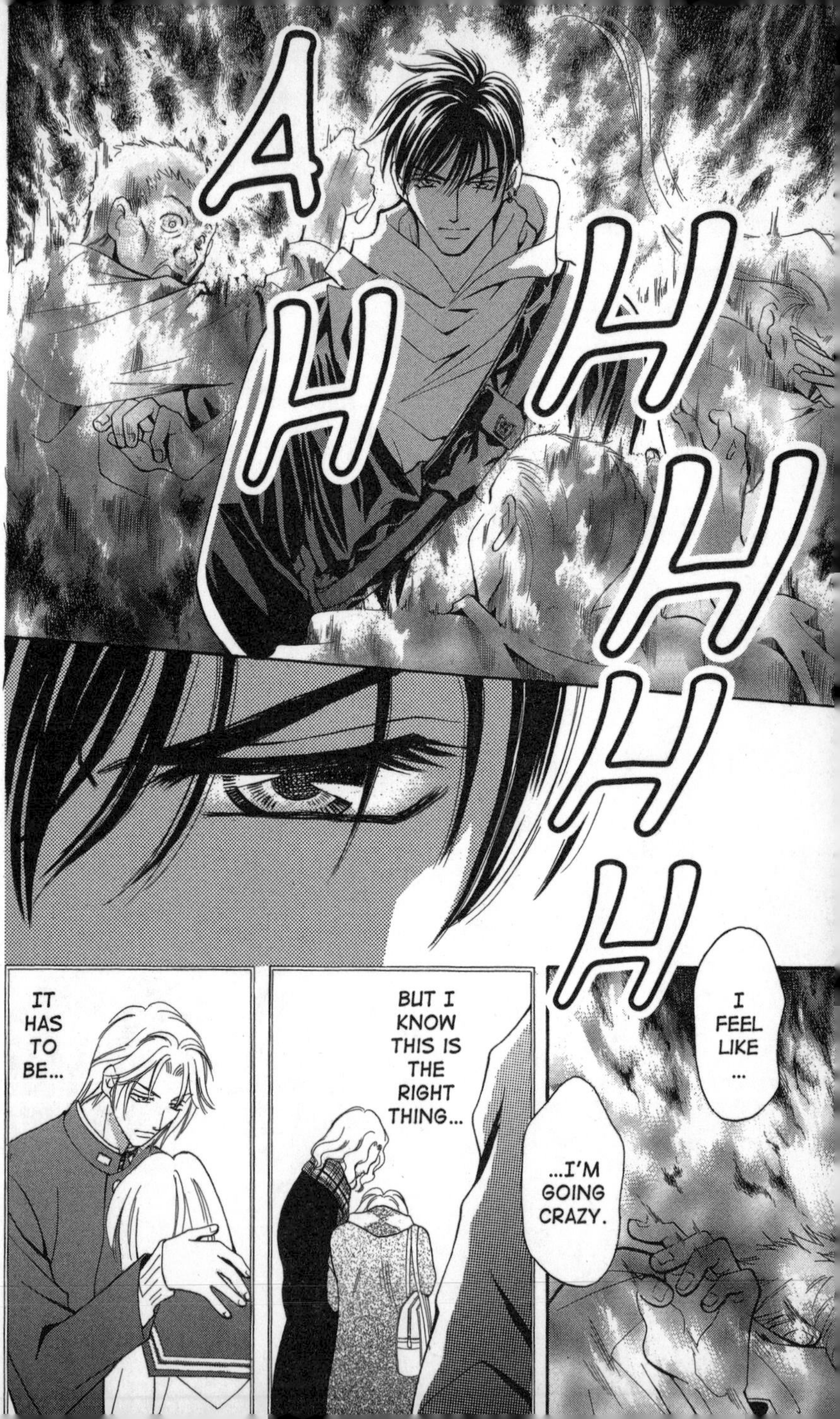
AHHHHHHH
I FEEL LIKE ...
...I'M GOING CRAZY.
BUT I KNOW THIS IS THE RIGHT THING...
IT HAS TO BE...

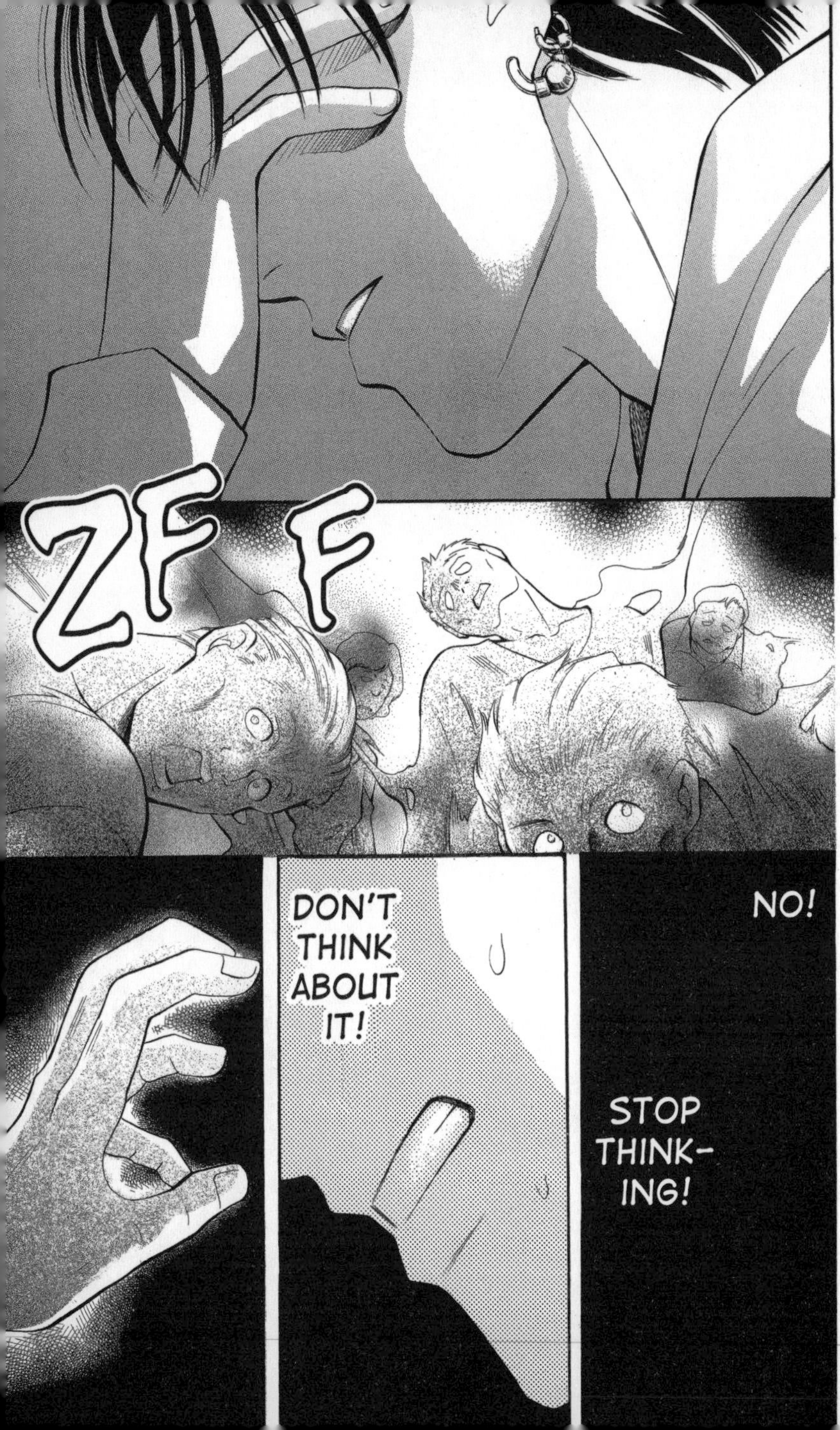
ZFF
NO!
STOP THINKING!
DON'T THINK ABOUT IT!

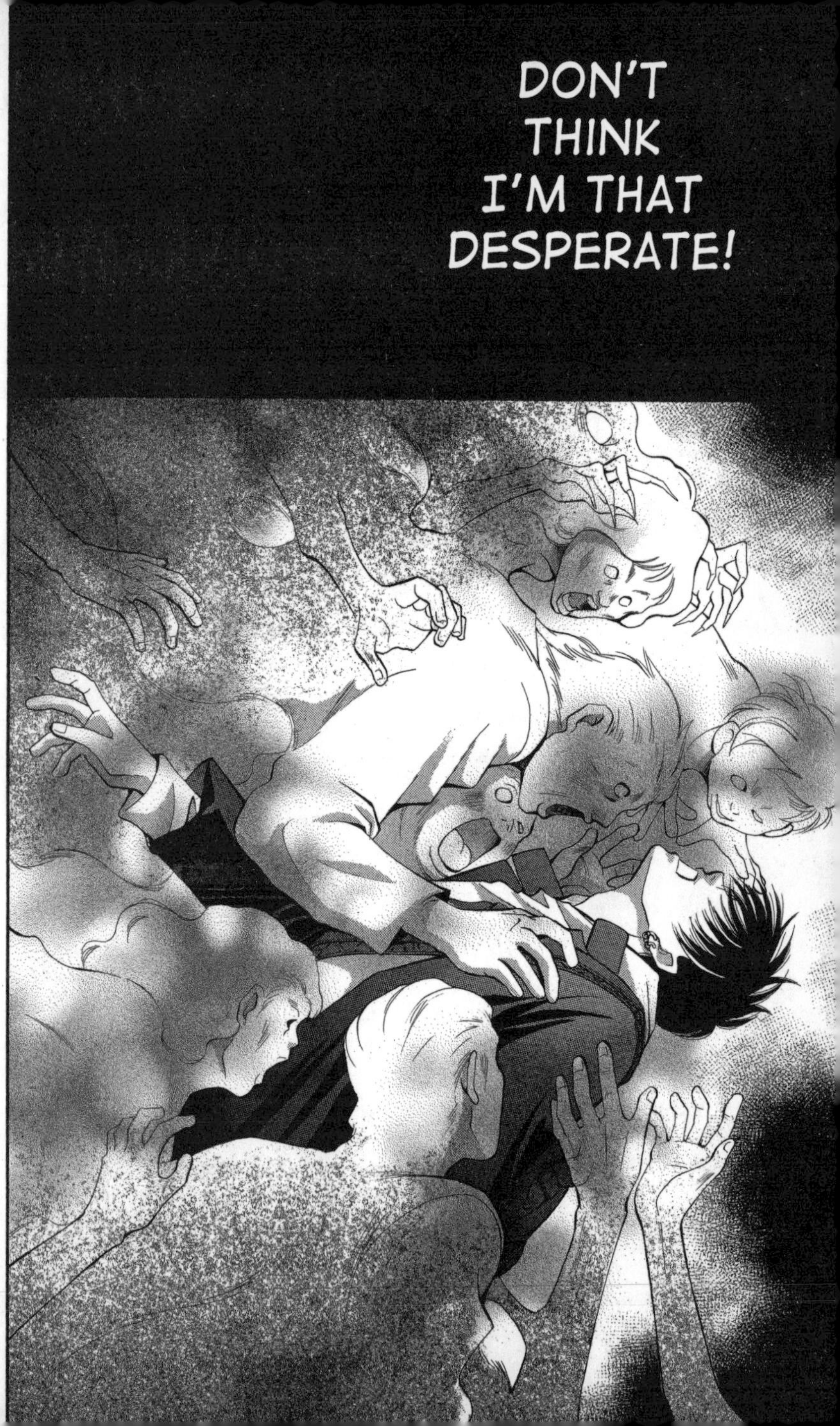
DON'T THINK I'M THAT DESPERATE!

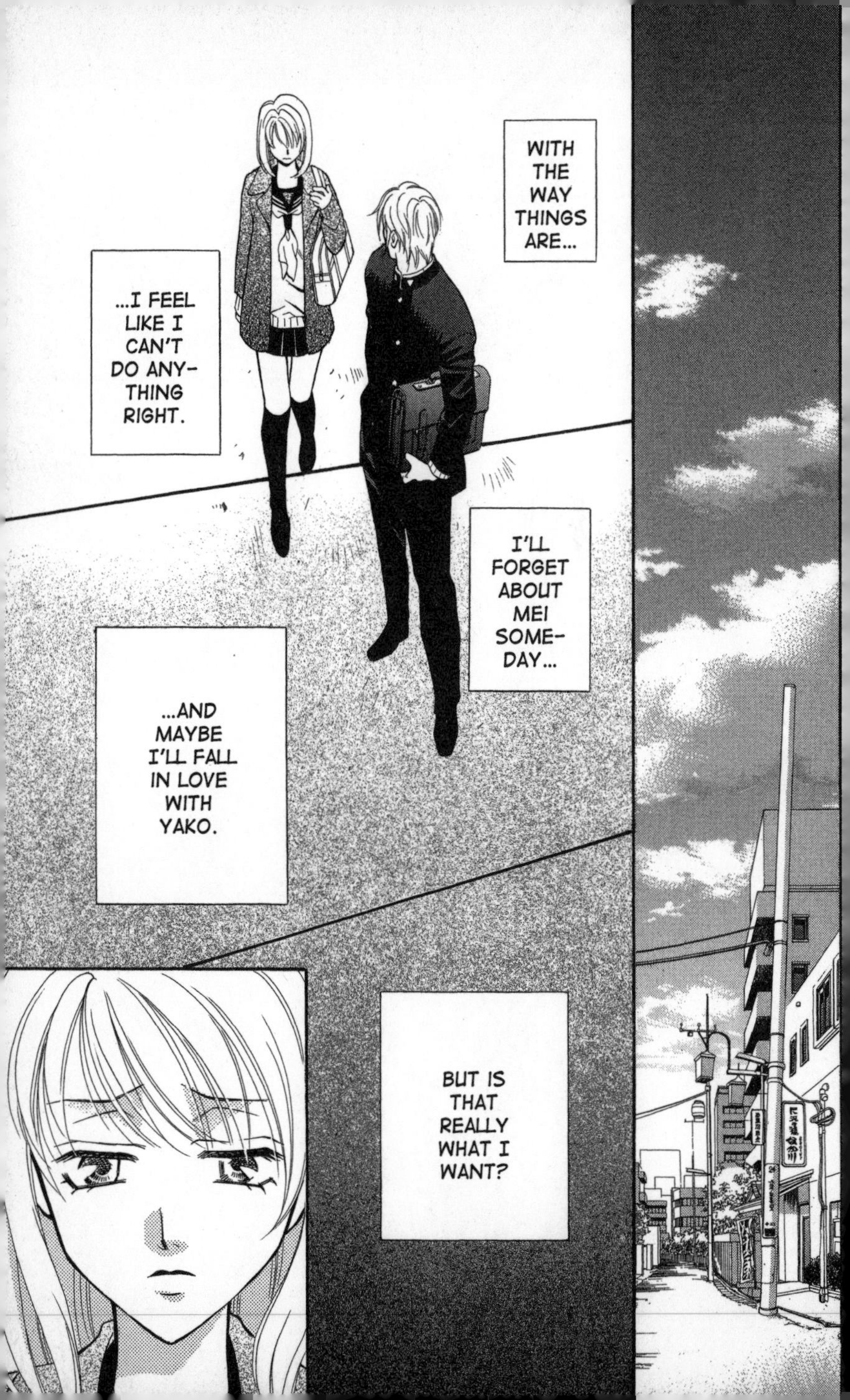
WITH THE WAY THINGS ARE...
...I FEEL LIKE I CAN'T DO ANYTHING RIGHT.
I'LL FORGET ABOUT MEI SOMEDAY...
...AND MAYBE I'LL FALL IN LOVE WITH YAKO.
BUT IS THAT REALLY WHAT I WANT?

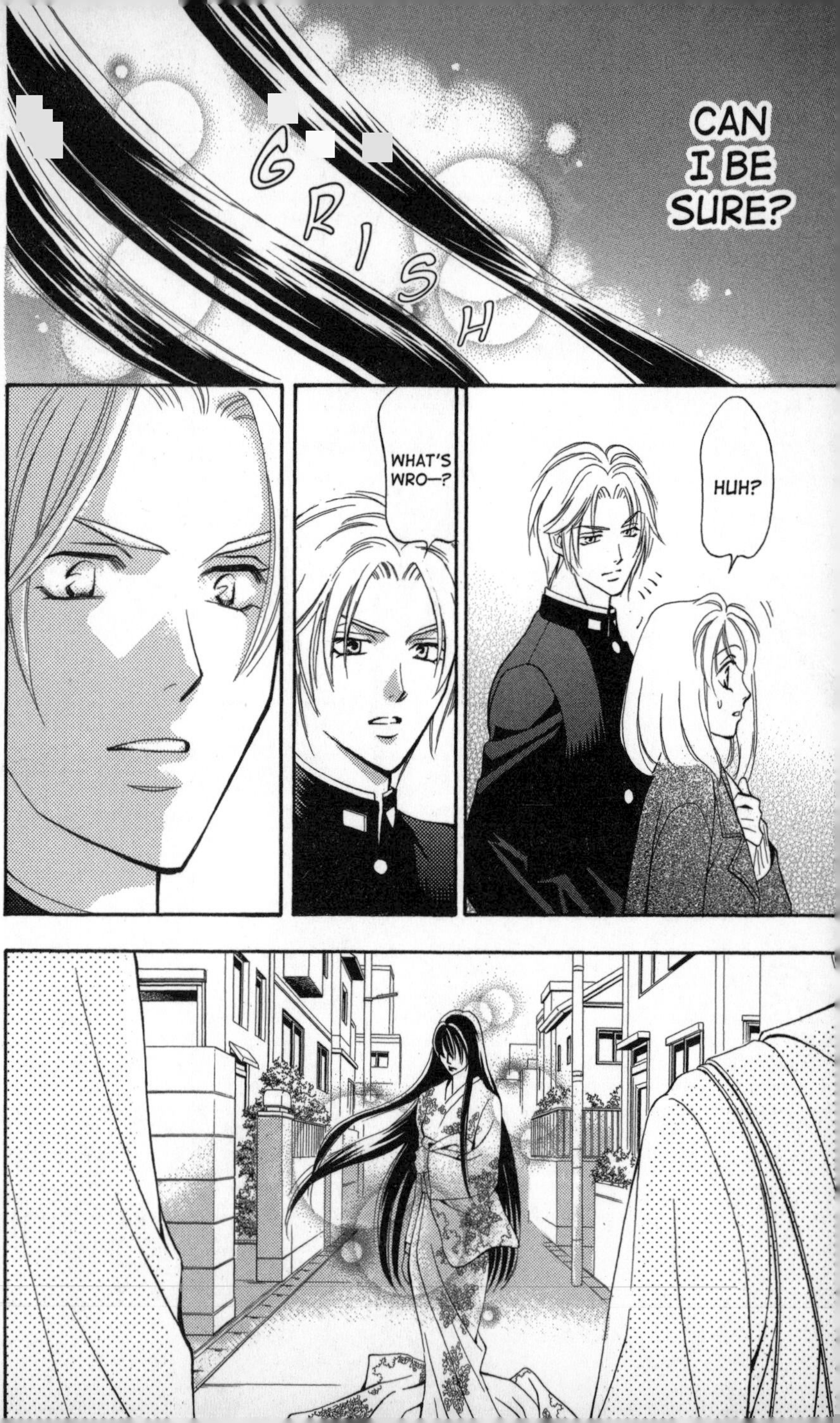
CAN I BE SURE?
GRISH
HUH?
WHAT'S WRO—?

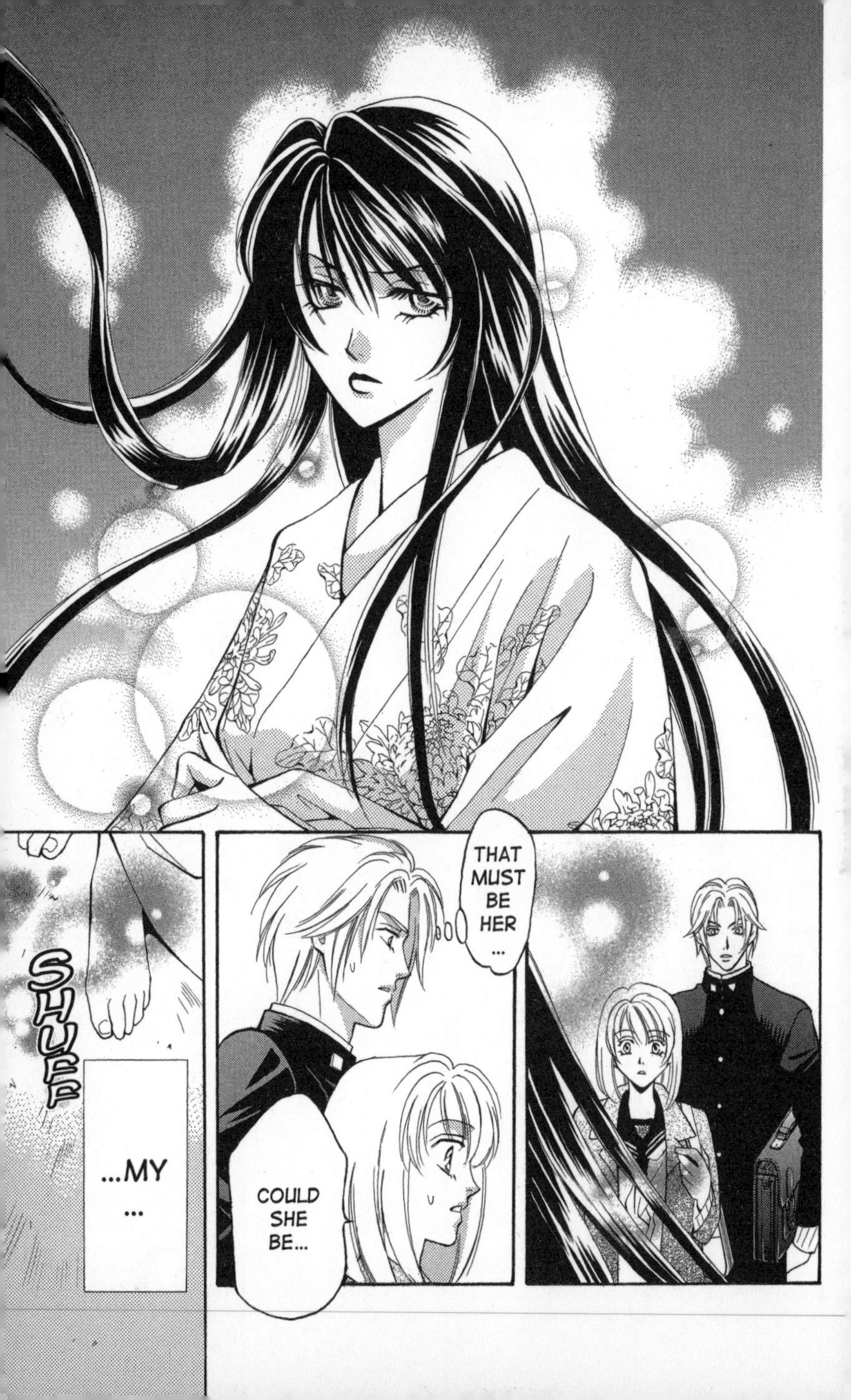
THAT MUST BE HER ...
COULD SHE BE...
SHUFF
...MY ...

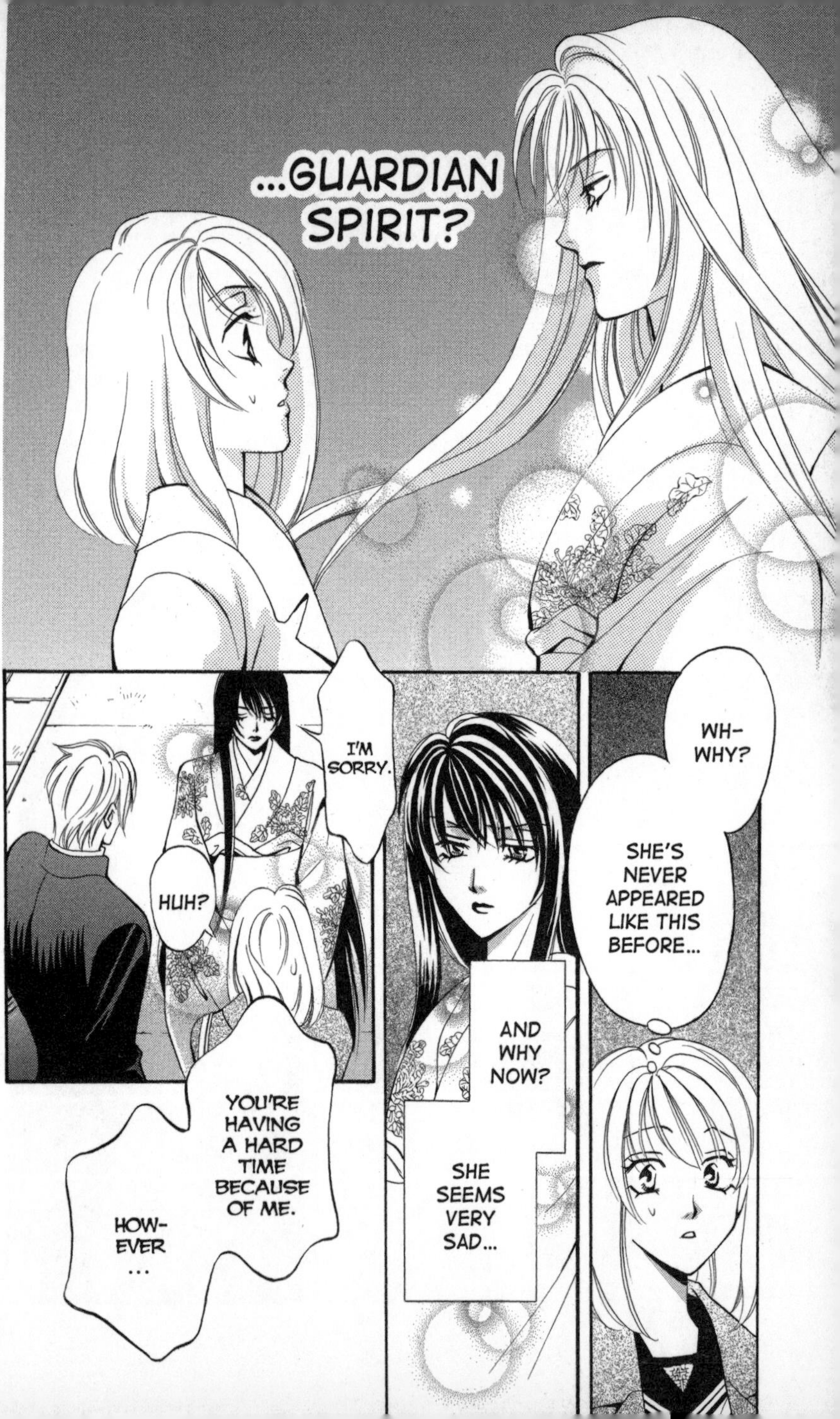
...GUARDIAN SPIRIT?
WH- WHY?
SHE'S NEVER APPEARED LIKE THIS BEFORE...
AND WHY NOW?
SHE SEEMS VERY SAD...
I'M SORRY.
HUH?
YOU'RE HAVING A HARD TIME BECAUSE OF ME.
HOW- EVER ...

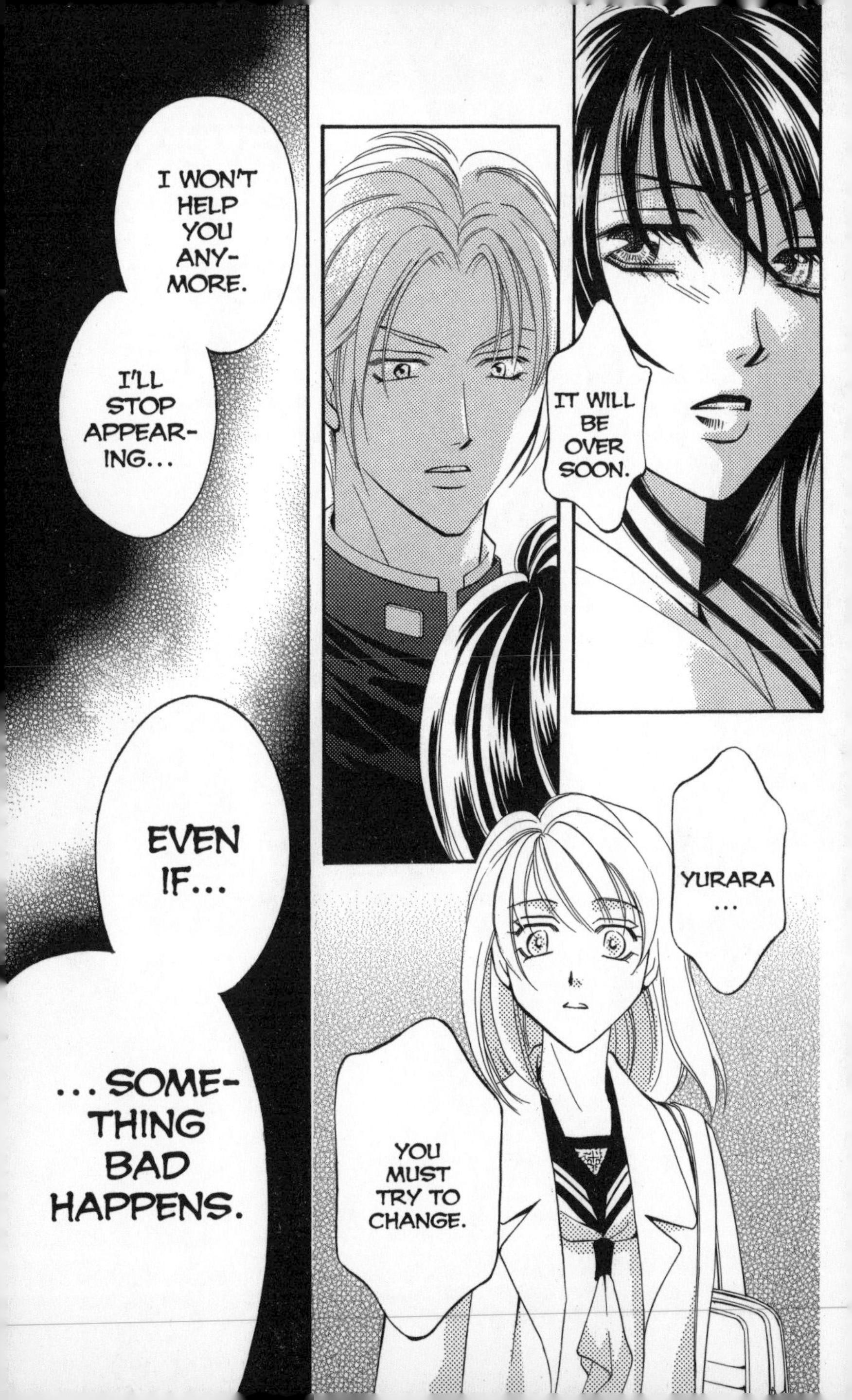
IT WILL BE OVER SOON.
YURARA ...
YOU MUST TRY TO CHANGE.
I WON'T HELP YOU ANY-MORE.
I'LL STOP APPEAR-ING...
EVEN IF...
...SOME-THING BAD HAPPENS.

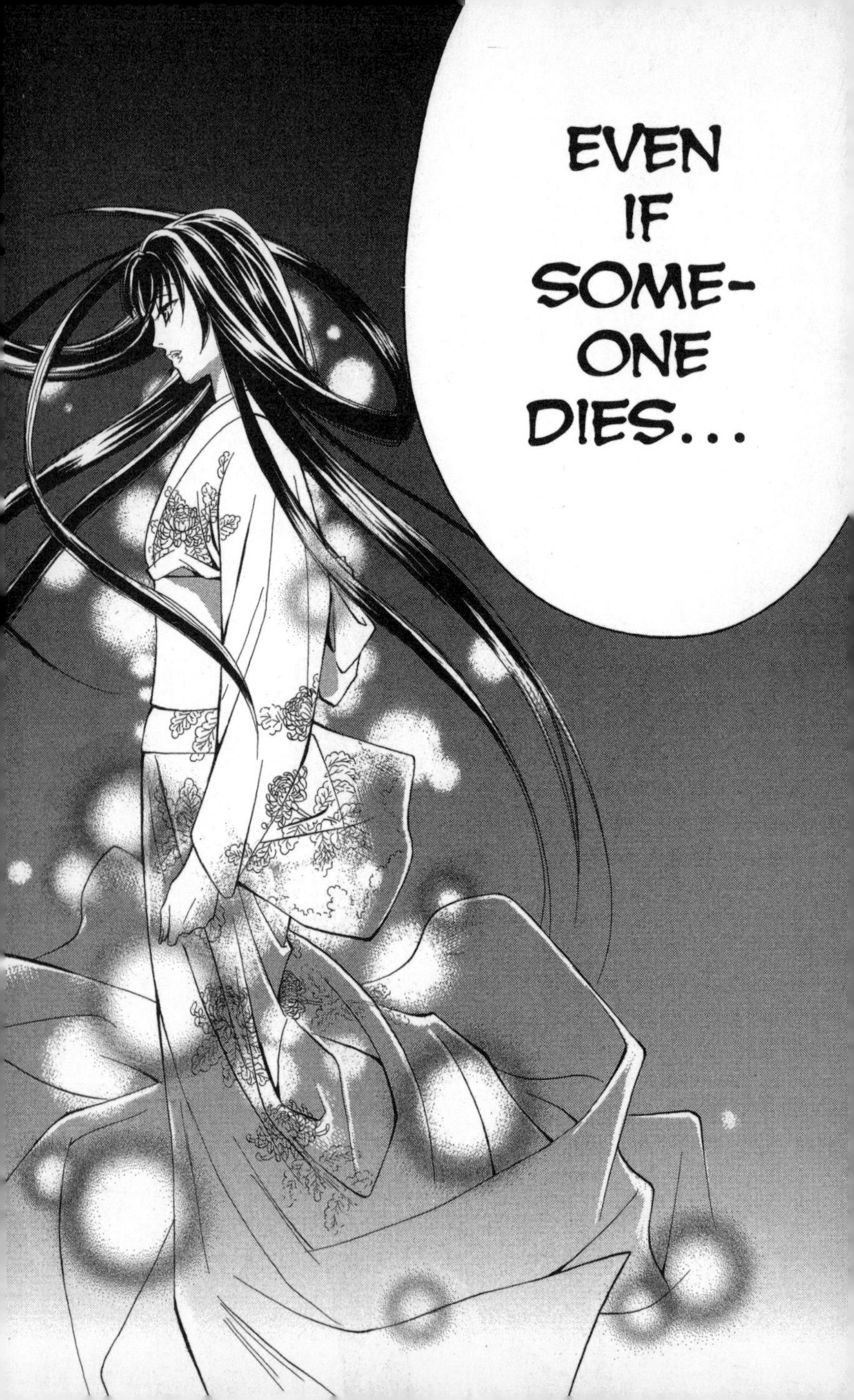
EVEN IF SOME-ONE DIES...

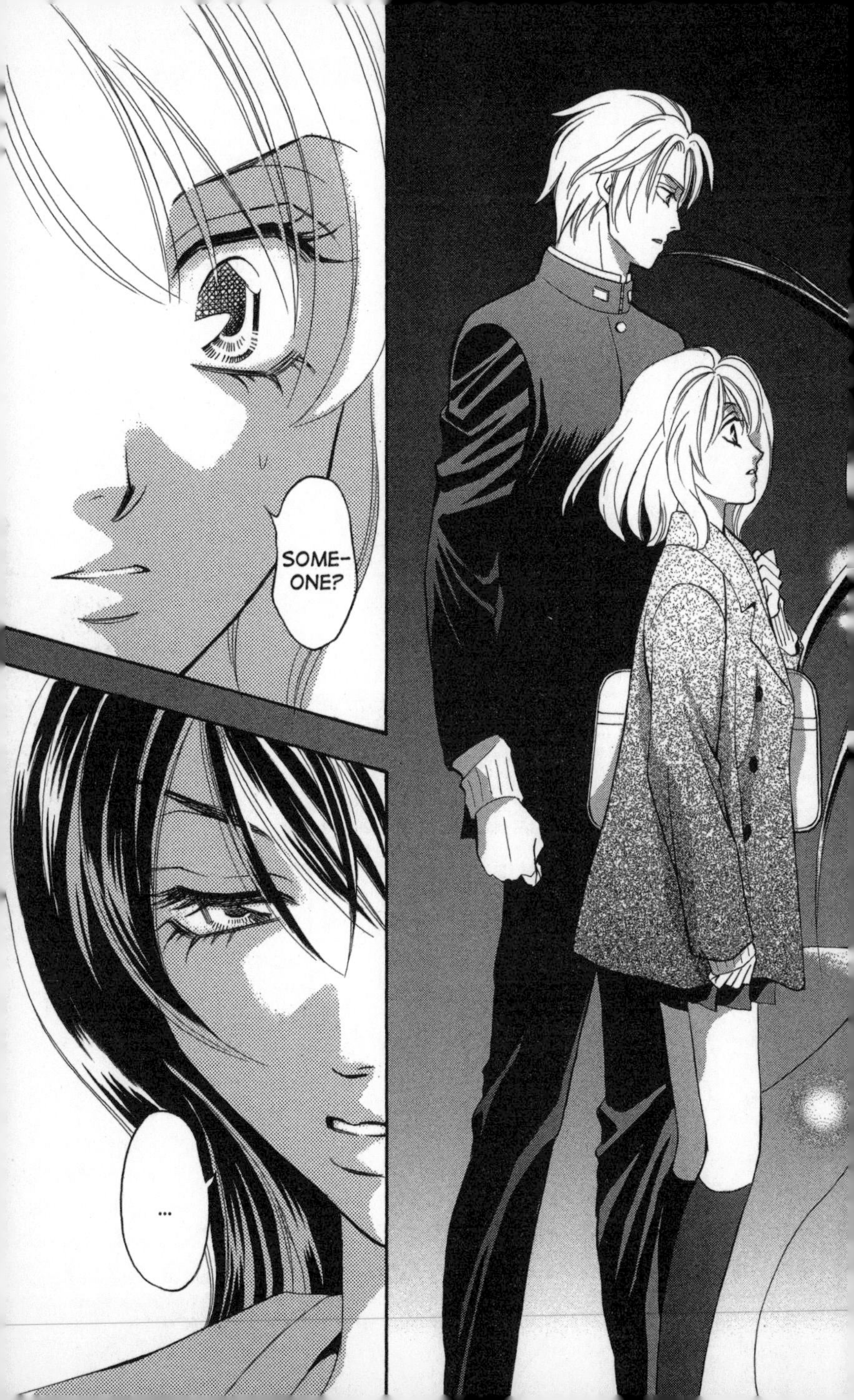
SOME-
ONE?
...

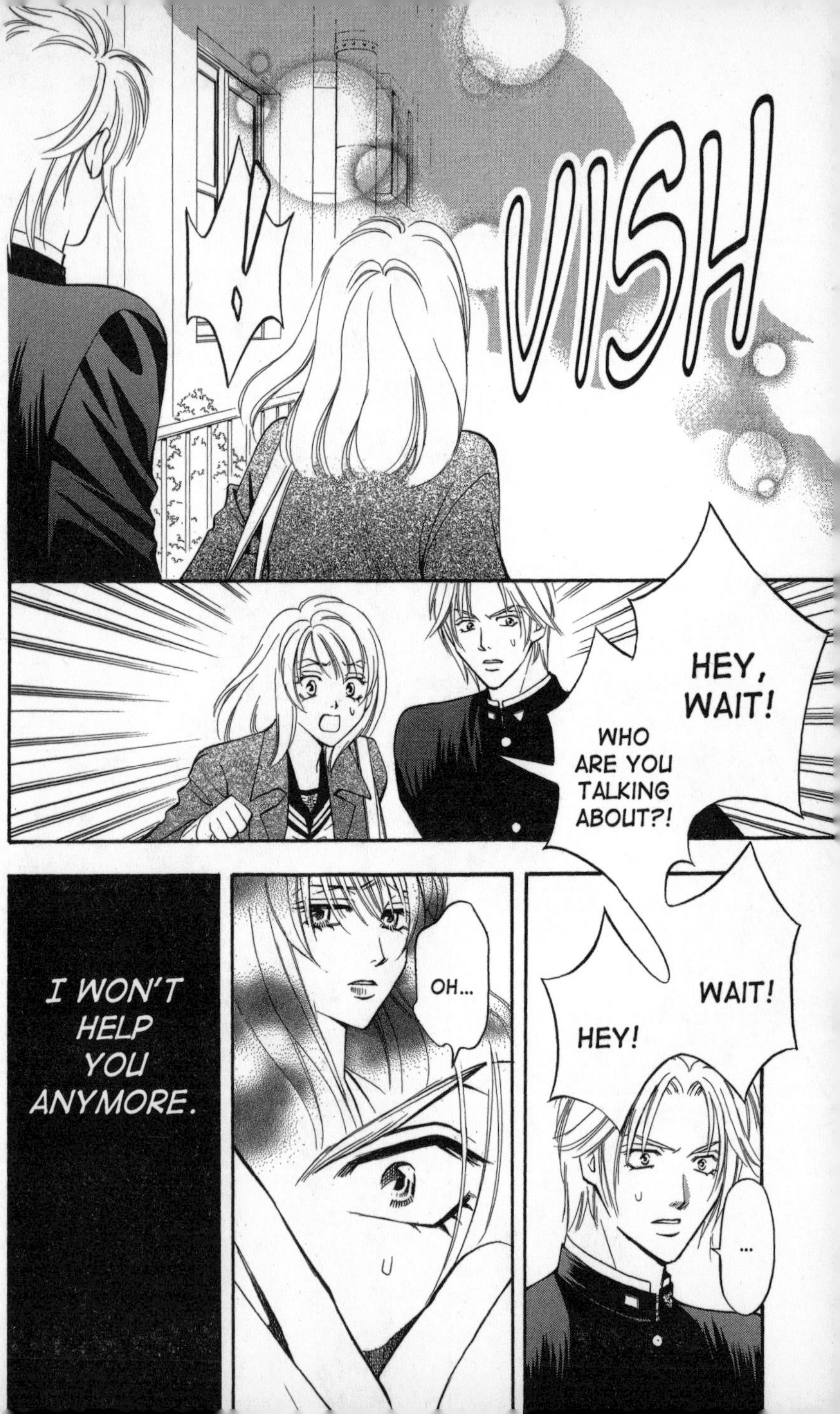
VISH
!
HEY, WAIT!
WHO ARE YOU TALKING ABOUT?!
WAIT!
HEY!
...
OH...
I WON'T HELP YOU ANYMORE.

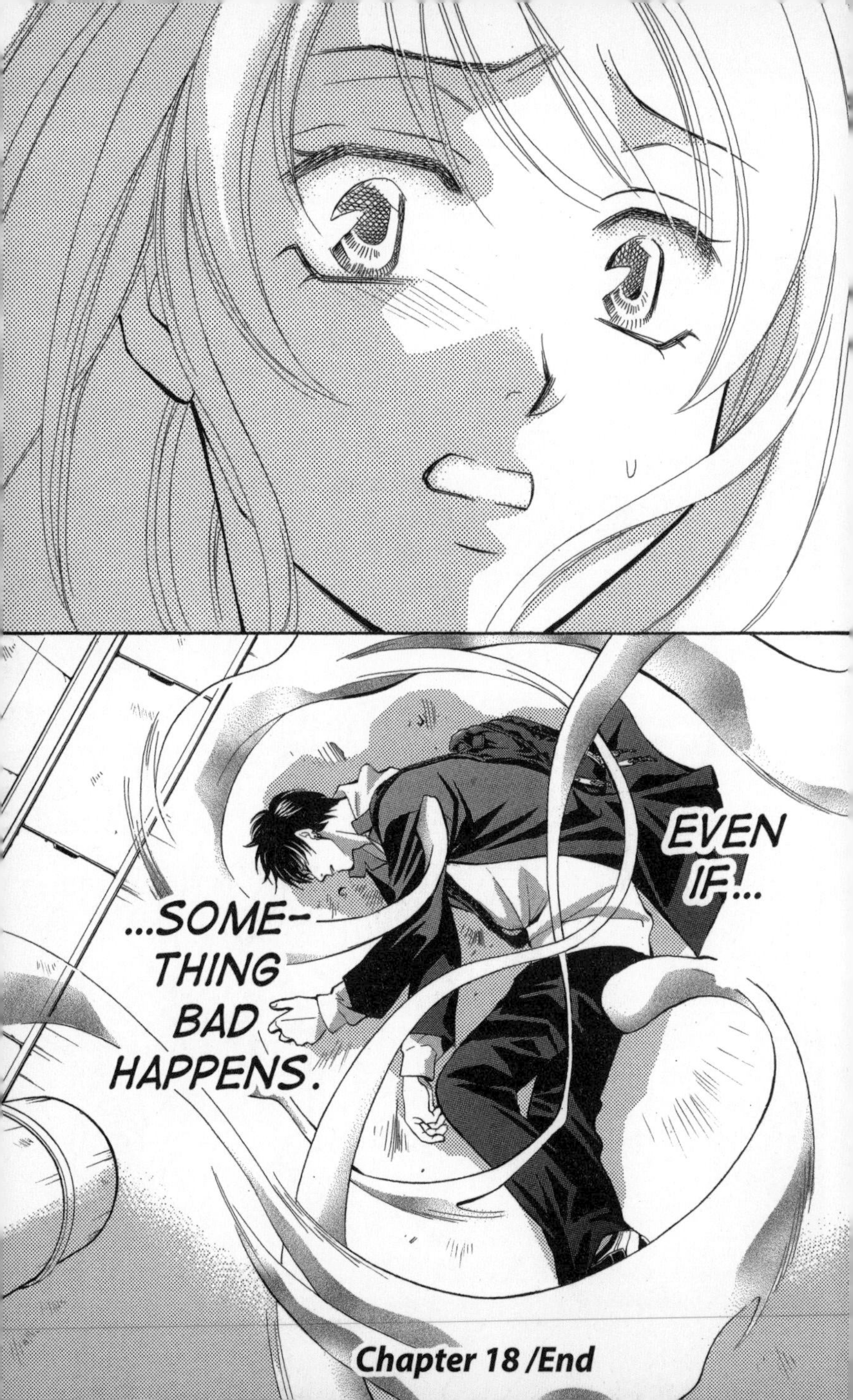
EVEN IF...
...SOME-
THING
BAD
HAPPENS.
Chapter 18 /End

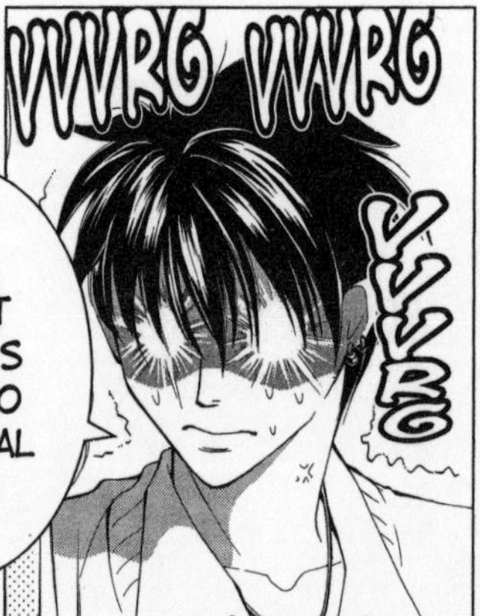
VVVRG VVVRG
WHAT MAKES ME SO SPECIAL ?!

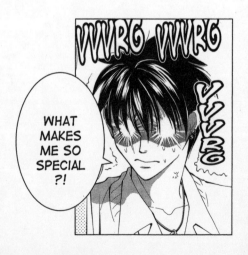

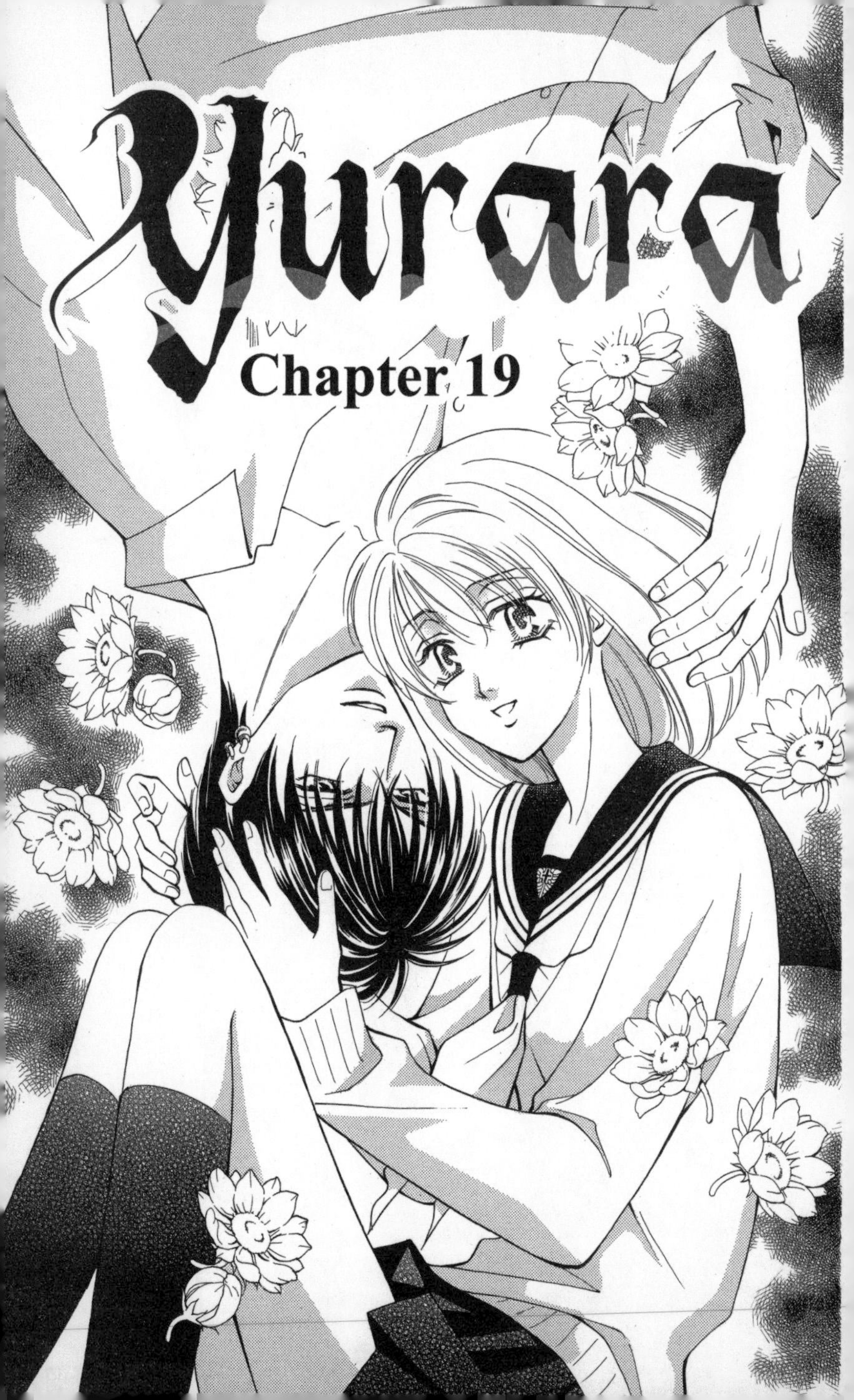
Yurara
Chapter 19

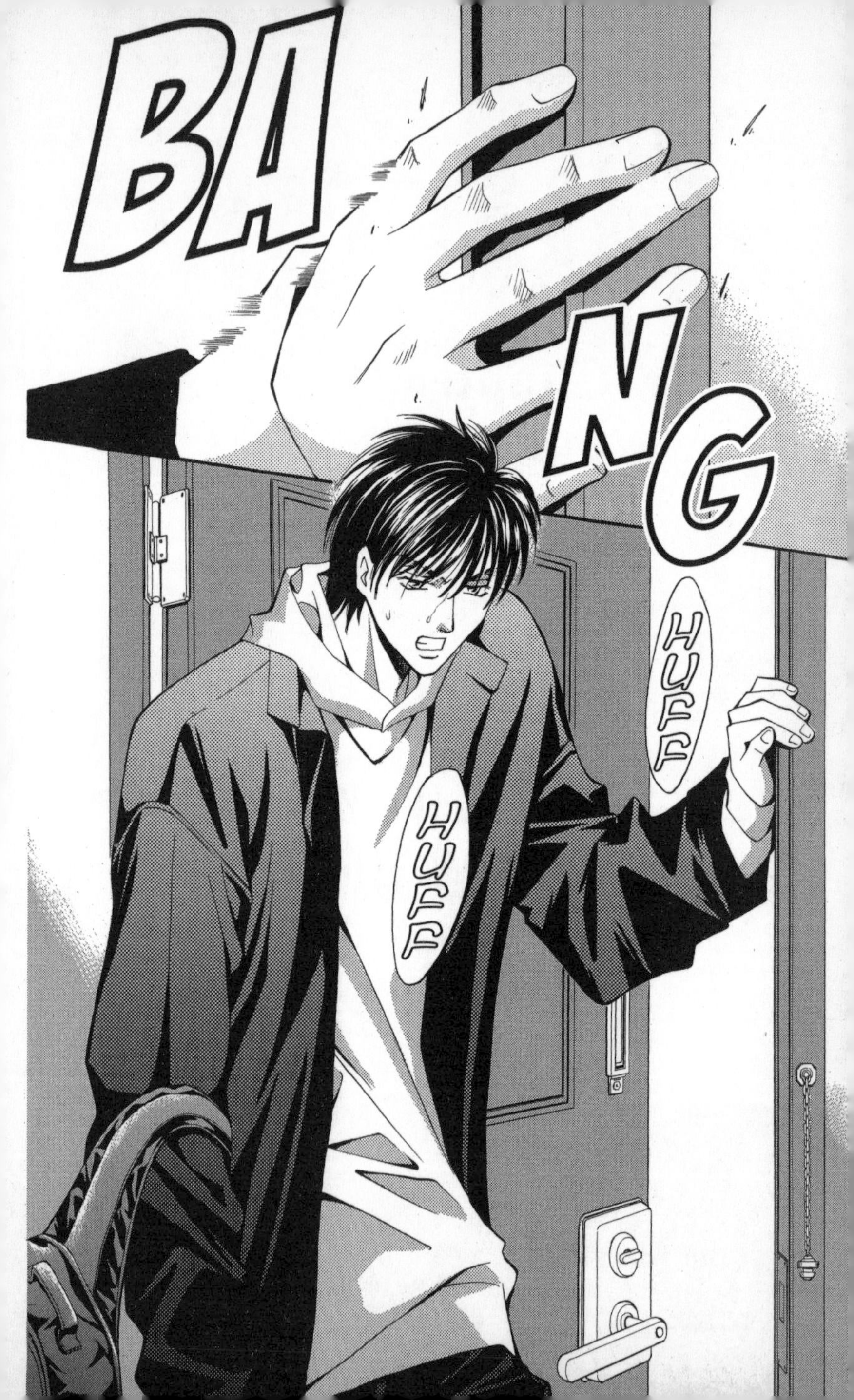
BANG
HUFF
HUFF

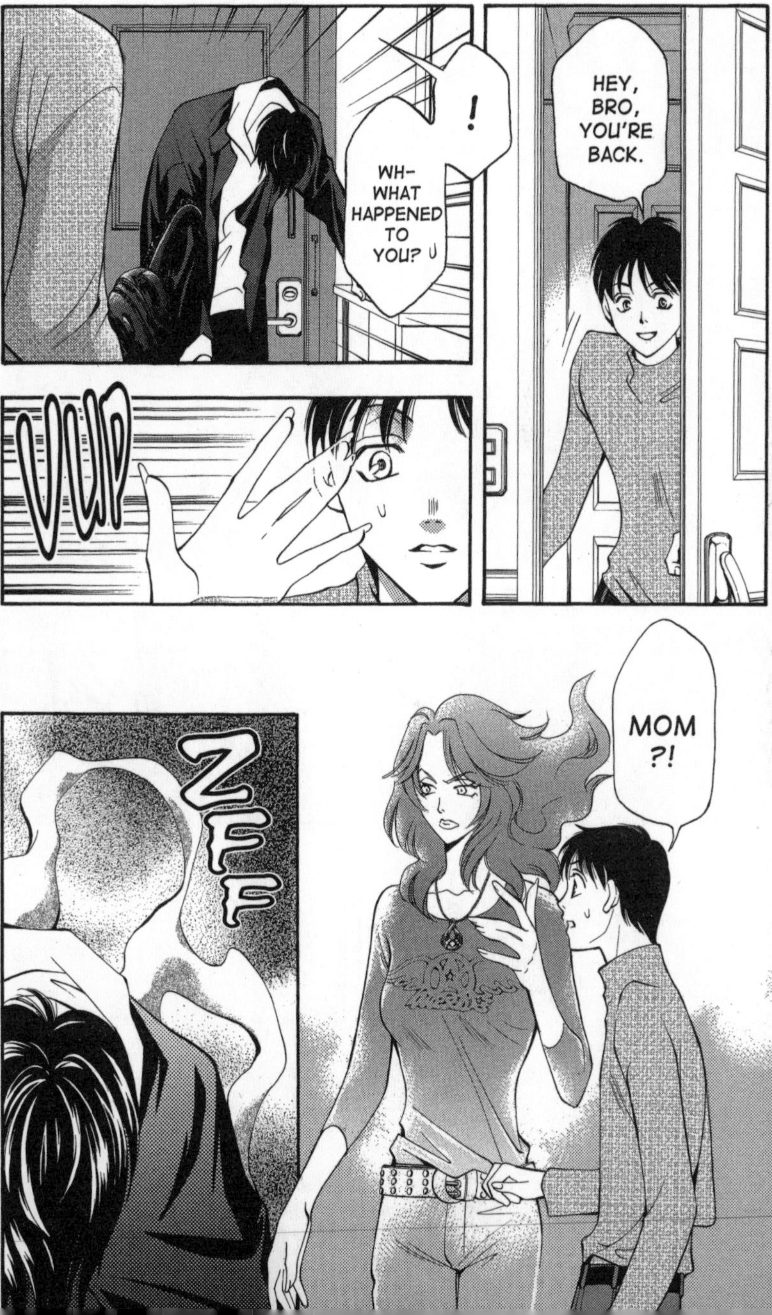
HEY, BRO, YOU'RE BACK.
!
WH-WHAT HAPPENED TO YOU?
VUP
MOM ?!
ZFF

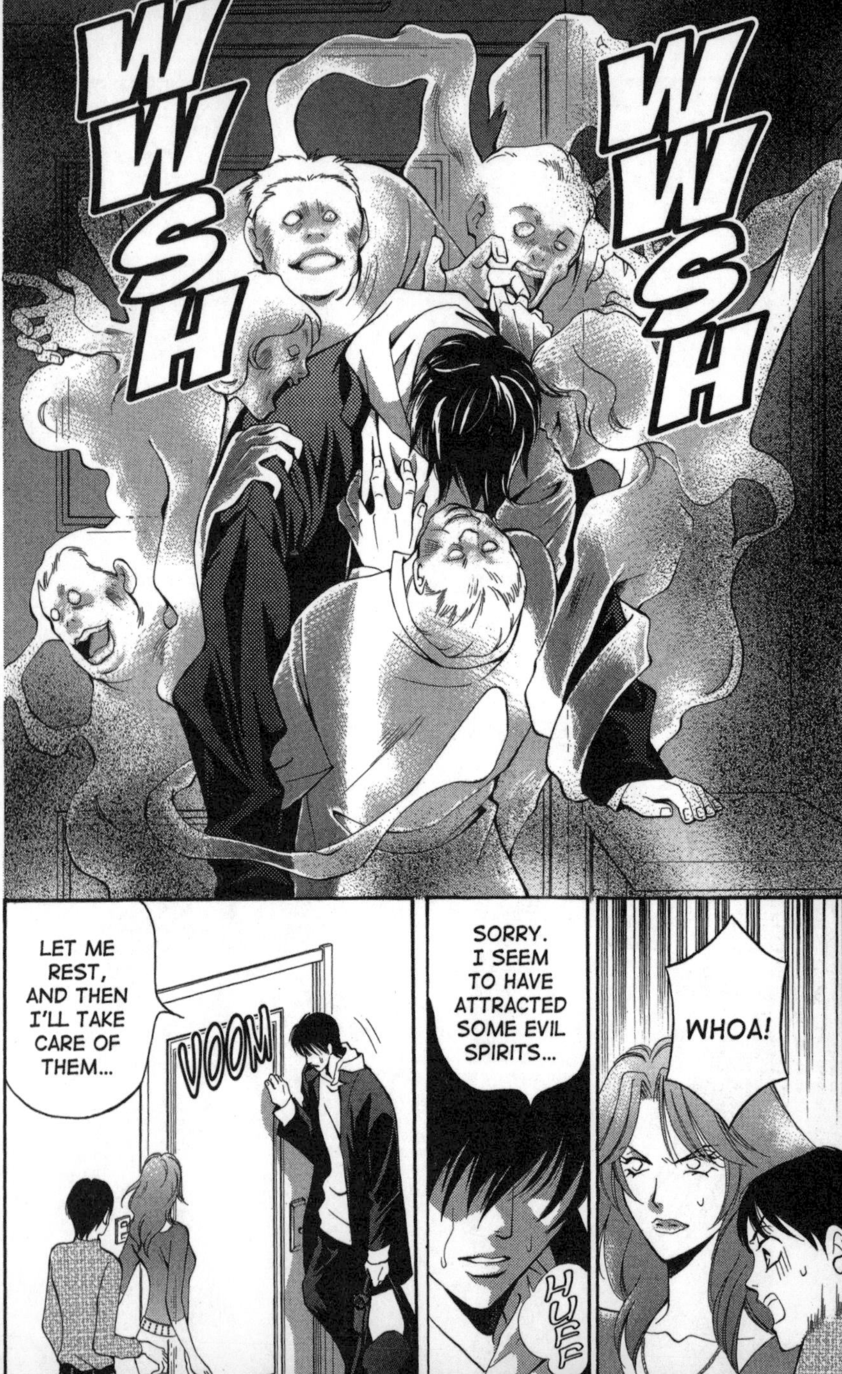
WWSH
WWSH
WHOA!
SORRY. I SEEM TO HAVE ATTRACTED SOME EVIL SPIRITS...
HUFF
LET ME REST, AND THEN I'LL TAKE CARE OF THEM...
VOOM

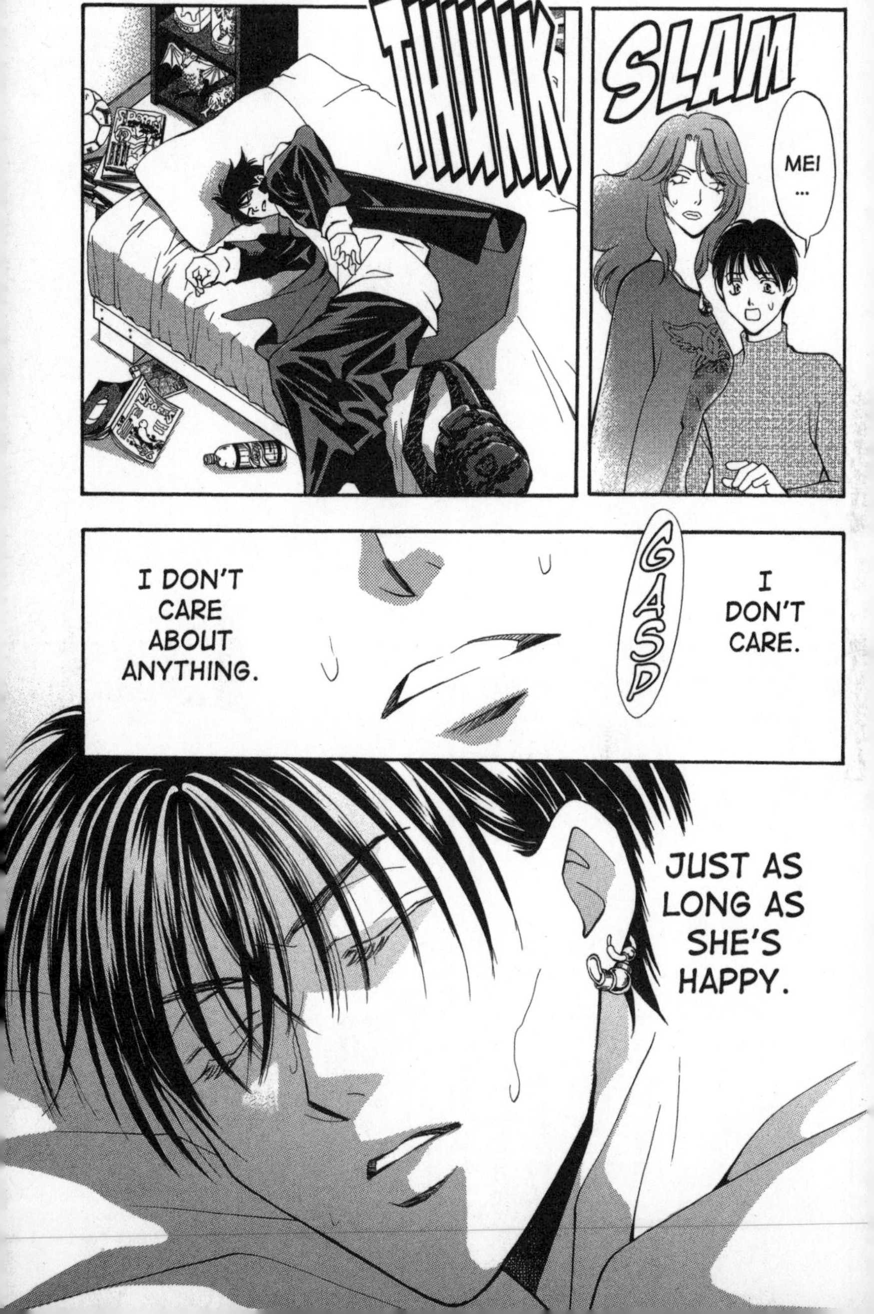
SLAM
MEI ...
THUNK
I DON'T CARE.
GASP
I DON'T CARE ABOUT ANYTHING.
JUST AS LONG AS SHE'S HAPPY.

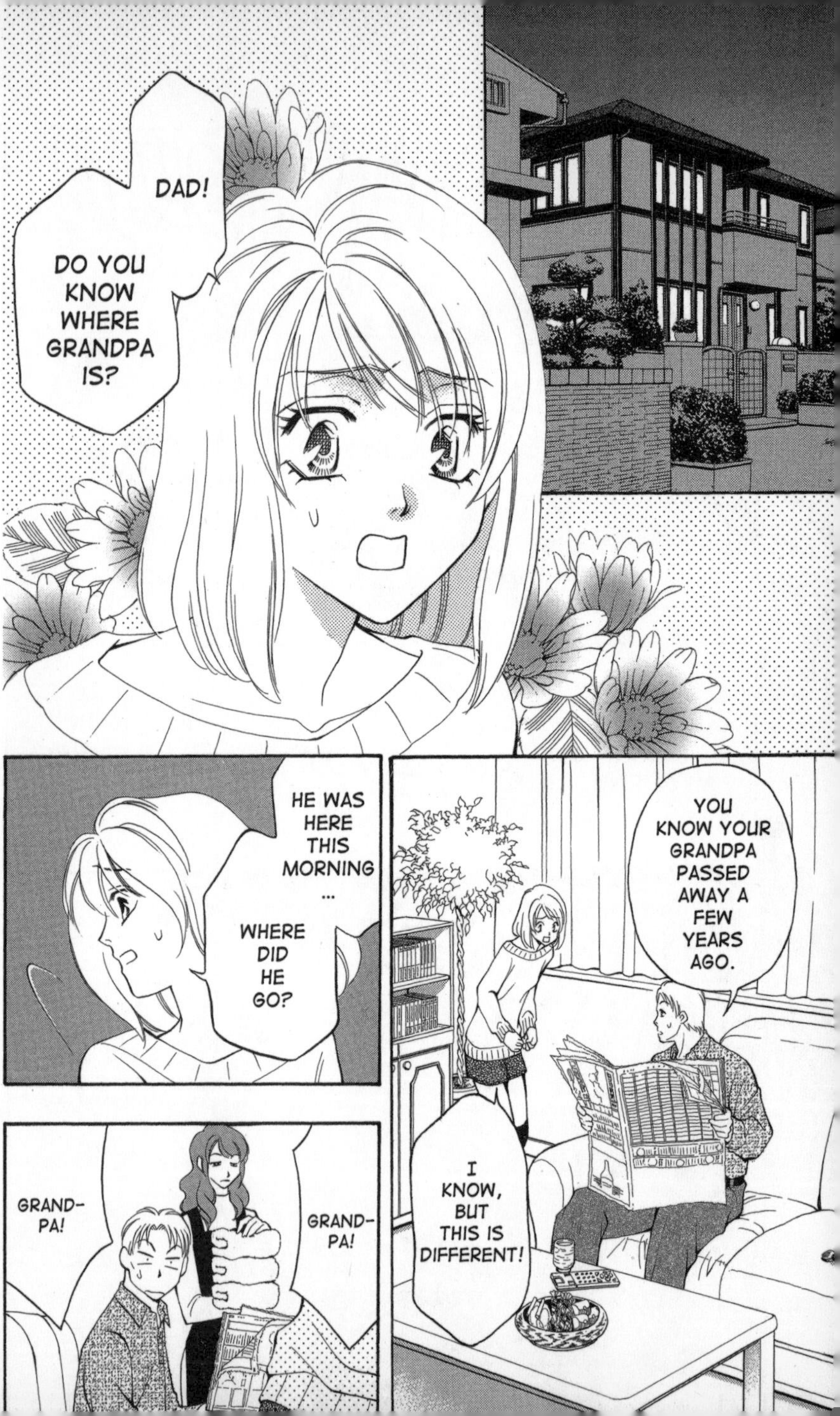
DAD!
DO YOU KNOW WHERE GRANDPA IS?
YOU KNOW YOUR GRANDPA PASSED AWAY A FEW YEARS AGO.
I KNOW, BUT THIS IS DIFFERENT!
HE WAS HERE THIS MORNING ...
WHERE DID HE GO?
GRAND-PA!
GRAND-PA!

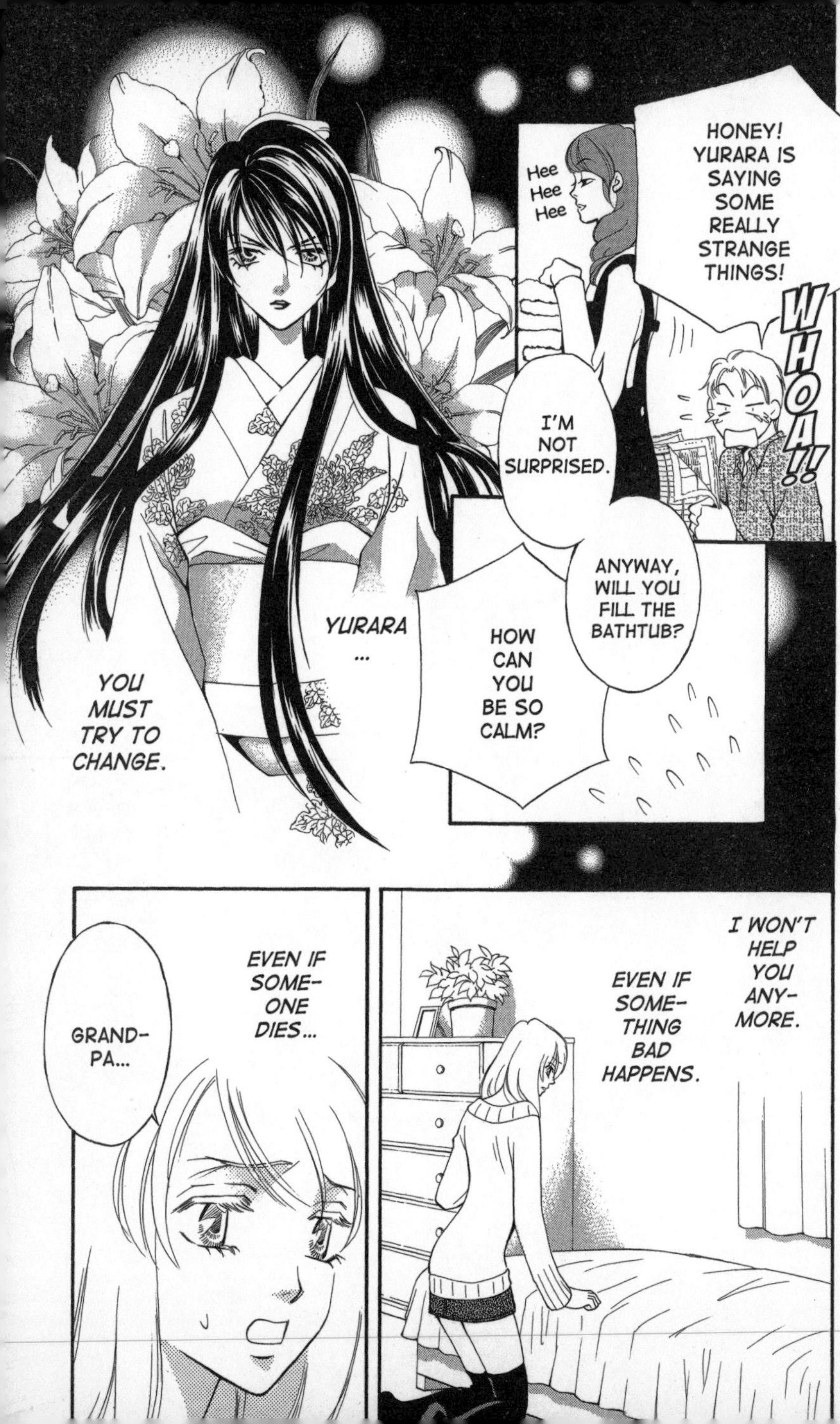
HONEY! YURARA IS SAYING SOME REALLY STRANGE THINGS!
Hee Hee Hee
WHOA!!
I'M NOT SURPRISED.
ANYWAY, WILL YOU FILL THE BATHTUB?
HOW CAN YOU BE SO CALM?
YURARA ...
YOU MUST TRY TO CHANGE.
I WON'T HELP YOU ANY-MORE.
EVEN IF SOME-THING BAD HAPPENS.
EVEN IF SOME-ONE DIES...
GRAND-PA...

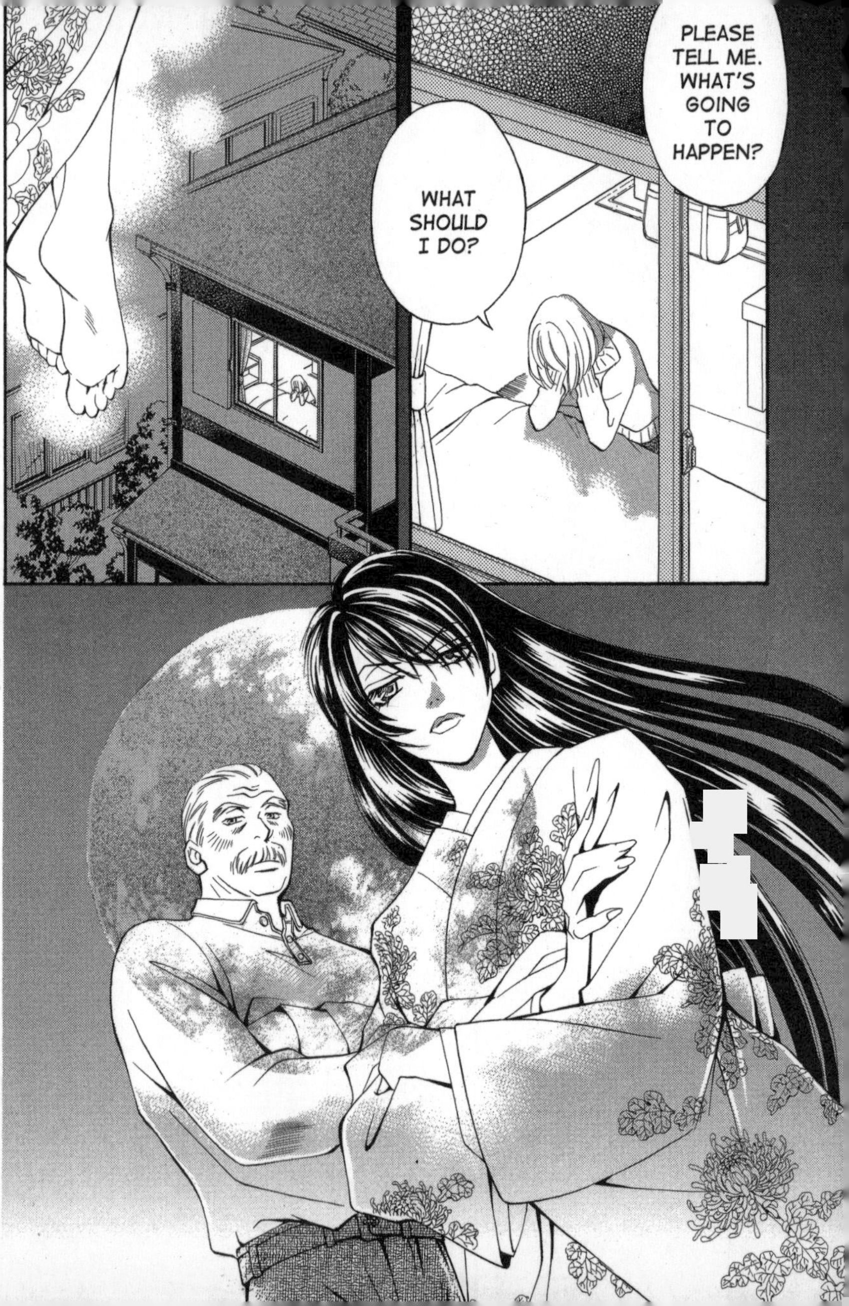
PLEASE TELL ME. WHAT'S GOING TO HAPPEN?
WHAT SHOULD I DO?

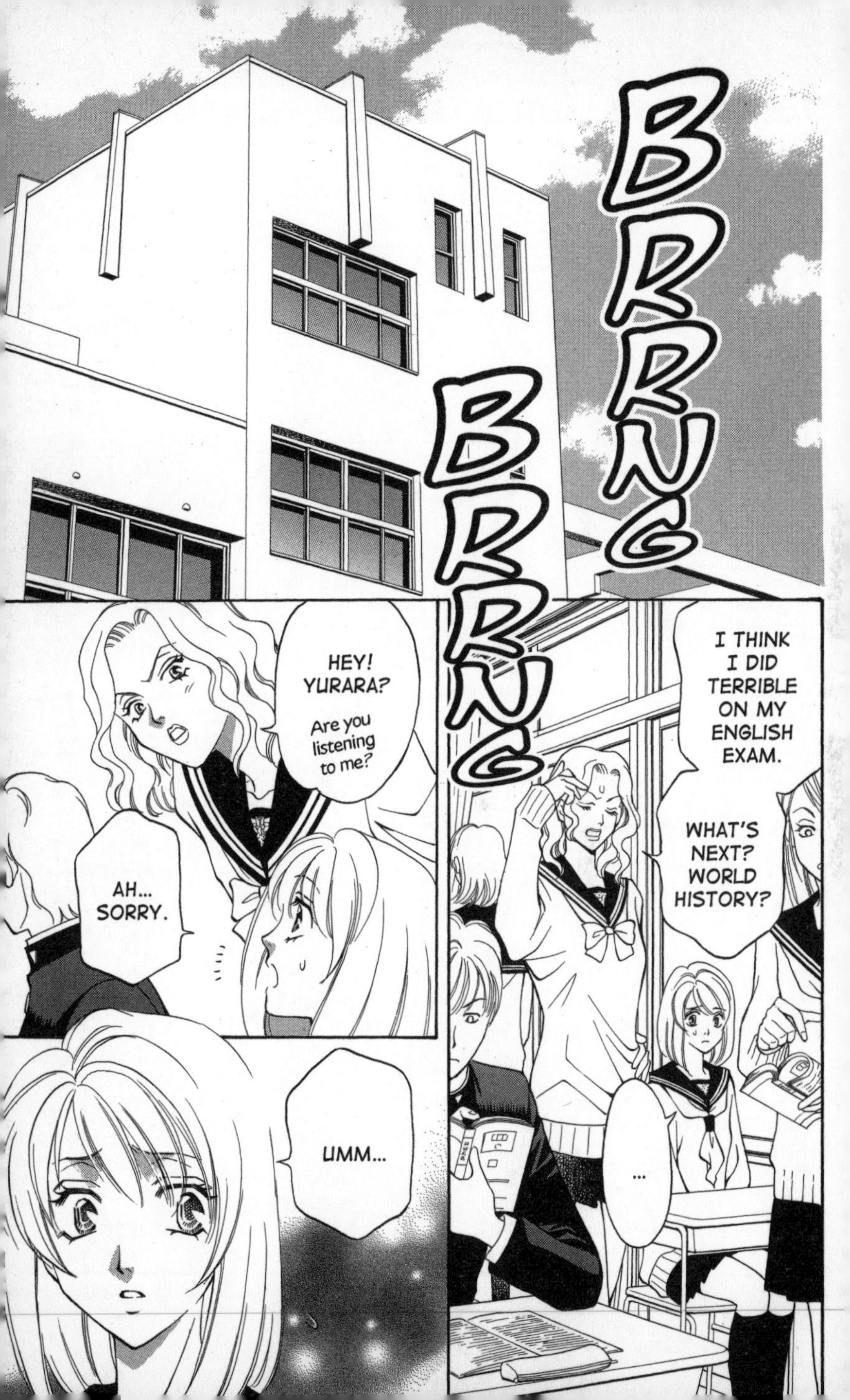
BRRRNG
BRRRNG
I THINK I DID TERRIBLE ON MY ENGLISH EXAM.
WHAT'S NEXT? WORLD HISTORY?
...
HEY! YURARA?
Are you listening to me?
AH... SORRY.
UMM...

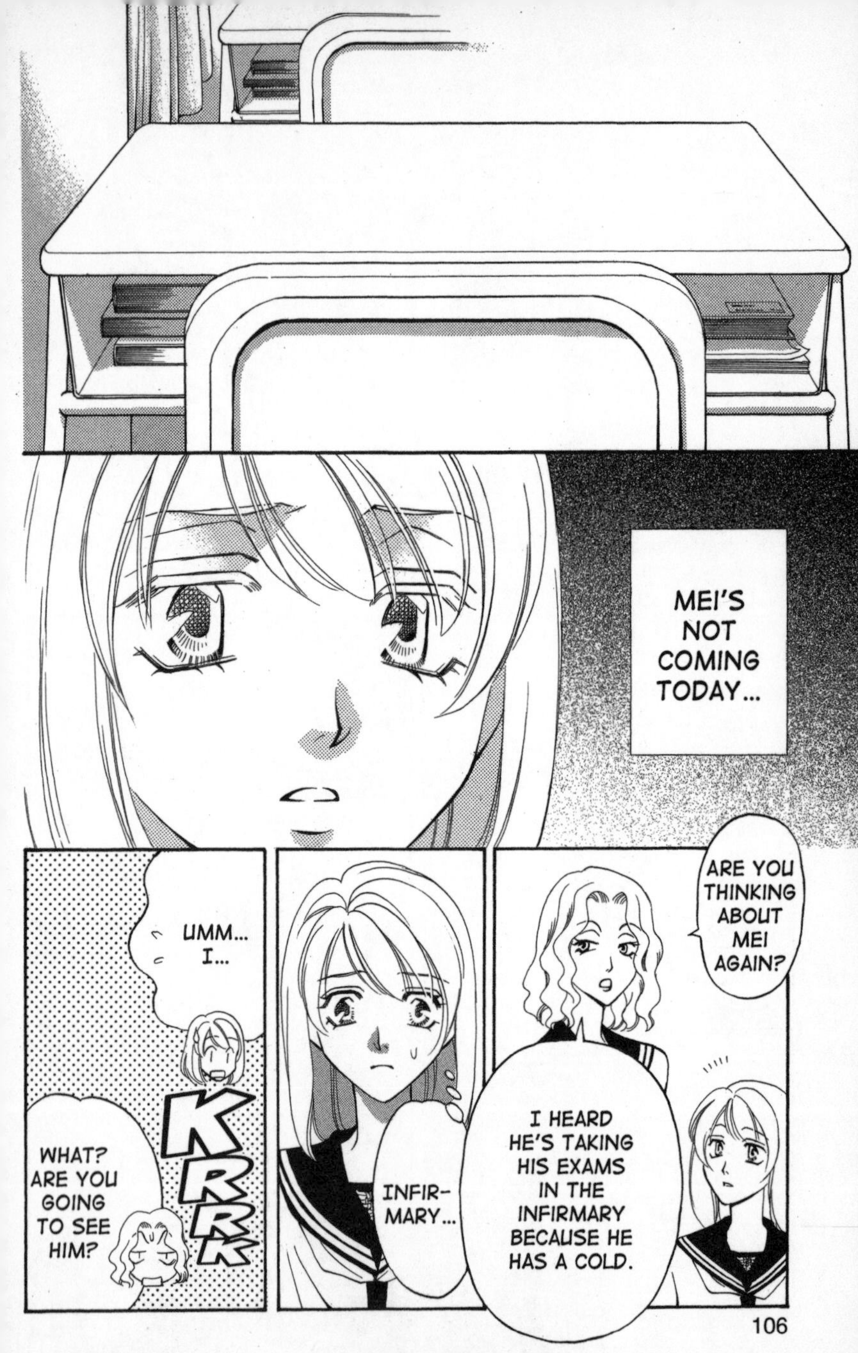
MEI'S NOT COMING TODAY...
ARE YOU THINKING ABOUT MEI AGAIN?
I HEARD HE'S TAKING HIS EXAMS IN THE INFIRMARY BECAUSE HE HAS A COLD.
INFIR-MARY...
UMM... I...
KRRK
WHAT? ARE YOU GOING TO SEE HIM?

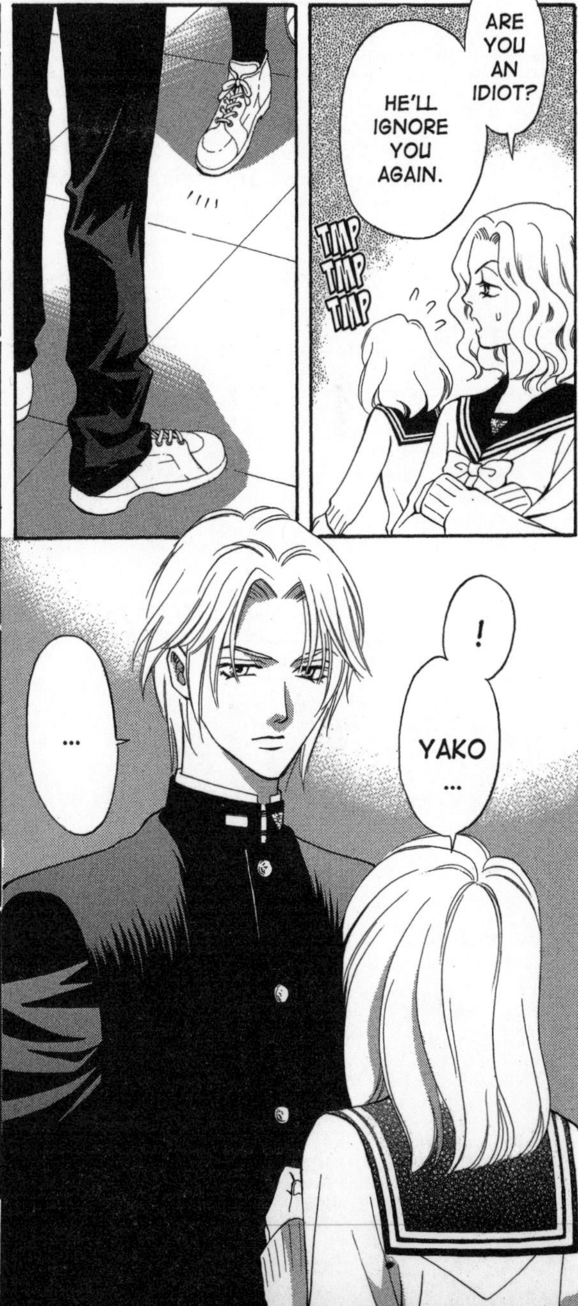
ARE YOU AN IDIOT?
HE'LL IGNORE YOU AGAIN.
TMP TMP TMP
!
YAKO ...
...

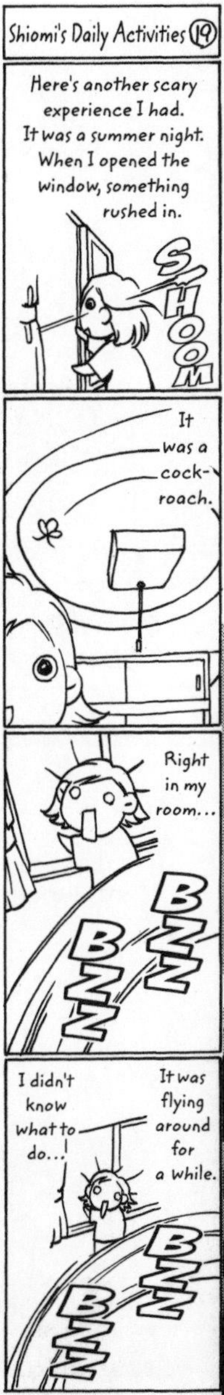
Shiomi's Daily Activities 19
Here's another scary experience I had. It was a summer night. When I opened the window, something rushed in.
SHOOM
It was a cock-roach.
Right in my room...
BZZ BZZ
It was flying around for a while.
I didn't know what to do...!
BZZ BZZ

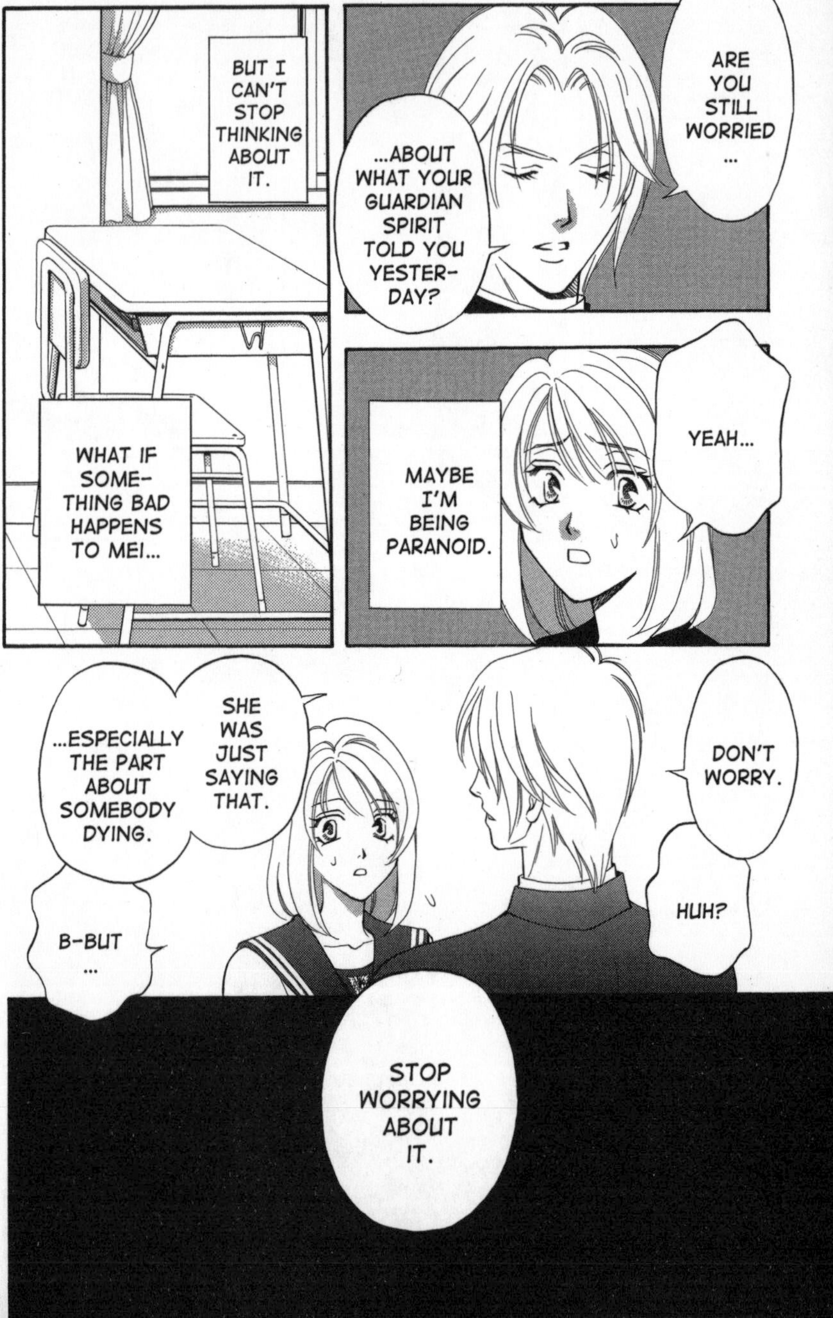
ARE YOU STILL WORRIED ...
...ABOUT WHAT YOUR GUARDIAN SPIRIT TOLD YOU YESTER-DAY?
YEAH...
MAYBE I'M BEING PARANOID.
BUT I CAN'T STOP THINKING ABOUT IT.
WHAT IF SOME-THING BAD HAPPENS TO MEI...
DON'T WORRY.
SHE WAS JUST SAYING THAT.
...ESPECIALLY THE PART ABOUT SOMEBODY DYING.
HUH?
B-BUT ...
STOP WORRYING ABOUT IT.

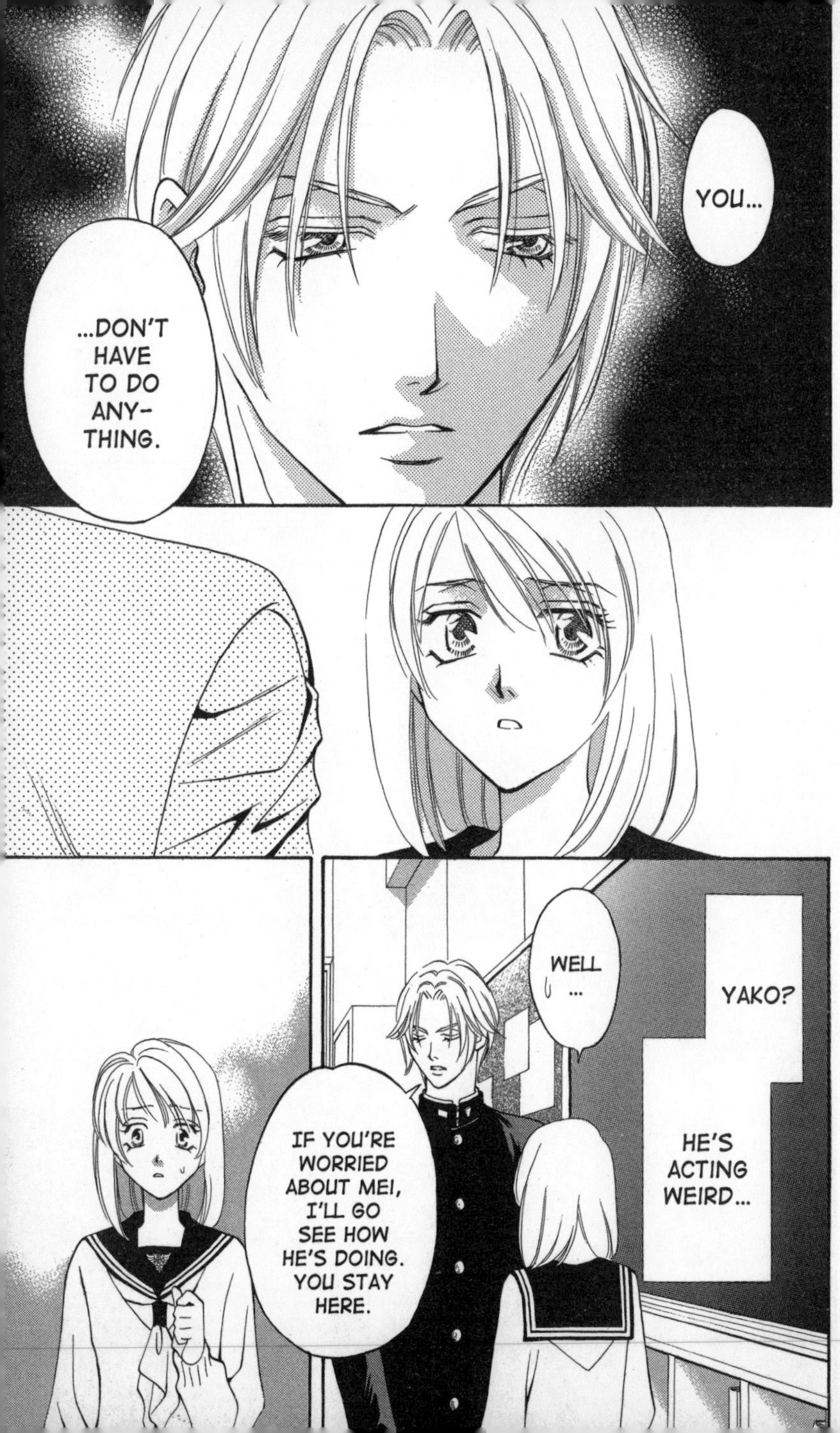
YOU...
...DON'T HAVE TO DO ANY-THING.
YAKO?
HE'S ACTING WEIRD...
WELL ...
IF YOU'RE WORRIED ABOUT MEI, I'LL GO SEE HOW HE'S DOING. YOU STAY HERE.

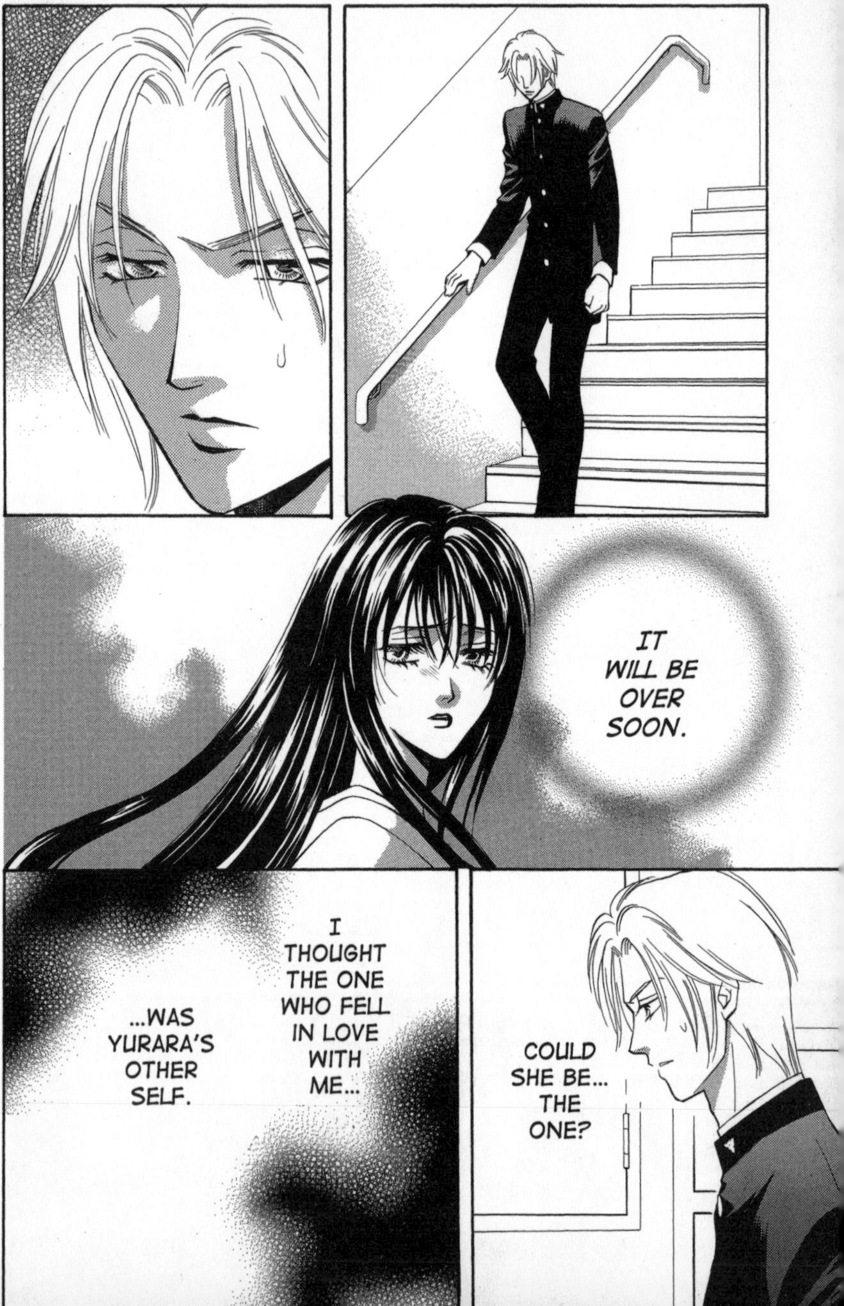
IT WILL BE OVER SOON.
COULD SHE BE... THE ONE?
I THOUGHT THE ONE WHO FELL IN LOVE WITH ME...
...WAS YURARA'S OTHER SELF.

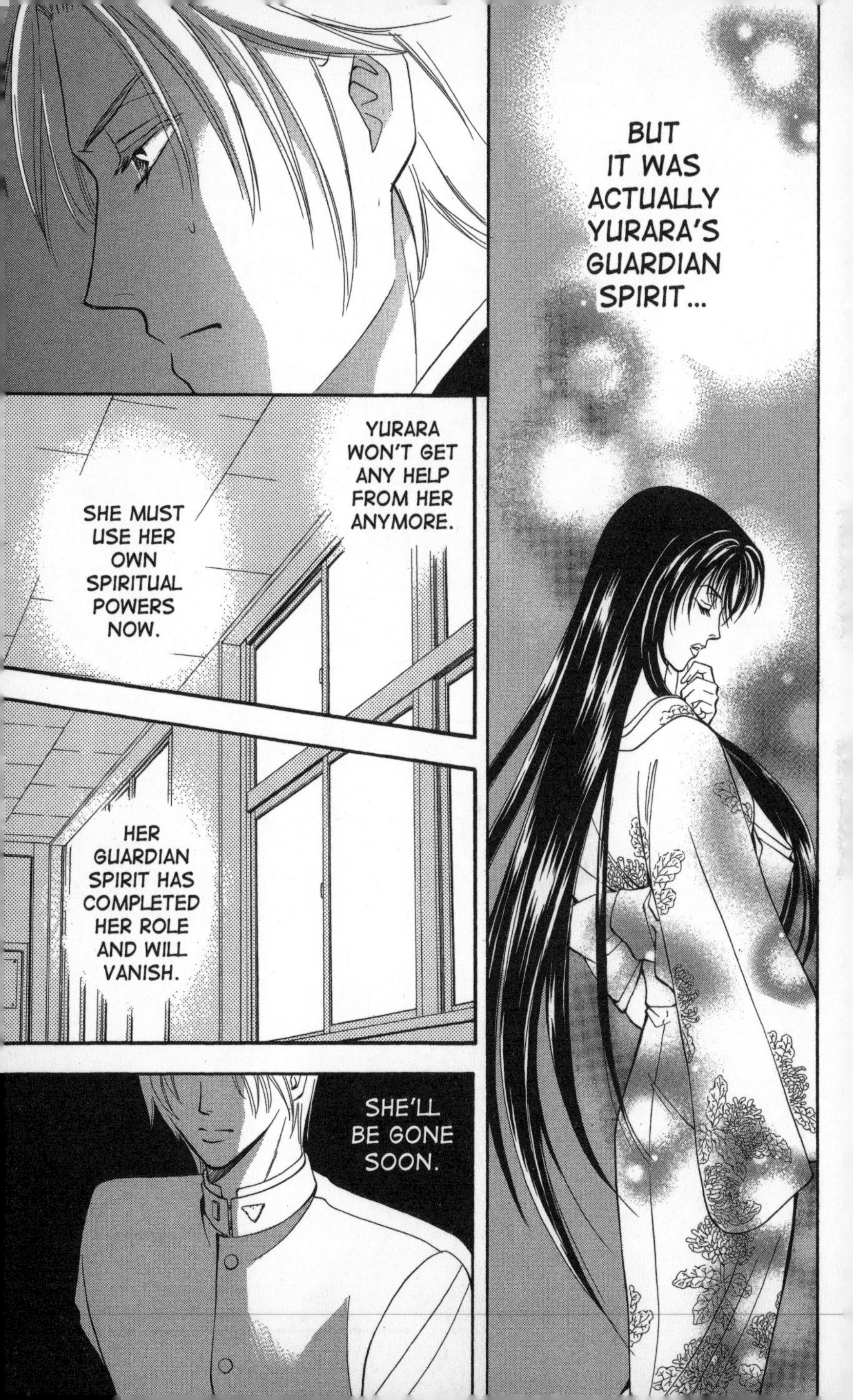
BUT IT WAS ACTUALLY YURARA'S GUARDIAN SPIRIT...
YURARA WON'T GET ANY HELP FROM HER ANYMORE.
SHE MUST USE HER OWN SPIRITUAL POWERS NOW.
HER GUARDIAN SPIRIT HAS COMPLETED HER ROLE AND WILL VANISH.
SHE'LL BE GONE SOON.

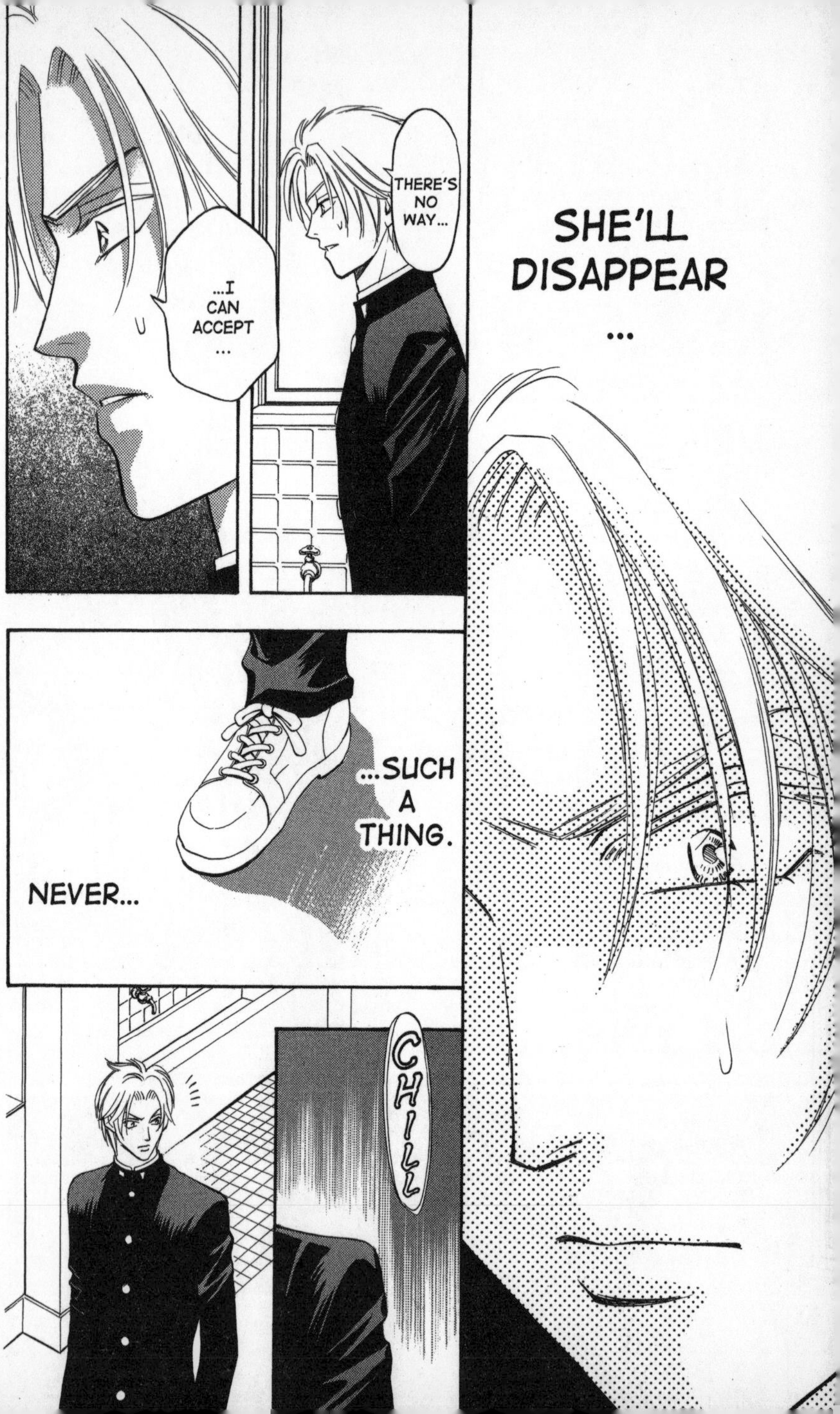
SHE'LL DISAPPEAR ...
THERE'S NO WAY...
...I CAN ACCEPT ...
...SUCH A THING.
NEVER...
CHILL

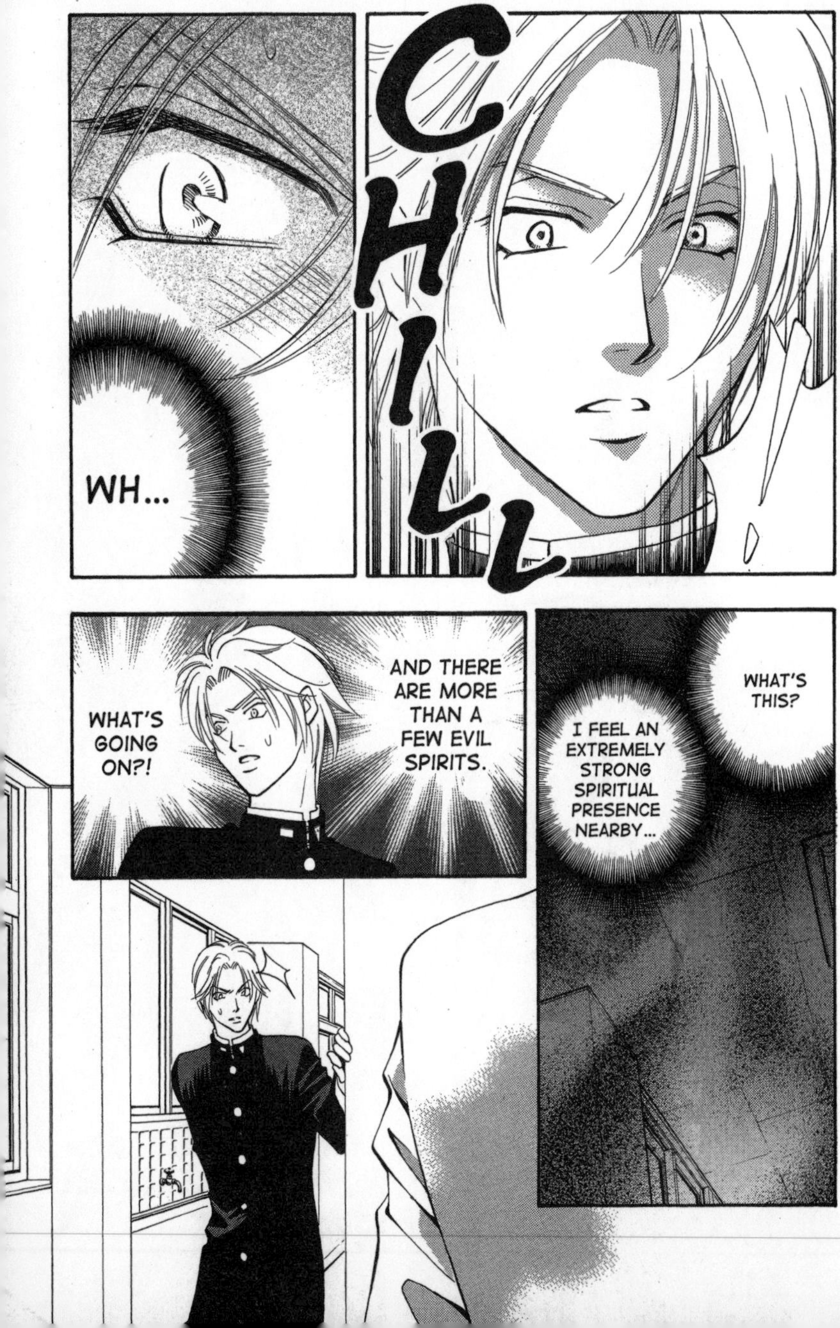
CHILL
WH...
WHAT'S THIS?
I FEEL AN EXTREMELY STRONG SPIRITUAL PRESENCE NEARBY...
AND THERE ARE MORE THAN A FEW EVIL SPIRITS.
WHAT'S GOING ON?!

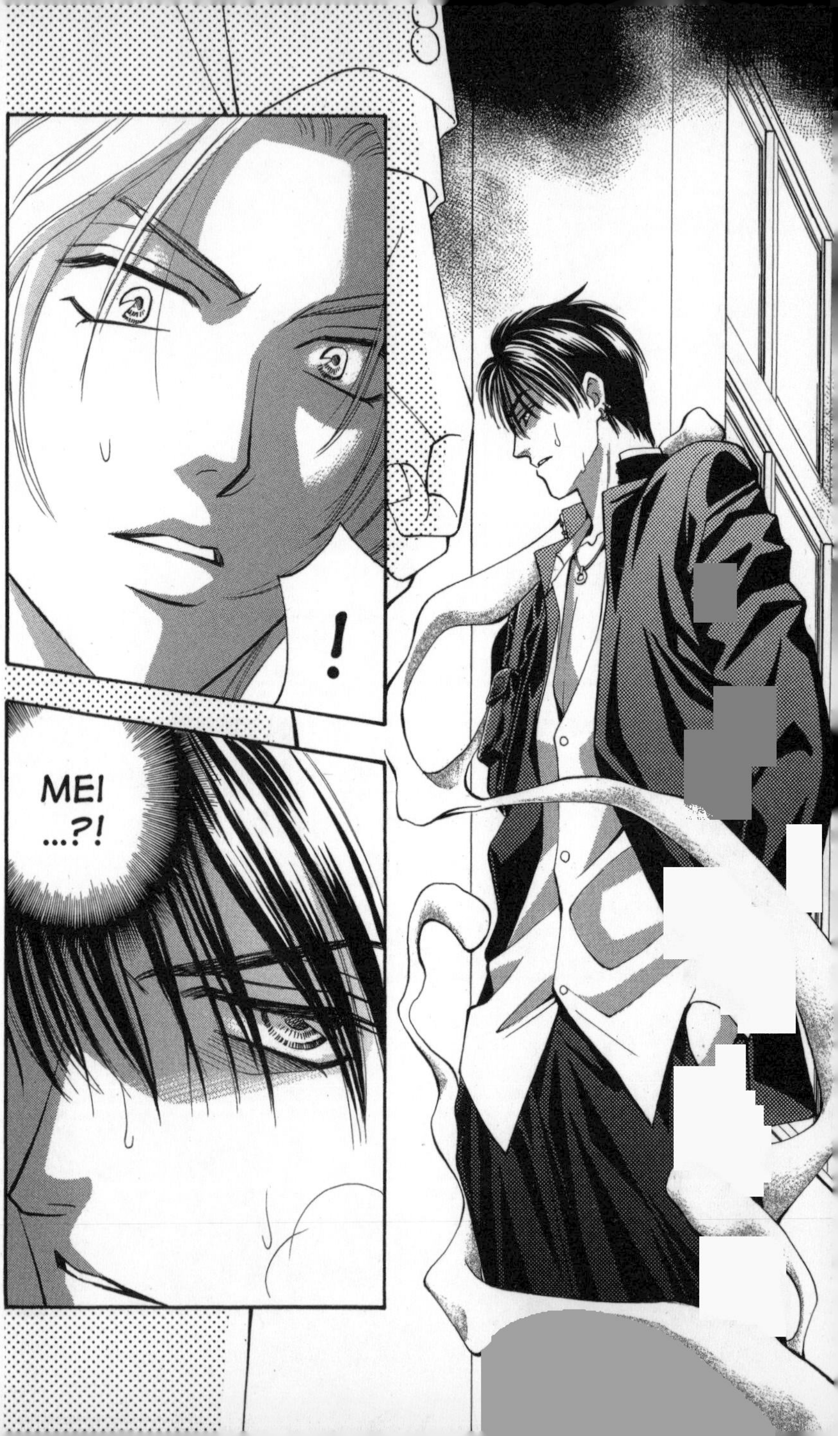
!
MEI ...?!

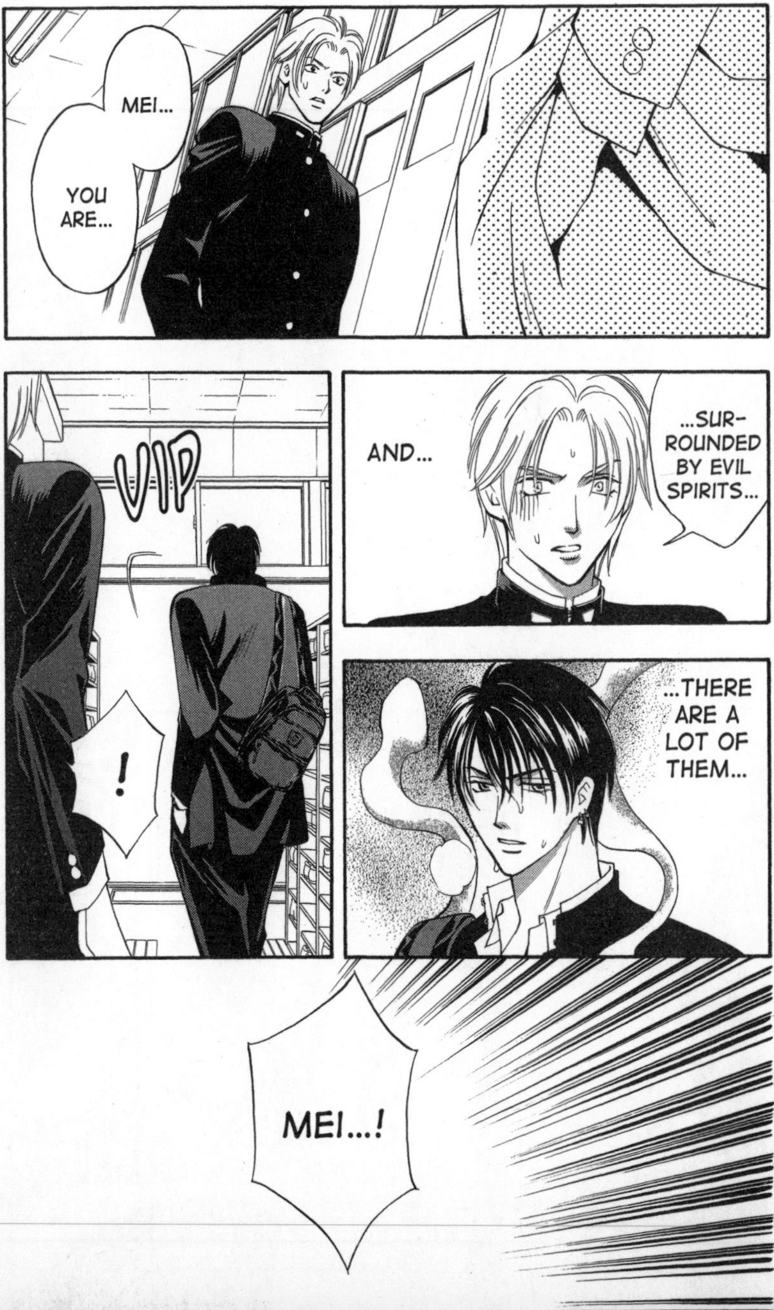
MEI...
YOU ARE...
...SUR-ROUNDED BY EVIL SPIRITS...
AND...
...THERE ARE A LOT OF THEM...
VIP
!
MEI...!

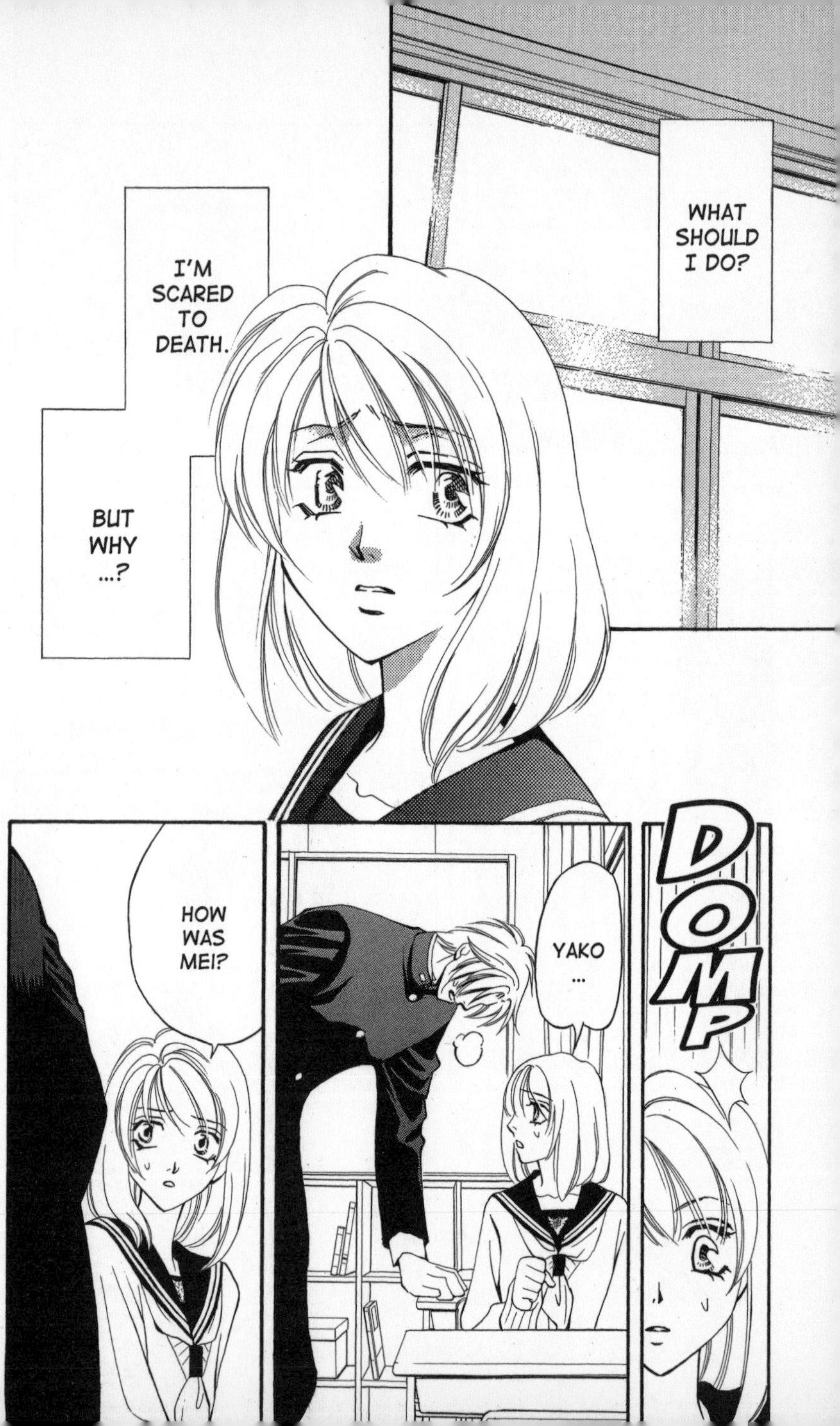
WHAT SHOULD I DO?
I'M SCARED TO DEATH.
BUT WHY ...?
DOMP
YAKO ...
HOW WAS MEI?

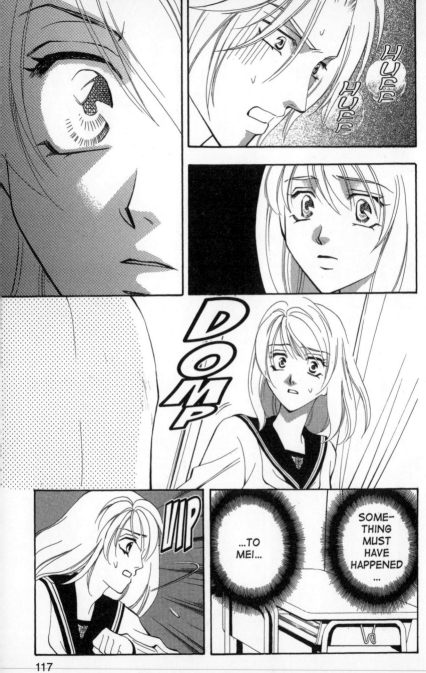

HUFF
HUFF
HUFF

D
O
M
P

VIP

...TO MEI...

SOME-
THING
MUST
HAVE
HAPPENED
...

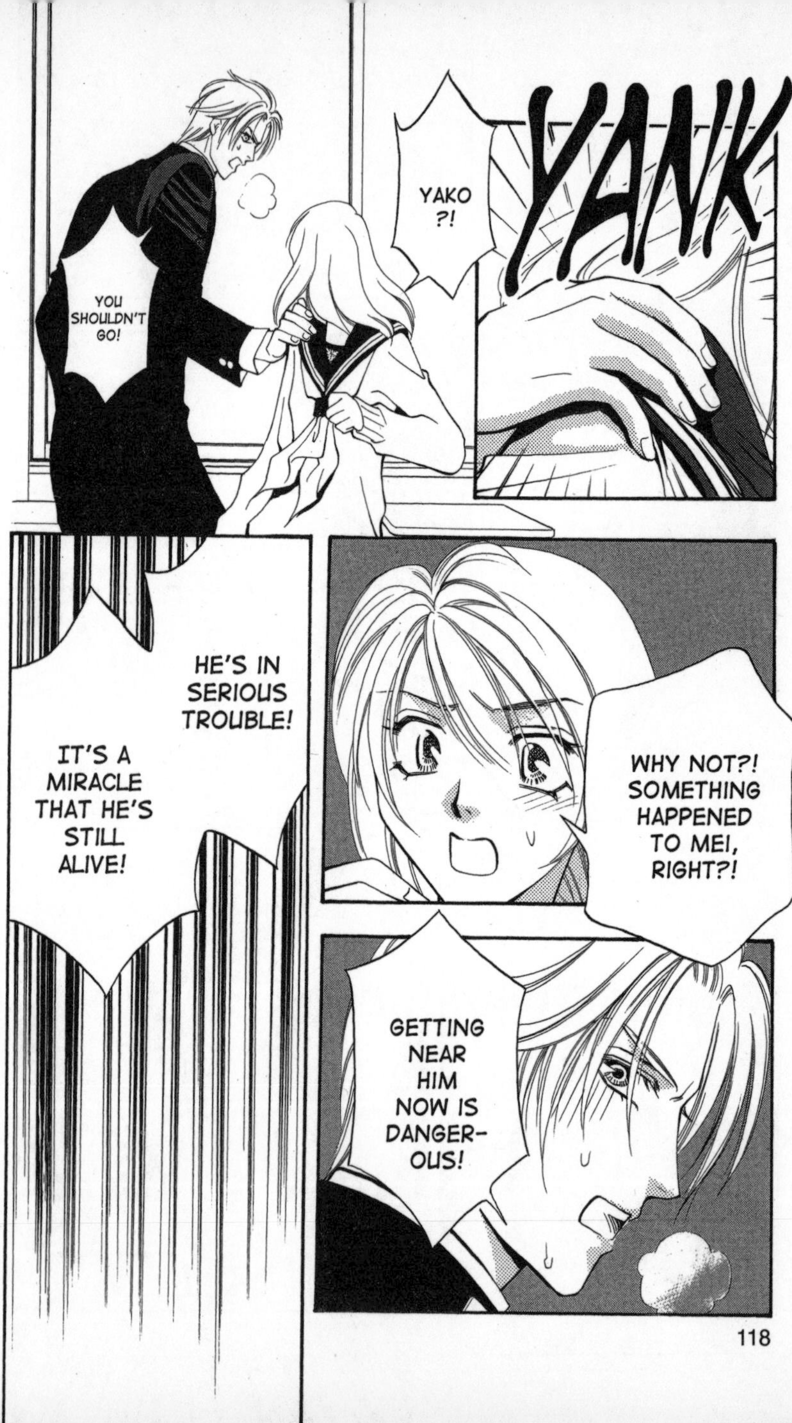
YANK
YAKO ?!
YOU SHOULDN'T GO!
WHY NOT?! SOMETHING HAPPENED TO MEI, RIGHT?!
GETTING NEAR HIM NOW IS DANGER-OUS!
HE'S IN SERIOUS TROUBLE!
IT'S A MIRACLE THAT HE'S STILL ALIVE!

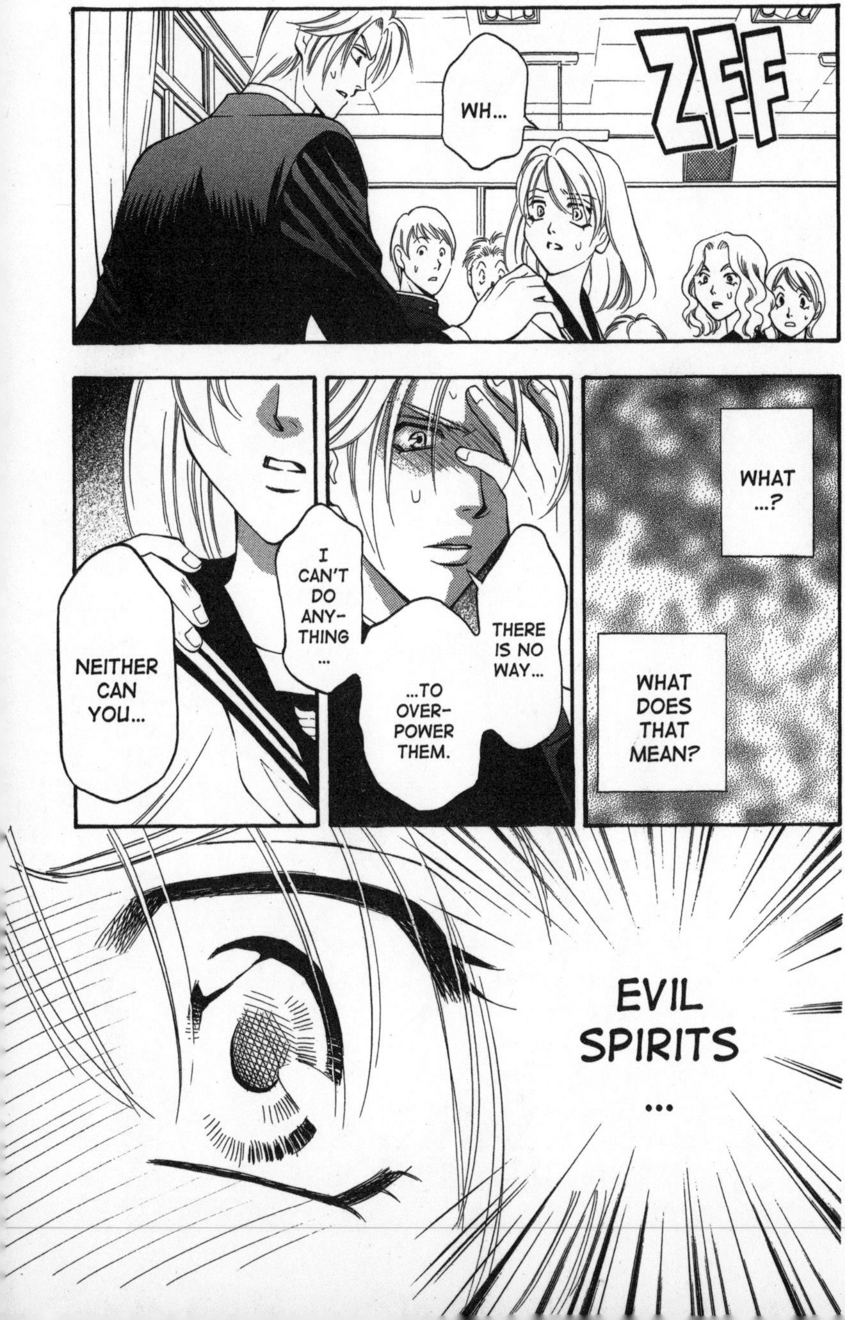
ZFF
WH...
WHAT ...?
WHAT DOES THAT MEAN?
THERE IS NO WAY...
...TO OVER-POWER THEM.
I CAN'T DO ANY-THING ...
NEITHER CAN YOU...
EVIL SPIRITS ...

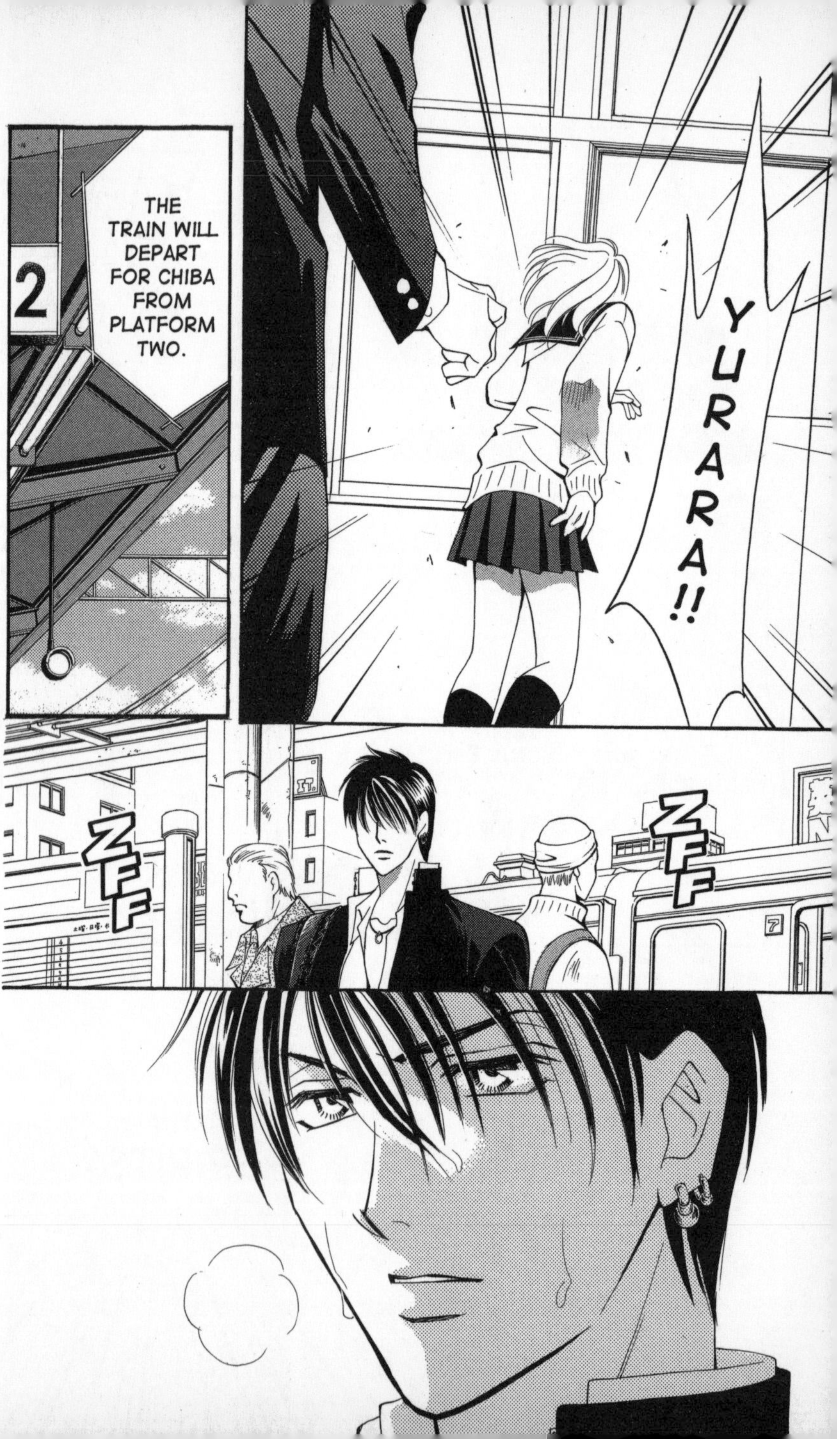
YURARA!!
THE TRAIN WILL DEPART FOR CHIBA FROM PLATFORM TWO.
2
ZFF
ZFF

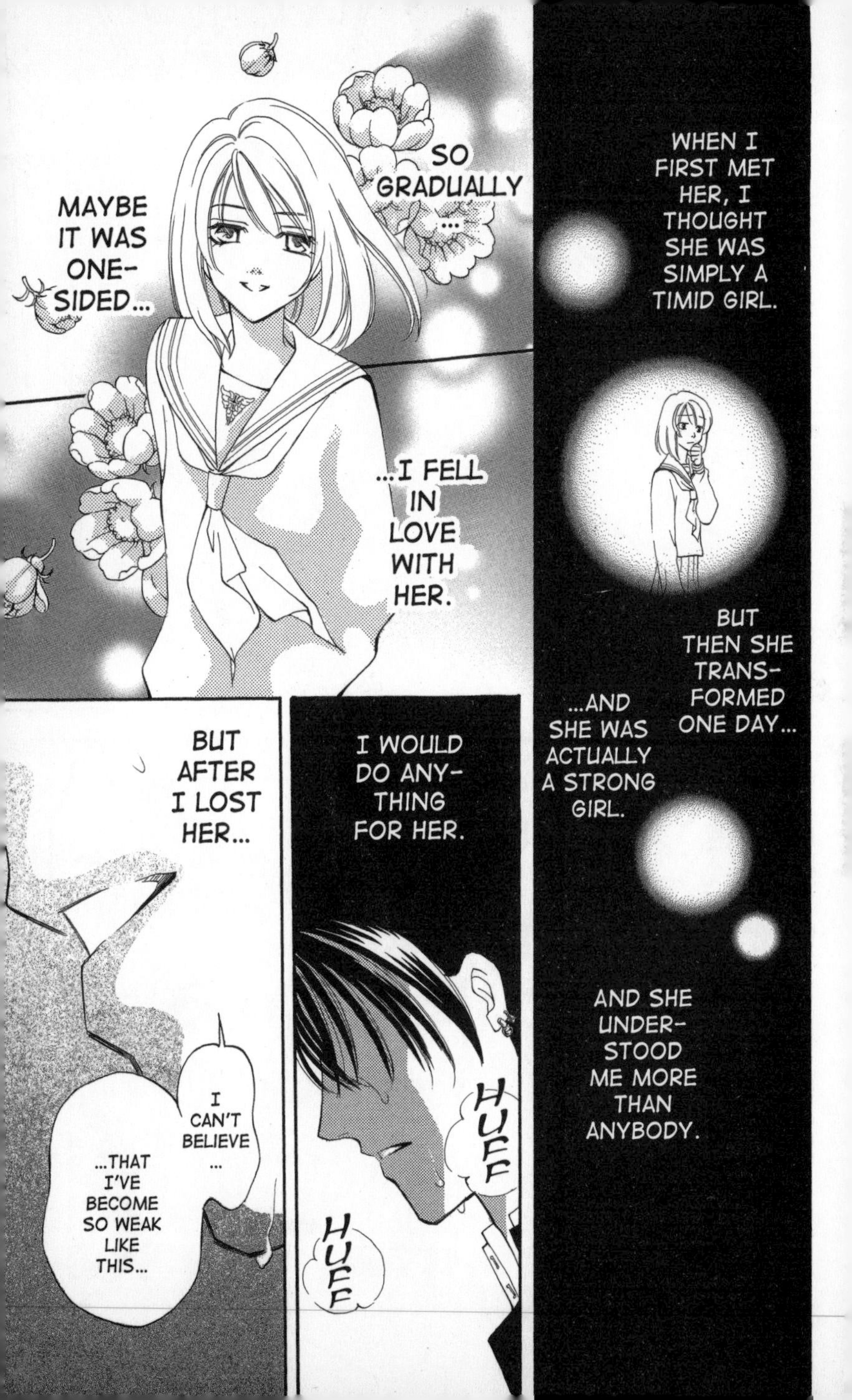
WHEN I FIRST MET HER, I THOUGHT SHE WAS SIMPLY A TIMID GIRL.
BUT THEN SHE TRANSFORMED ONE DAY...
...AND SHE WAS ACTUALLY A STRONG GIRL.
AND SHE UNDERSTOOD ME MORE THAN ANYBODY.
SO GRADUALLY...
MAYBE IT WAS ONE-SIDED...
...I FELL IN LOVE WITH HER.
I WOULD DO ANYTHING FOR HER.
HUFF
HUFF
BUT AFTER I LOST HER...
I CAN'T BELIEVE...
...THAT I'VE BECOME SO WEAK LIKE THIS...

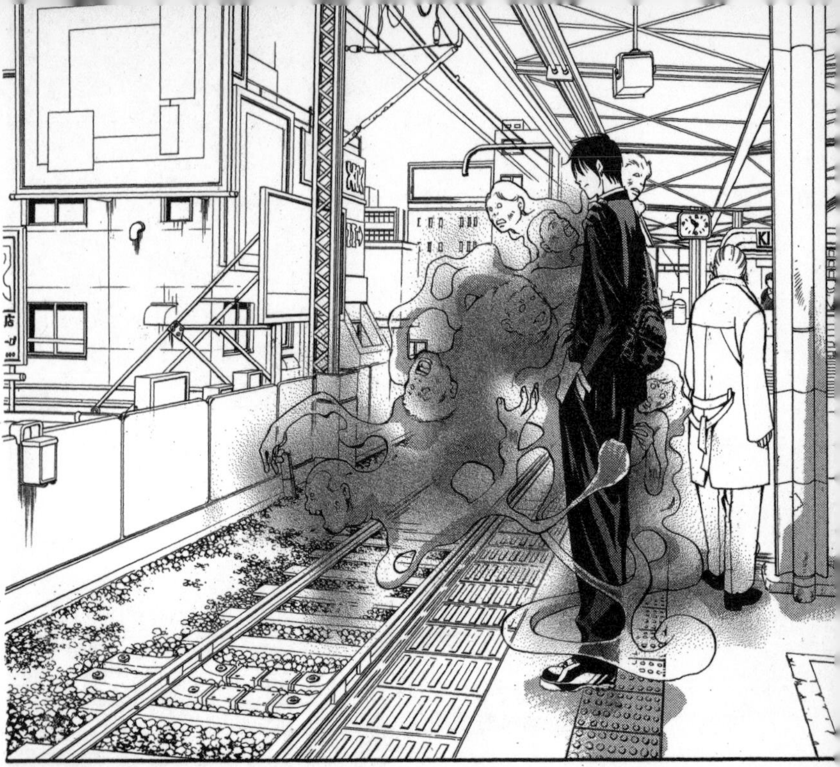

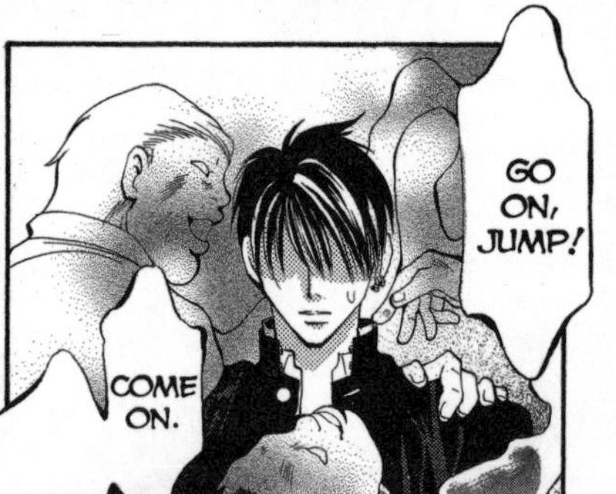
GO ON, JUMP!
COME ON.
NOW ...!
DIE!

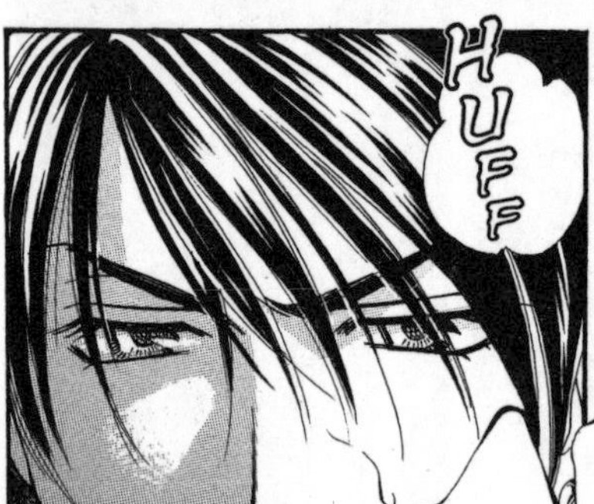
HUFF
HUFF

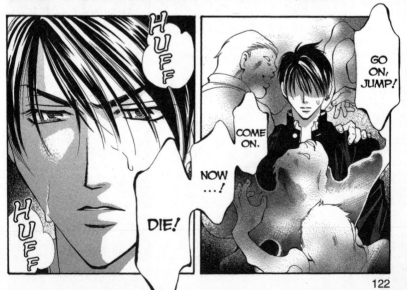

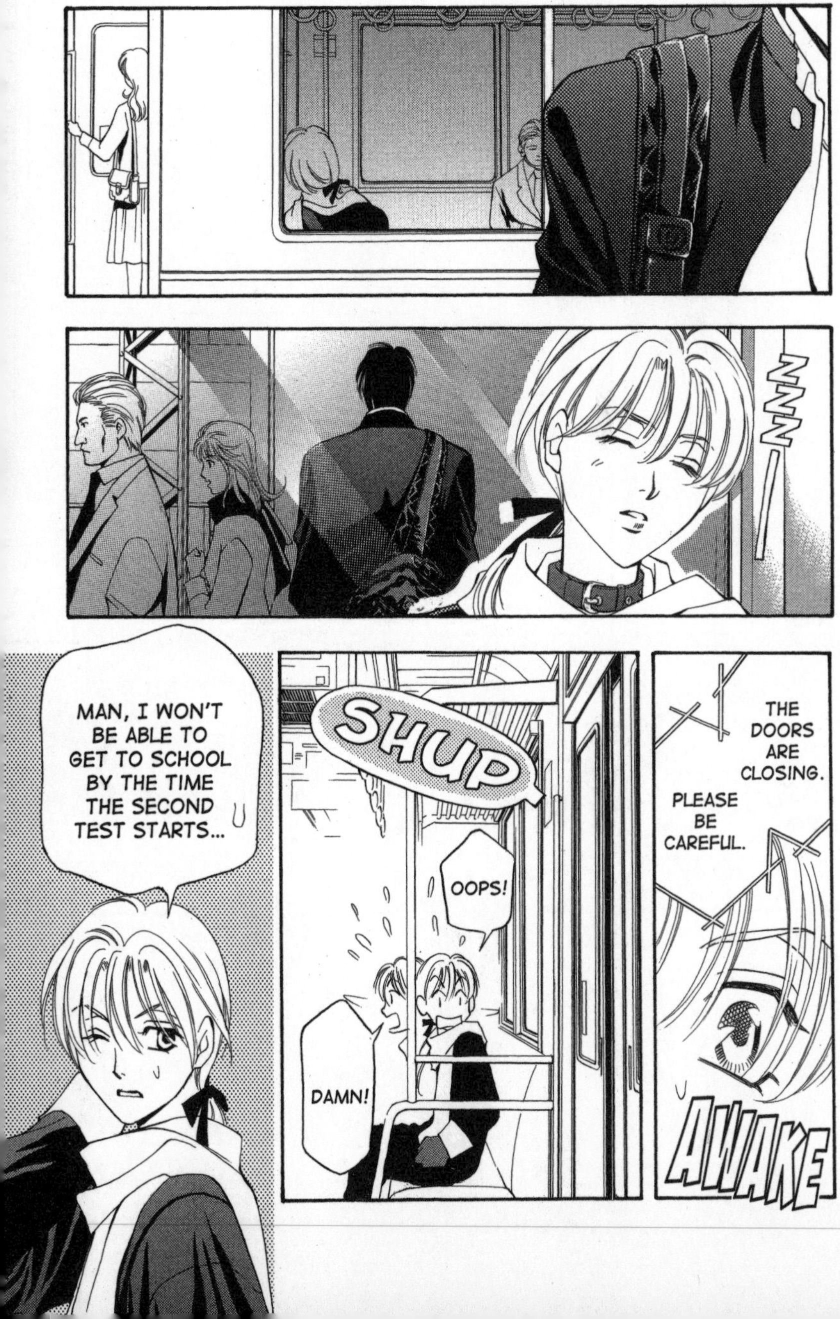
ZZZ
THE DOORS ARE CLOSING.
PLEASE BE CAREFUL.
AWAKE
SHUP
OOPS!
DAMN!
MAN, I WON'T BE ABLE TO GET TO SCHOOL BY THE TIME THE SECOND TEST STARTS...

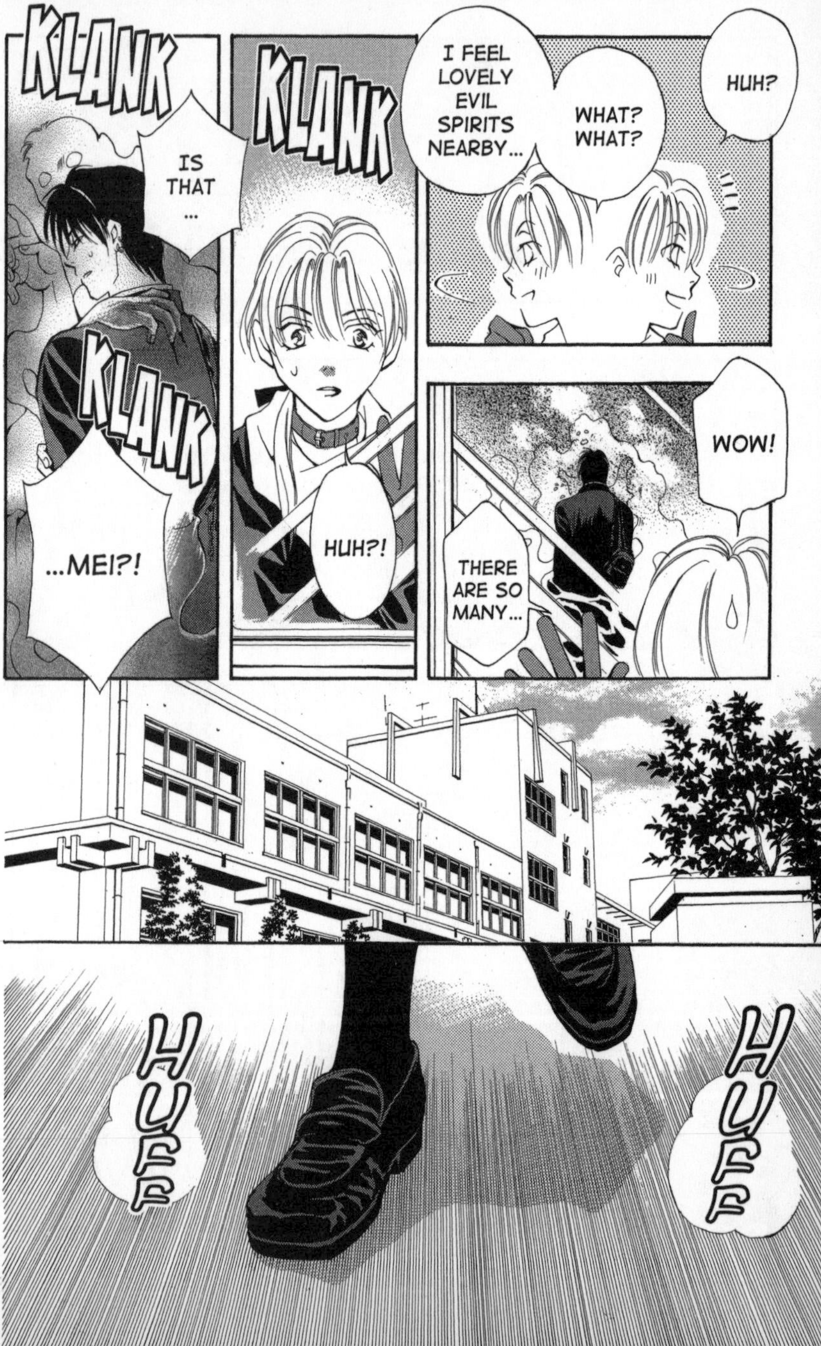

I FEEL LOVELY EVIL SPIRITS NEARBY...
WHAT? WHAT?
HUH?
WOW!
THERE ARE SO MANY...
KLANK
HUH?!
KLANK
IS THAT ...
KLANK
...MEI?!
HUFF
HUFF

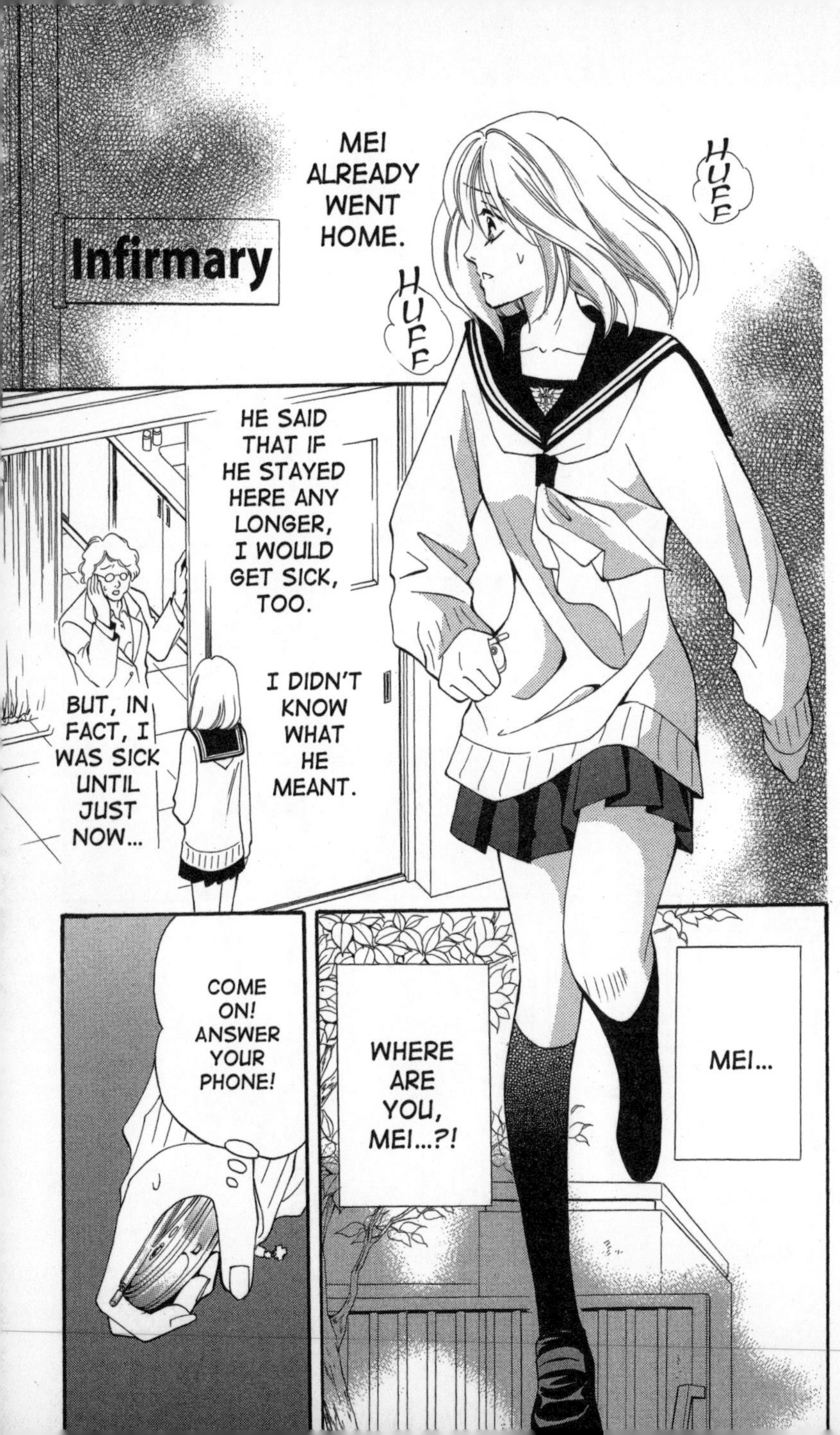
HUFF
MEI ALREADY WENT HOME.
HUFF
Infirmary
HE SAID THAT IF HE STAYED HERE ANY LONGER, I WOULD GET SICK, TOO.
I DIDN'T KNOW WHAT HE MEANT.
BUT, IN FACT, I WAS SICK UNTIL JUST NOW...
MEI...
WHERE ARE YOU, MEI...?!
COME ON! ANSWER YOUR PHONE!

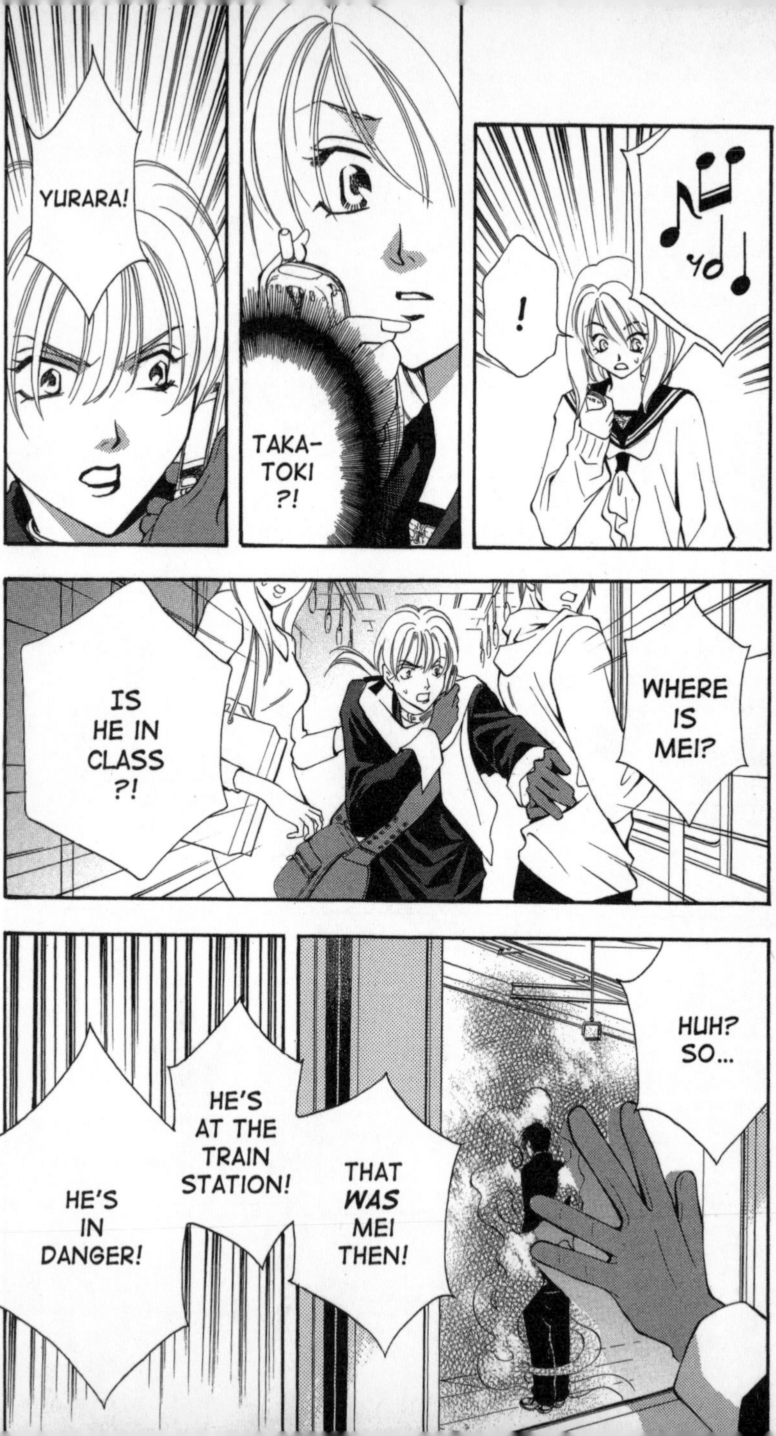
!
TAKA-TOKI ?!
YURARA!
WHERE IS MEI?
IS HE IN CLASS ?!
HUH? SO...
THAT *WAS* MEI THEN!
HE'S AT THE TRAIN STATION!
HE'S IN DANGER!

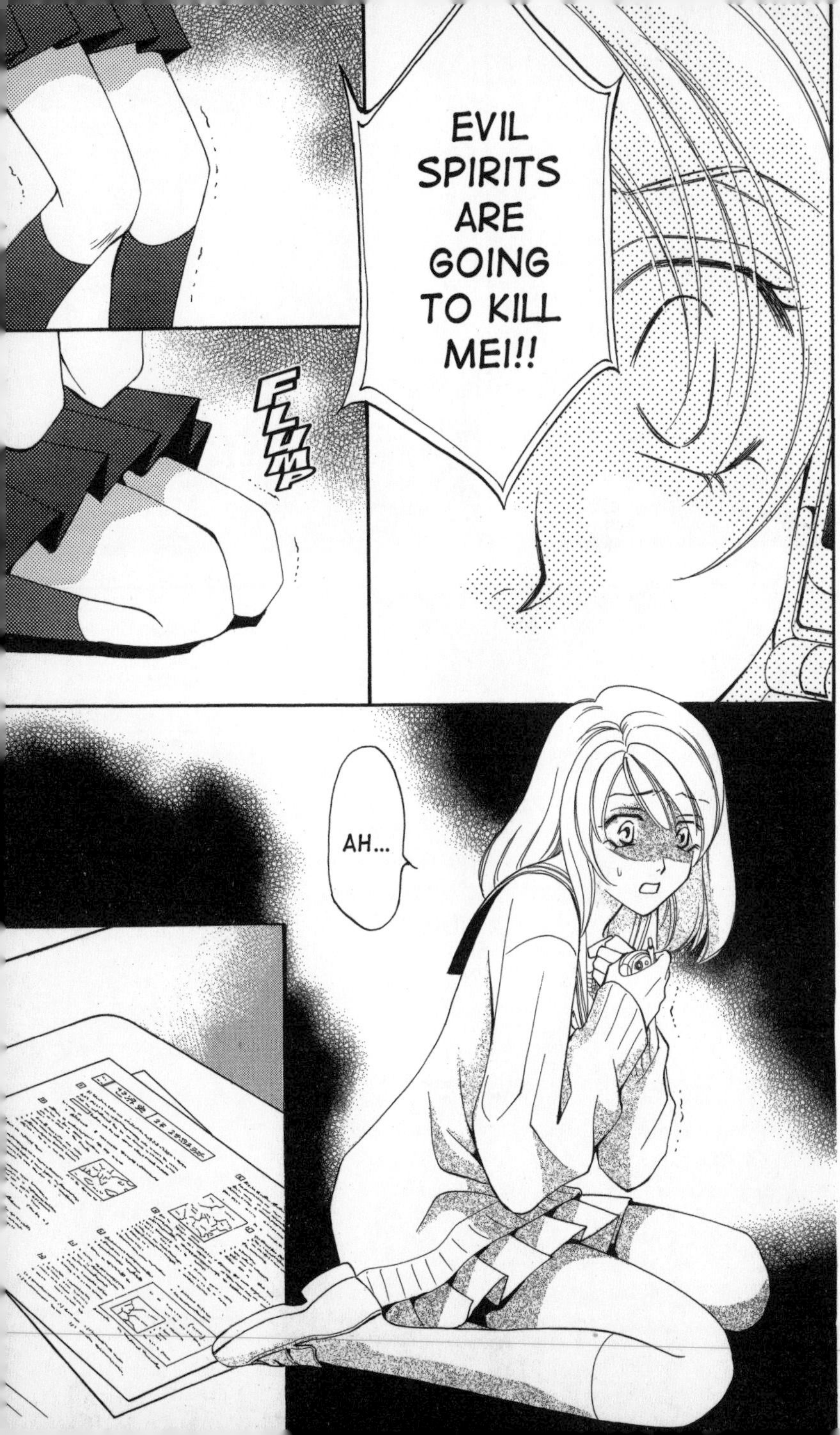
EVIL SPIRITS ARE GOING TO KILL MEI!!
FLUMP
AH...

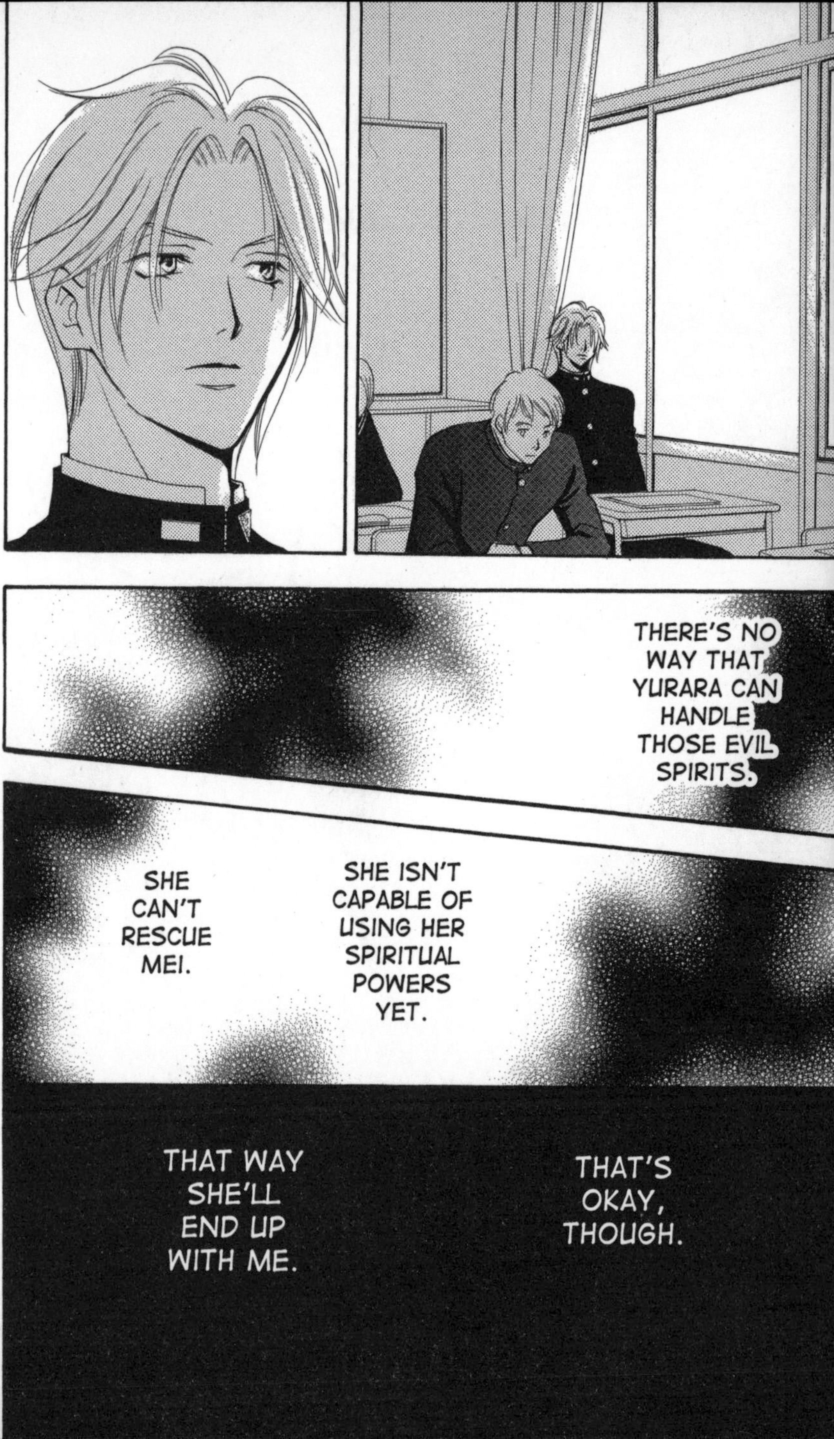
THERE'S NO WAY THAT YURARA CAN HANDLE THOSE EVIL SPIRITS.
SHE ISN'T CAPABLE OF USING HER SPIRITUAL POWERS YET.
SHE CAN'T RESCUE MEI.
THAT'S OKAY, THOUGH.
THAT WAY SHE'LL END UP WITH ME.

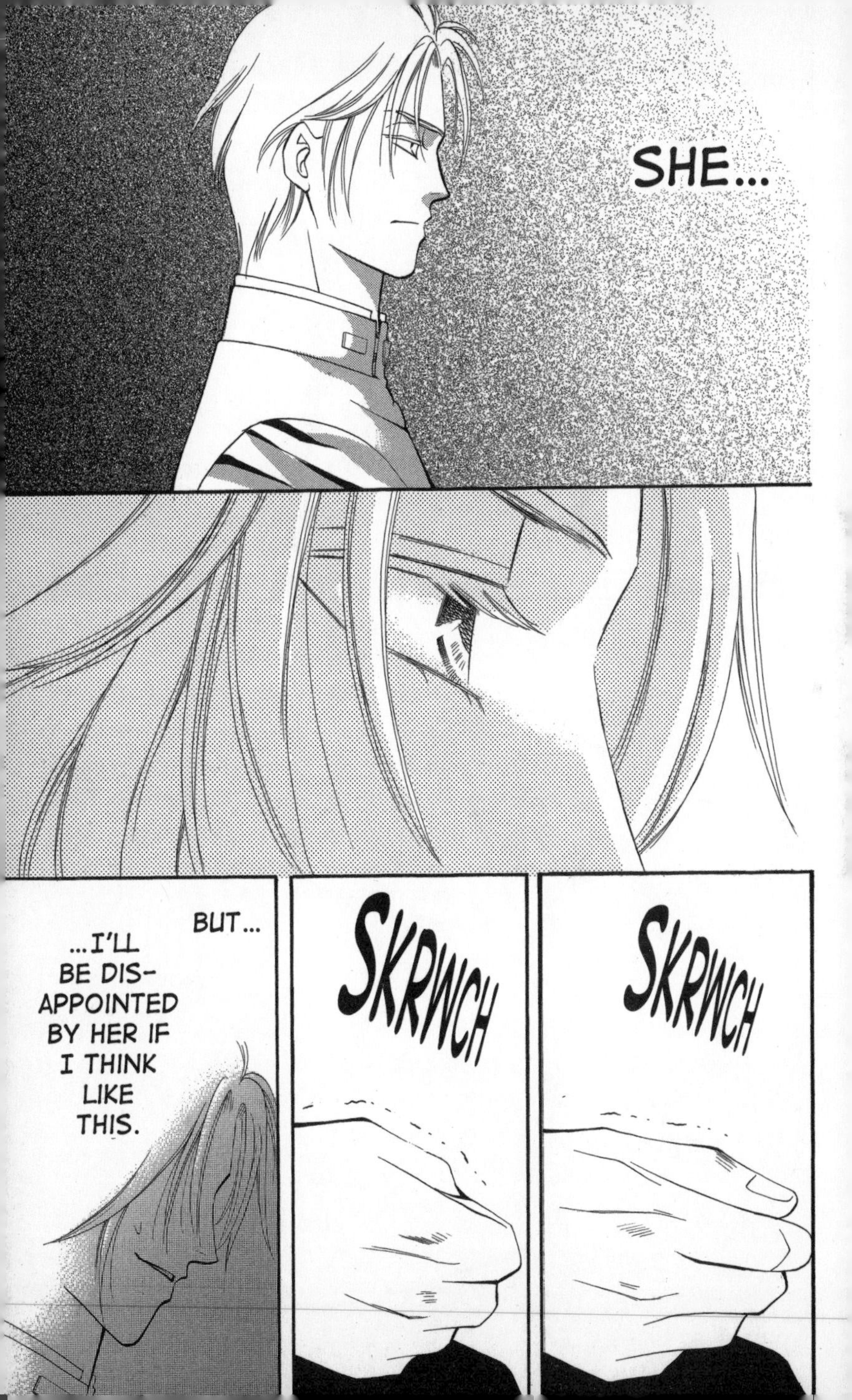
SHE...
SKRWCH
SKRWCH
BUT...
...I'LL BE DIS-APPOINTED BY HER IF I THINK LIKE THIS.

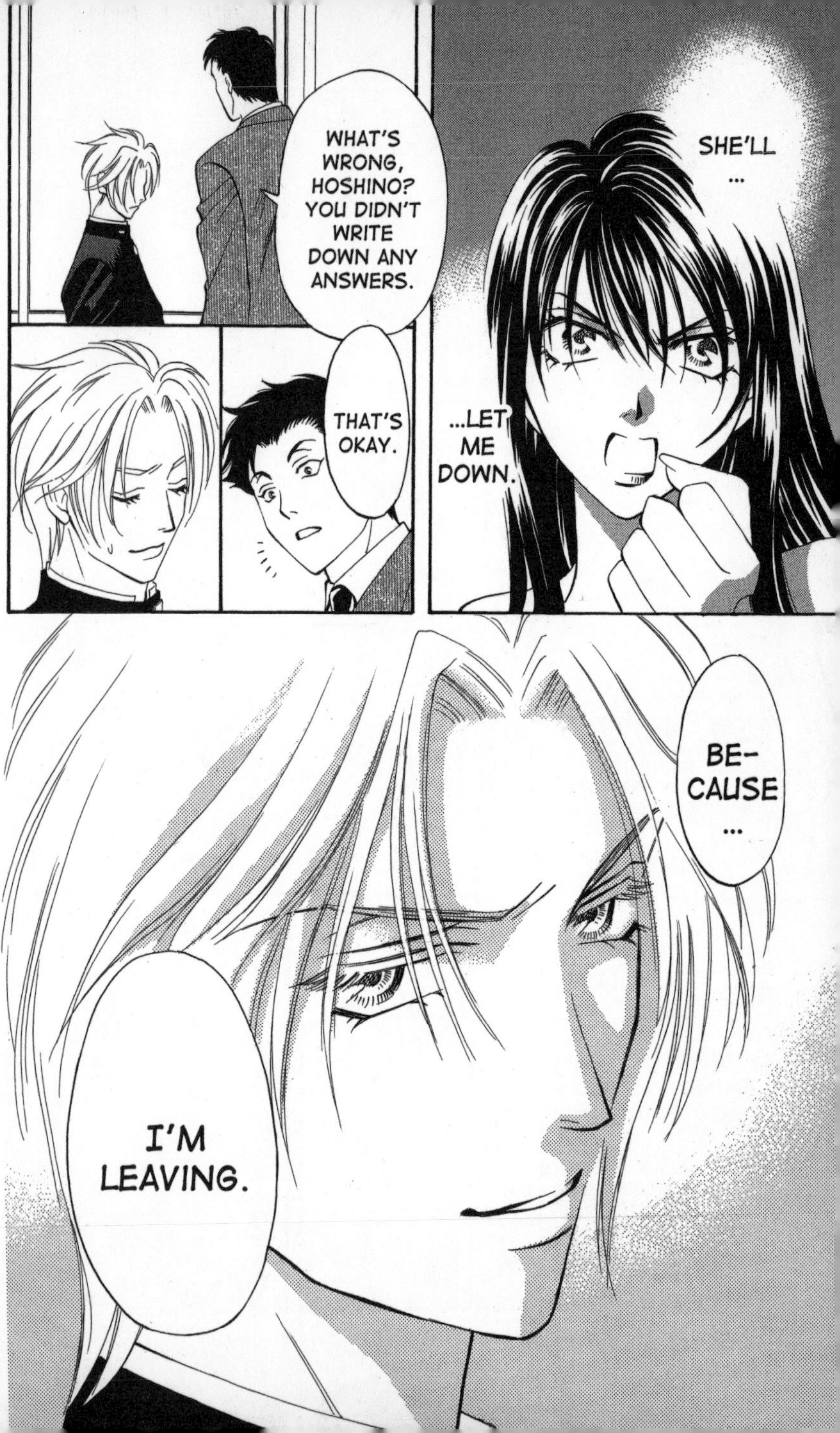
SHE'LL ...
...LET ME DOWN.
WHAT'S WRONG, HOSHINO? YOU DIDN'T WRITE DOWN ANY ANSWERS.
THAT'S OKAY.
BE-CAUSE ...
I'M LEAVING.

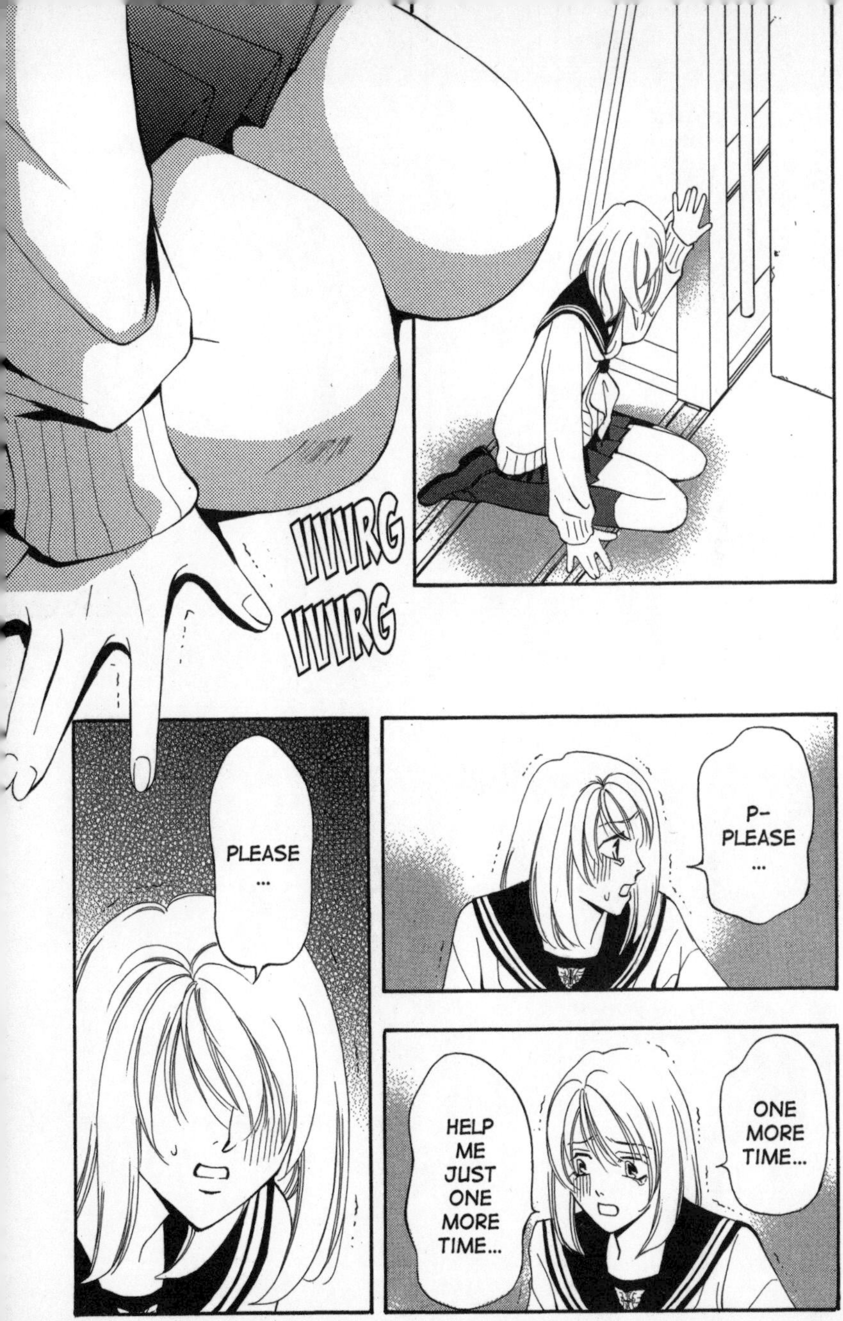
VVVRG
VVVRG
P-PLEASE ...
ONE MORE TIME...
HELP ME JUST ONE MORE TIME...
PLEASE ...

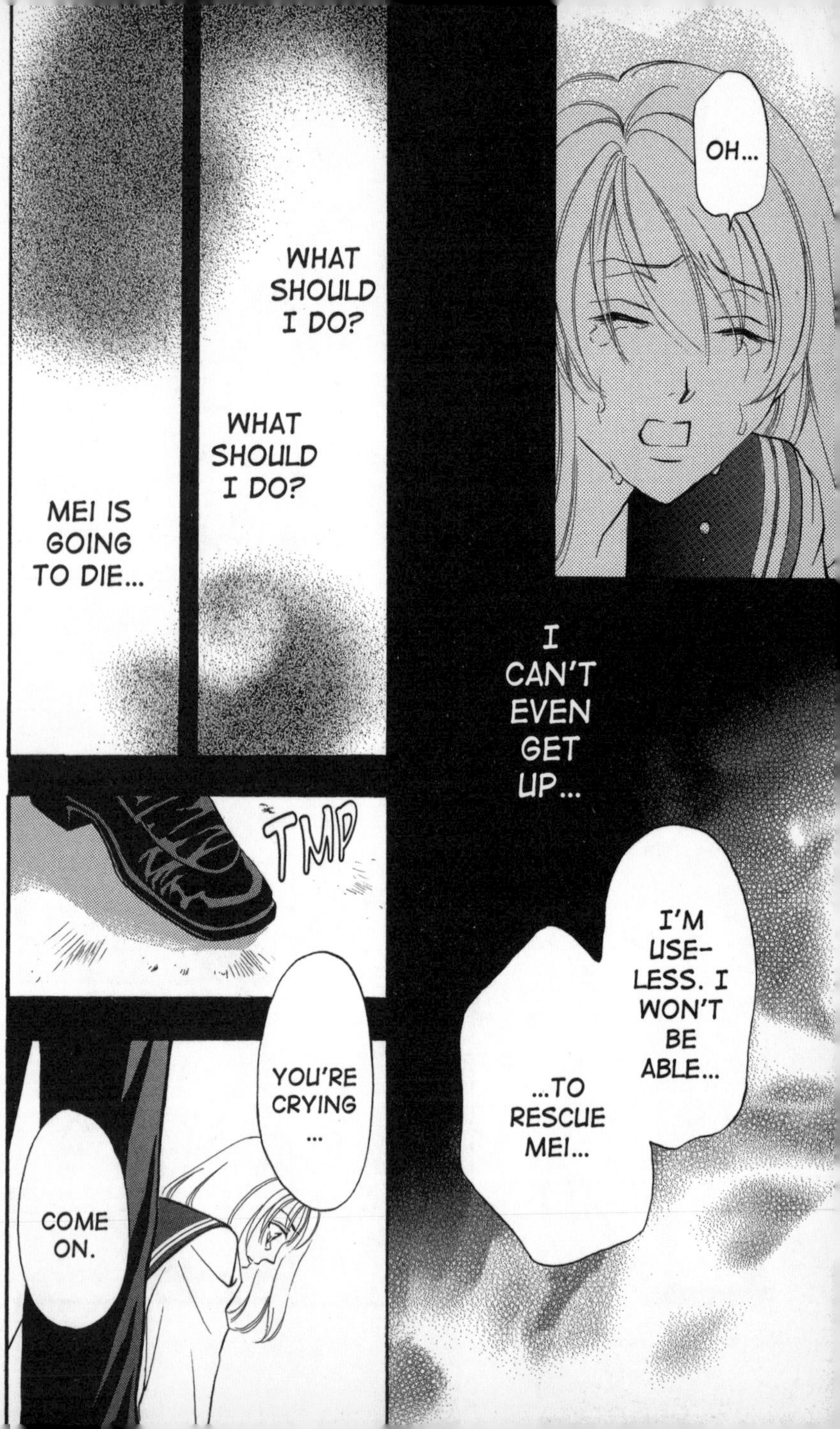
OH...
I CAN'T EVEN GET UP...
I'M USE-LESS. I WON'T BE ABLE...
...TO RESCUE MEI...
WHAT SHOULD I DO?
WHAT SHOULD I DO?
MEI IS GOING TO DIE...
TMP
YOU'RE CRYING...
COME ON.

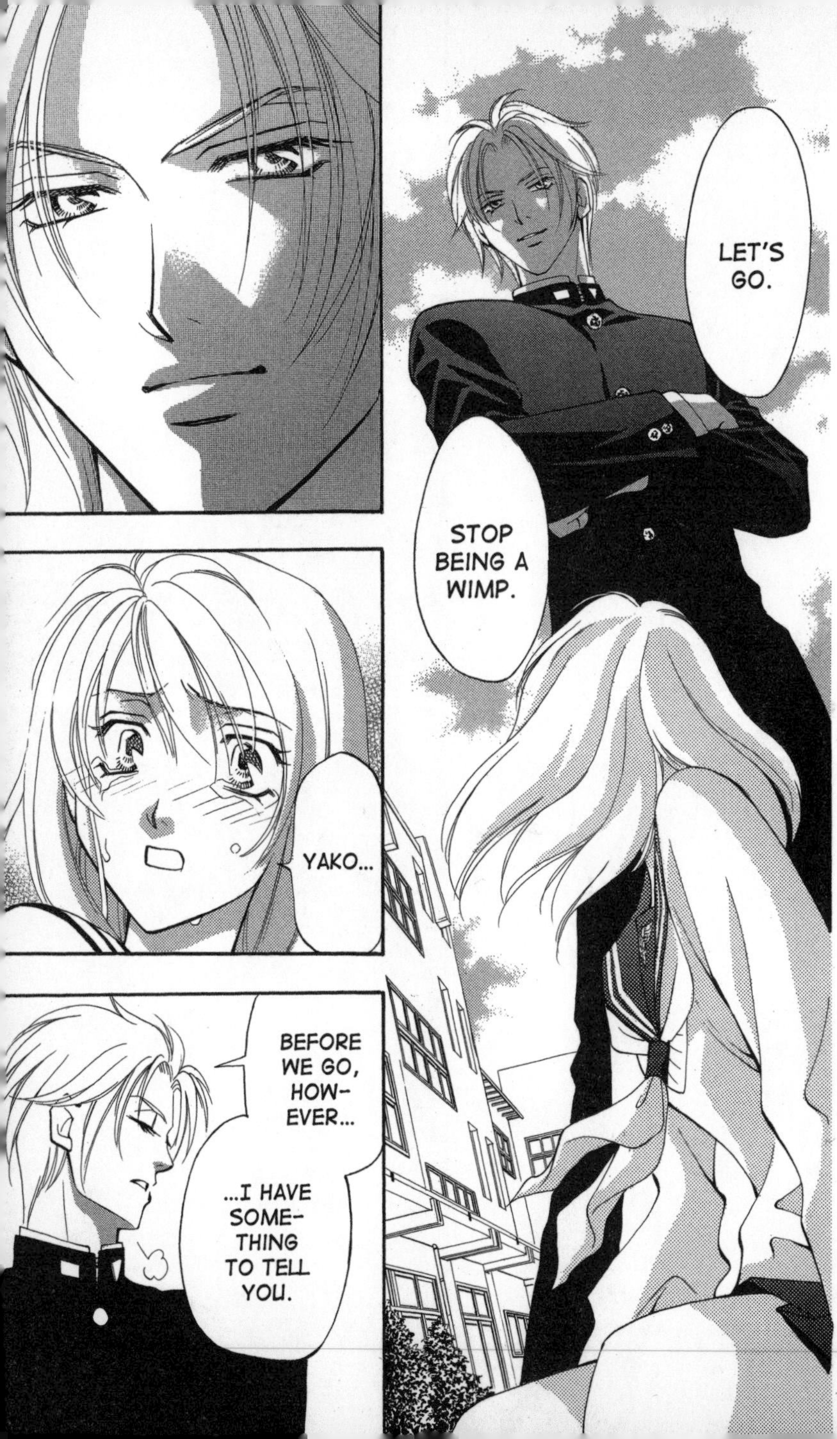
LET'S GO.
STOP BEING A WIMP.
YAKO...
BEFORE WE GO, HOW-EVER...
...I HAVE SOME-THING TO TELL YOU.

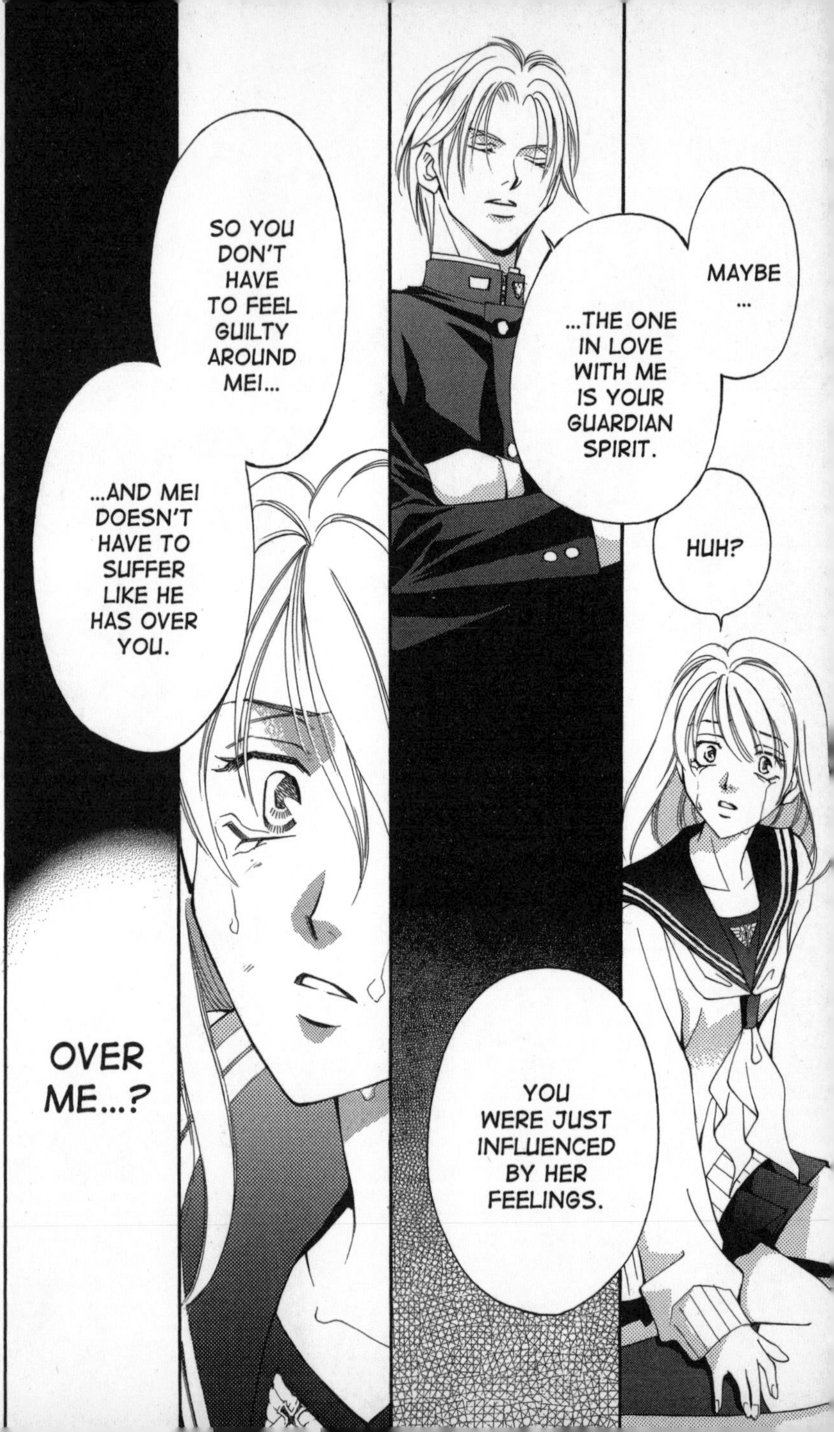
MAYBE ...
...THE ONE IN LOVE WITH ME IS YOUR GUARDIAN SPIRIT.
HUH?
YOU WERE JUST INFLUENCED BY HER FEELINGS.
SO YOU DON'T HAVE TO FEEL GUILTY AROUND MEI...
...AND MEI DOESN'T HAVE TO SUFFER LIKE HE HAS OVER YOU.
OVER ME...?

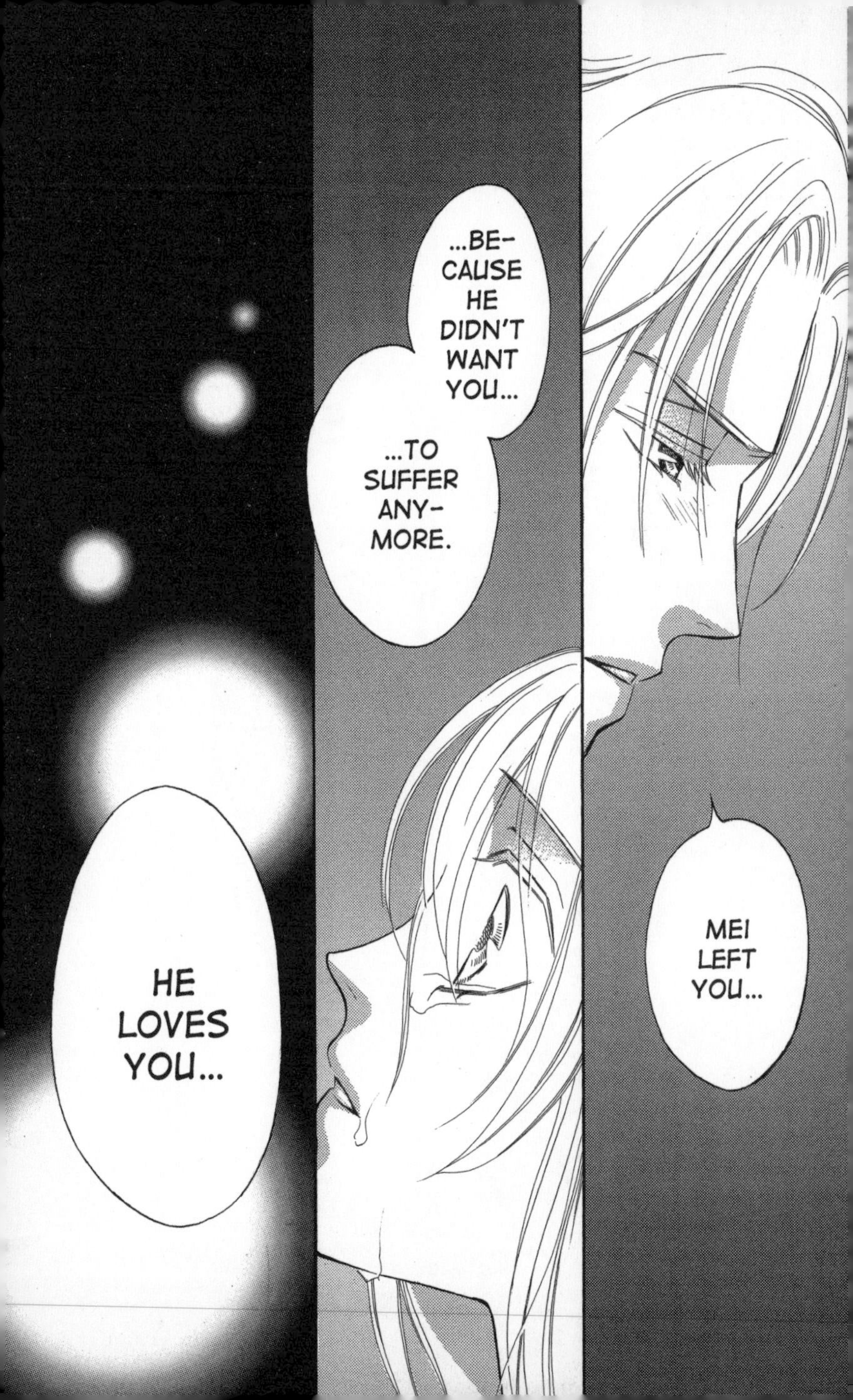
MEI LEFT YOU...
...BE-CAUSE HE DIDN'T WANT YOU...
...TO SUFFER ANY-MORE.
HE LOVES YOU...

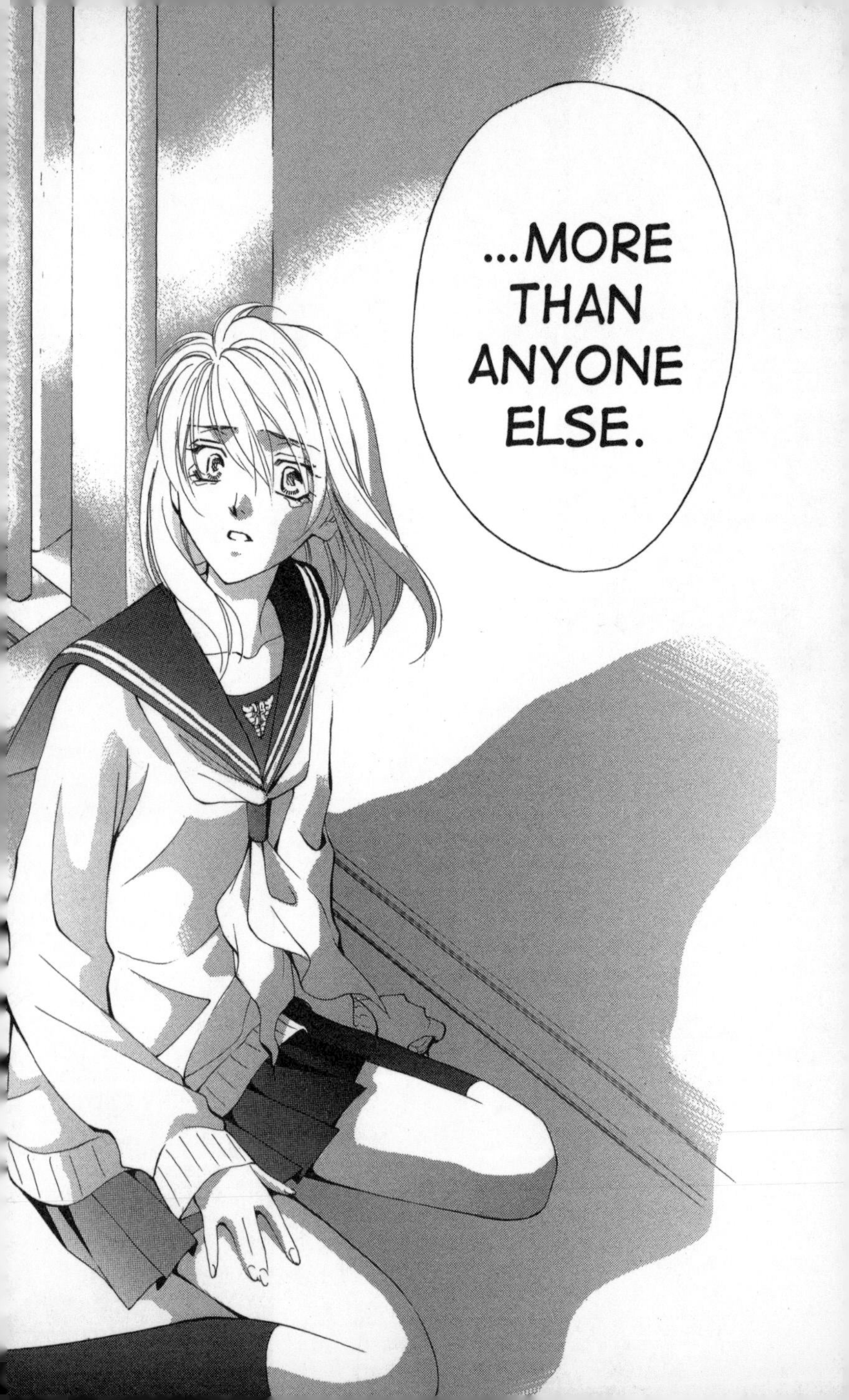
...MORE THAN ANYONE ELSE.

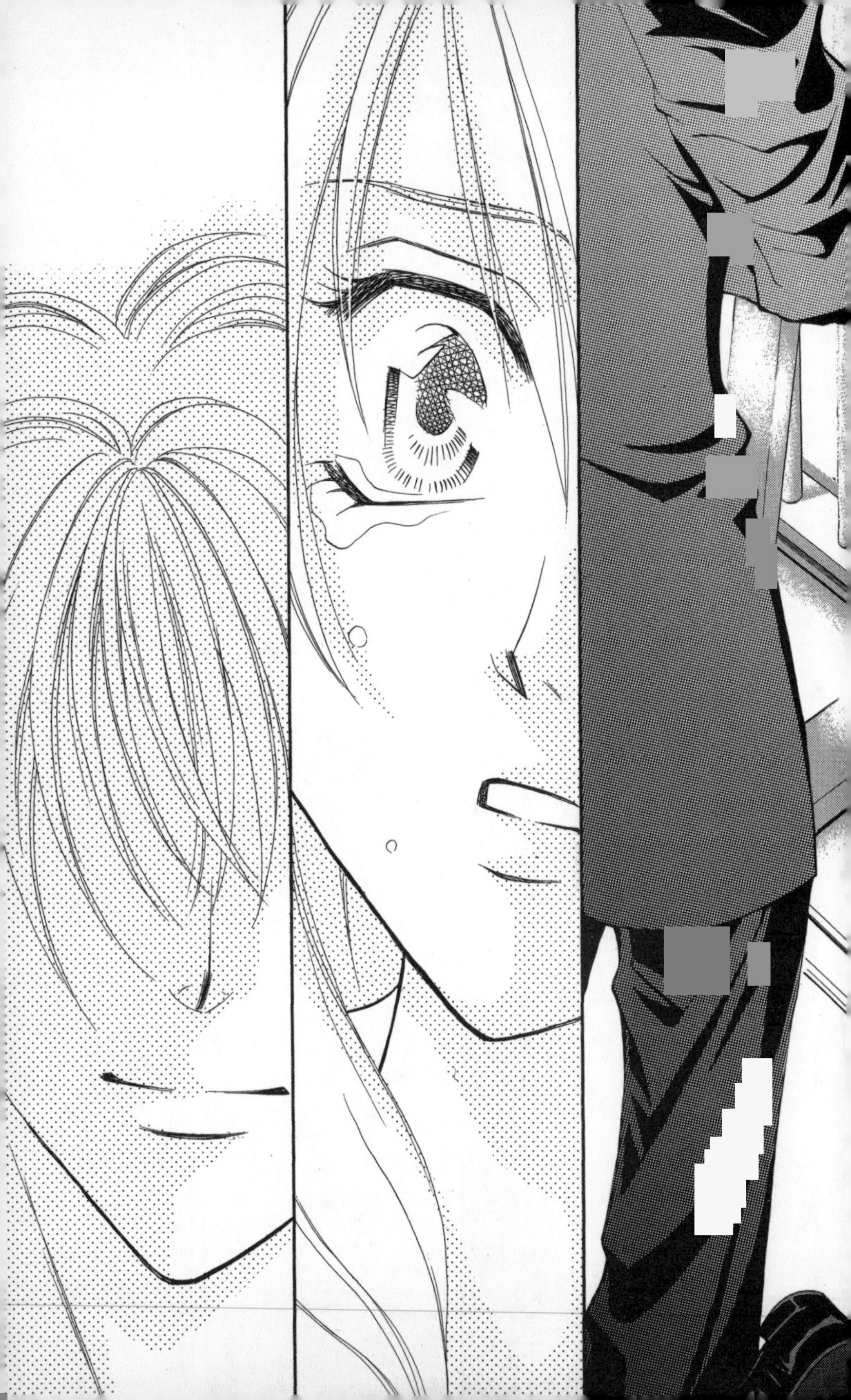

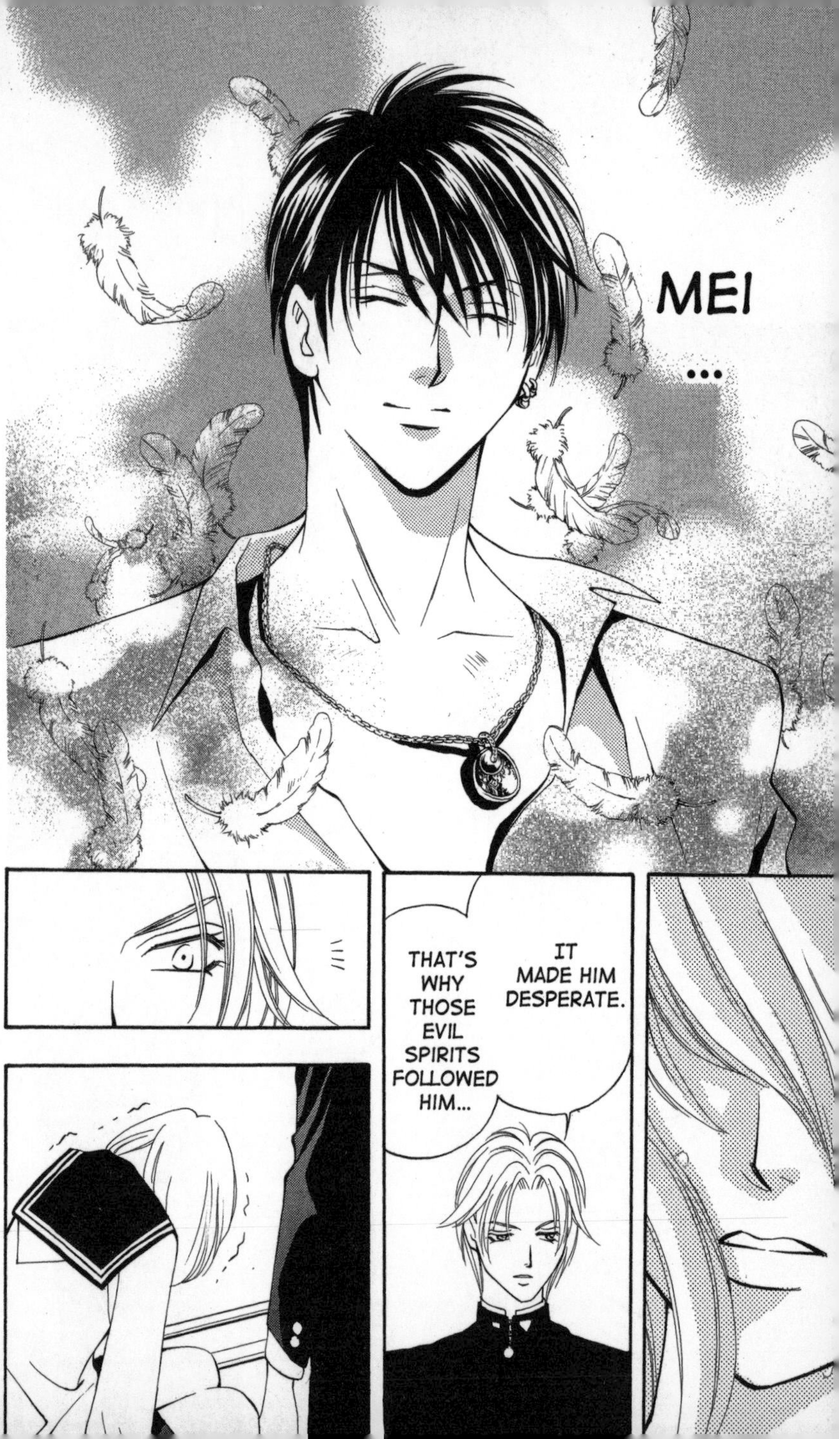
MEI
...
IT MADE HIM DESPERATE.
THAT'S WHY THOSE EVIL SPIRITS FOLLOWED HIM...

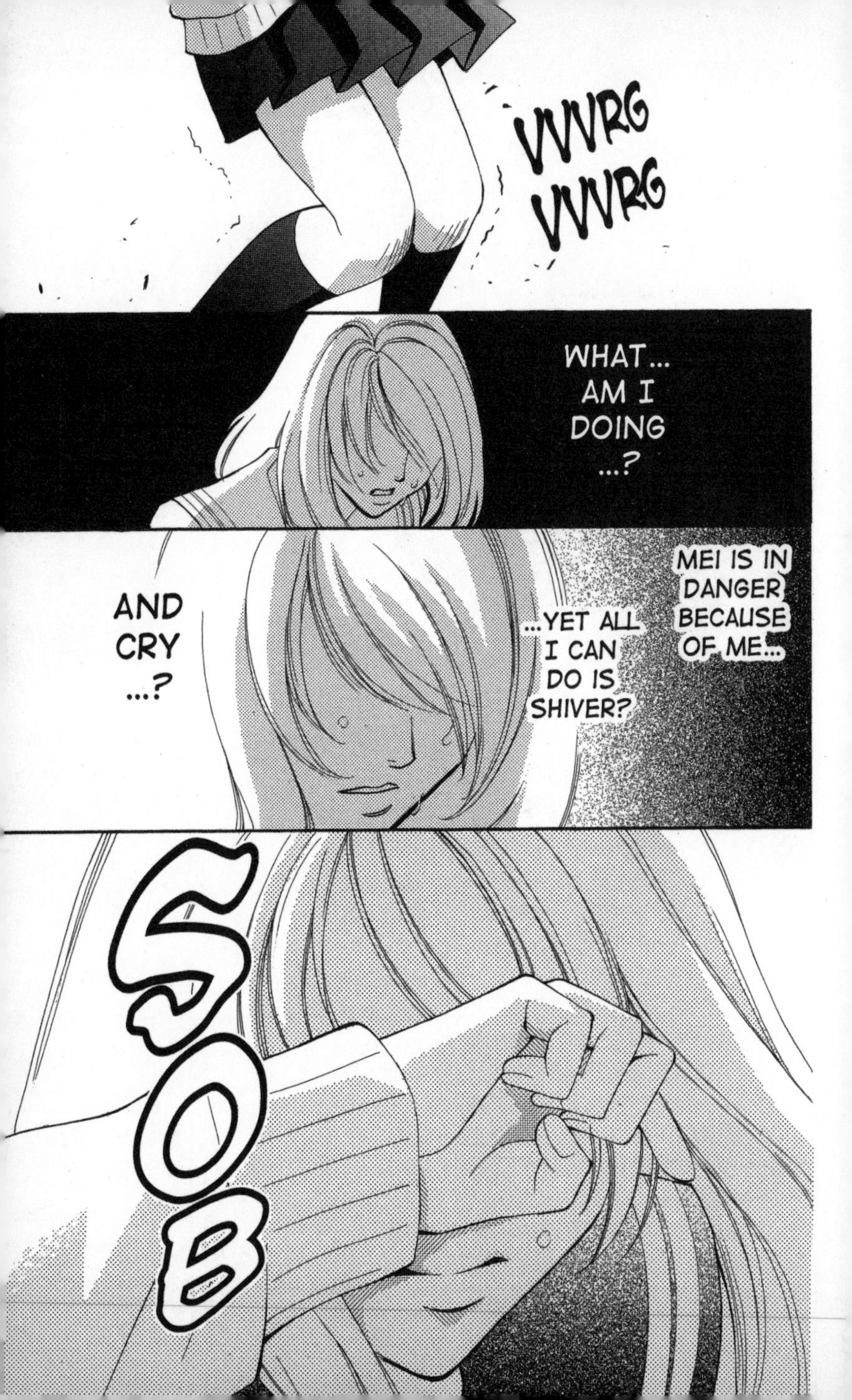
VVVRG VVVRG
WHAT... AM I DOING ...?
MEI IS IN DANGER BECAUSE OF ME...
...YET ALL I CAN DO IS SHIVER?
AND CRY ...?
SOB

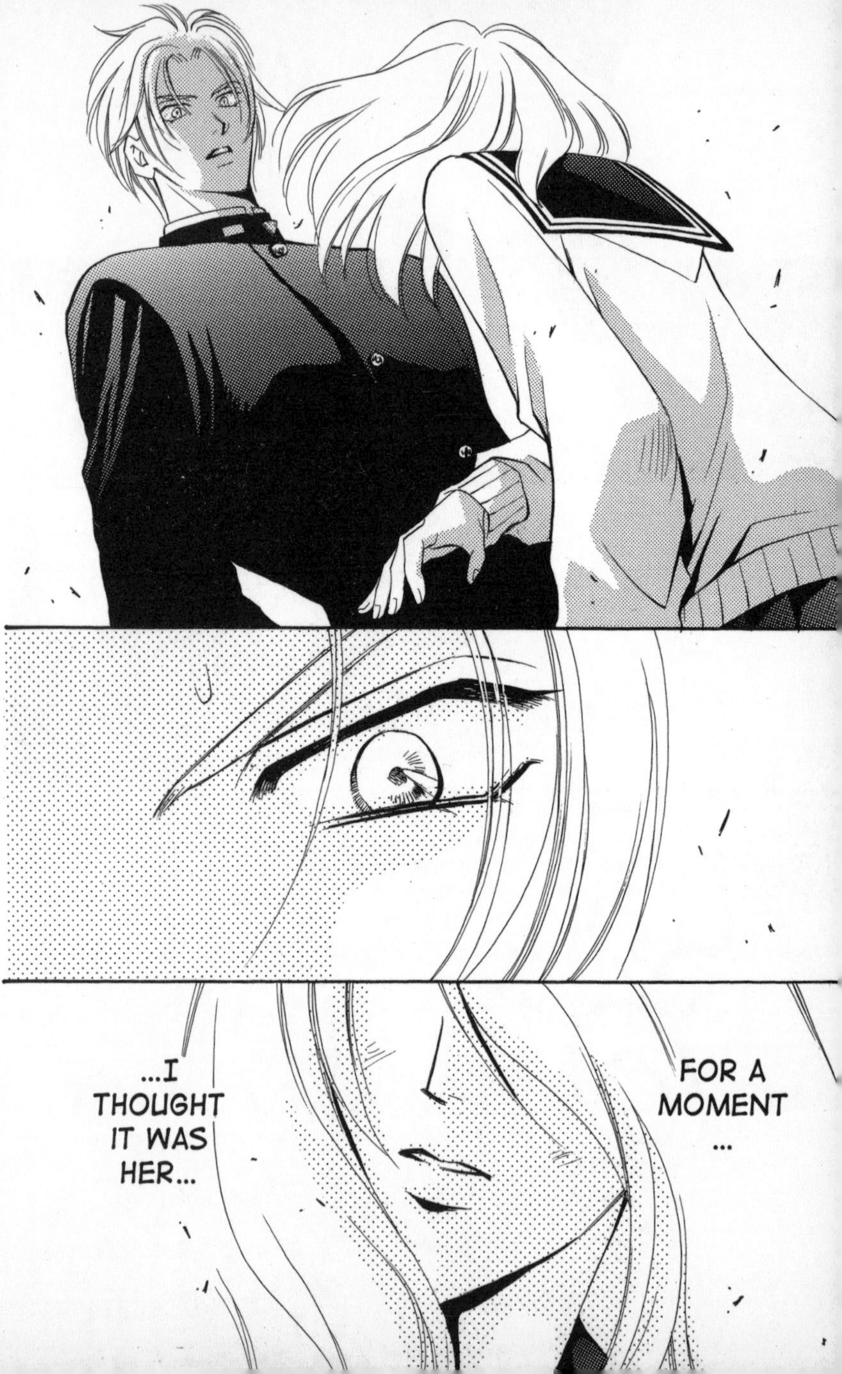
FOR A MOMENT ...
...I THOUGHT IT WAS HER...

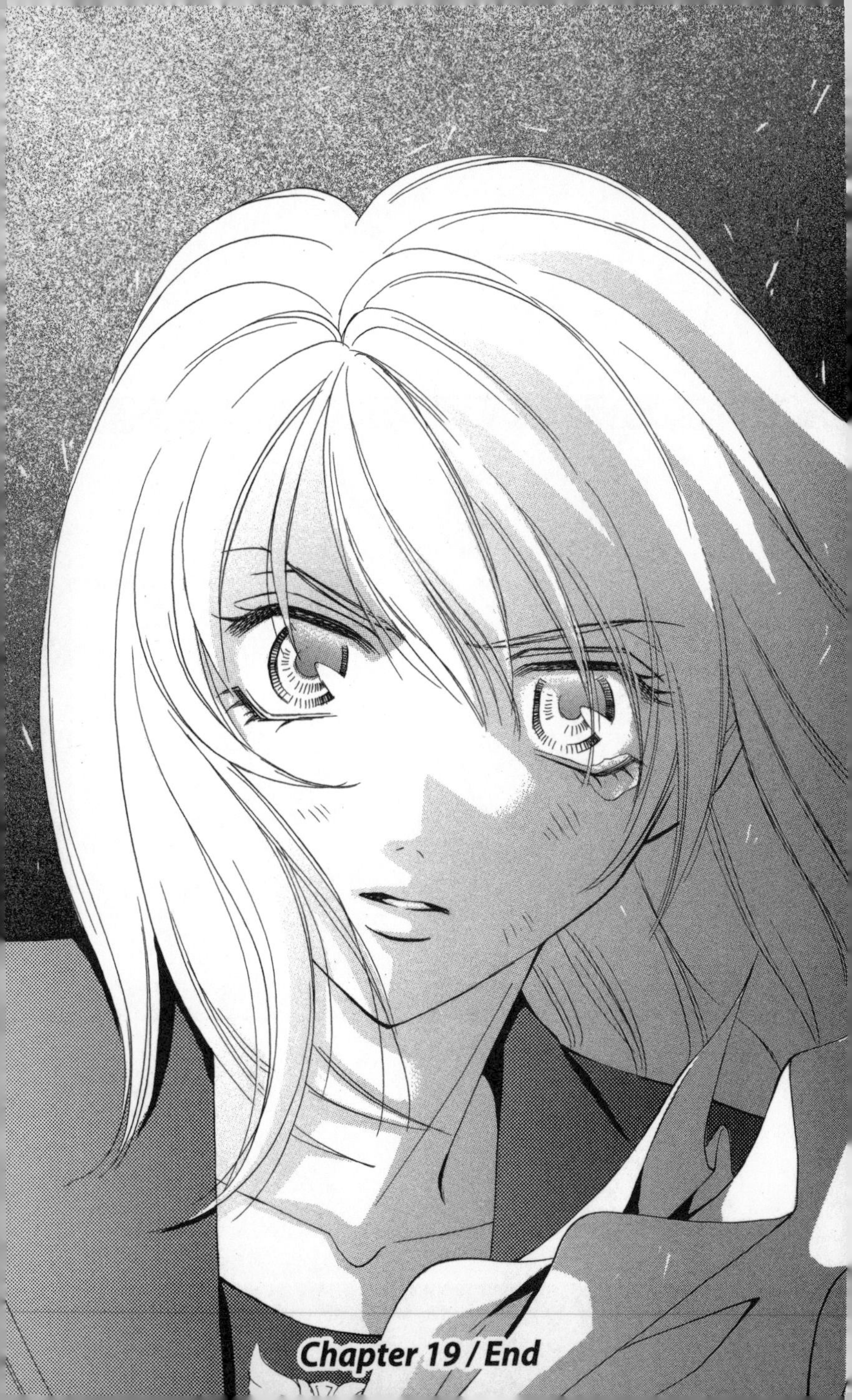
Chapter 19 / End

BONUS MANGA

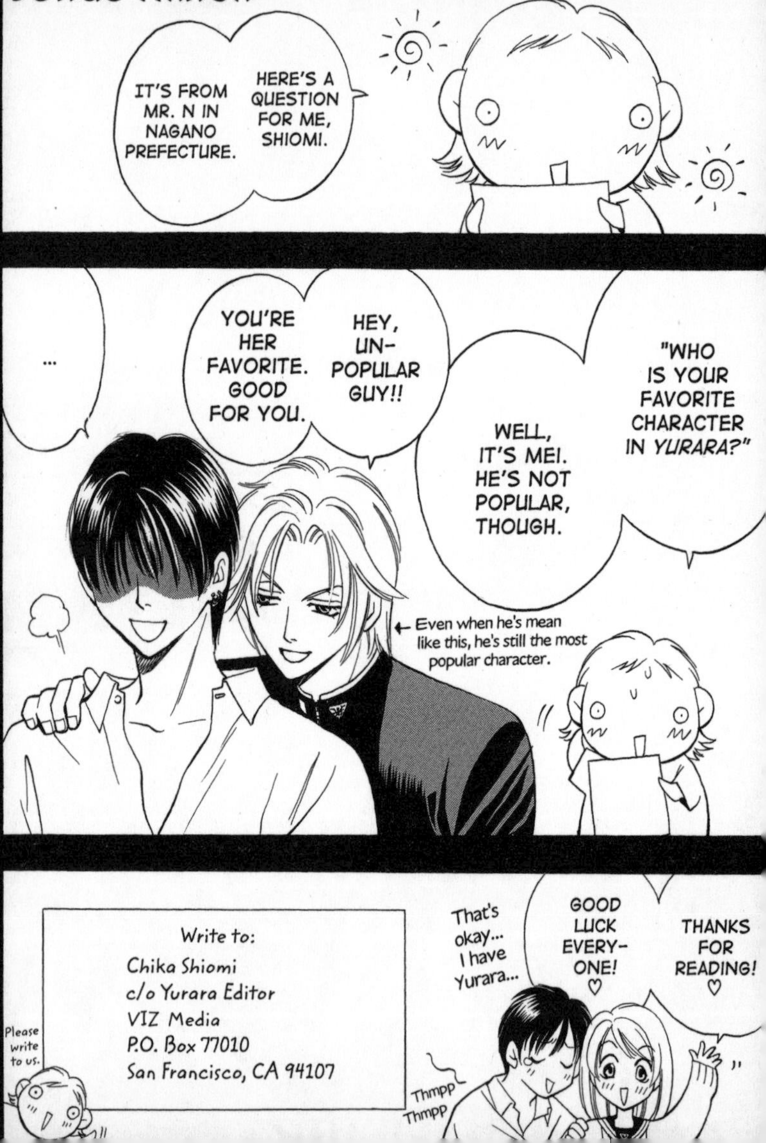
HERE'S A QUESTION FOR ME, SHIOMI.
IT'S FROM MR. N IN NAGANO PREFECTURE.
"WHO IS YOUR FAVORITE CHARACTER IN *YURARA?*"
WELL, IT'S MEI. HE'S NOT POPULAR, THOUGH.
HEY, UN-POPULAR GUY!!
YOU'RE HER FAVORITE. GOOD FOR YOU.
...
← Even when he's mean like this, he's still the most popular character.
THANKS FOR READING! ♡
GOOD LUCK EVERY-ONE! ♡
That's okay... I have Yurara...
Thmpp Thmpp
Write to:
Chika Shiomi
c/o Yurara Editor
VIZ Media
P.O. Box 77010
San Francisco, CA 94107
Please write to us.

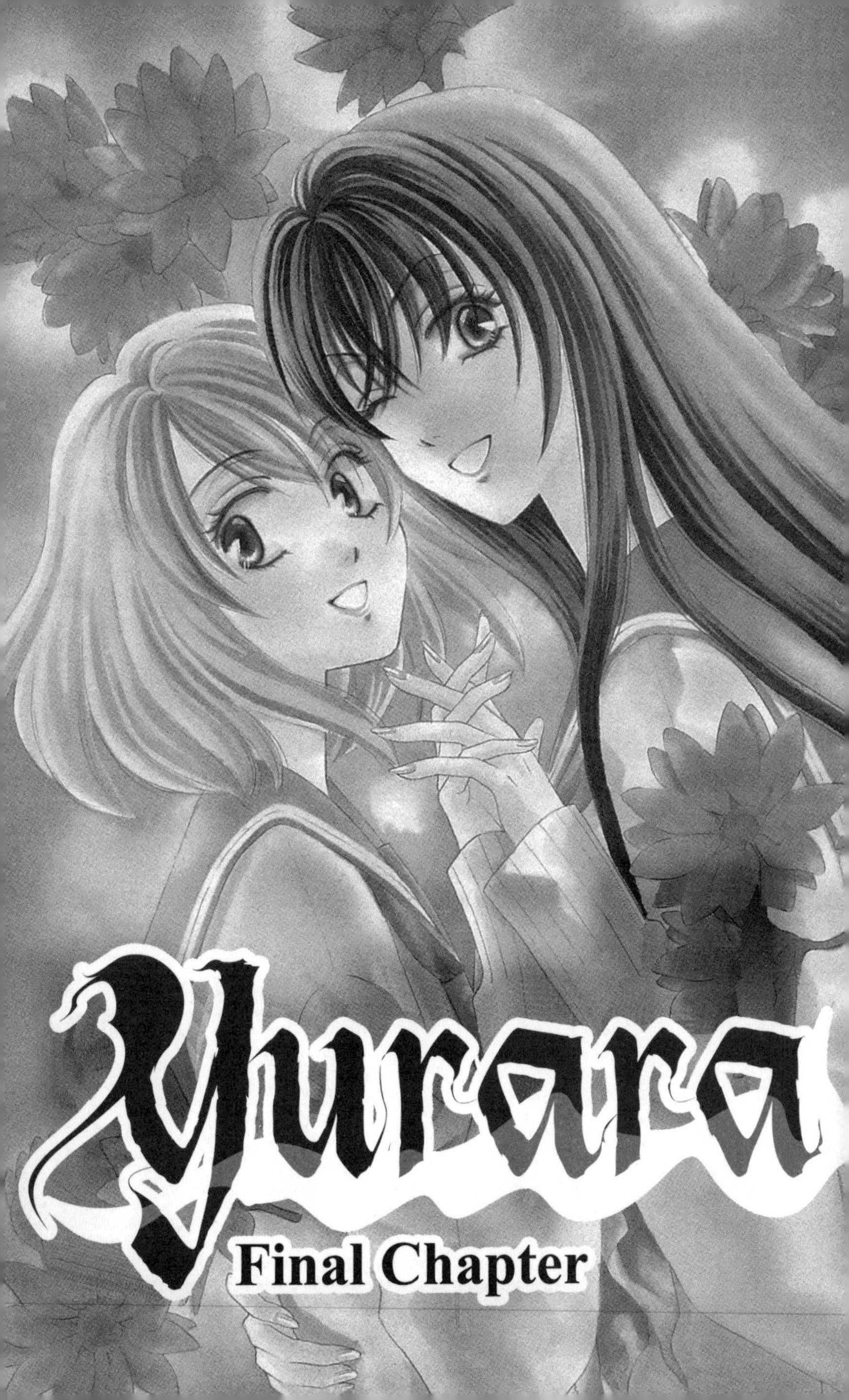
Yurara
Final Chapter

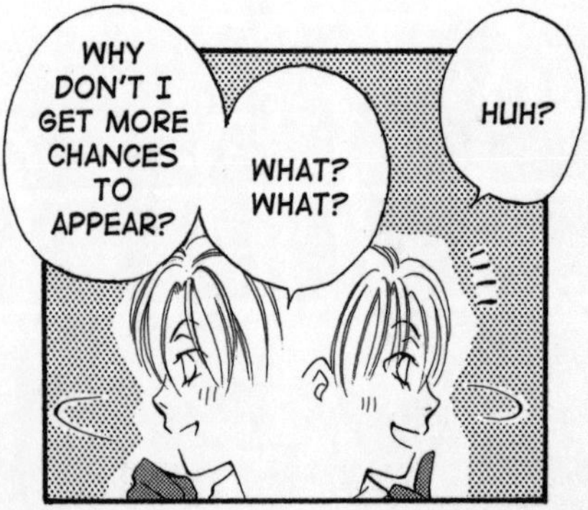
HUH?
WHAT? WHAT?
WHY DON'T I GET MORE CHANCES TO APPEAR?

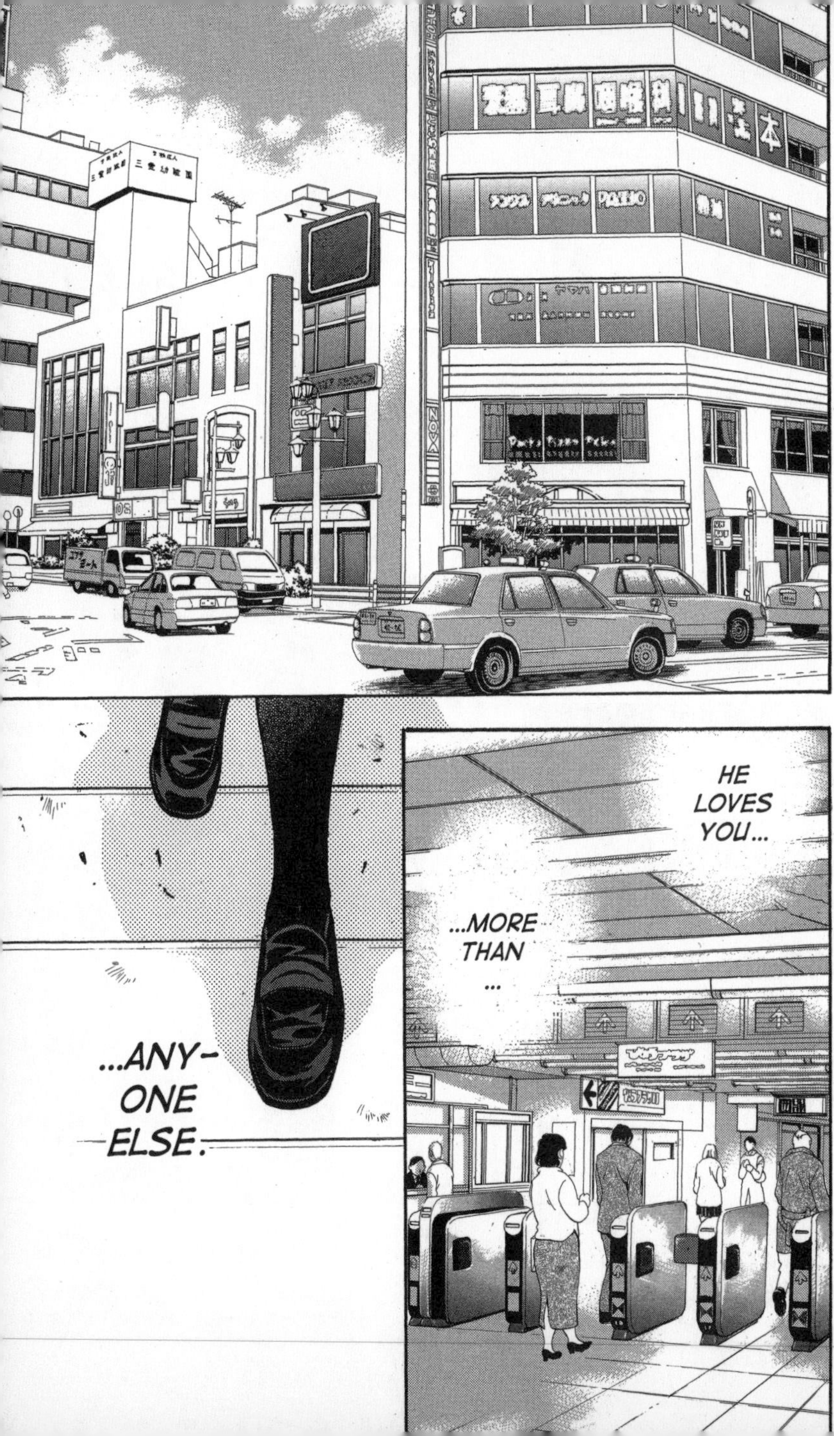
HE LOVES YOU...
...MORE THAN ...
...ANY-ONE ELSE.

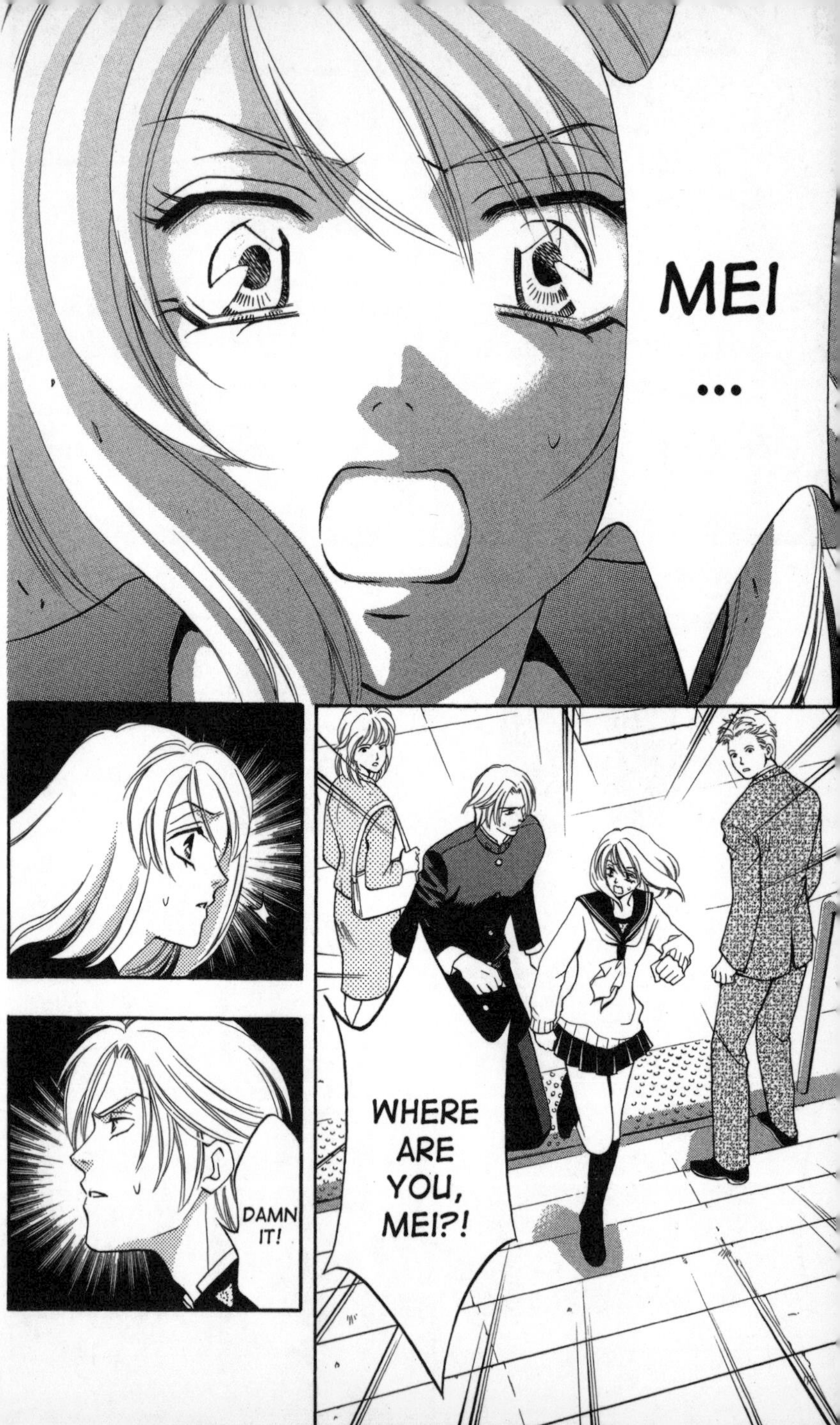
MEI
...
WHERE ARE YOU, MEI?!
DAMN IT!

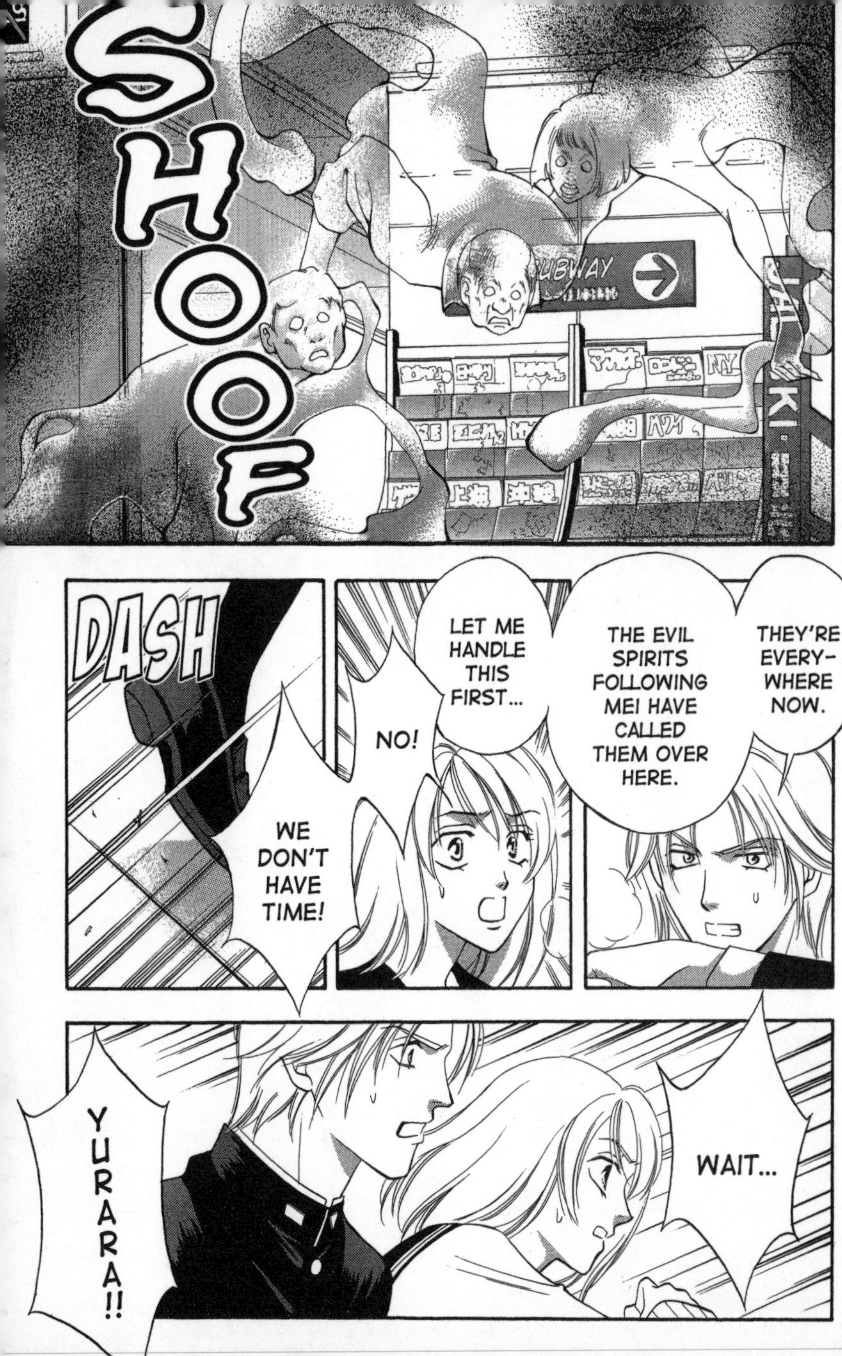
SHOOF
SUBWAY
THEY'RE EVERY-WHERE NOW.
THE EVIL SPIRITS FOLLOWING MEI HAVE CALLED THEM OVER HERE.
LET ME HANDLE THIS FIRST...
NO!
WE DON'T HAVE TIME!
DASH
WAIT...
YURARA!!

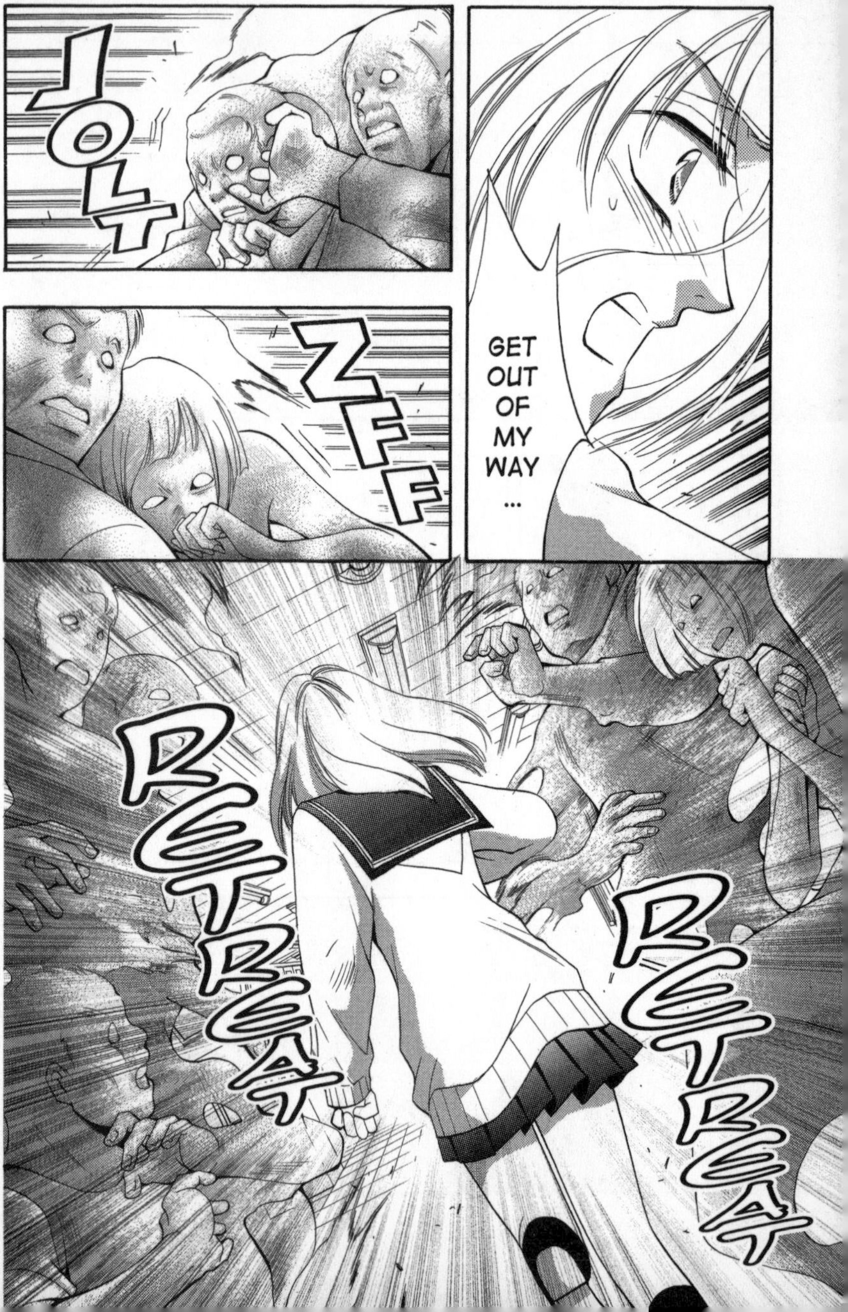
GET OUT OF MY WAY ...
JOLT
ZFFF
RETREAK
RETREAK

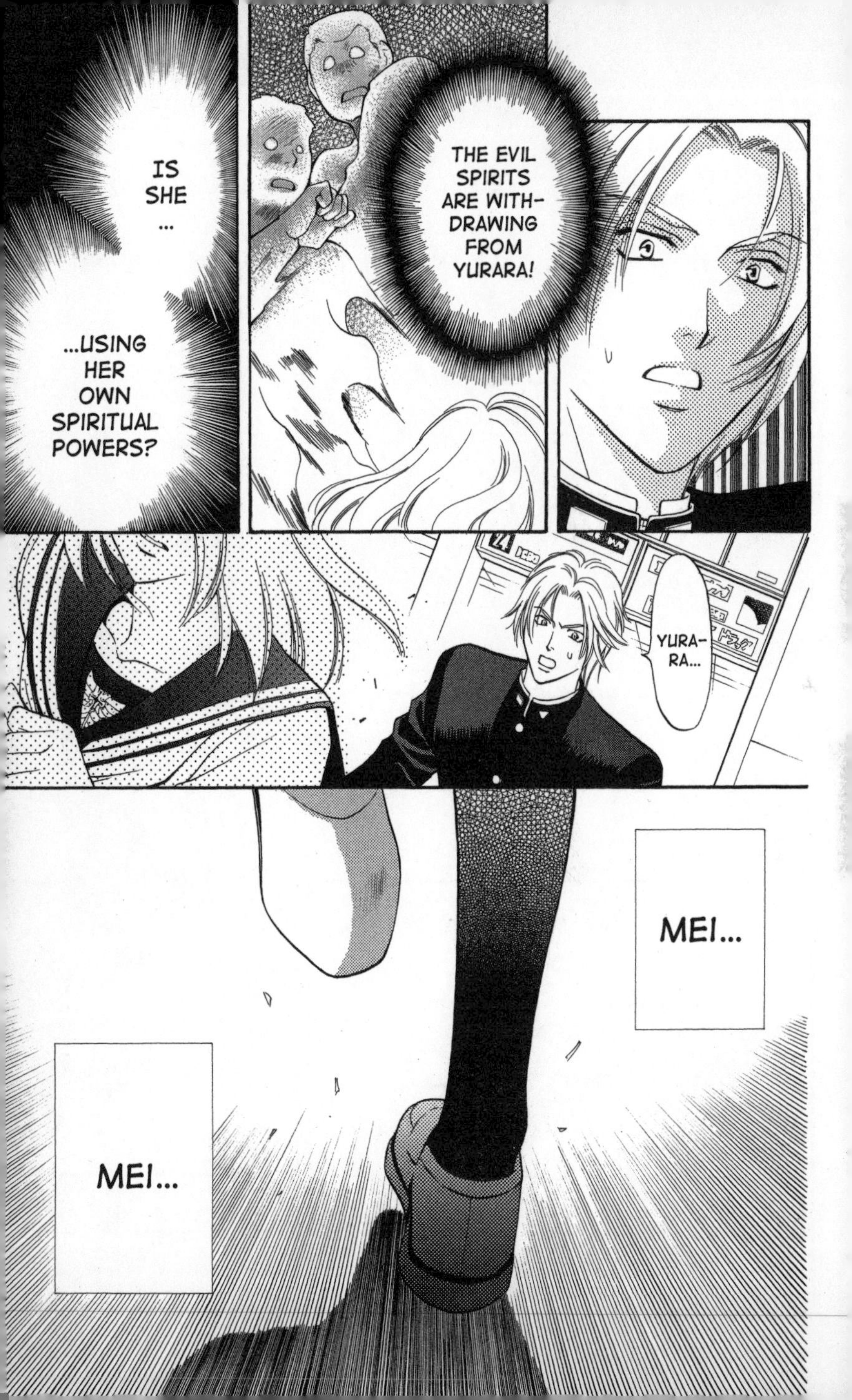
THE EVIL SPIRITS ARE WITH-DRAWING FROM YURARA!
IS SHE ...
...USING HER OWN SPIRITUAL POWERS?
YURA-RA...
MEI...
MEI...

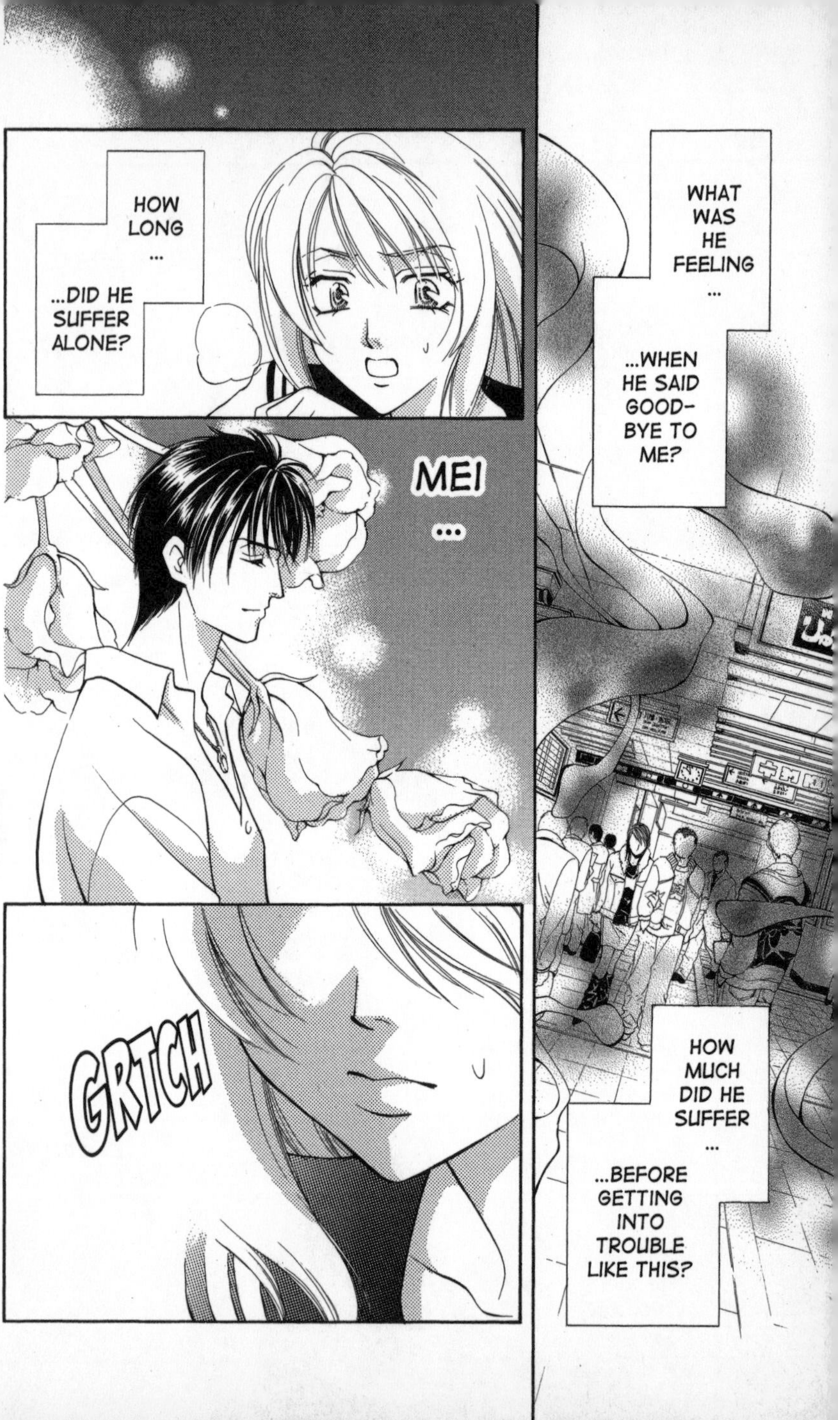
WHAT WAS HE FEELING ...
...WHEN HE SAID GOOD-BYE TO ME?
HOW MUCH DID HE SUFFER ...
...BEFORE GETTING INTO TROUBLE LIKE THIS?
HOW LONG ...
...DID HE SUFFER ALONE?
MEI ...
GRTCH

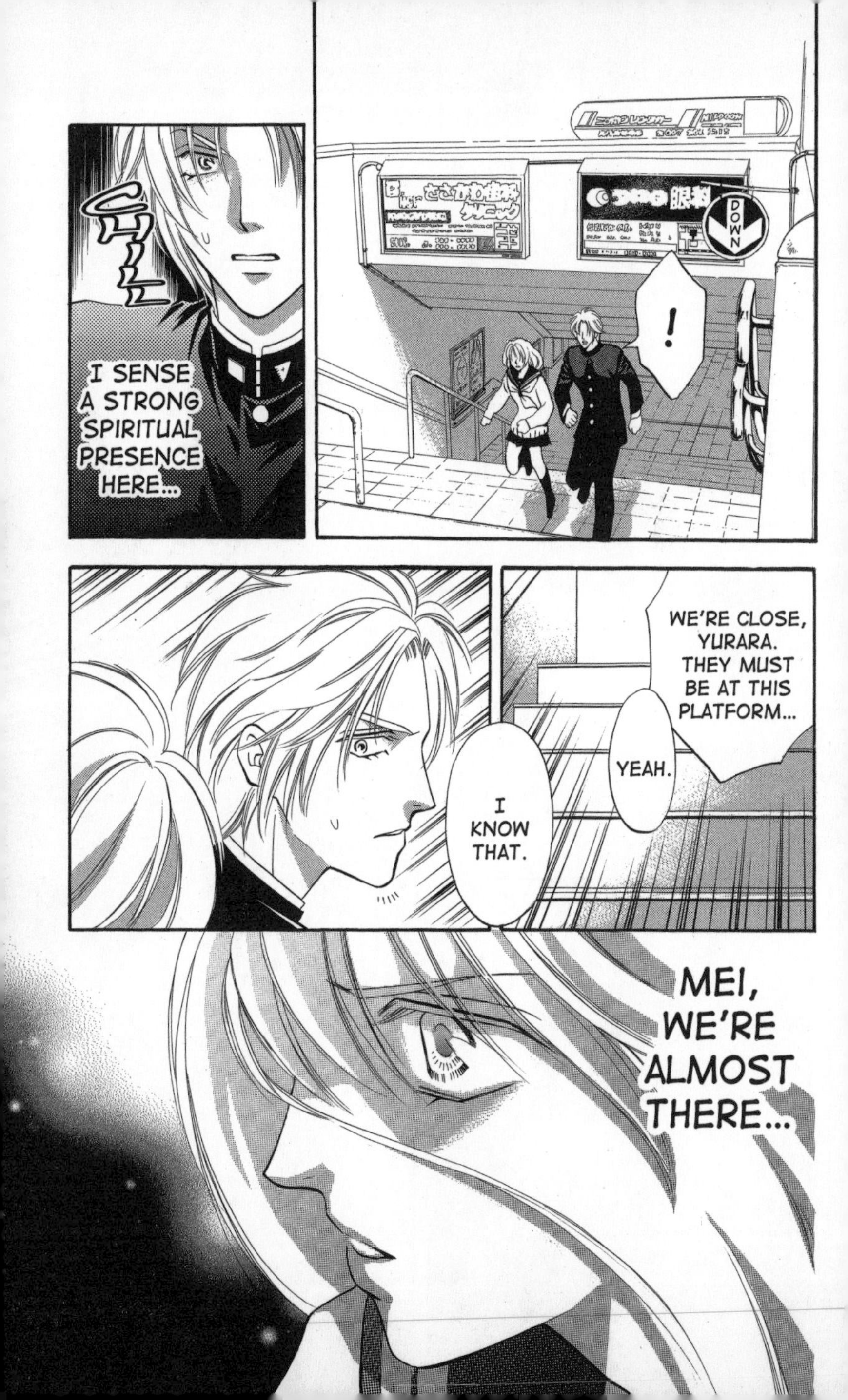

DOWN
!
CHILL
I SENSE A STRONG SPIRITUAL PRESENCE HERE...
WE'RE CLOSE, YURARA. THEY MUST BE AT THIS PLATFORM...
YEAH.
I KNOW THAT.
MEI, WE'RE ALMOST THERE...

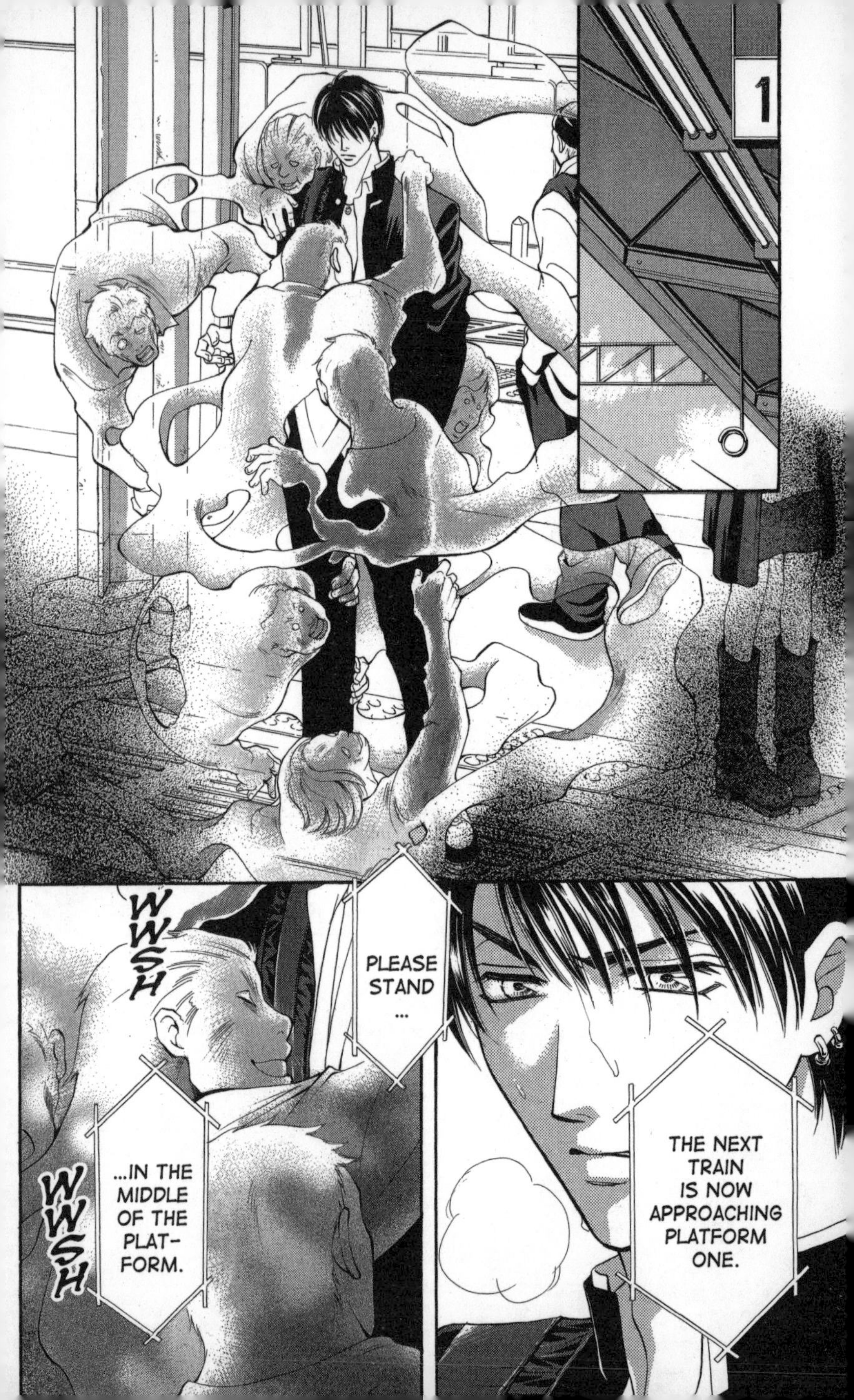
THE NEXT TRAIN IS NOW APPROACHING PLATFORM ONE.
PLEASE STAND ...
...IN THE MIDDLE OF THE PLAT-FORM.
WWSH
WWSH

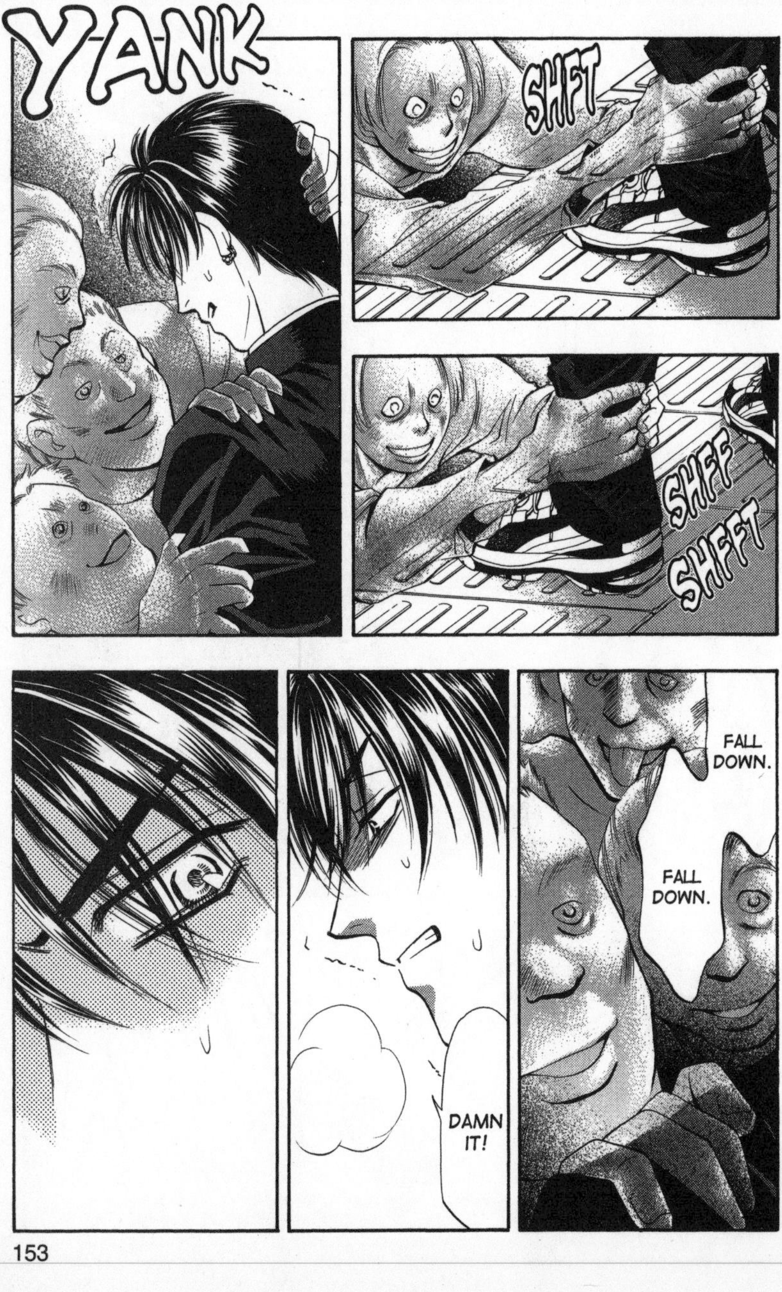
SHFT
SHFF
SHFFT
YANK
FALL DOWN.
FALL DOWN.
DAMN IT!

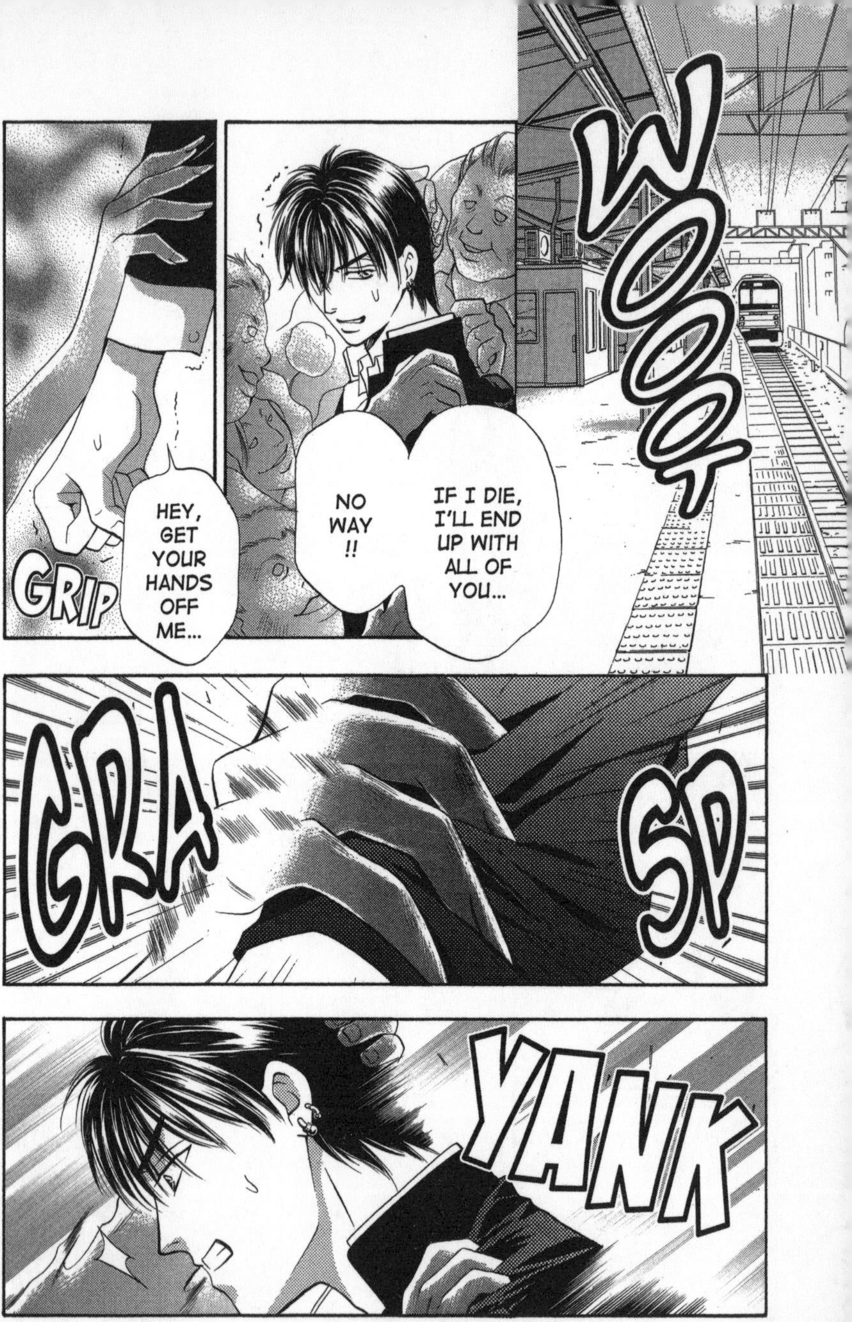
WOOOH
IF I DIE, I'LL END UP WITH ALL OF YOU...
NO WAY!!
HEY, GET YOUR HANDS OFF ME...
GRIP
GRA
SP
YANK

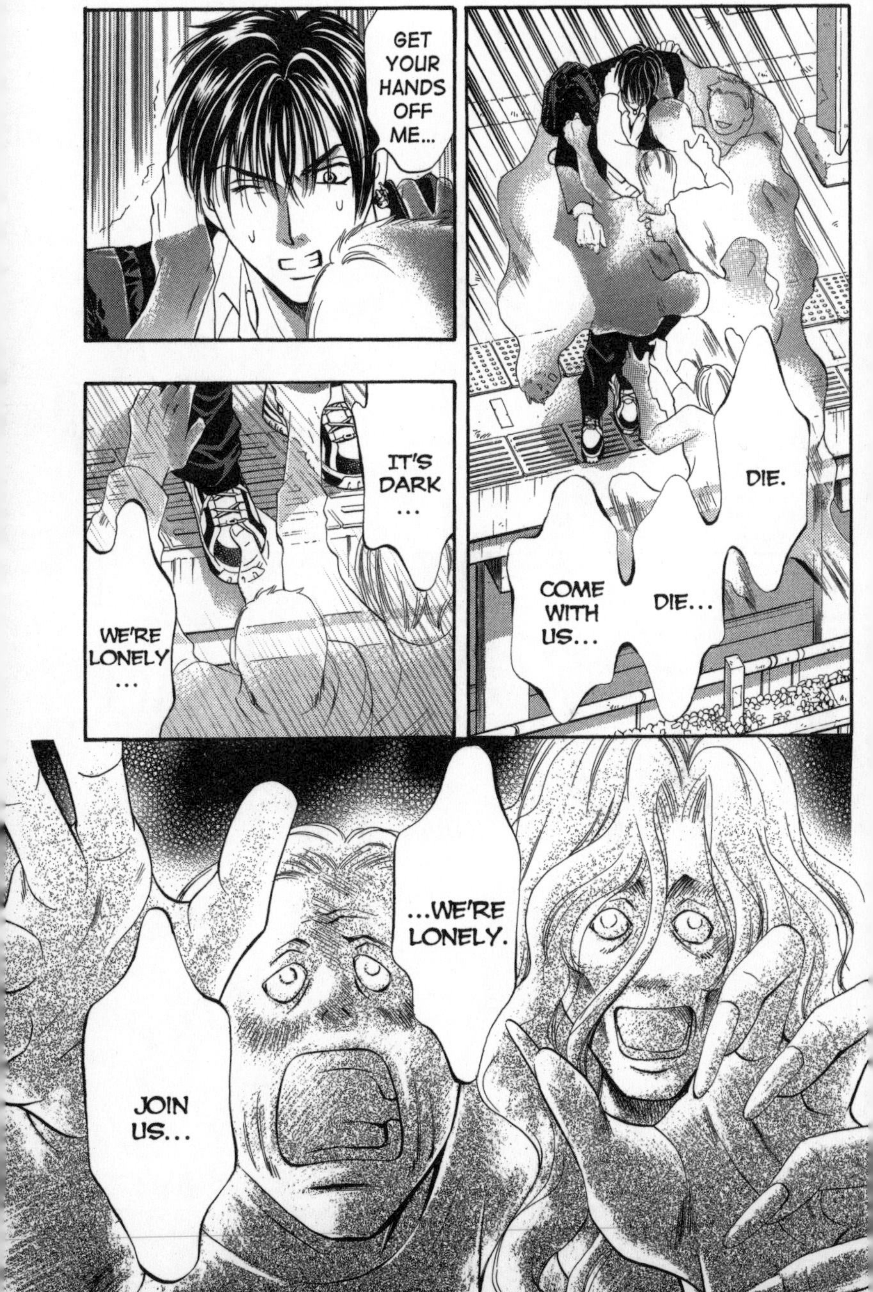
DIE.
DIE...
COME WITH US...
GET YOUR HANDS OFF ME...
IT'S DARK...
WE'RE LONELY...
...WE'RE LONELY.
JOIN US...

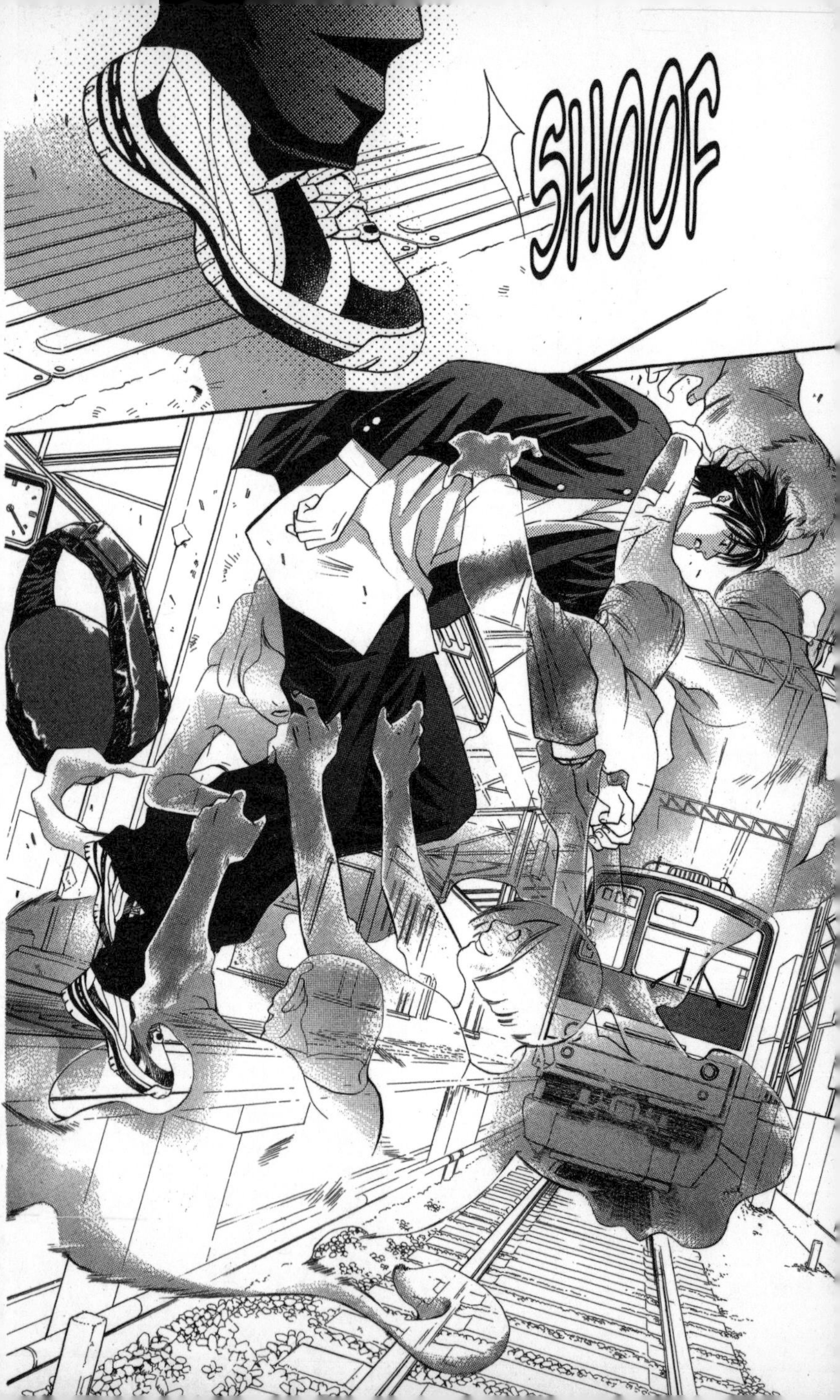
SHOOF

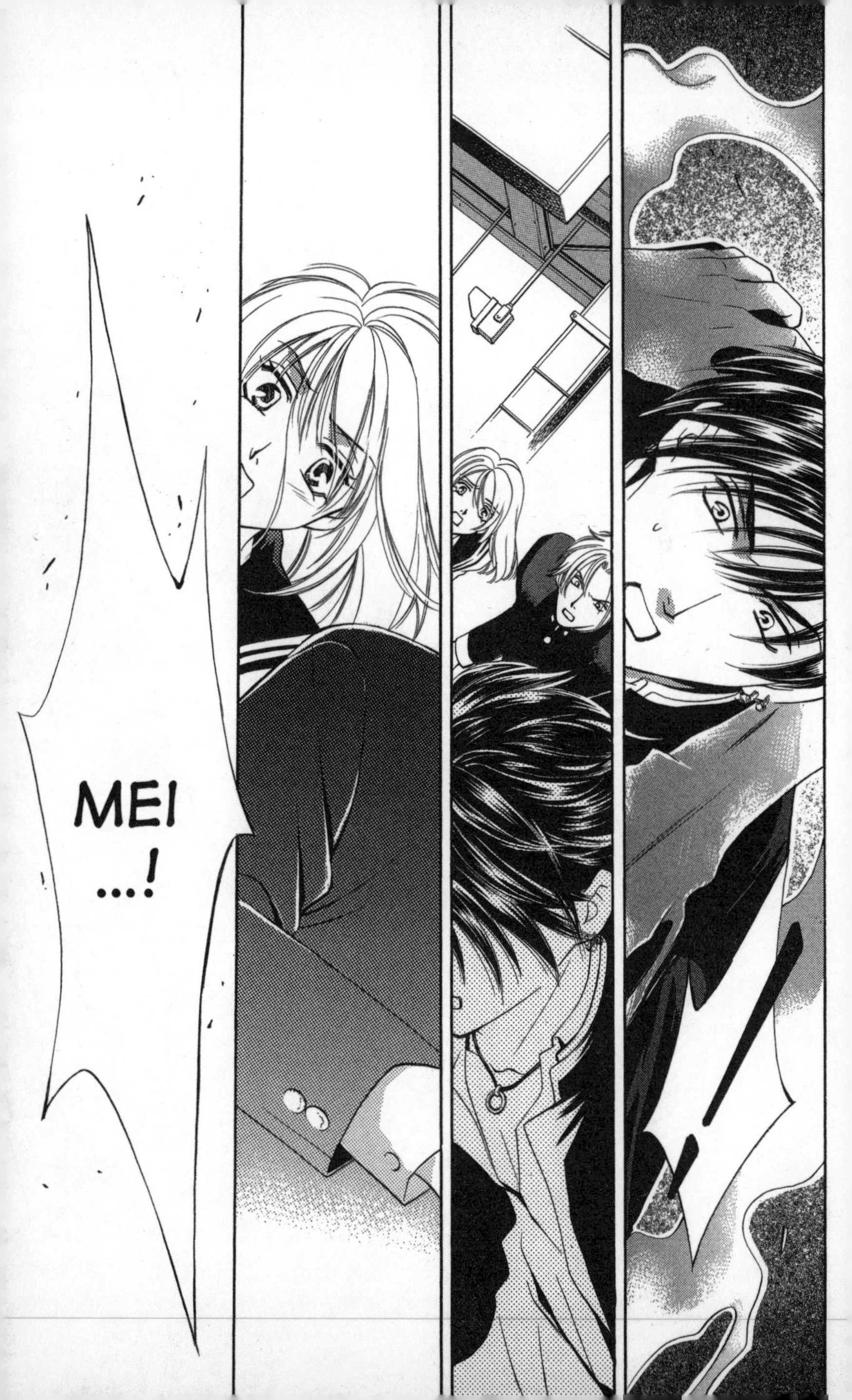
MEI
...!

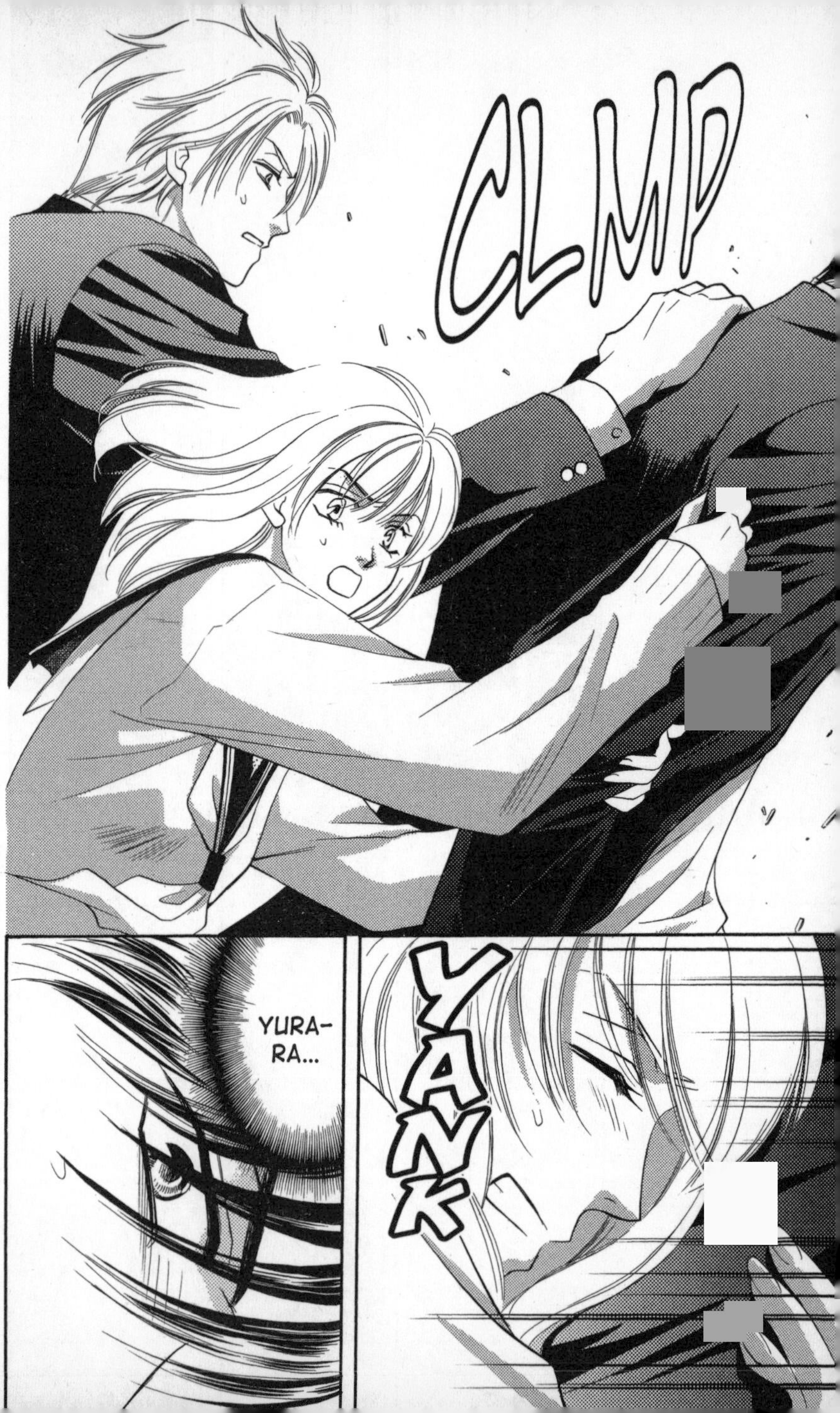
CLMP
YANK
YURA-RA...

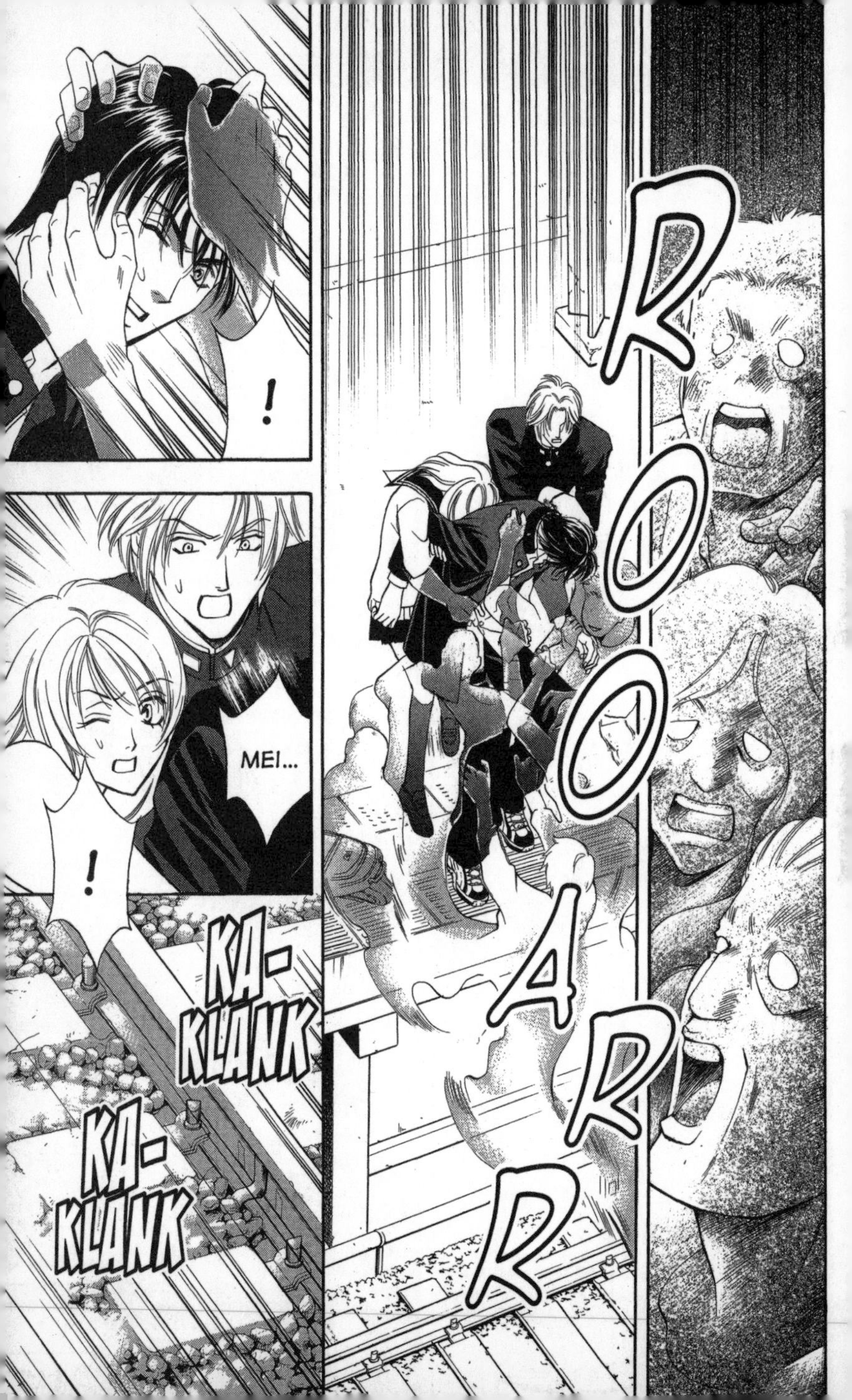
ROOOARRR
!
MEI...
!
KA-KLANK
KA-KLANK

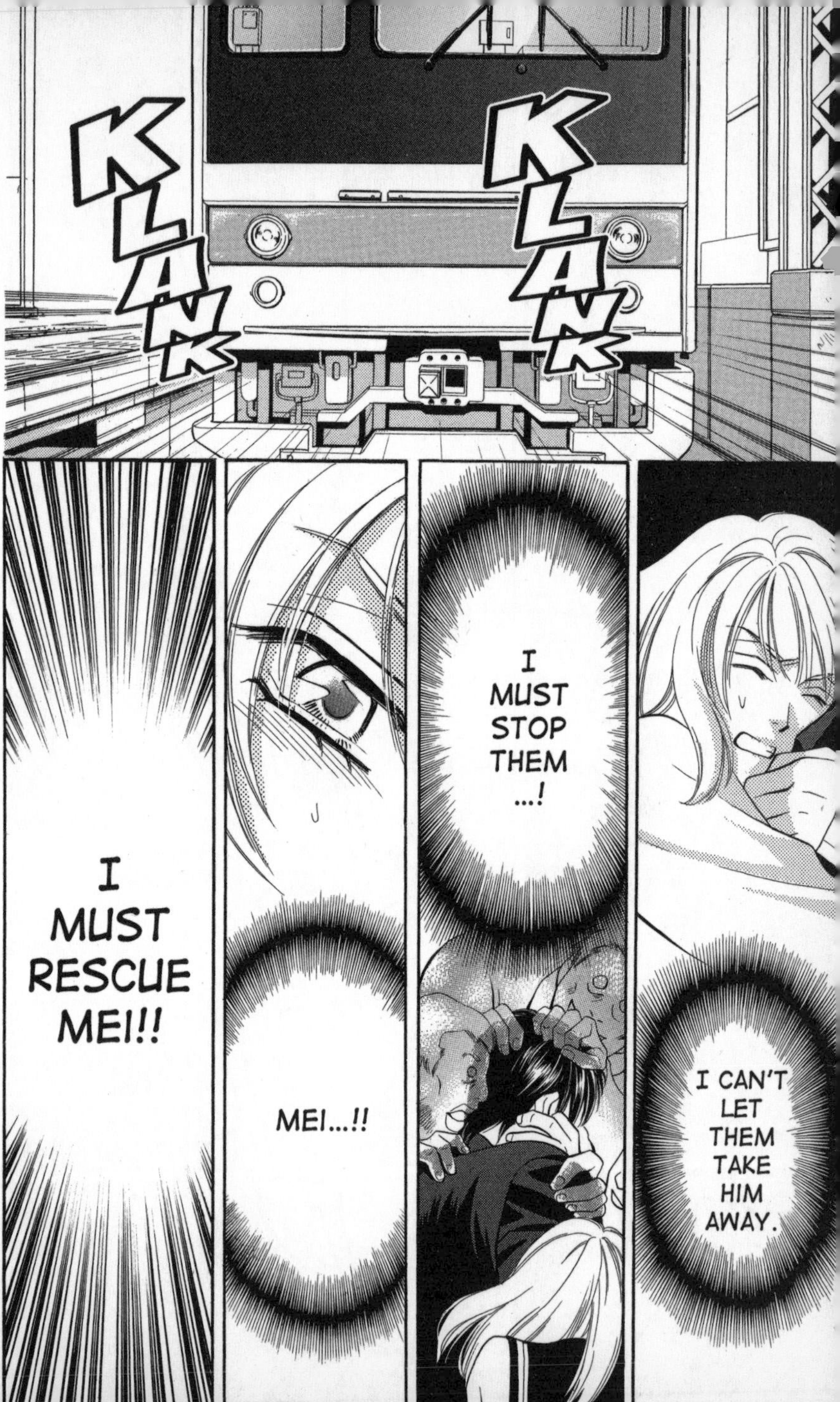
KLANK
KLANK
I CAN'T LET THEM TAKE HIM AWAY.
I MUST STOP THEM ...!
MEI...!!
I MUST RESCUE MEI!!

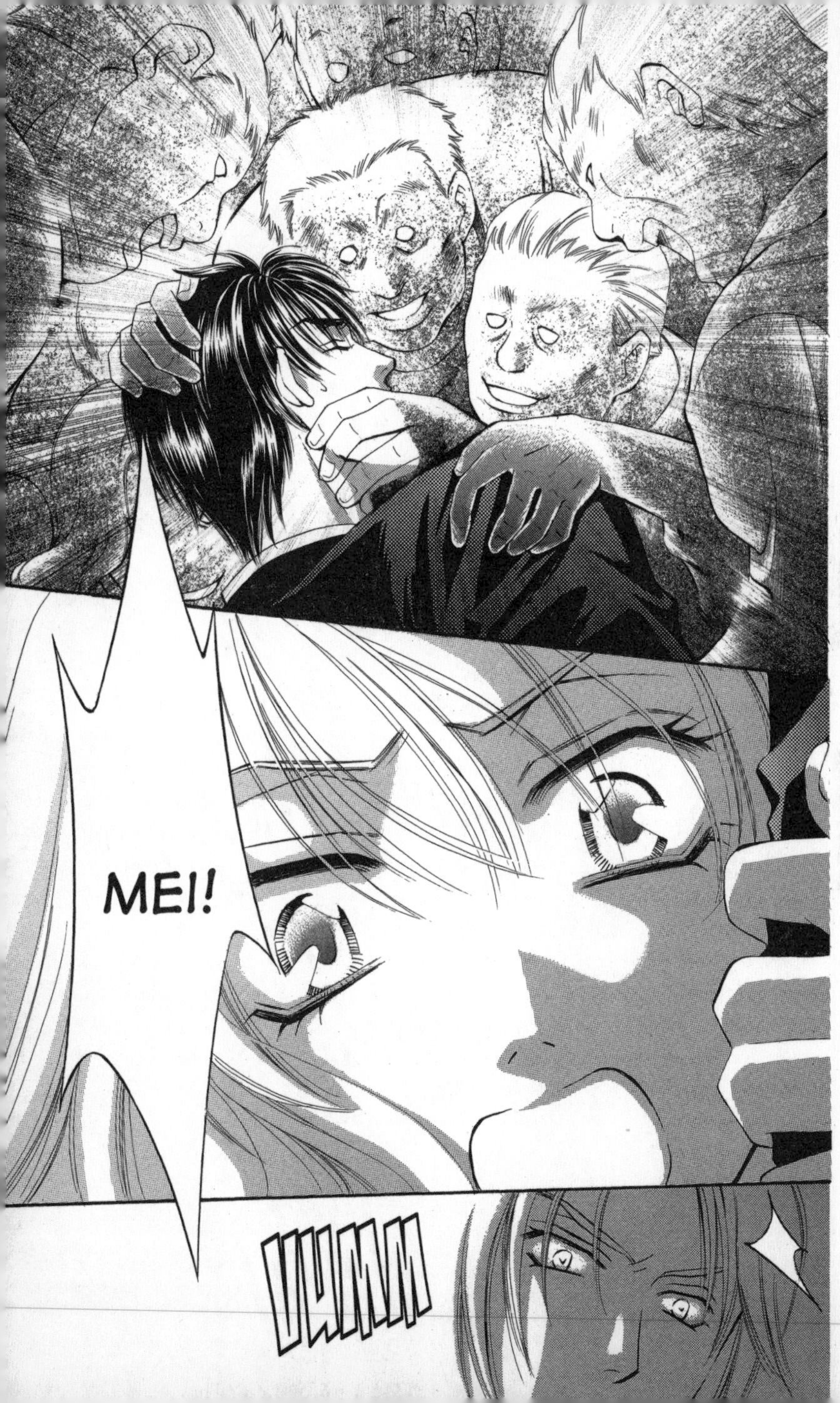
MEI!
VUMM

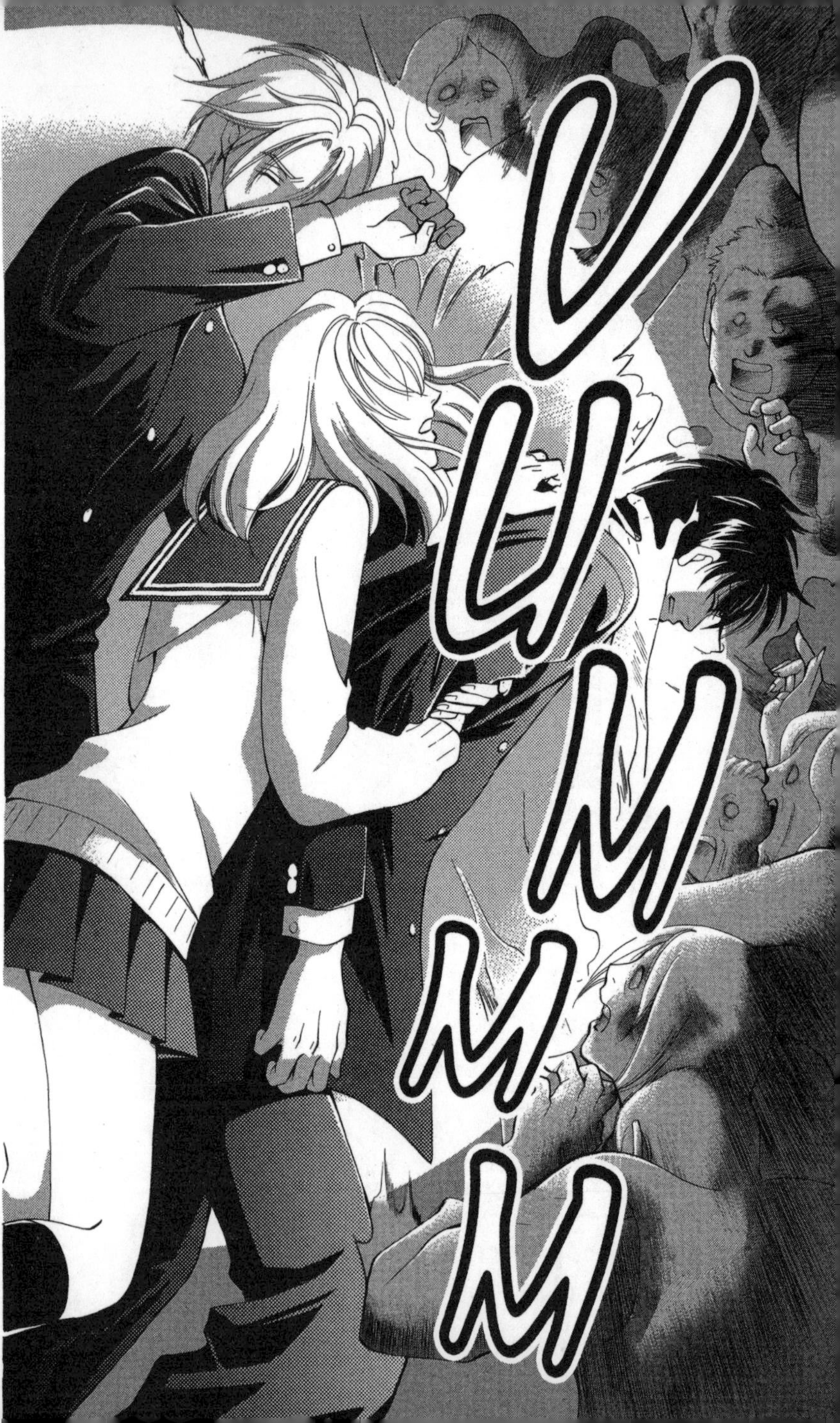
VUMMM

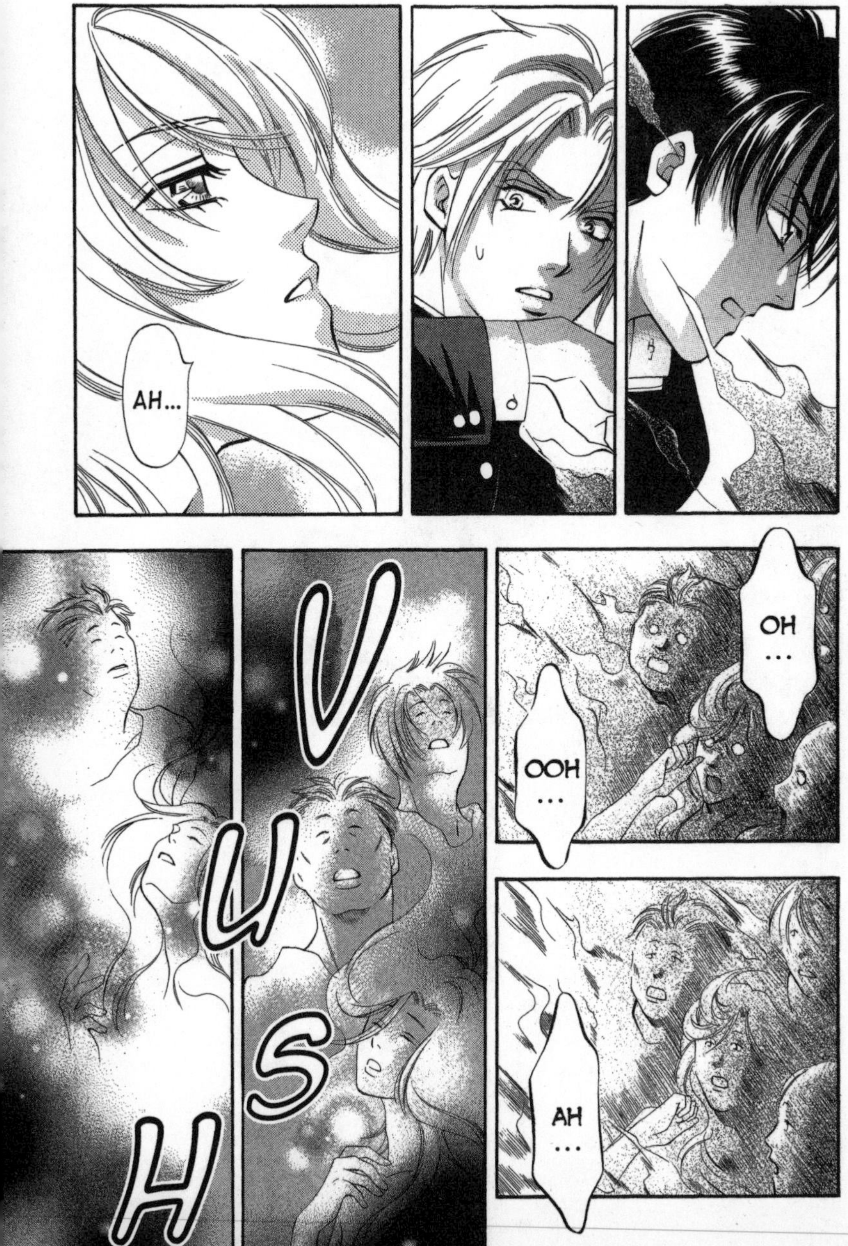
AH...
OH ...
OOH ...
AH ...
VUSH

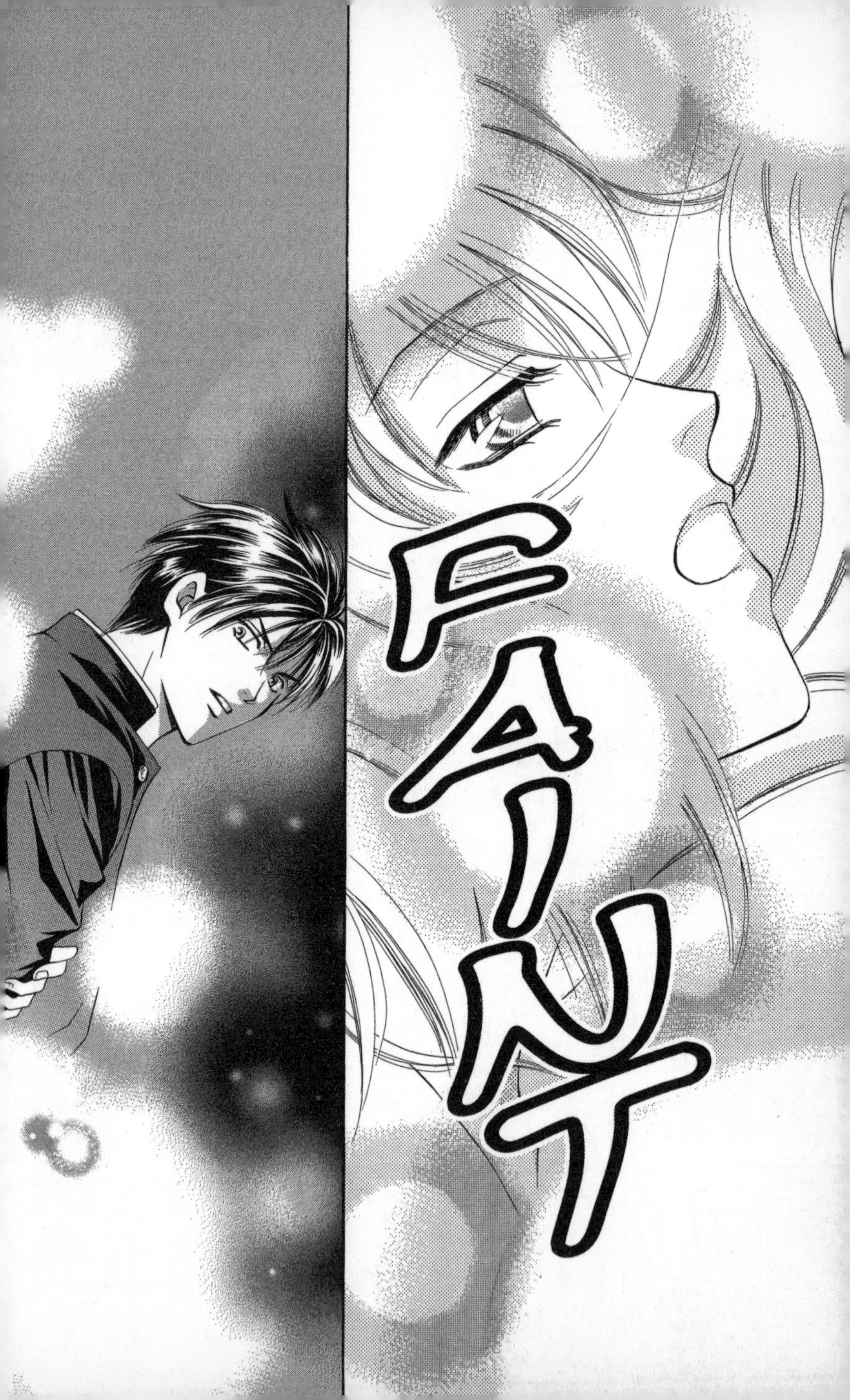
FAINT

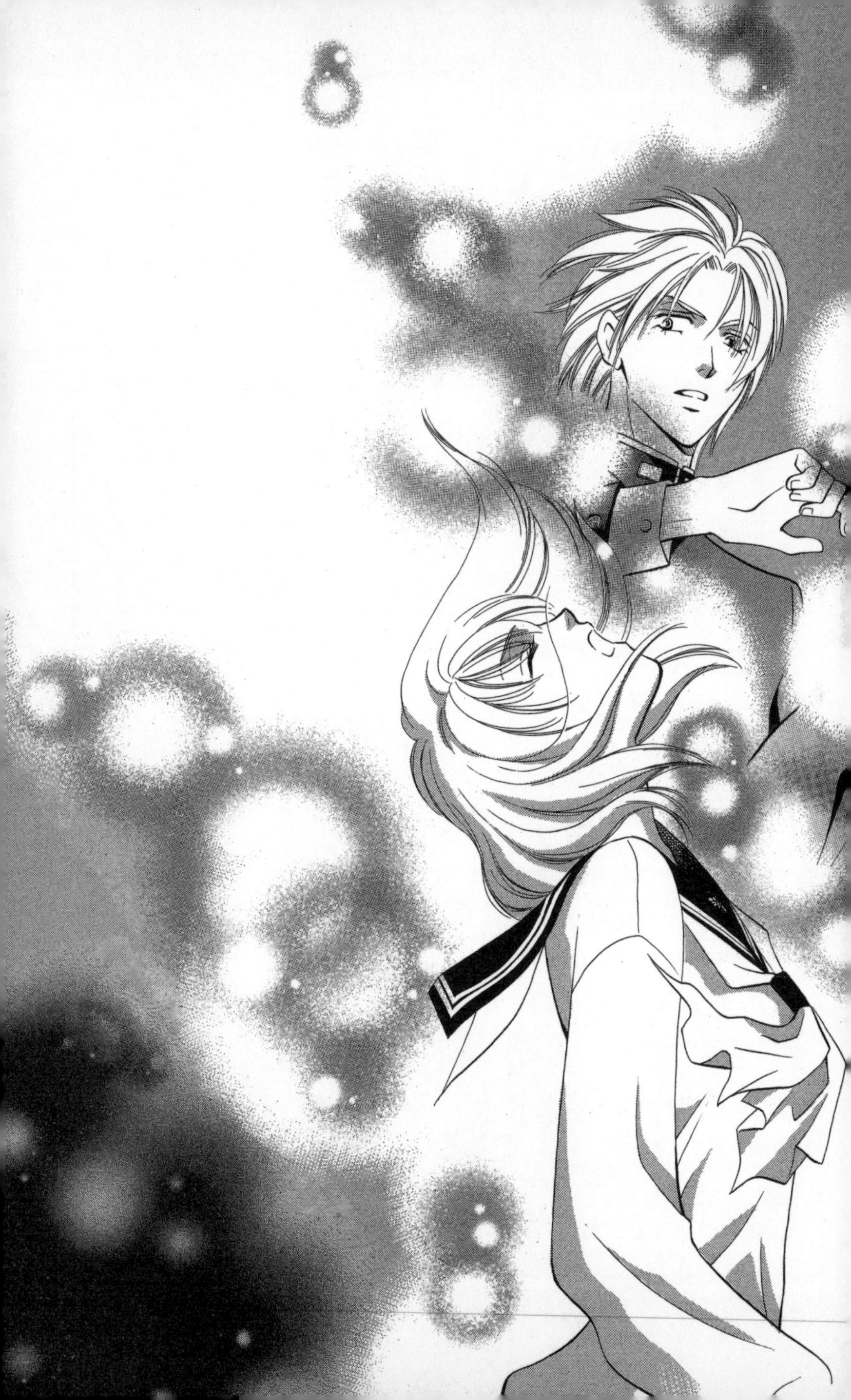

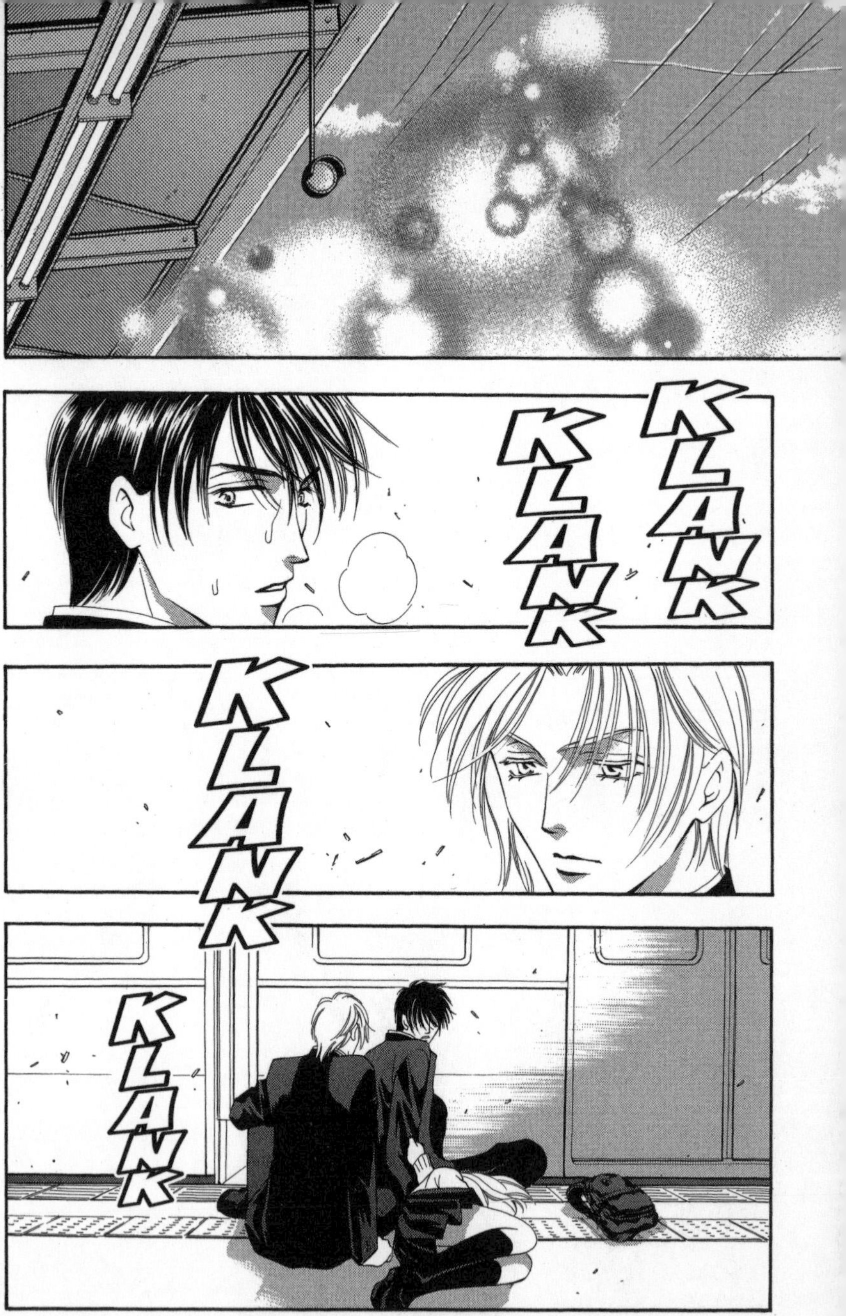
KLANK
KLANK
KLANK
KLANK

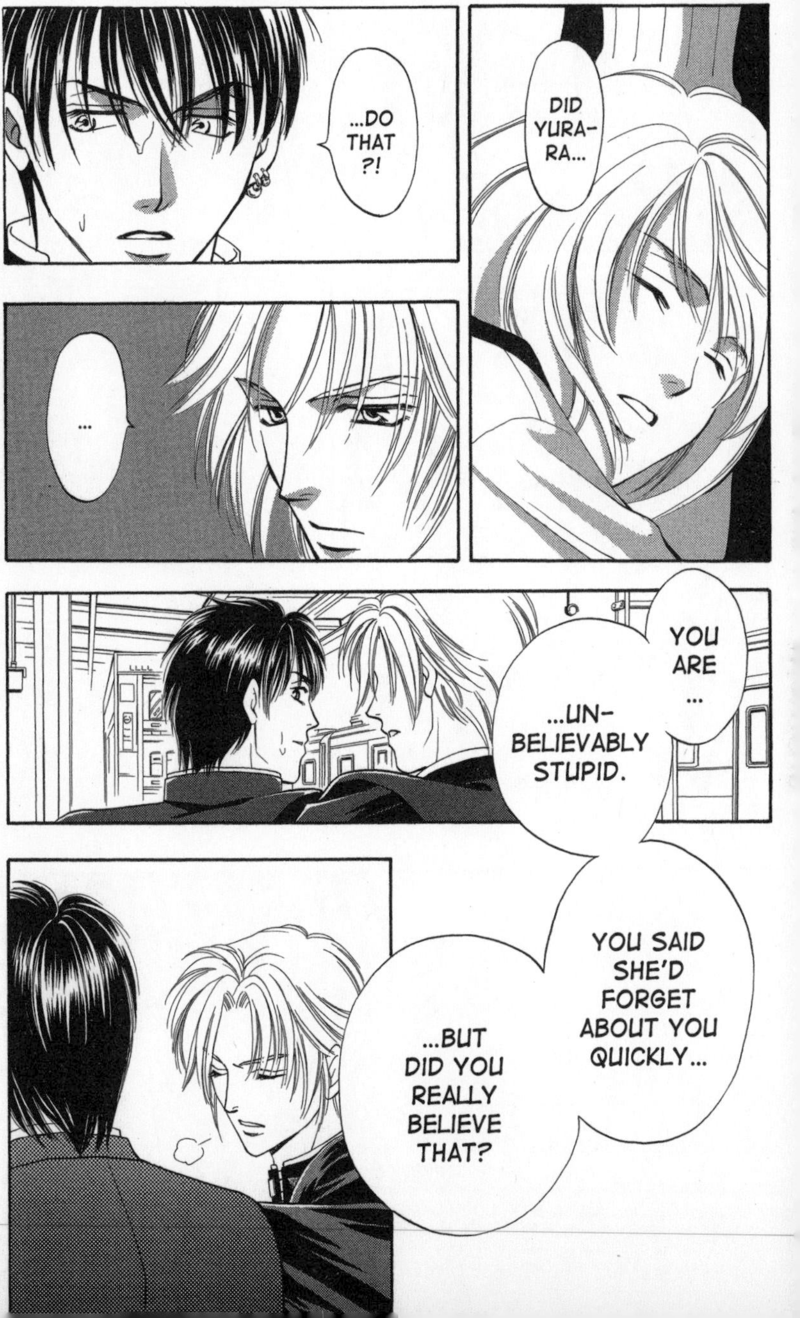
DID YURA-RA...
...DO THAT?!
...
YOU ARE ...
...UN-BELIEVABLY STUPID.
YOU SAID SHE'D FORGET ABOUT YOU QUICKLY...
...BUT DID YOU REALLY BELIEVE THAT?

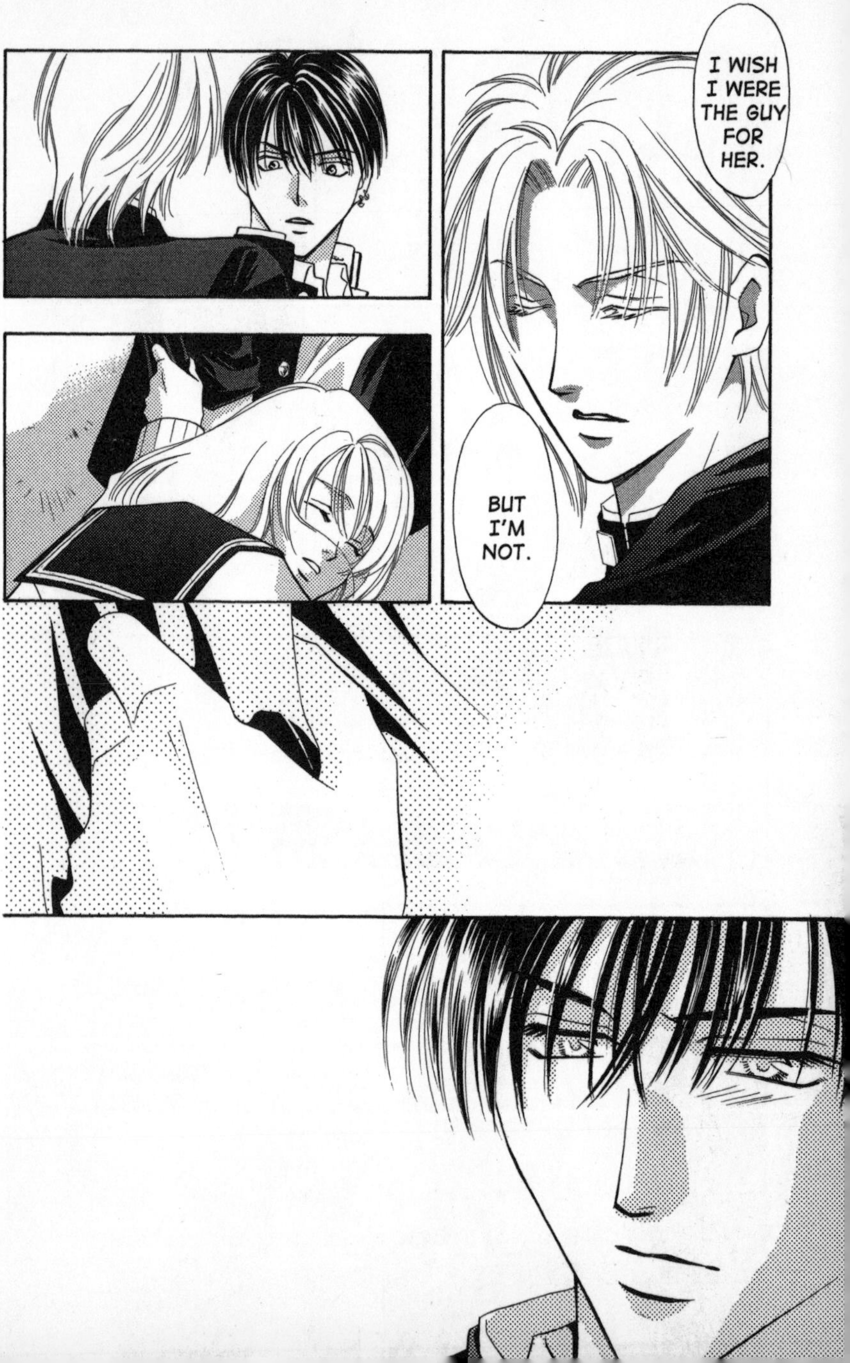
I WISH I WERE THE GUY FOR HER.
BUT I'M NOT.

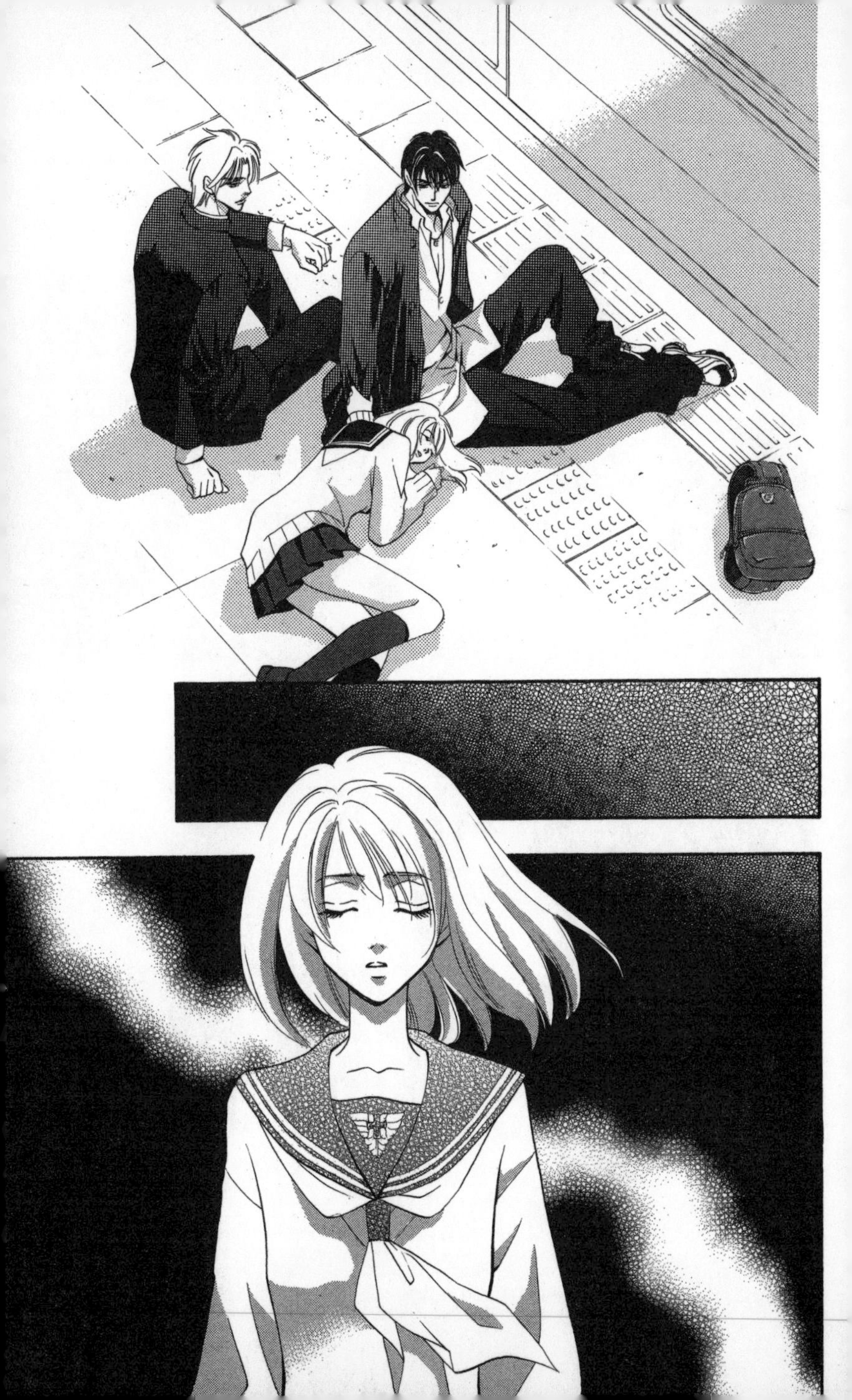

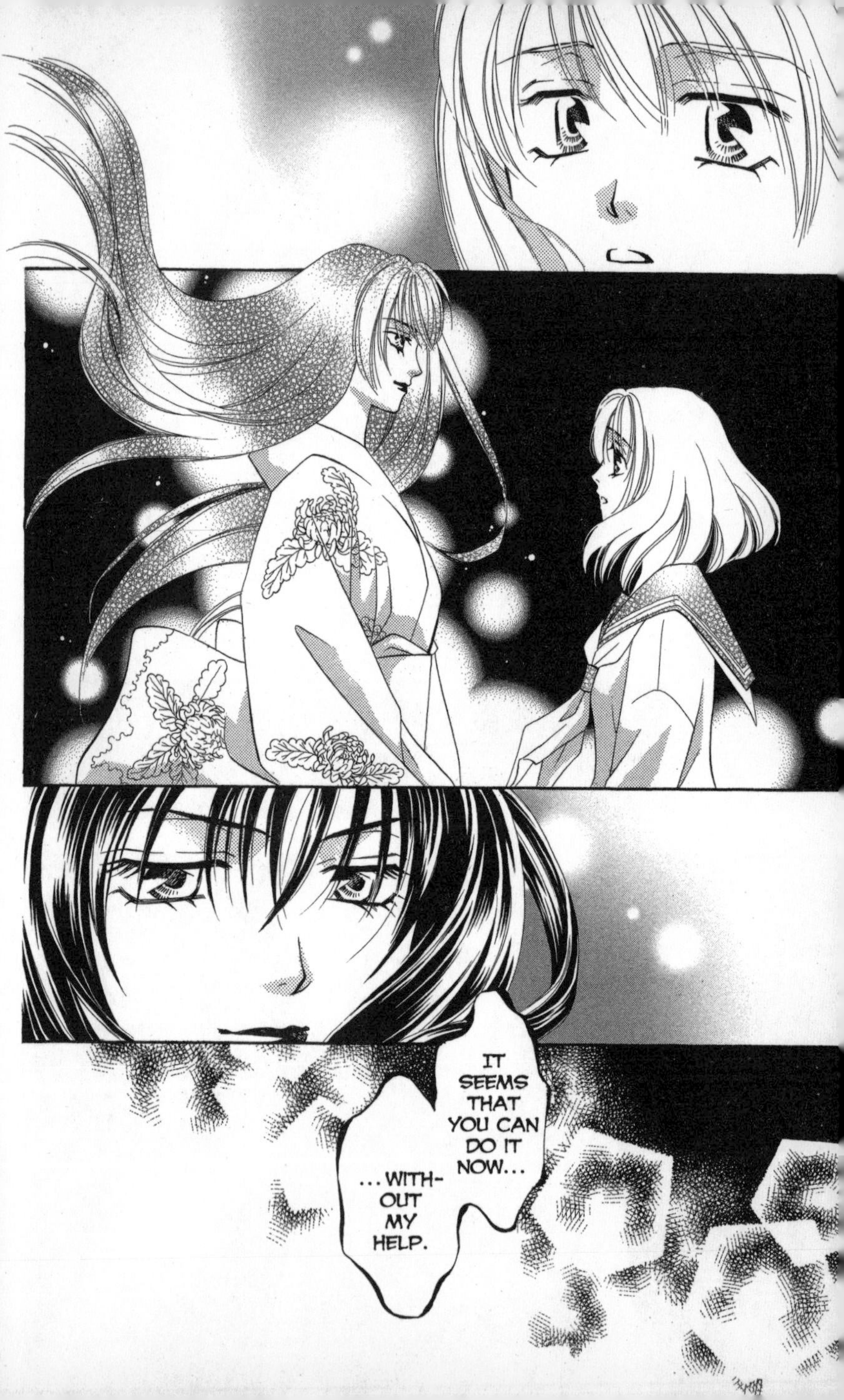
IT SEEMS THAT YOU CAN DO IT NOW...
...WITH-OUT MY HELP.

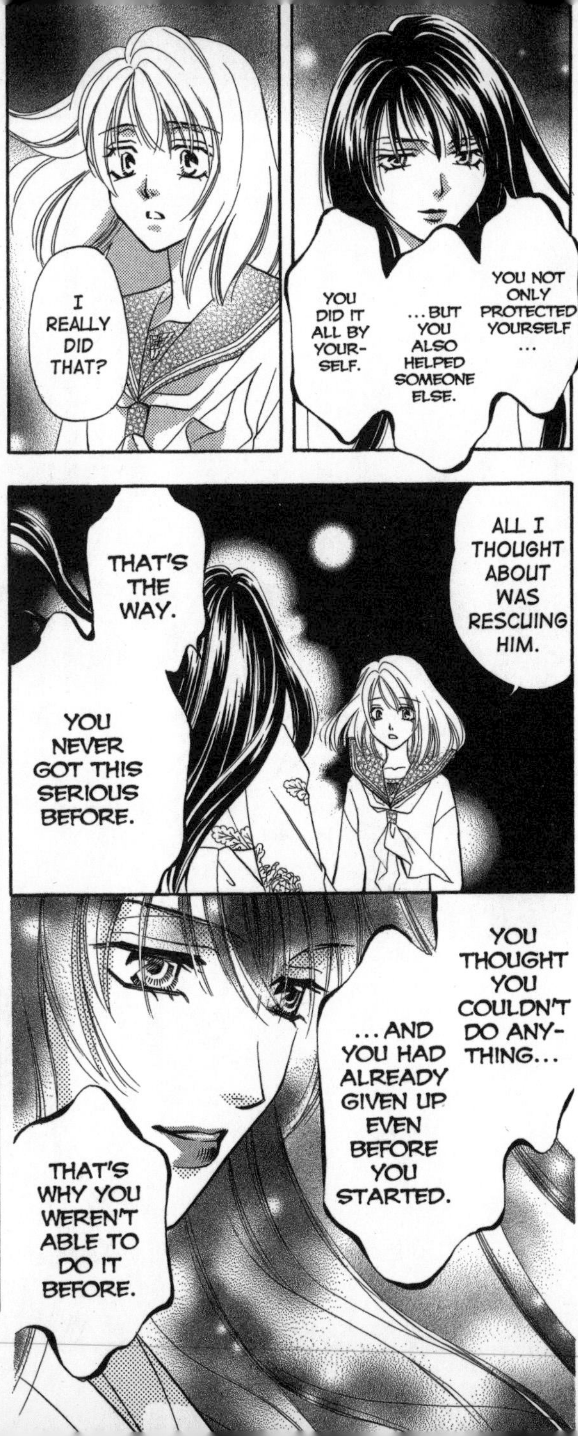
YOU NOT ONLY PROTECTED YOURSELF...
...BUT YOU ALSO HELPED SOMEONE ELSE.
YOU DID IT ALL BY YOUR-SELF.
I REALLY DID THAT?
ALL I THOUGHT ABOUT WAS RESCUING HIM.
THAT'S THE WAY.
YOU NEVER GOT THIS SERIOUS BEFORE.
YOU THOUGHT YOU COULDN'T DO ANY-THING...
...AND YOU HAD ALREADY GIVEN UP EVEN BEFORE YOU STARTED.
THAT'S WHY YOU WEREN'T ABLE TO DO IT BEFORE.

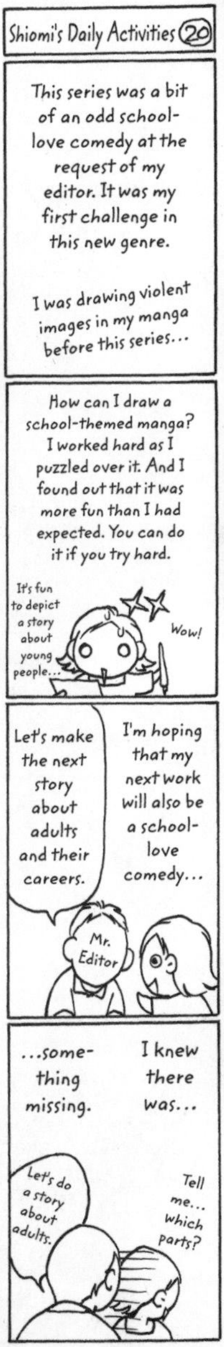
Shiomi's Daily Activities 20
This series was a bit of an odd school-love comedy at the request of my editor. It was my first challenge in this new genre.
I was drawing violent images in my manga before this series...
How can I draw a school-themed manga? I worked hard as I puzzled over it. And I found out that it was more fun than I had expected. You can do it if you try hard.
It's fun to depict a story about young people...
Wow!
I'm hoping that my next work will also be a school-love comedy...
Let's make the next story about adults and their careers.
Mr. Editor
I knew there was...
...some-thing missing.
Tell me... which parts?
Let's do a story about adults.

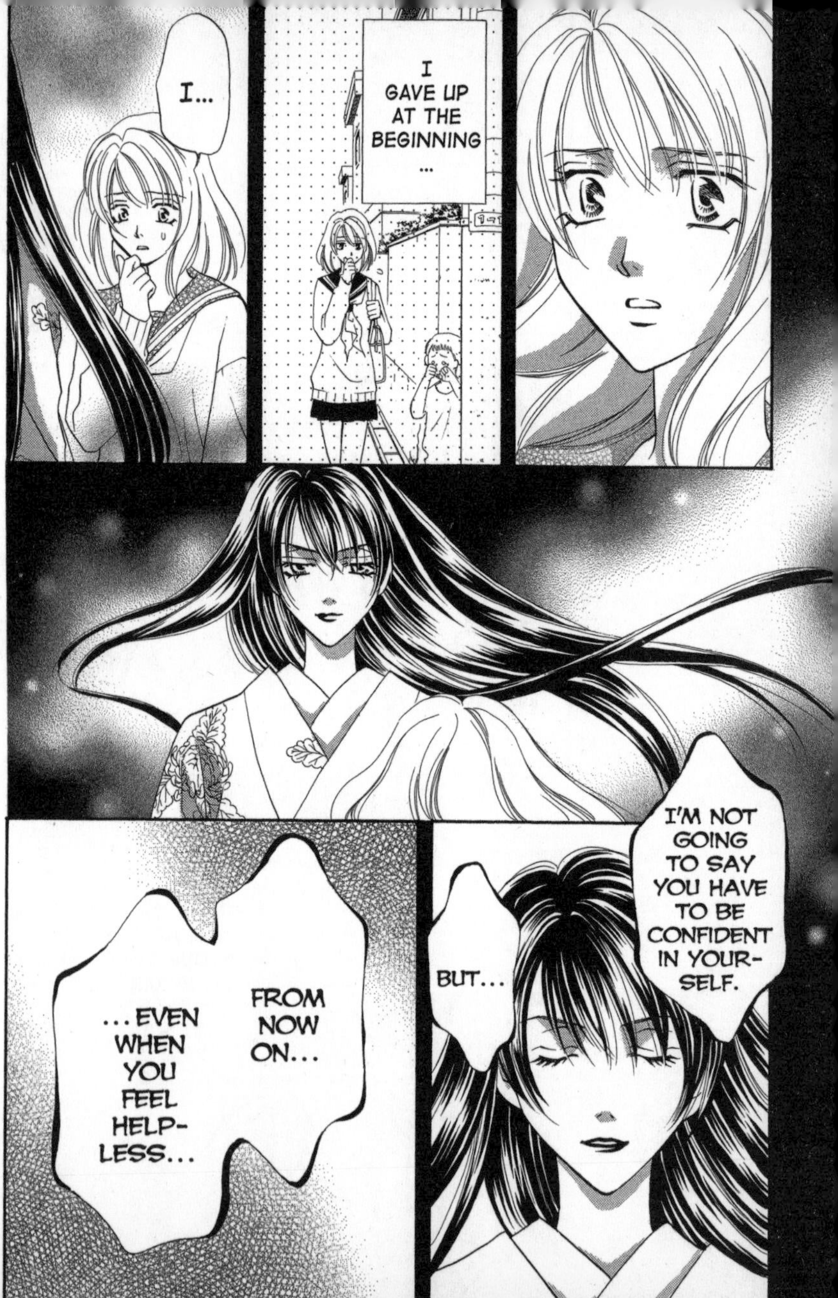
I GAVE UP AT THE BEGINNING...
I...
I'M NOT GOING TO SAY YOU HAVE TO BE CONFIDENT IN YOUR-SELF.
BUT...
FROM NOW ON...
...EVEN WHEN YOU FEEL HELP-LESS...

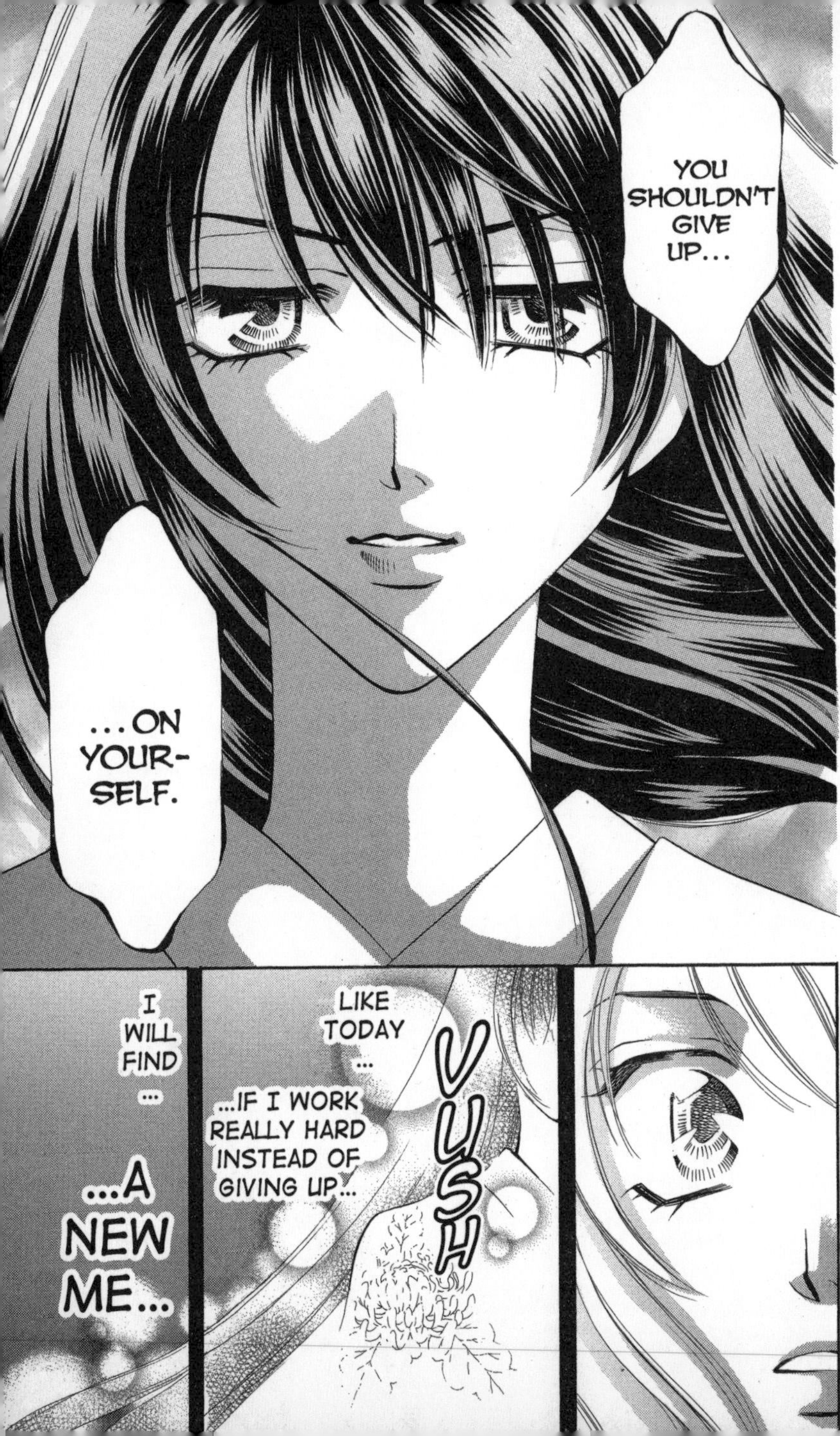
YOU SHOULDN'T GIVE UP...
...ON YOUR-SELF.
LIKE TODAY ...
...IF I WORK REALLY HARD INSTEAD OF GIVING UP...
VUSH
I WILL FIND ...
...A NEW ME...

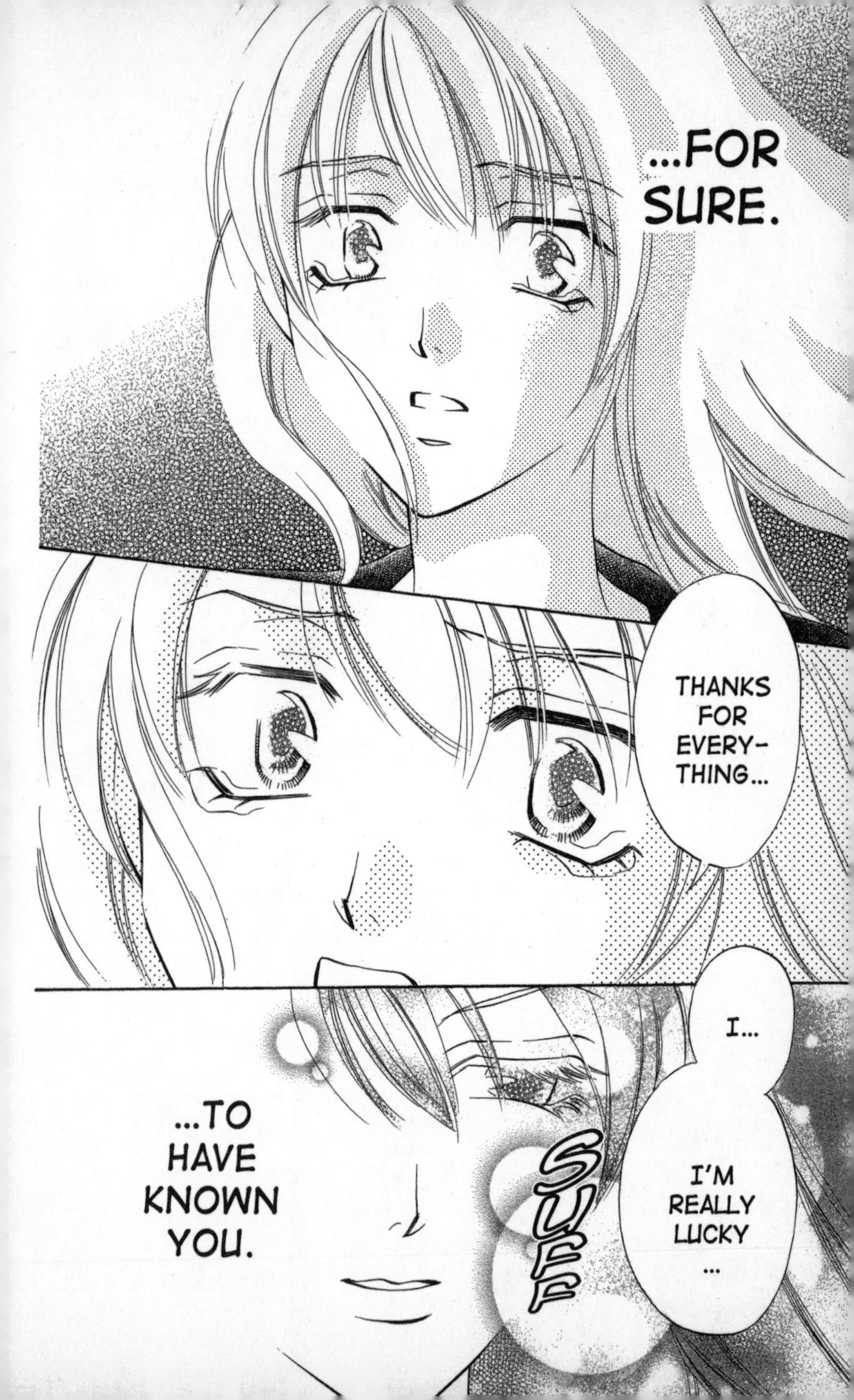
...FOR SURE.
THANKS FOR EVERY-THING...
I...
I'M REALLY LUCKY ...
SUFF
...TO HAVE KNOWN YOU.

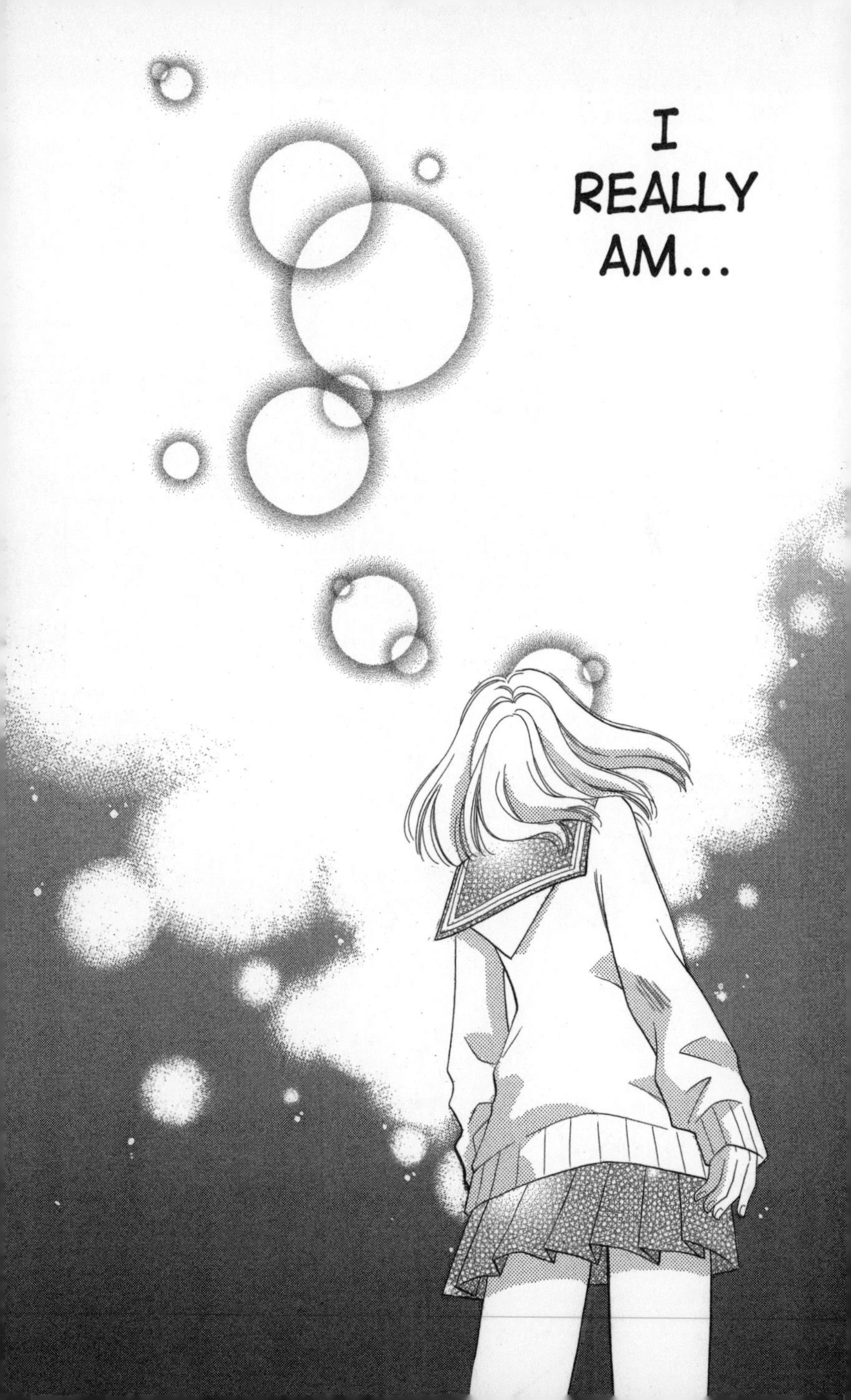
I REALLY AM...

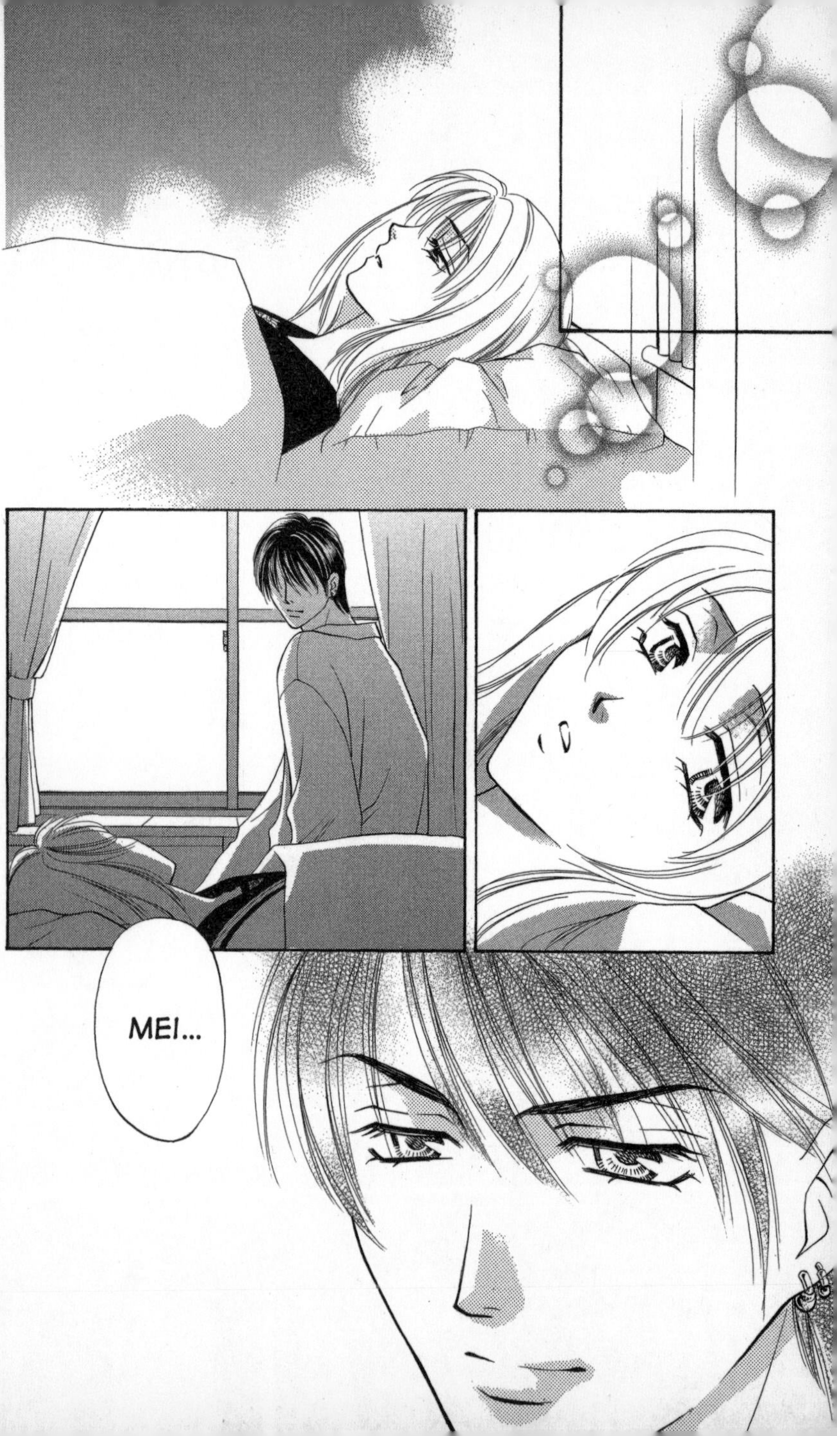
MEI...

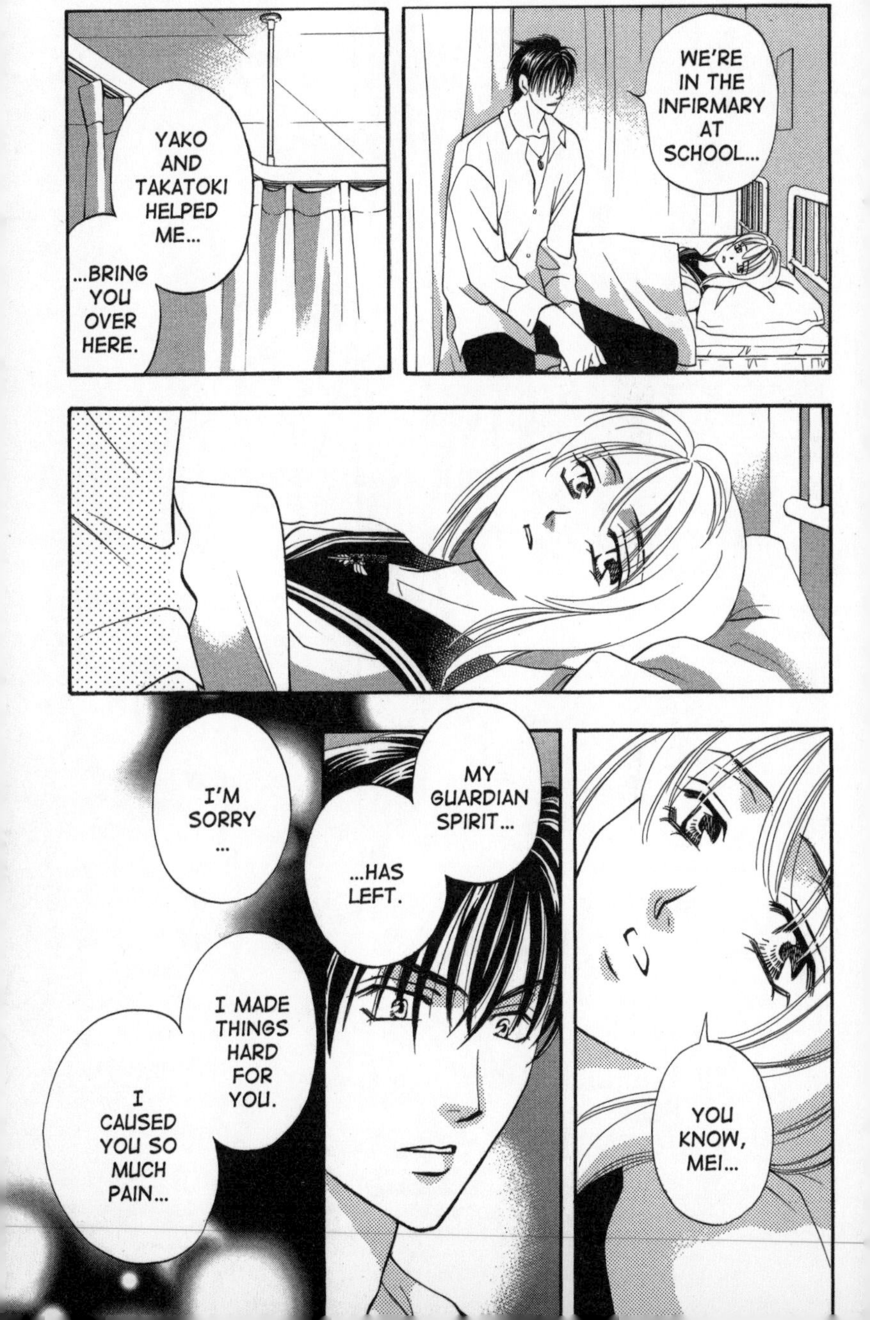
WE'RE IN THE INFIRMARY AT SCHOOL...
YAKO AND TAKATOKI HELPED ME...
...BRING YOU OVER HERE.
YOU KNOW, MEI...
MY GUARDIAN SPIRIT...
...HAS LEFT.
I'M SORRY ...
I MADE THINGS HARD FOR YOU.
I CAUSED YOU SO MUCH PAIN...

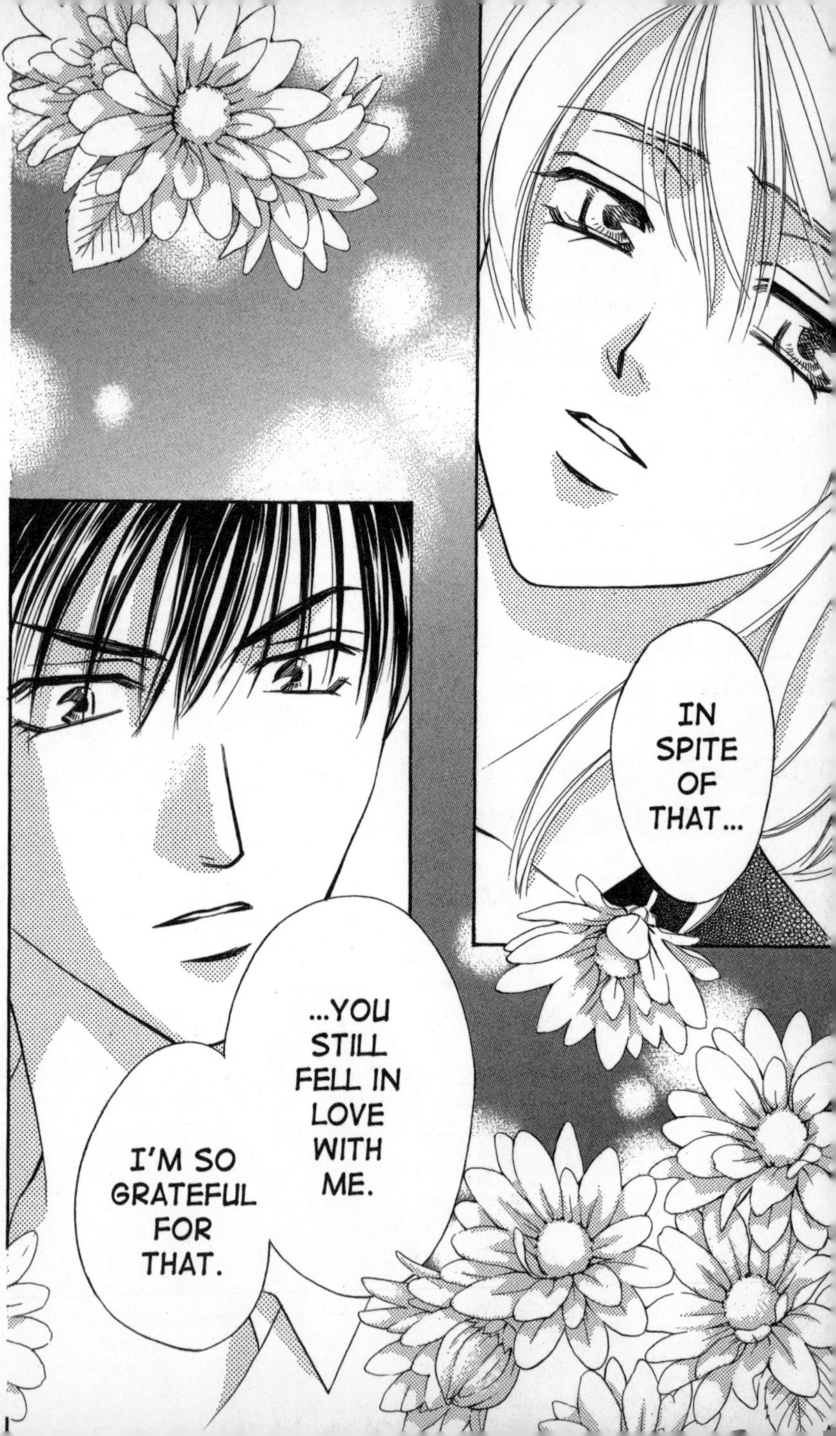
IN SPITE OF THAT...
...YOU STILL FELL IN LOVE WITH ME.
I'M SO GRATEFUL FOR THAT.

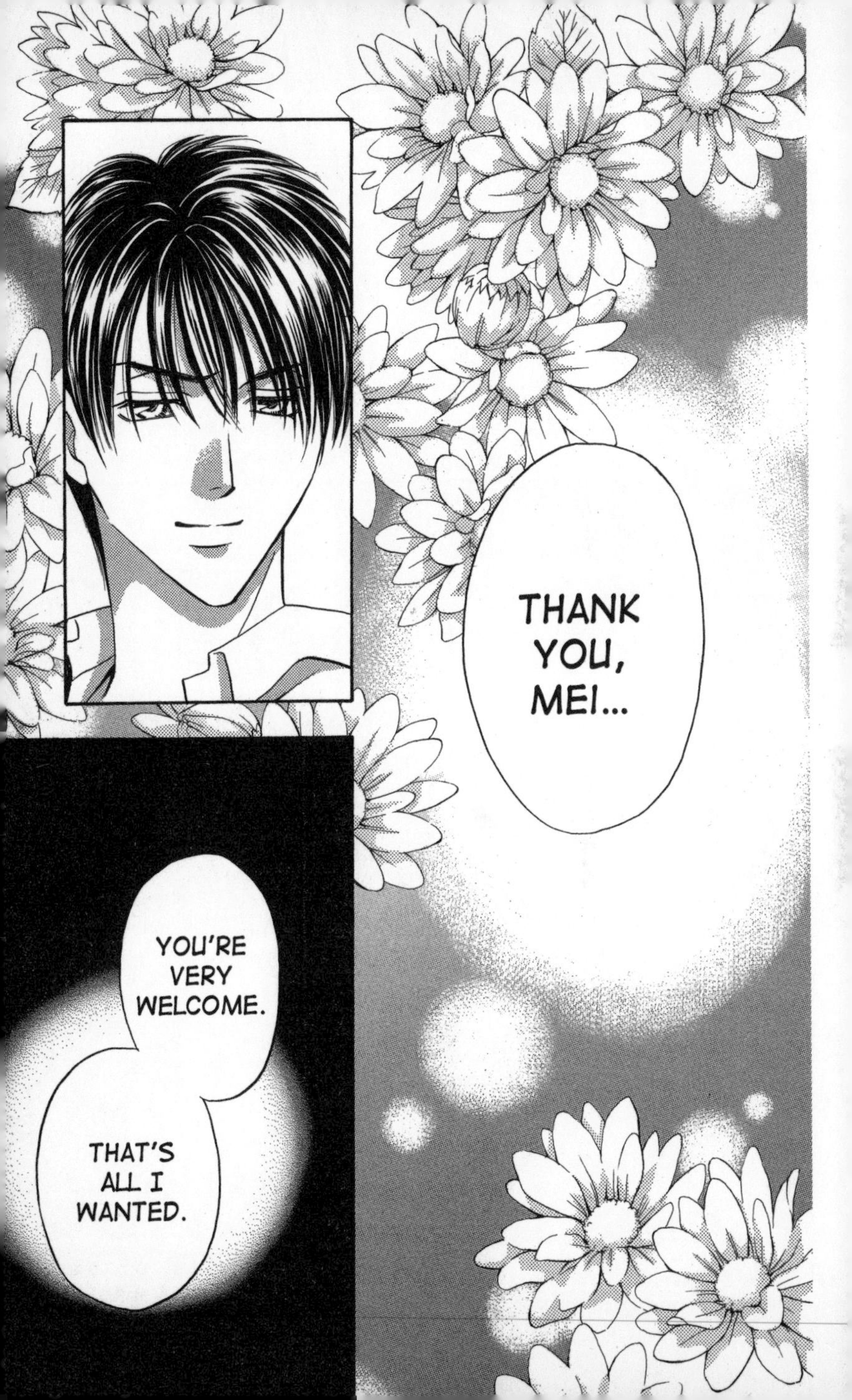
THANK YOU, MEI...
YOU'RE VERY WELCOME.
THAT'S ALL I WANTED.

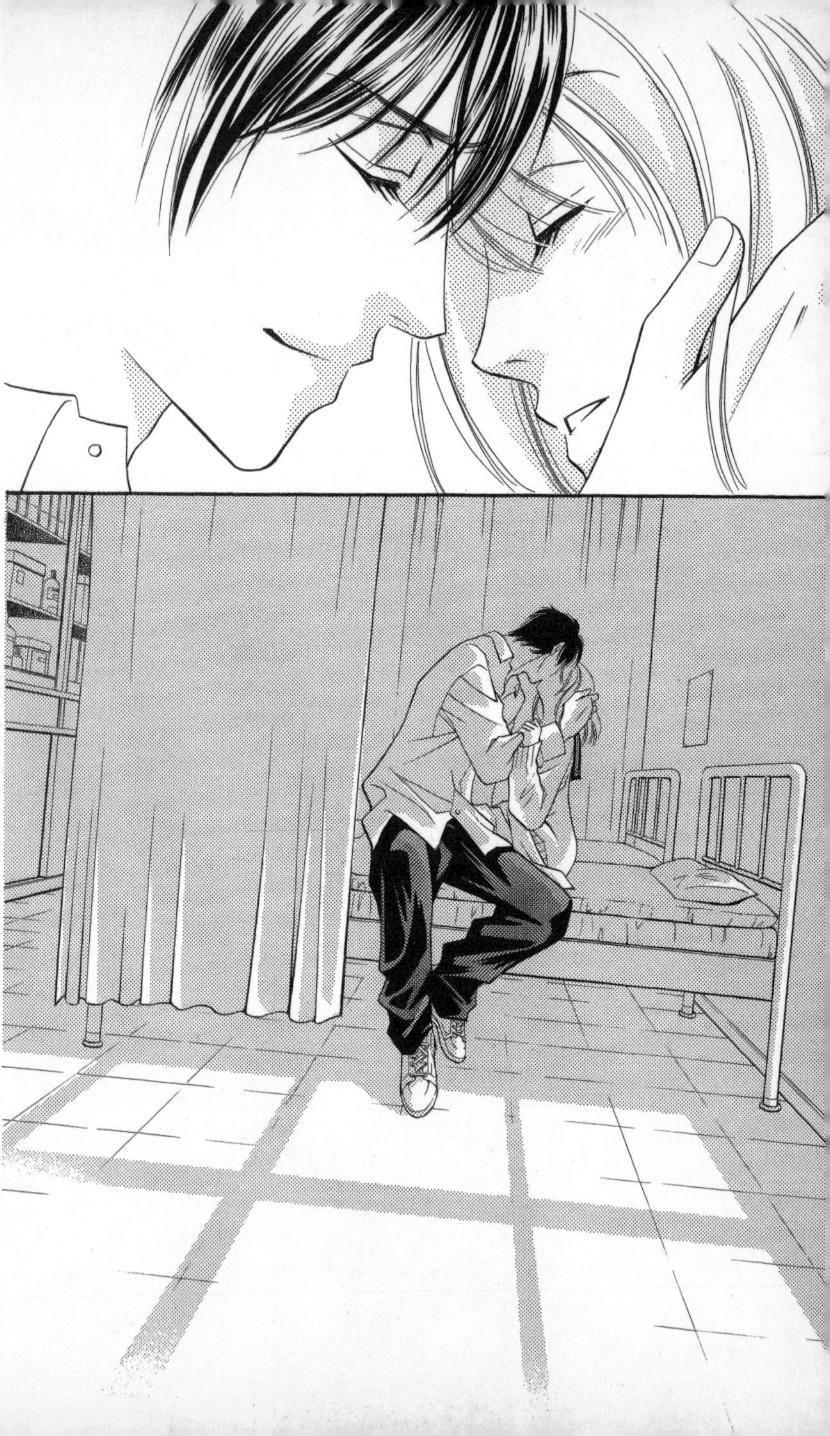

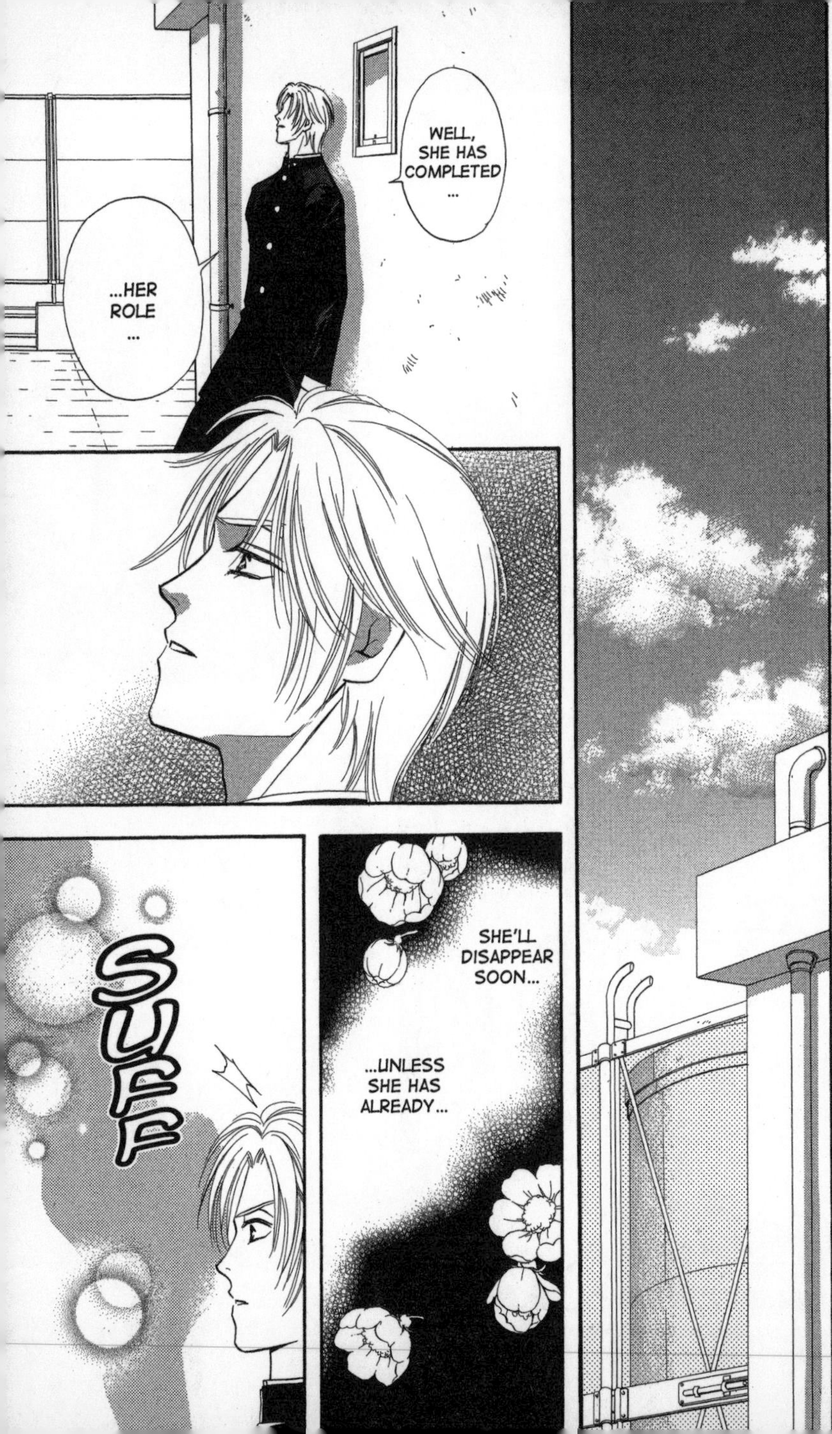

WELL, SHE HAS COMPLETED ...
...HER ROLE ...
SHE'LL DISAPPEAR SOON...
...UNLESS SHE HAS ALREADY...
SUFF

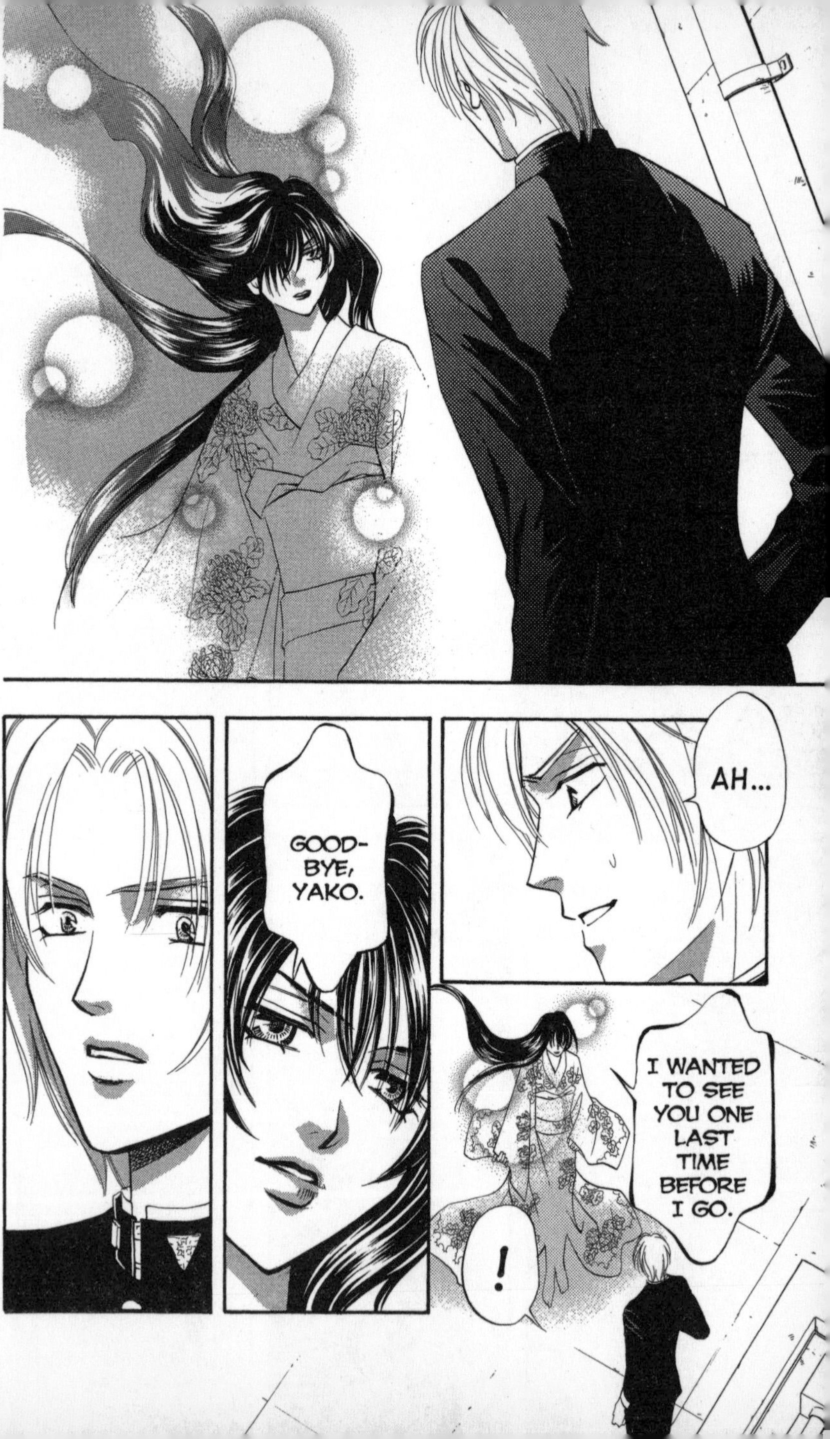
AH...
I WANTED TO SEE YOU ONE LAST TIME BEFORE I GO.
!
GOOD-BYE, YAKO.

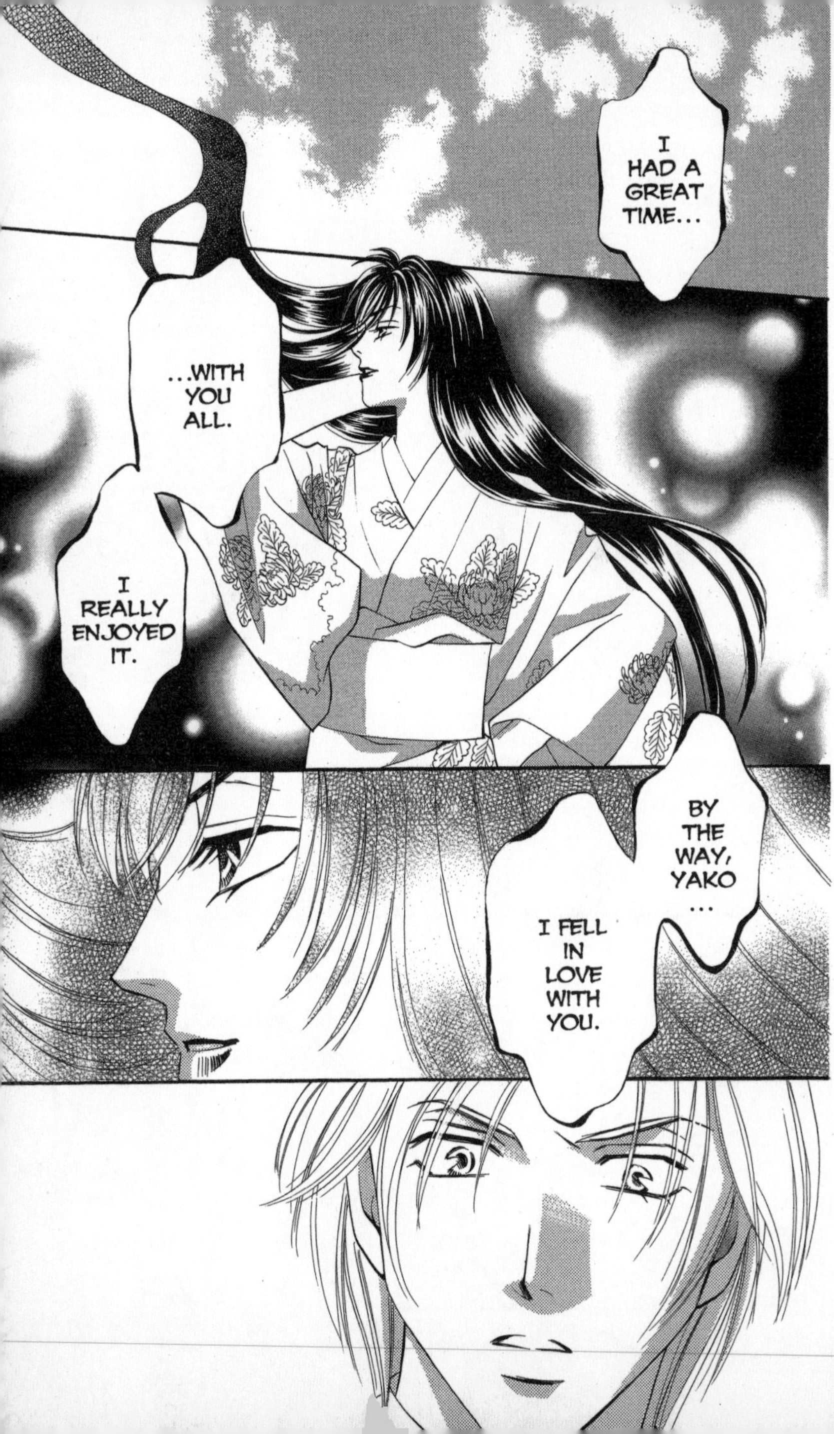
I HAD A GREAT TIME...
...WITH YOU ALL.
I REALLY ENJOYED IT.
BY THE WAY, YAKO...
I FELL IN LOVE WITH YOU.

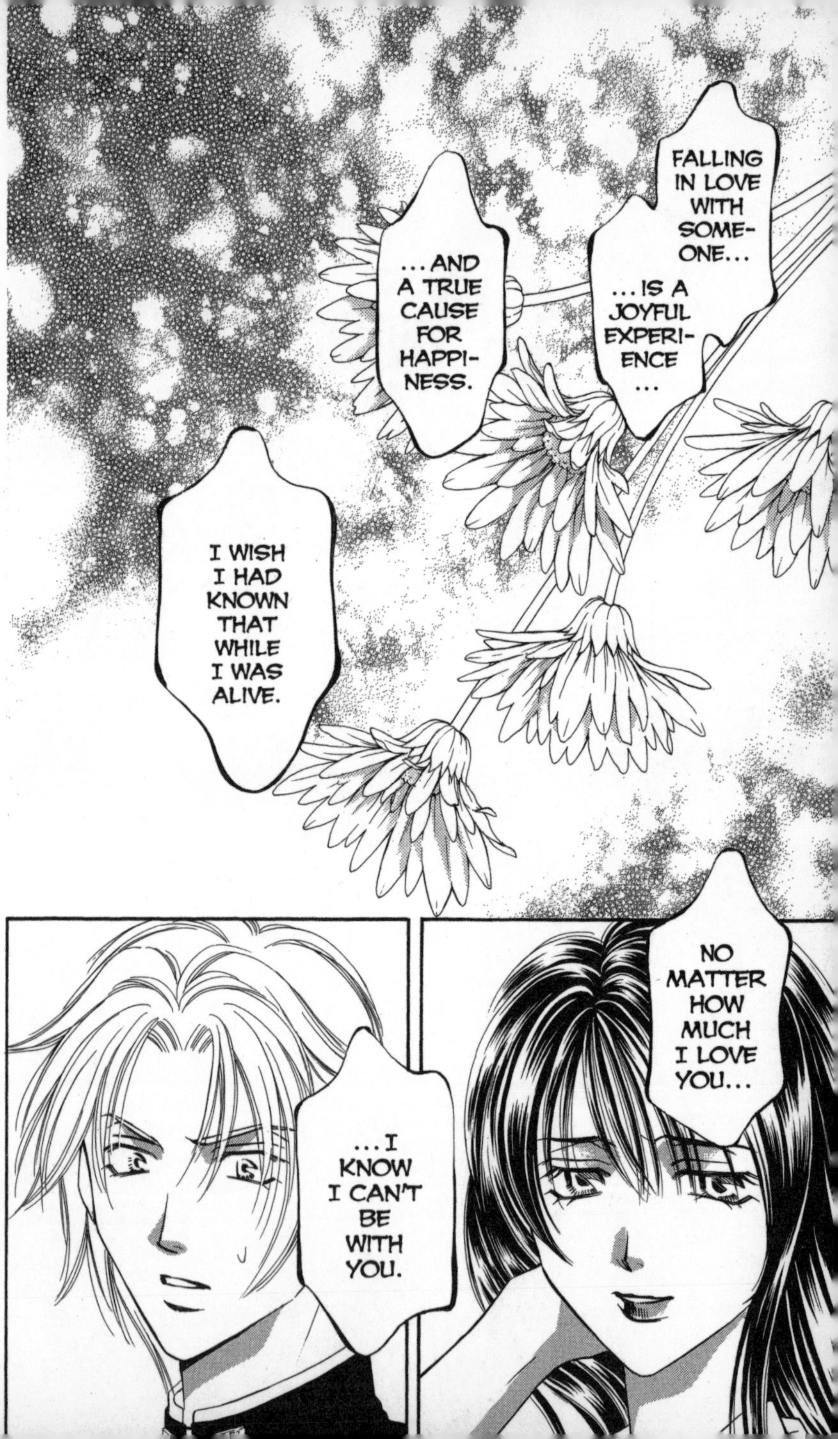
FALLING IN LOVE WITH SOMEONE...
...IS A JOYFUL EXPERIENCE...
...AND A TRUE CAUSE FOR HAPPINESS.
I WISH I HAD KNOWN THAT WHILE I WAS ALIVE.
NO MATTER HOW MUCH I LOVE YOU...
...I KNOW I CAN'T BE WITH YOU.

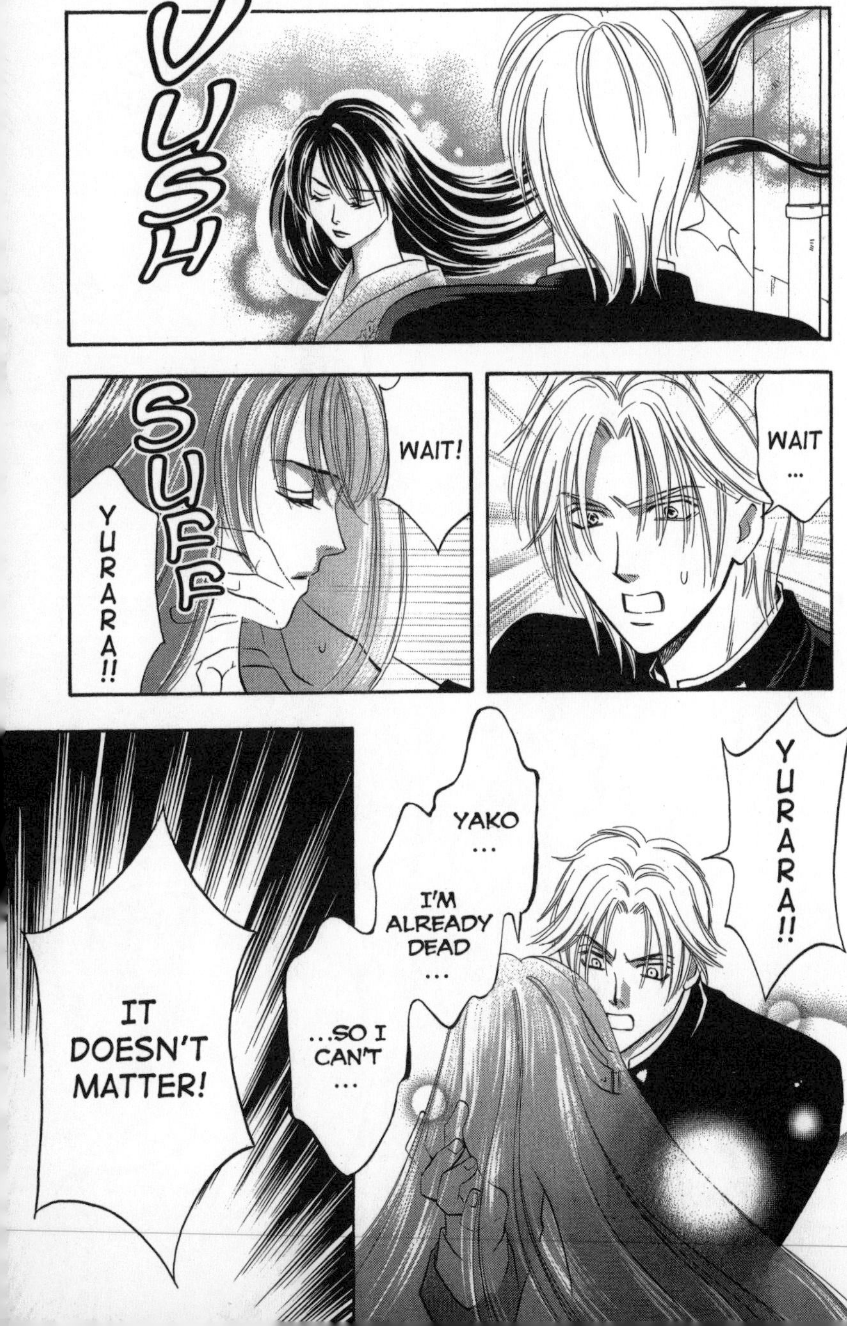
VUSH
WAIT ...
WAIT!
SUFF
YURARA!!
YURARA!!
YAKO ...
I'M ALREADY DEAD ...
...SO I CAN'T ...
IT DOESN'T MATTER!

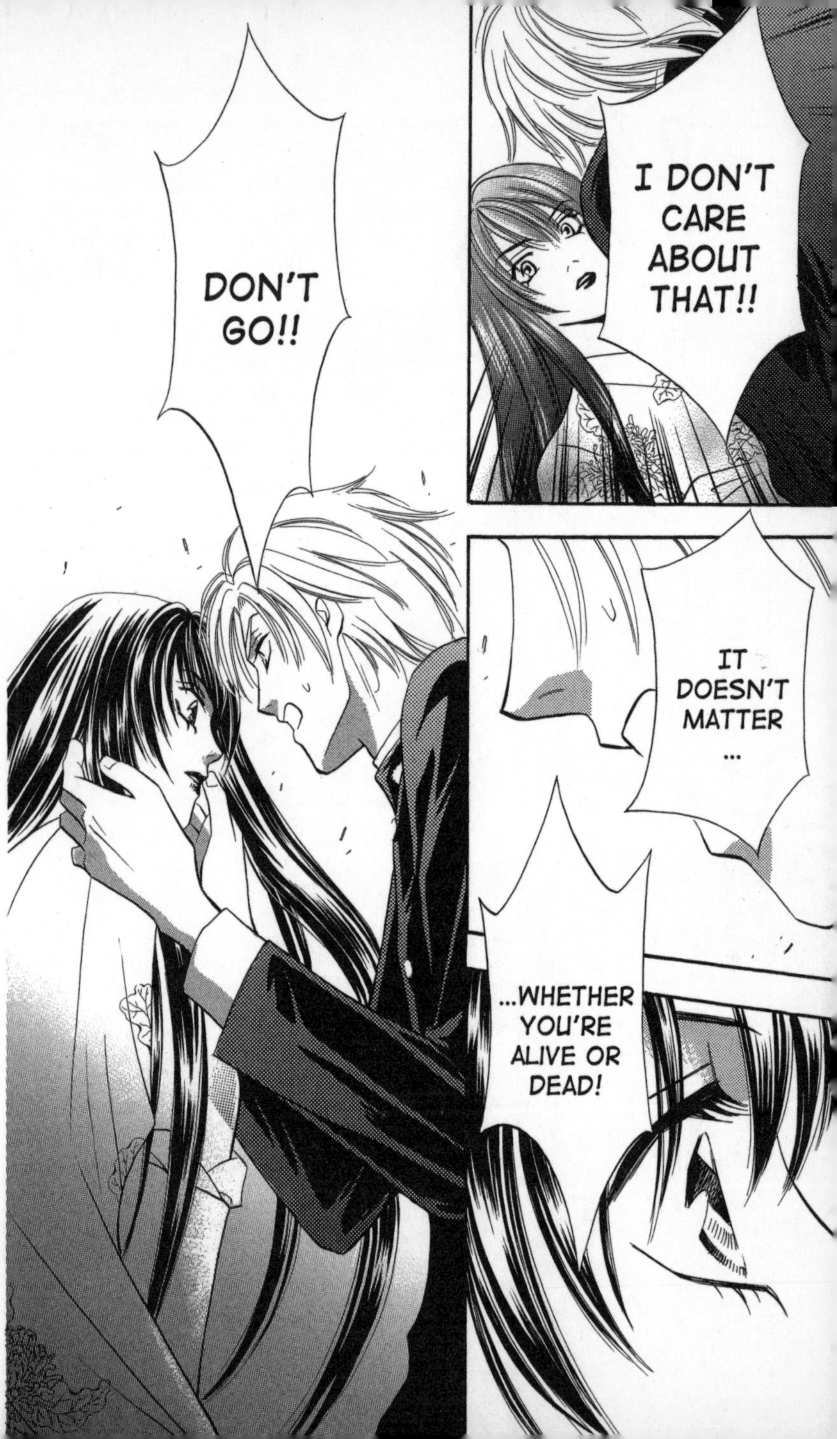
I DON'T CARE ABOUT THAT!!
IT DOESN'T MATTER ...
...WHETHER YOU'RE ALIVE OR DEAD!
DON'T GO!!

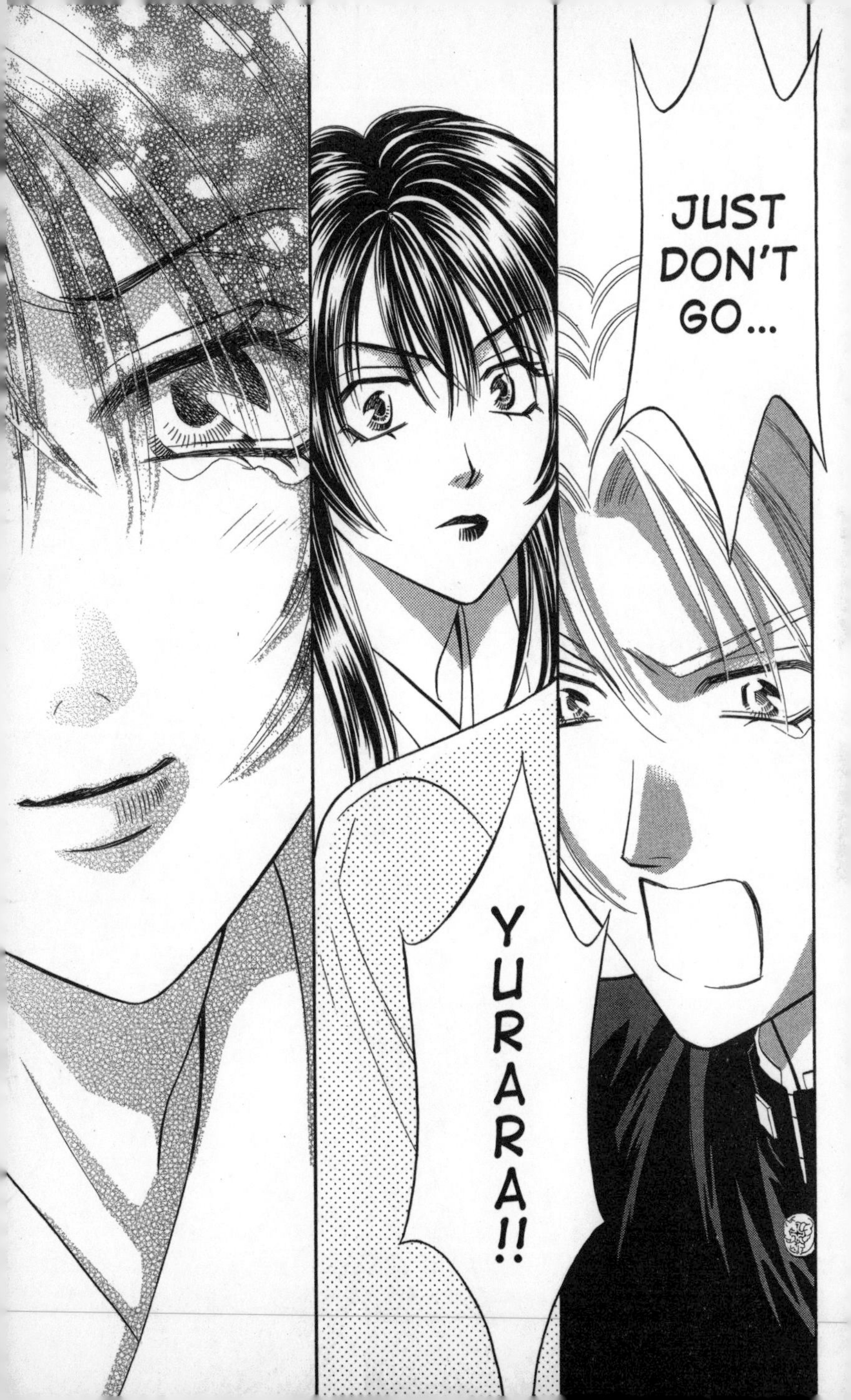
JUST DON'T GO...
YURARA!!

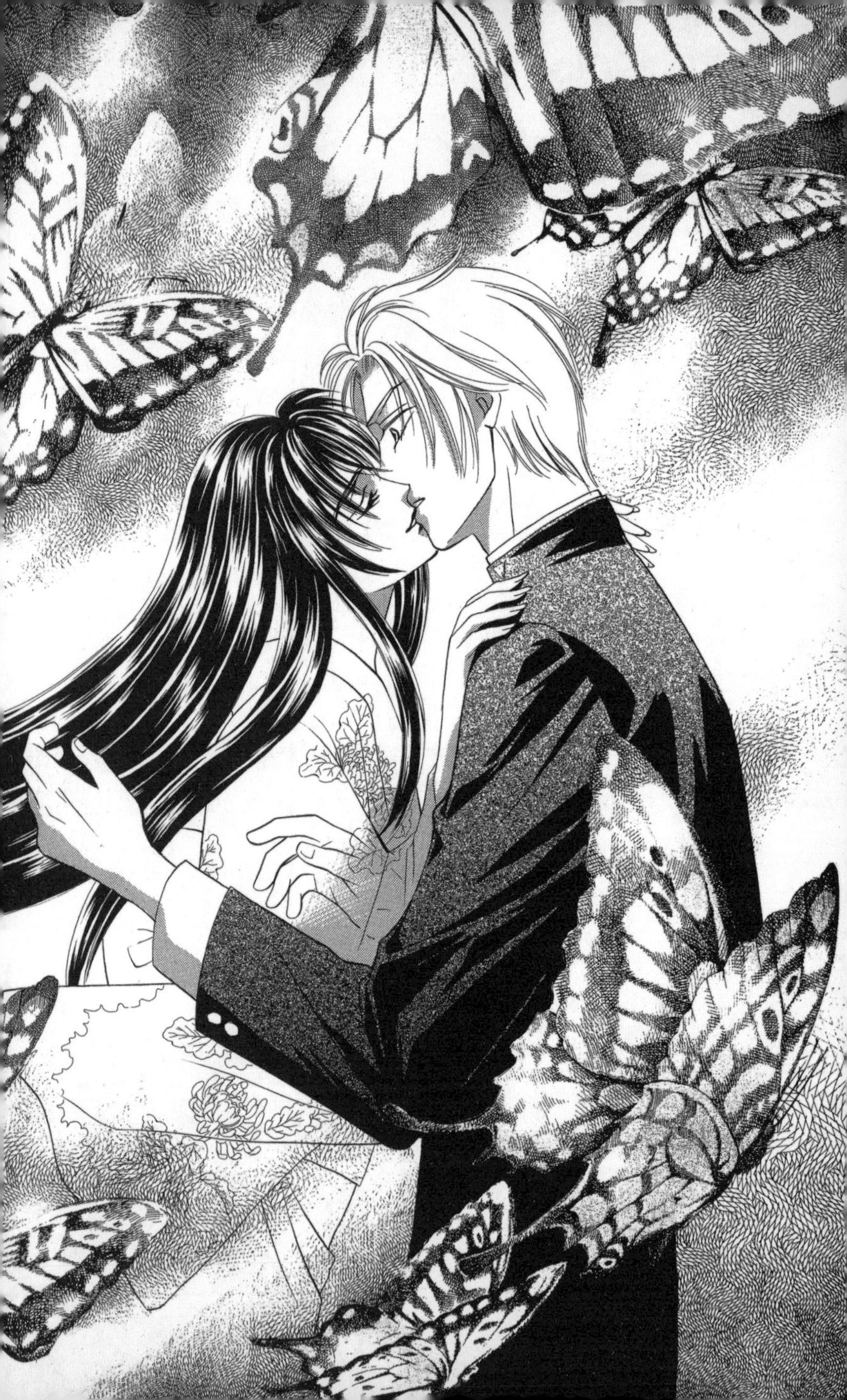

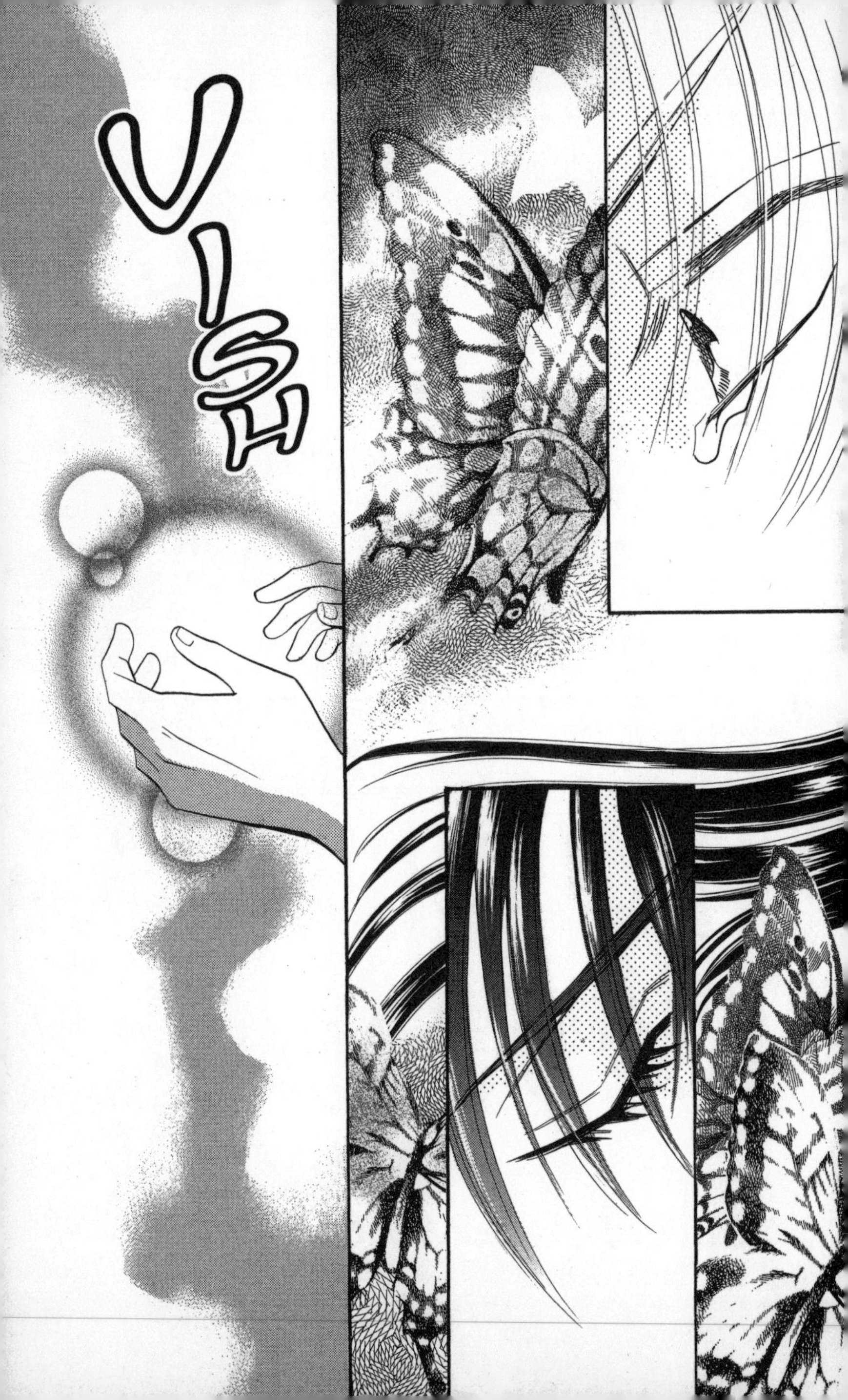
VISH

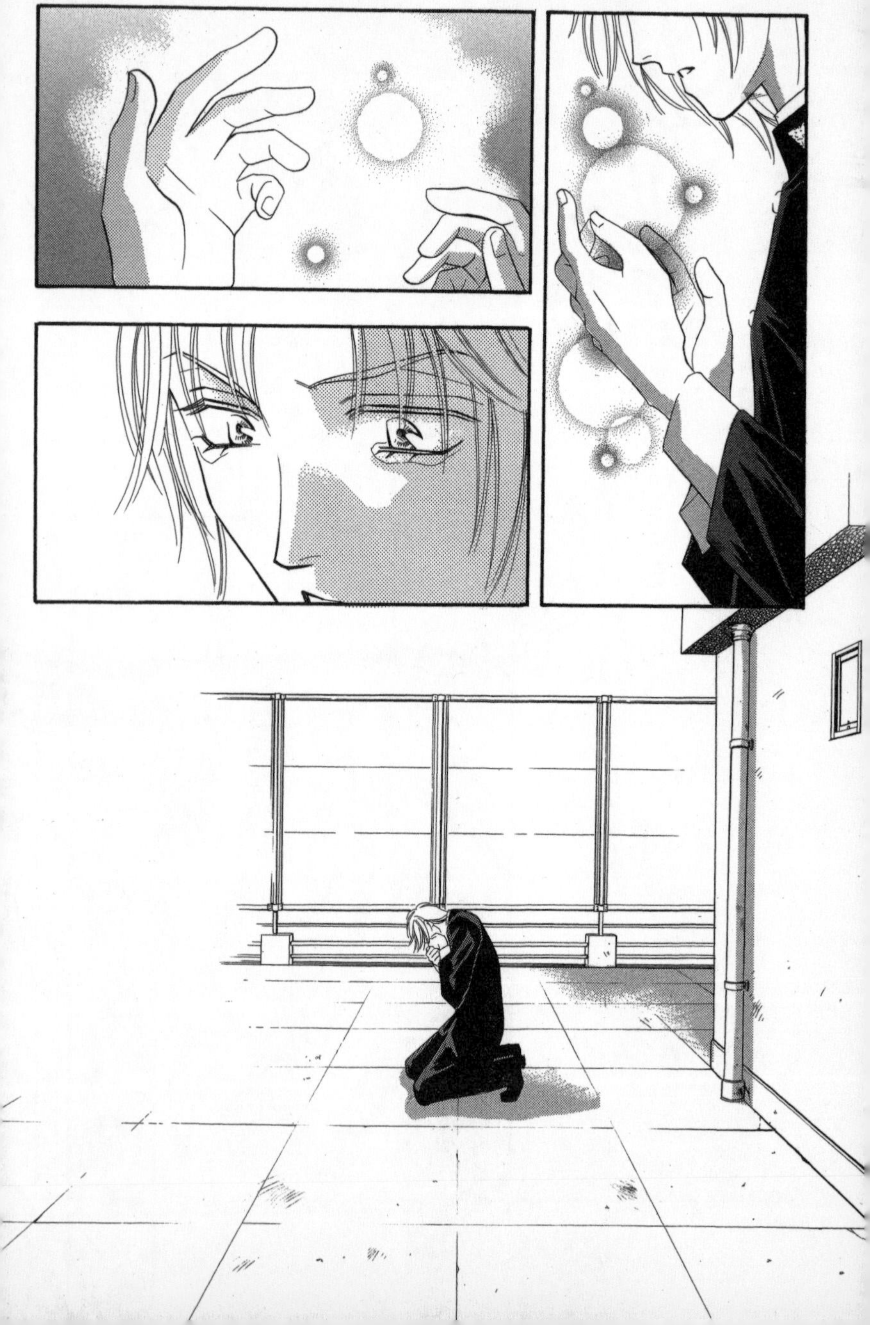

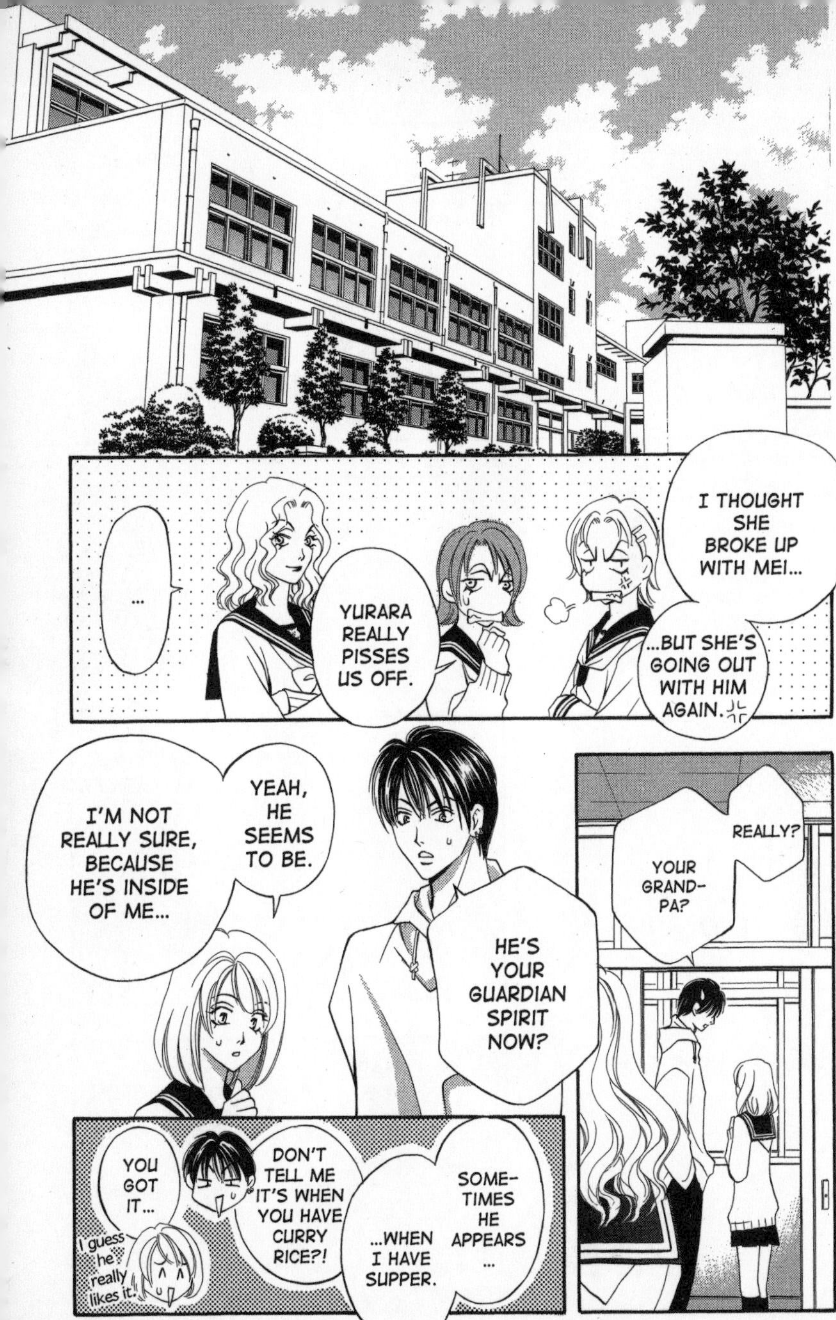
I THOUGHT SHE BROKE UP WITH MEI...
...BUT SHE'S GOING OUT WITH HIM AGAIN.
YURARA REALLY PISSES US OFF.
...
REALLY?
YOUR GRANDPA?
HE'S YOUR GUARDIAN SPIRIT NOW?
YEAH, HE SEEMS TO BE.
I'M NOT REALLY SURE, BECAUSE HE'S INSIDE OF ME...
SOME-TIMES HE APPEARS ...
...WHEN I HAVE SUPPER.
DON'T TELL ME IT'S WHEN YOU HAVE CURRY RICE?!
YOU GOT IT...
I guess he really likes it.

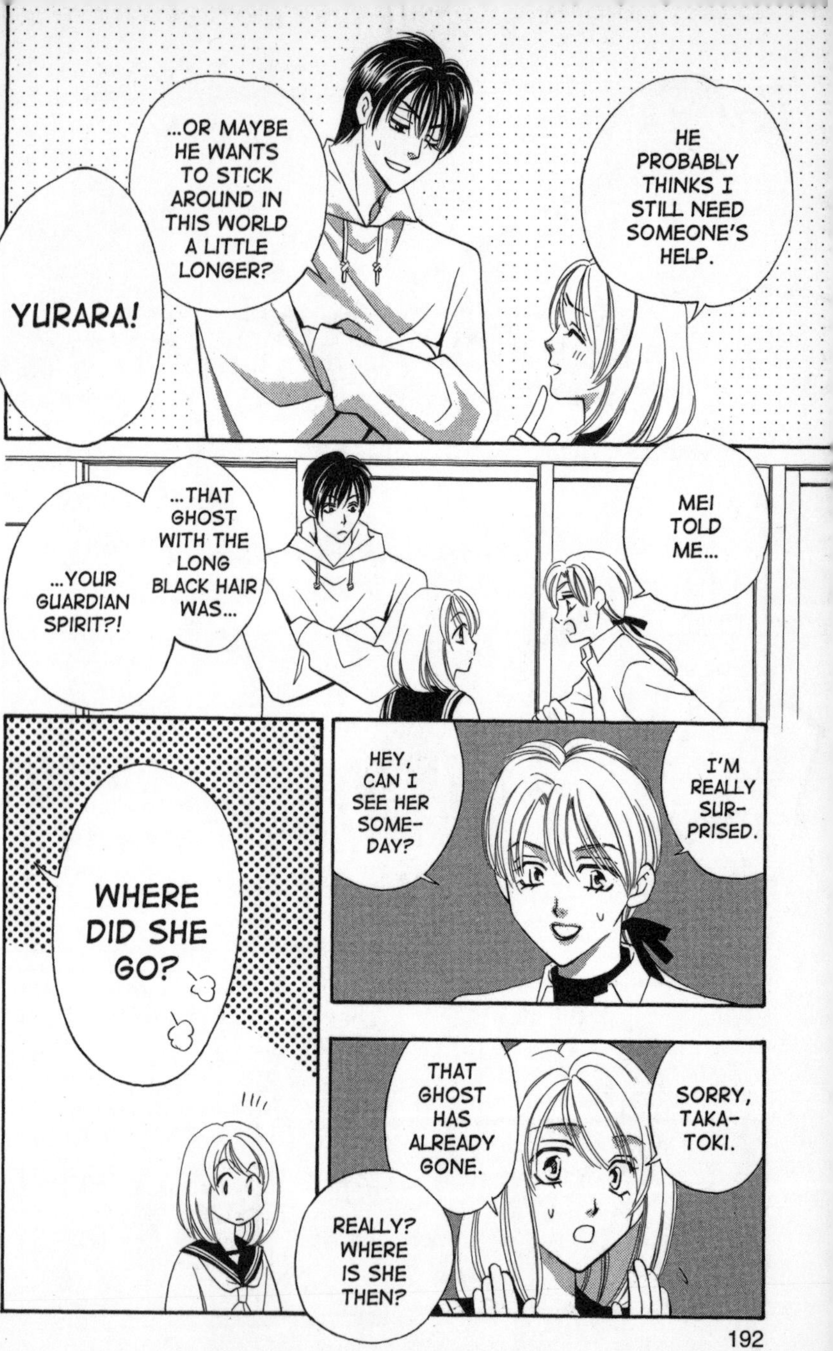
HE PROBABLY THINKS I STILL NEED SOMEONE'S HELP.
...OR MAYBE HE WANTS TO STICK AROUND IN THIS WORLD A LITTLE LONGER?
YURARA!
MEI TOLD ME...
...THAT GHOST WITH THE LONG BLACK HAIR WAS...
...YOUR GUARDIAN SPIRIT?!
I'M REALLY SUR-PRISED.
HEY, CAN I SEE HER SOME-DAY?
SORRY, TAKA-TOKI.
THAT GHOST HAS ALREADY GONE.
REALLY? WHERE IS SHE THEN?
WHERE DID SHE GO?

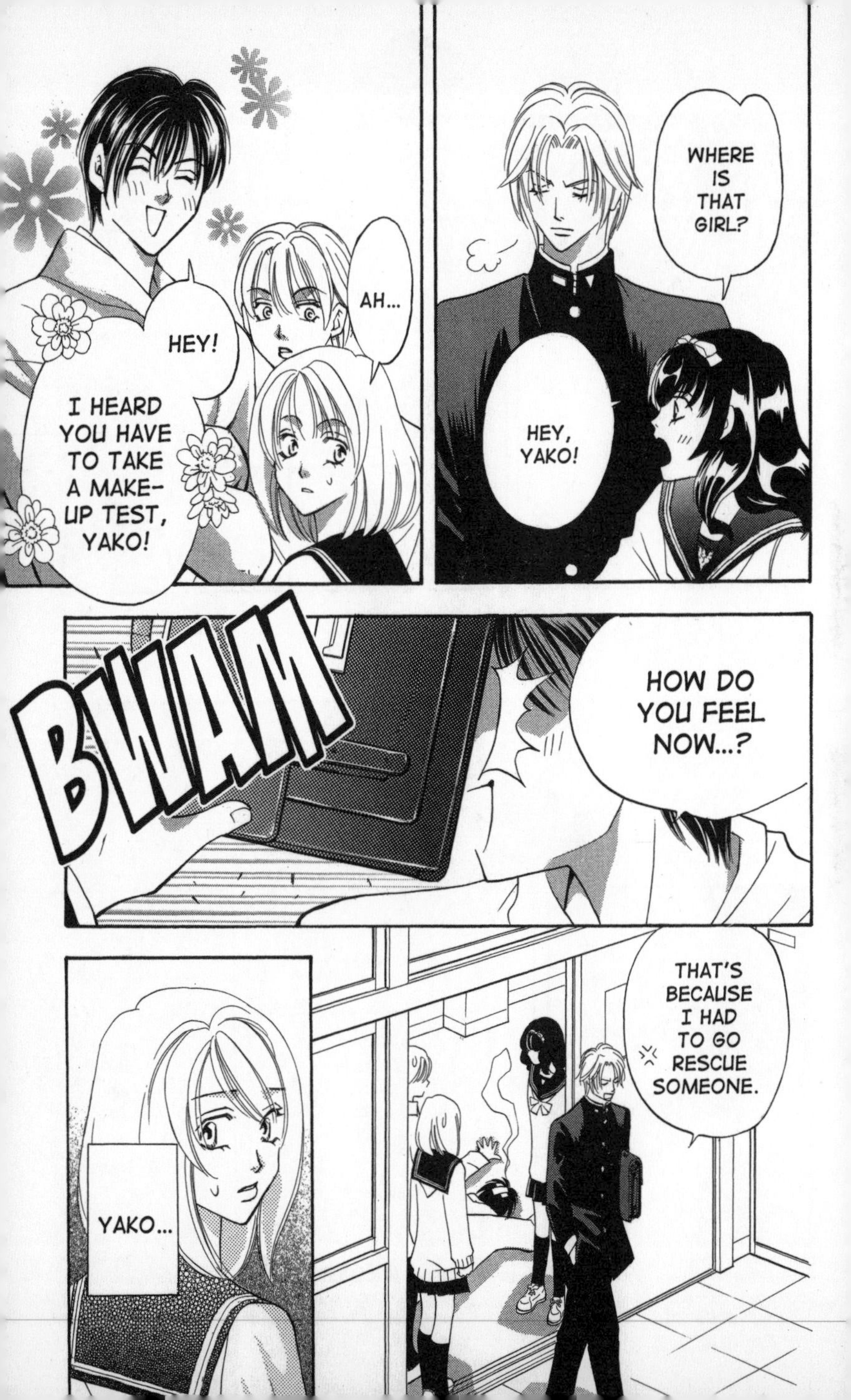
WHERE IS THAT GIRL?
HEY, YAKO!
AH...
HEY!
I HEARD YOU HAVE TO TAKE A MAKE-UP TEST, YAKO!
HOW DO YOU FEEL NOW...?
BWAM
THAT'S BECAUSE I HAD TO GO RESCUE SOMEONE.
YAKO...

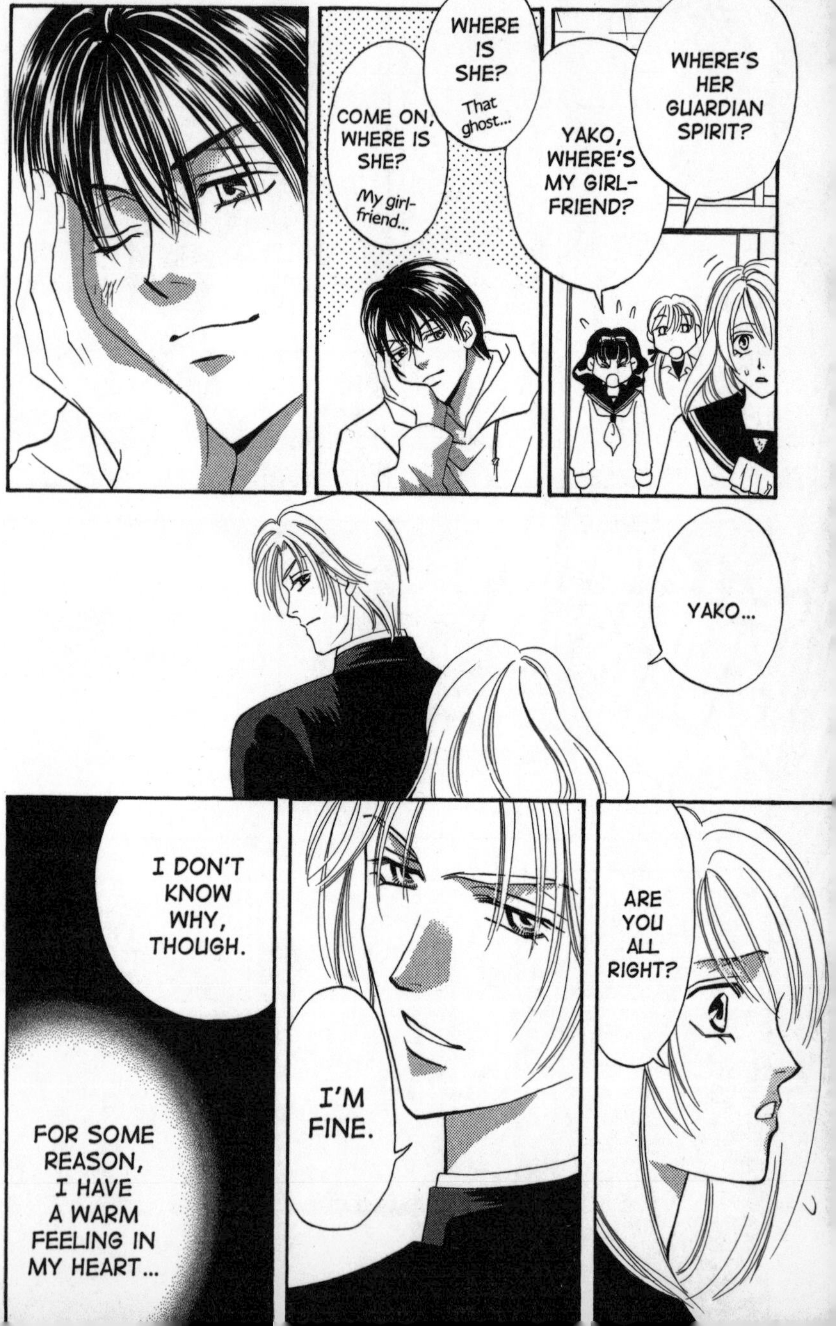
WHERE'S HER GUARDIAN SPIRIT?
YAKO, WHERE'S MY GIRL-FRIEND?
WHERE IS SHE?
That ghost...
COME ON, WHERE IS SHE?
My girl-friend...
YAKO...
ARE YOU ALL RIGHT?
I'M FINE.
I DON'T KNOW WHY, THOUGH.
FOR SOME REASON, I HAVE A WARM FEELING IN MY HEART...

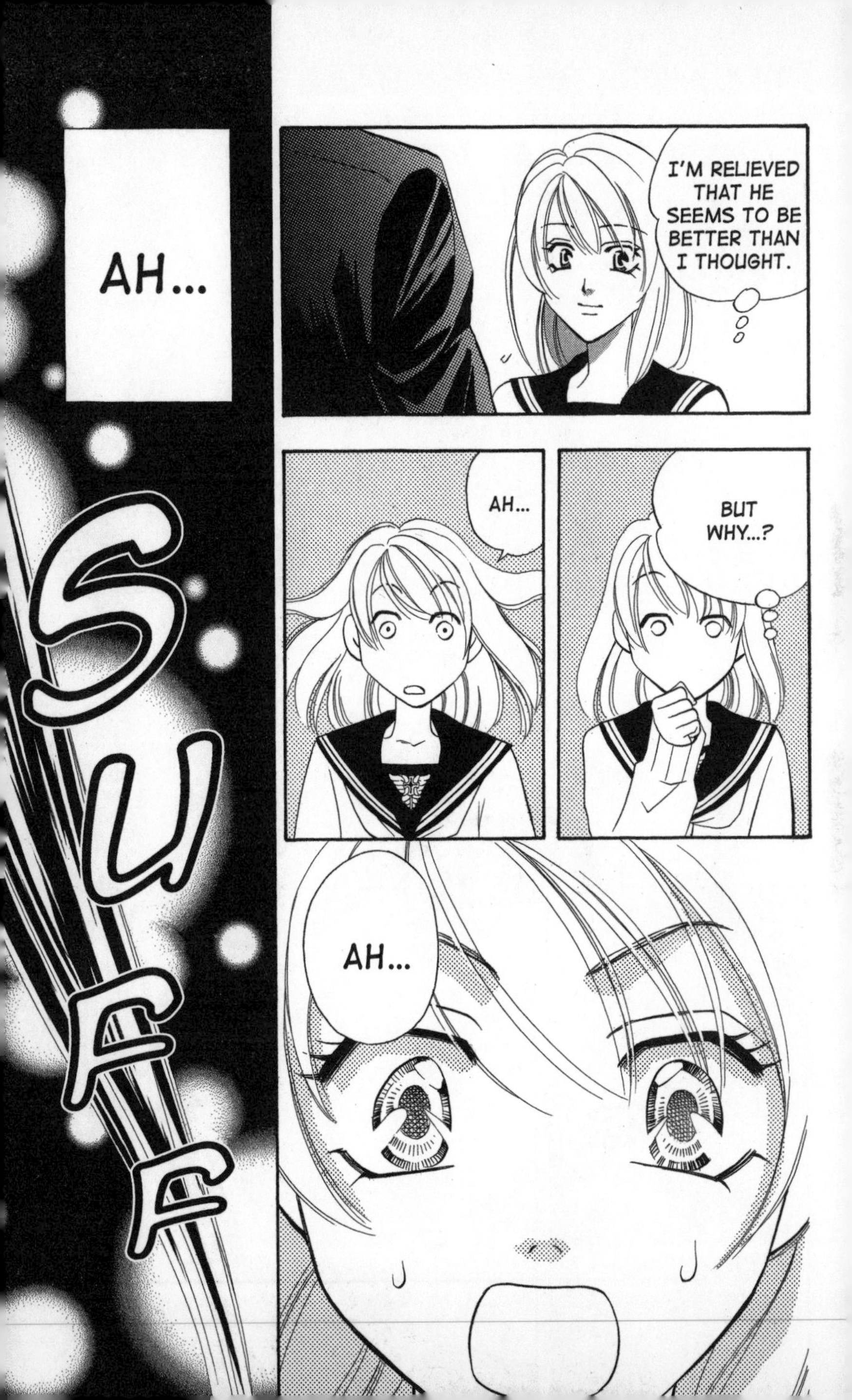
I'M RELIEVED THAT HE SEEMS TO BE BETTER THAN I THOUGHT.
BUT WHY...?
AH...
AH...
AH...
SUFF

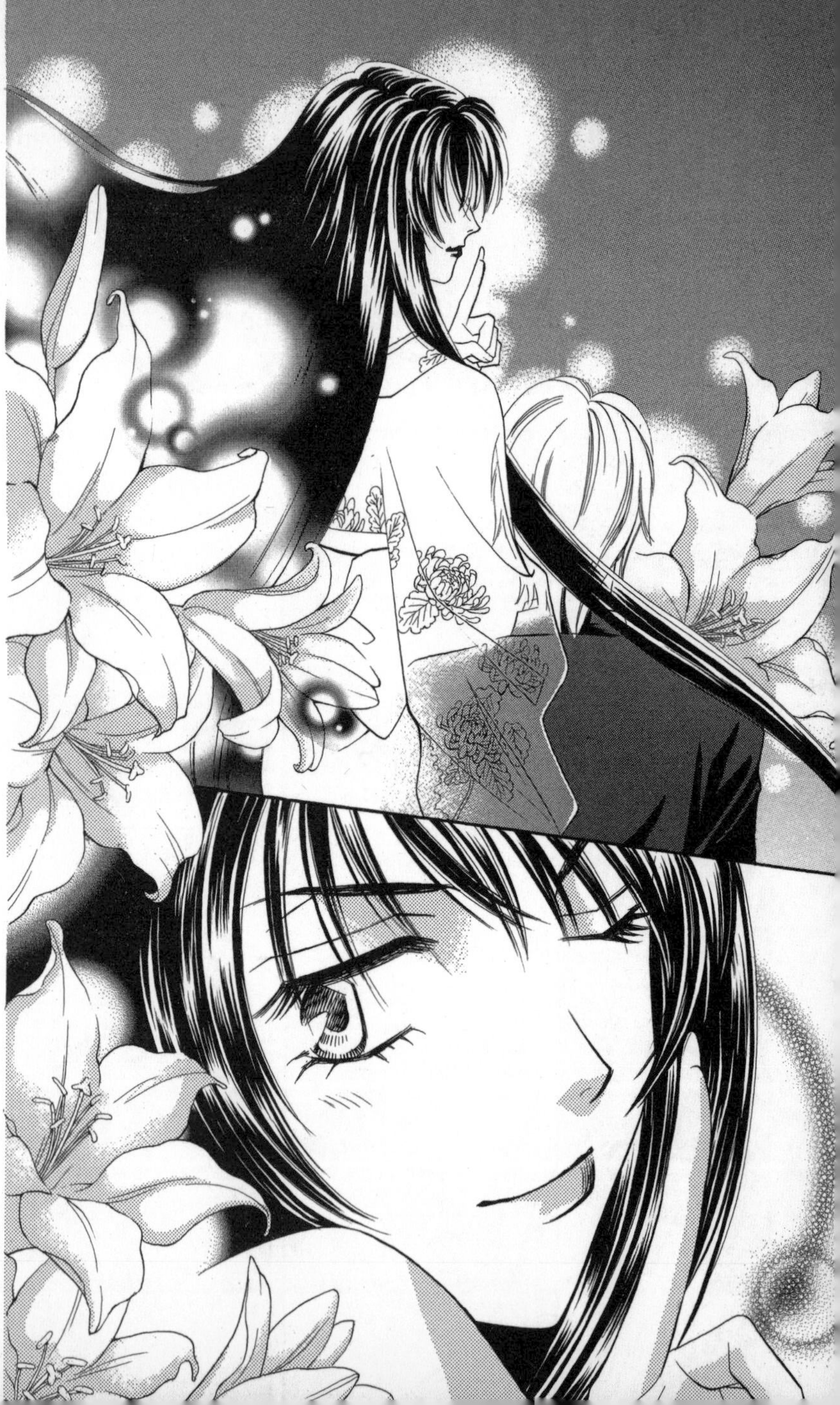

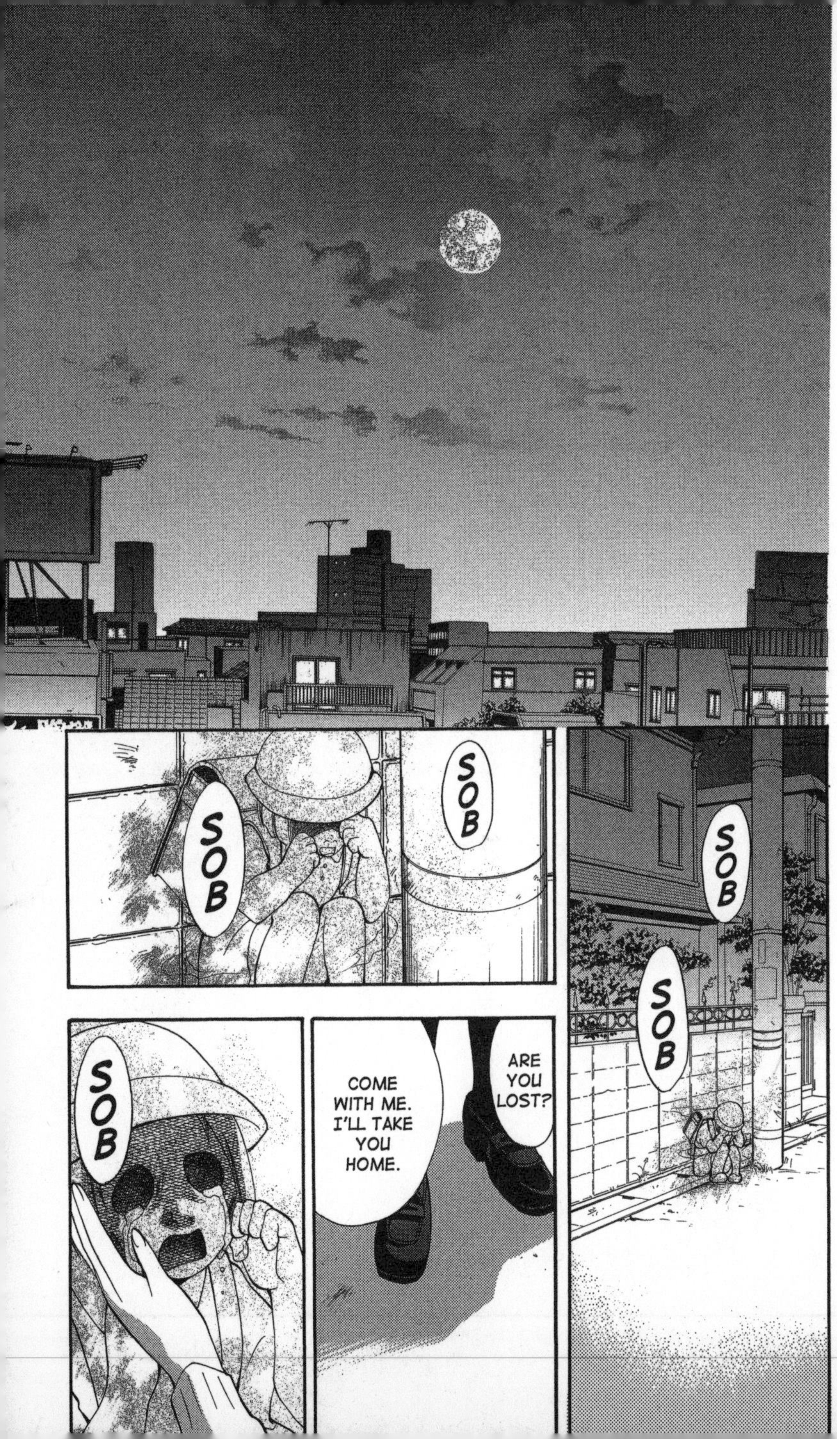
SOB
SOB
SOB
SOB
ARE YOU LOST?
COME WITH ME. I'LL TAKE YOU HOME.
SOB

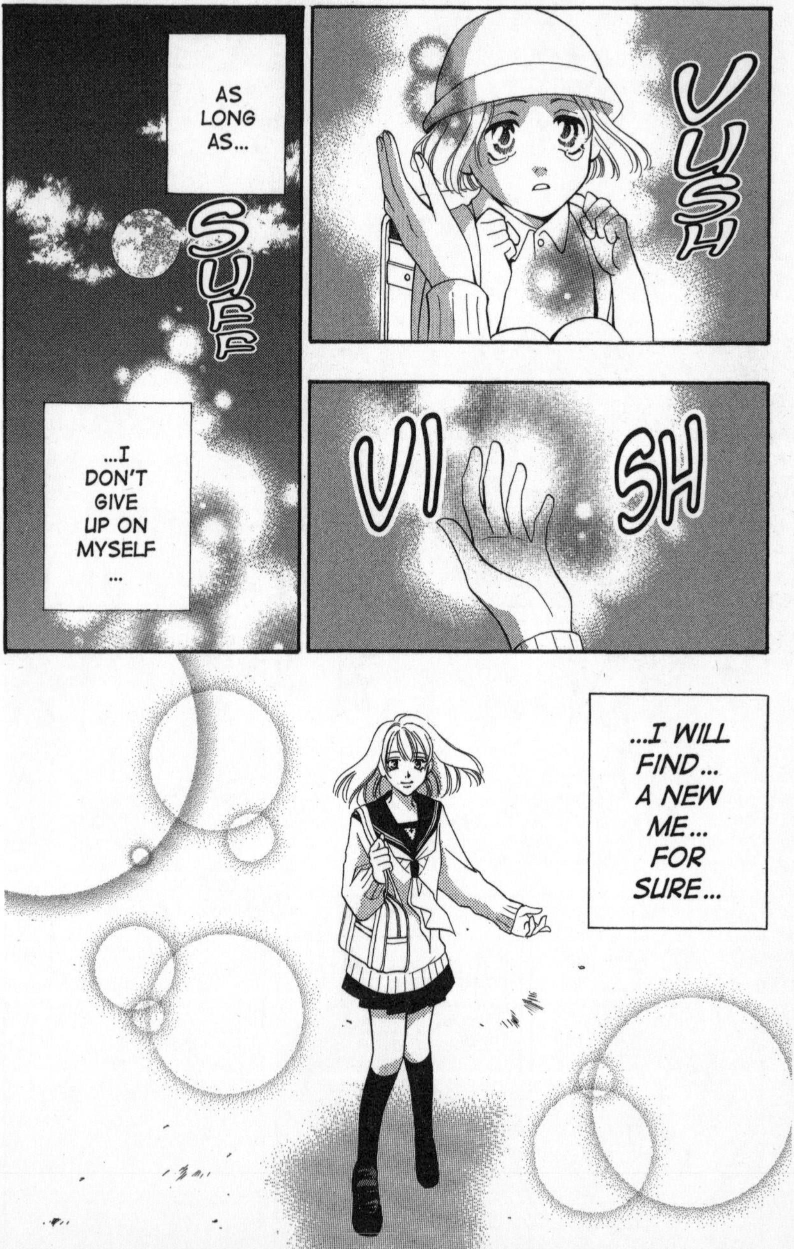
VUSH
VI SH
AS LONG AS...
SUFF
...I DON'T GIVE UP ON MYSELF ...
...I WILL FIND... A NEW ME... FOR SURE...

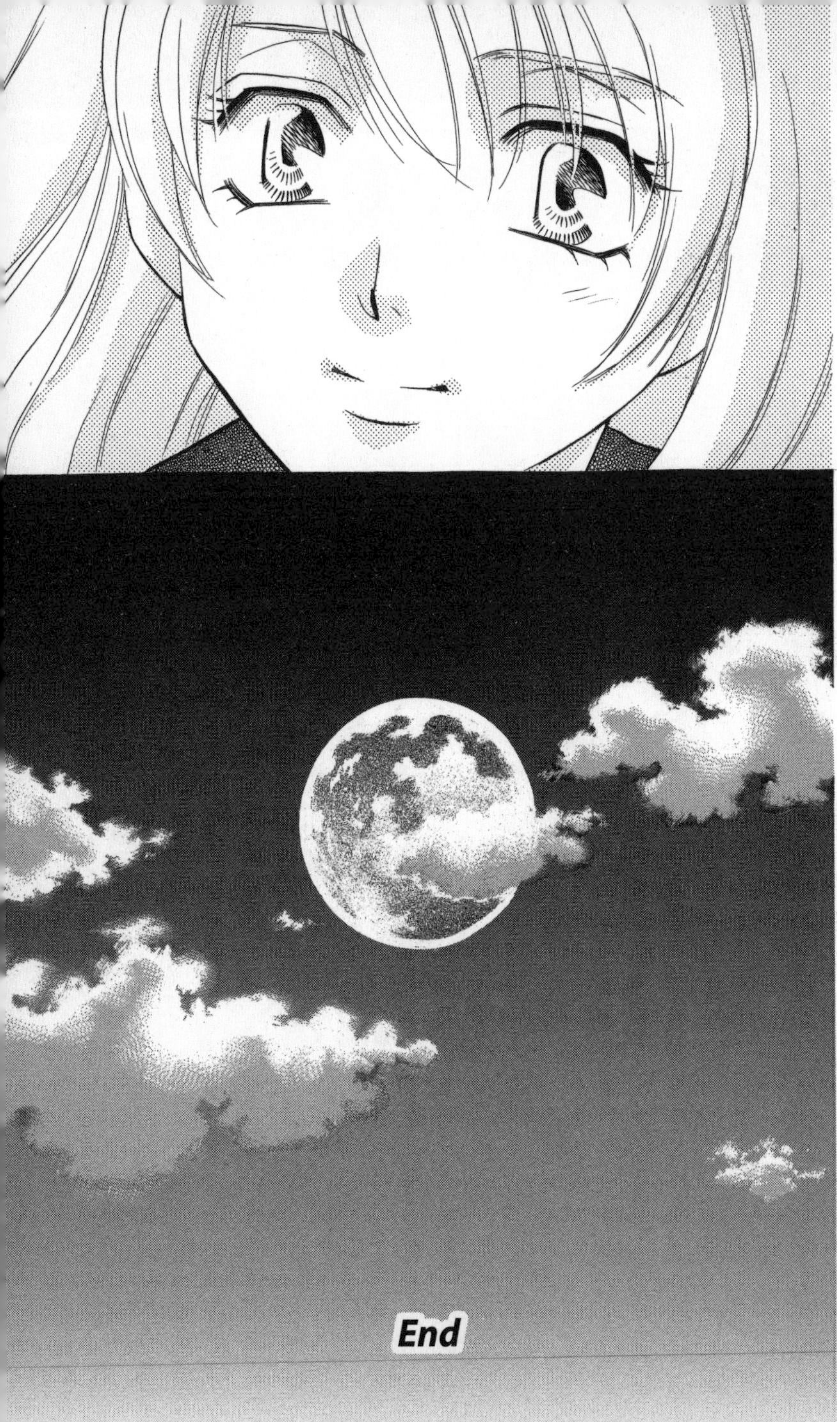
End

Chika Shiomi lives in the Aichi Prefecture
of Japan. She debuted with the manga
Todokeru Toki o Sugitemo (Even If the
Time for Deliverance Passes), and her work
is currently running in two magazines,
Bessatsu Hana to Yume and *Mystery Bonita*.
She loves reading manga, traveling, and
listening to music by Aerosmith, Hyde, and
Guns N' Roses. Her favorite artists include
Michelangelo, Hokusai, Bernini, and Gustav
Klimt.

Yurara

Vol. 5
The Shojo Beat Manga Edition

STORY & ART BY
CHIKA SHIOMI

English Adaptation/Heidi Vivolo
Translation/JN Productions
Touch-up Art & Lettering/Freeman Wong
Design/Izumi Hirayama
Editor/Mike Montesa

Editor in Chief, Books/Alvin Lu
Editor in Chief, Magazines/Marc Weidenbaum
VP of Publishing Licensing/Rika Inouye
VP of Sales/Gonzalo Ferreyra
Sr. VP of Marketing/Liza Coppola
Publisher/Hyoe Narita

Yurara no Tsuki by Chika Shiomi © Chika Shiomi 2004. All rights reserved.
First published in Japan in 2005 by HAKUSENSHA, Inc., Tokyo. English
language translation rights arranged with HAKUSENSHA, Inc., Tokyo. The
stories, characters and incidents mentioned in this publication are entirely fictional.

Printed in Canada

Published by VIZ Media, LLC
P.O. Box 77064
San Francisco, CA 94107

Shojo Beat Manga Edition
10 9 8 7 6 5 4 3 2 1
First printing, June 2008

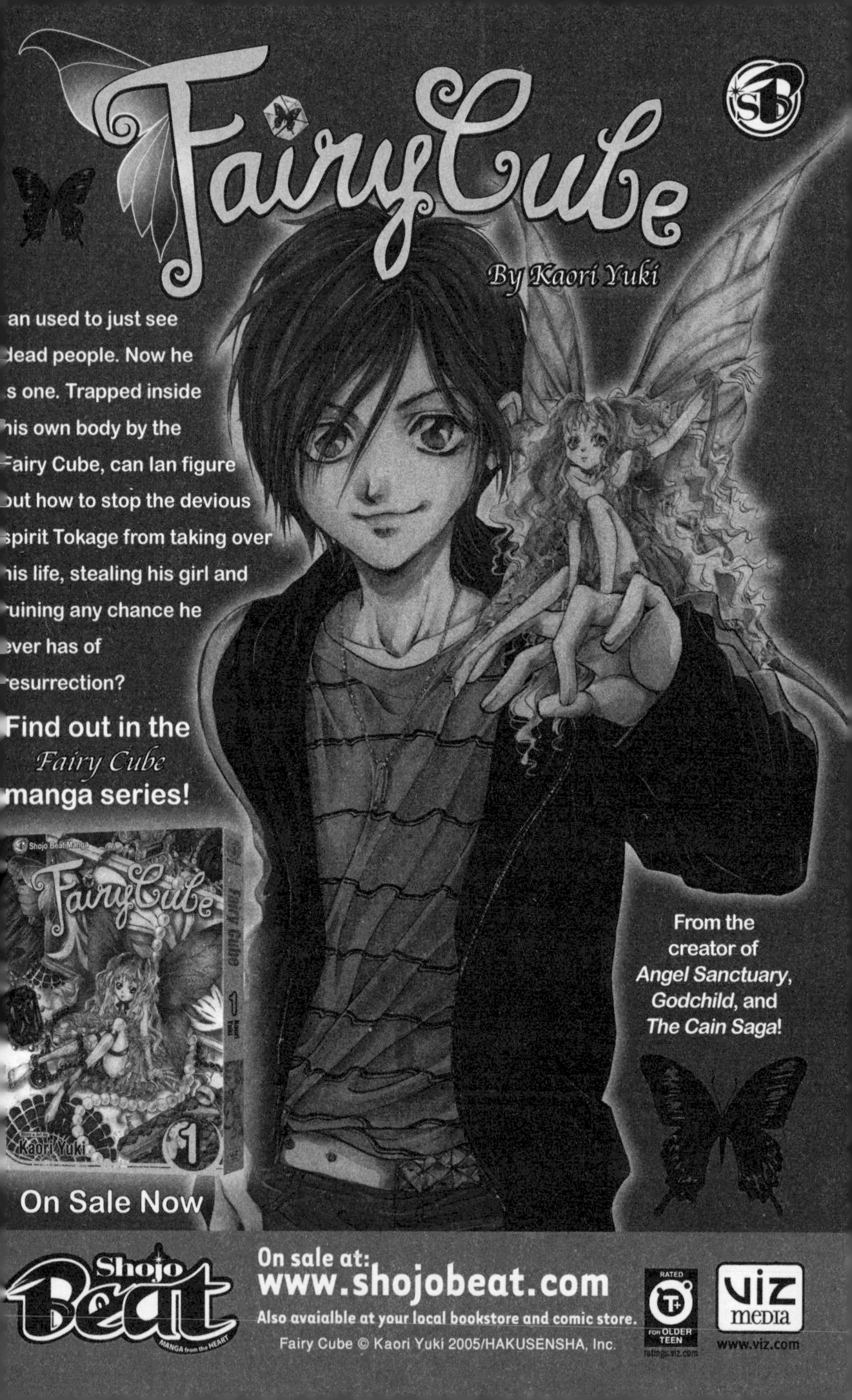
Fairy Cube
By Kaori Yuki
an used to just see
dead people. Now he
s one. Trapped inside
his own body by the
Fairy Cube, can Ian figure
out how to stop the devious
spirit Tokage from taking over
his life, stealing his girl and
ruining any chance he
ever has of
resurrection?
Find out in the
Fairy Cube
manga series!
Shojo Beat Manga
Fairy Cube
Kaori Yuki
1
On Sale Now
From the
creator of
Angel Sanctuary,
Godchild, and
The Cain Saga!
Shojo Beat
MANGA from the HEART
On sale at:
www.shojobeat.com
Also avaialble at your local bookstore and comic store.
Fairy Cube © Kaori Yuki 2005/HAKUSENSHA, Inc.
RATED
T+
FOR OLDER TEEN
ratings.viz.com
VIZ media
www.viz.com

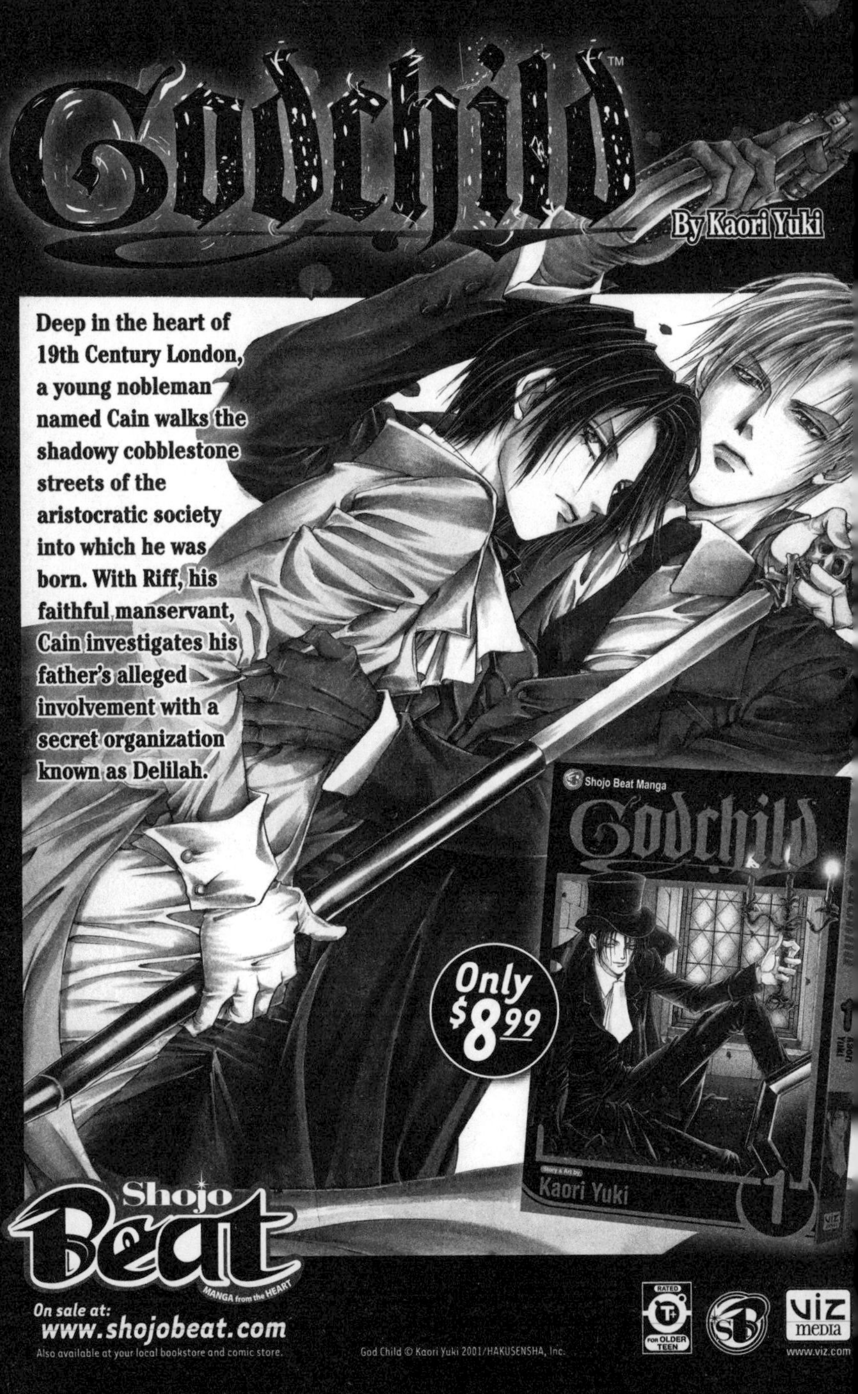
Godchild™
By Kaori Yuki
Deep in the heart of 19th Century London, a young nobleman named Cain walks the shadowy cobblestone streets of the aristocratic society into which he was born. With Riff, his faithful manservant, Cain investigates his father's alleged involvement with a secret organization known as Delilah.
Shojo Beat Manga
Godchild
Story & Art by
Kaori Yuki
1
Only $8.99
Shojo Beat
MANGA from the HEART
On sale at:
www.shojobeat.com
Also available at your local bookstore and comic store.
God Child © Kaori Yuki 2001/HAKUSENSHA, Inc.
RATED T+ FOR OLDER TEEN
viz media
www.viz.com

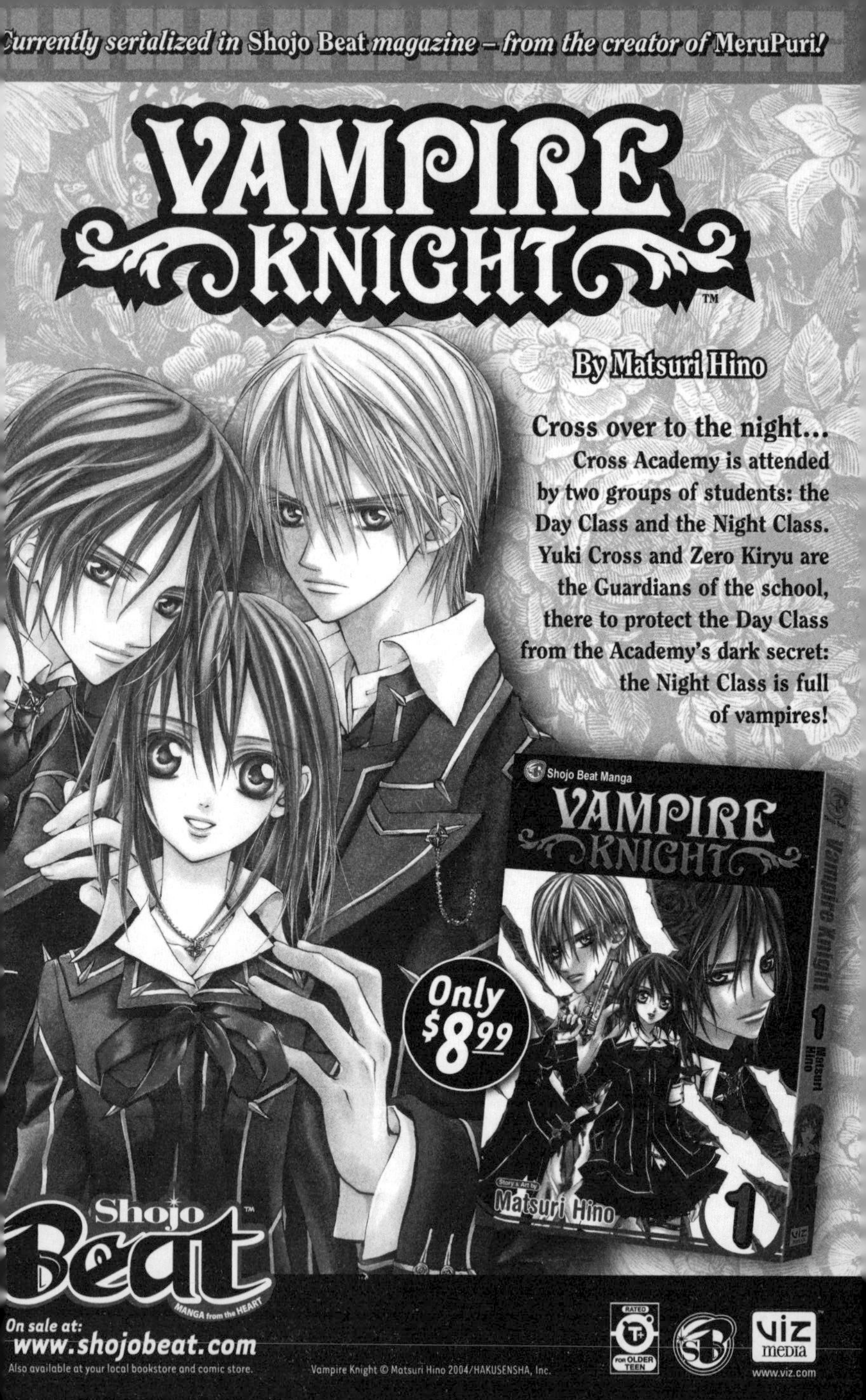

Currently serialized in Shojo Beat magazine – from the creator of MeruPuri!
VAMPIRE KNIGHT™
By Matsuri Hino
Cross over to the night...
Cross Academy is attended by two groups of students: the Day Class and the Night Class. Yuki Cross and Zero Kiryu are the Guardians of the school, there to protect the Day Class from the Academy's dark secret: the Night Class is full of vampires!
Shojo Beat Manga
VAMPIRE KNIGHT
Story & Art by Matsuri Hino
1
Vampire Knight 1 Matsuri Hino
Only $8.99
Shojo Beat™ MANGA from the HEART
On sale at:
www.shojobeat.com
Also available at your local bookstore and comic store.
Vampire Knight © Matsuri Hino 2004/HAKUSENSHA, Inc.
RATED T+ FOR OLDER TEEN
VIZ media
www.viz.com

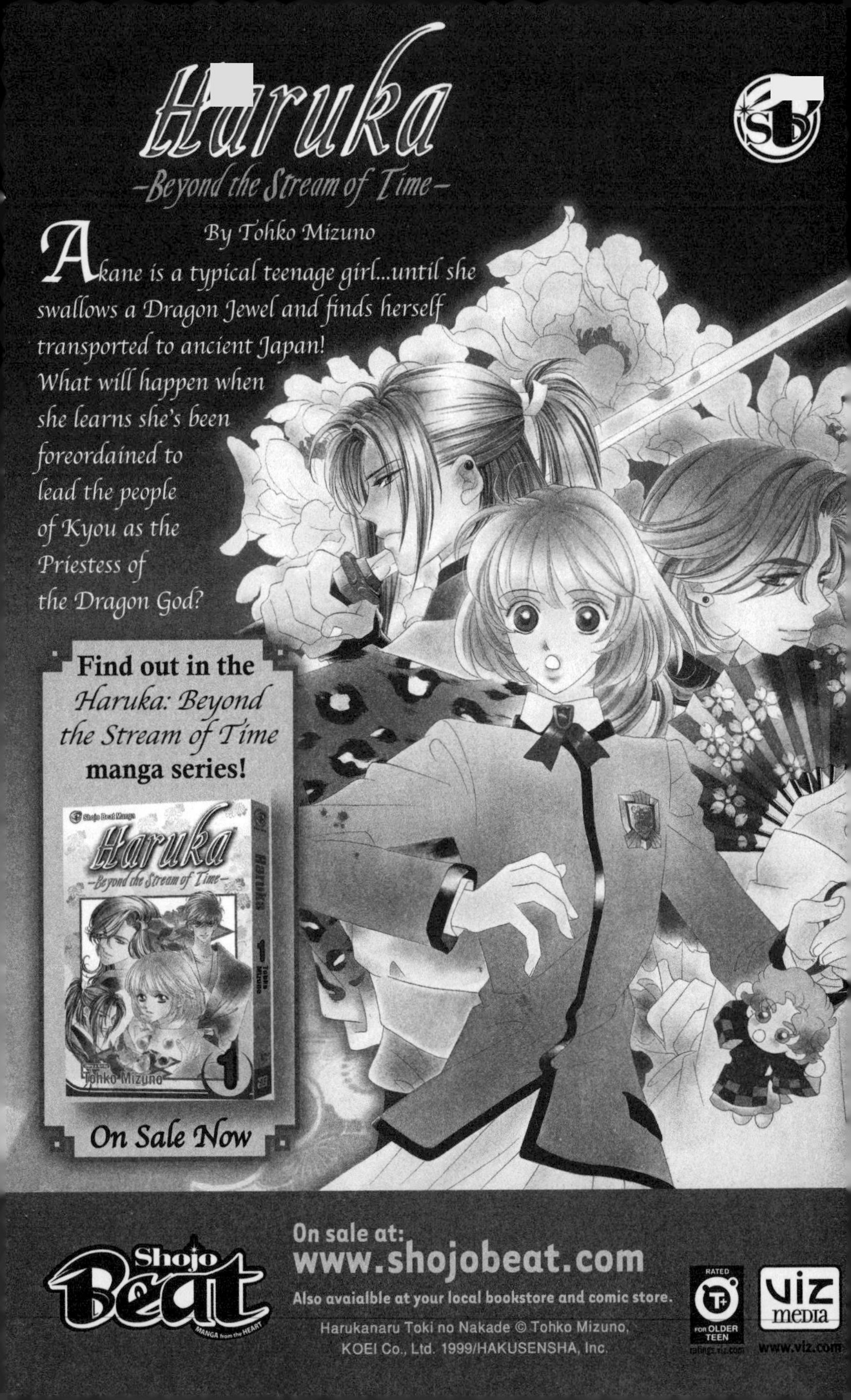

Haruka
-Beyond the Stream of Time-
By Tohko Mizuno
Akane is a typical teenage girl...until she swallows a Dragon Jewel and finds herself transported to ancient Japan! What will happen when she learns she's been foreordained to lead the people of Kyou as the Priestess of the Dragon God?
Find out in the Haruka: Beyond the Stream of Time manga series!
Shojo Beat Manga
Haruka
-Beyond the Stream of Time-
Tohko Mizuno
1
On Sale Now
Shojo Beat
MANGA from the HEART
On sale at:
www.shojobeat.com
Also avaialble at your local bookstore and comic store.
Harukanaru Toki no Nakade © Tohko Mizuno, KOEI Co., Ltd. 1999/HAKUSENSHA, Inc.
RATED
T+
FOR OLDER TEEN
ratings.viz.com
VIZ MEDIA
www.viz.com

MANGA from the HEART

12 GIANT issues for ONLY $34.99*

The Shojo Manga Authority

The most ADDICTIVE shojo manga stories from Japan PLUS unique editorial coverage on the arts, music, culture, fashion, and much more!

That's 51% OFF the cover price!

Shojo Beat
VAMPIRE KNIGHT
CELEBRATE BOYS
VISUAL KEI
Shojo Beat
MANGA from the HEART
August 2007
THE MANY STYLES OF GOTHIC LOLITA
SUMMER HOROSCOPE ALERT!
DANCE WITH THE DEAD
GACKT SPEAKS
LIVE BEAUTIFUL
Exclusive Story by Superstar Arina Tanemura!
TIPS FROM A TOKYO VIDEOGAME INSIDER
BEAT BOX: MAKE YOUR VOICE HEARD!
WIN 185 PRIZES!
Shojo Beat
February 2007
SPECIAL MUSIC ISSUE
An exclusive interview with pop princess Nana Kitade
JAPAN'S FASHION ICON
New Manga by the Creator of FULL MOON!
GENTLEMEN'S ALLIANCE
Shojo Beat
June 2007
OVER 340 PAGES

Subscribe NOW and become a member of the SB Sub Club!

- SAVE 51% OFF the cover price
- ALWAYS get every issue
- ACCESS exclusive areas of www.shojobeat.com
- FREE members-only gifts several times a year

Strictly VIP!

3 EASY WAYS TO SUBSCRIBE!

1) Send in the subscription order form from this book OR
2) Log on to: www.shojobeat.com OR
3) Call 1-800-541-7876